St. Thomas Aquinas on the Existence of God

St. Thomas Aquinas on the Existence of God

Collected Papers of Joseph Owens, C.Ss.R.

Edited by
JOHN R. CATAN

State University of New York Press
Albany

Library of Congress Cataloging in Publication Data

Owens, Joseph.
St. Thomas Aquinas on the Existence of God:
Collected Papers of Joseph Owens.

"Selected bibliography of Joseph Owens":
Includes Index.
CONTENTS: Aquinas as Aristotelian commentator.—
Aquinas on knowing existence.—Judgment and truth.—
[etc.]

1. God—Proof—History of doctrines—Addresses,
essays, lectures. 2. Thomas Aquinas, Saint,
1225?-1274—Addresses, essays, lectures.
I. Catan, John R. II. Title.
BT100.T4092   231'.042   79-13885
ISBN 0-87395-401-7

CONTENTS

FOREWORD

The present year marks the hundreth anniversary of the stimulus given Thomistic studies in 1879 by Leo XIII's encyclical *Aeterni Patris*. Only twice in the preceding centuries had comparable acclaim been showered upon the thought of Aquinas. One of the occasions was the euphoria surrounding his canonization in the early fourteenth century, the other the religious upheaval of the sixteenth. Both these were more interested in his theology than in his specifically philosophical achievements. Against the background of developments in the eighteenth and nineteenth centuries, however, the *Aeterni Patris* emphasized the philosophical worth of his thought. The elan that followed in the encyclical's wake crested throughout the twenties to the fifties of the present century in widely read works of Gilson and Maritain, and in numerous other commentators. The enthusiasm then subsided, as existentialism, phenomenology, structuralism, logical analysis and the philosophies of science and language captured the attention of the philosophic public during the recent decades. History had repeated the experience of flood and ebb tide.

Whether cresting or receding, the thought of Aquinas has nevertheless maintained unbroken attention during the seven hundred years since his death. The interest continues, in spite of the contemporary difficulties in understanding a mediaeval writer. The reasons for the interest may vary widely in accord with the different preoccupations of the readers. But for them all there is an ever-present appeal that is capable of guaranteeing continued attention in the future. It is the marvelous balance that prevails throughout in Aquinas' philosophical thinking. The fine equilibrium between judgment and conceptualization, between intuition and reasoning, and in the respective roles played by things and thought and language, is truly remarkable. From that viewpoint the work of Aquinas is unrivaled. It gives full promise of enduring as a prized heritage for future generations.

With these reflections may I express appreciation of the confidence in editor and publisher that contemporary interest is sufficient to justify the reprinting of these epistemological and metaphysical studies on the thought of Aquinas. The project was conceived by the editor, Professor John Catan, and carried through by his industry. The choice of papers was his. To the extent my own judgment may have any validity on this point, the selection represents accurately enough my thinking on Aquinas over the past three decades. Focus, I trust, has been sharpened with the years. But the direction has remained the same.

J. Owens

EDITOR'S PREFACE

For those who are aware of the field of Aquinian Studies, Father Joseph Owens' work needs no introduction. As a glance at the selected bibliography at the end of this volume will reveal, Father Owens has written many other articles on the theme of the existence of God which have not been included in the present volume. The principle of inclusion was both the relevance of the individual articles to the theme of the volume, namely, the existence of God and the contribution of the papers to the issue of the 'originality' of Saint Thomas' contributions to philosophy. The issues are intimately connected to and are most strikingly present in Saint Thomas' use of the genre of "commentary." The first article of Father Owens is a magisterial presentation and illumination of this issue. Given the centrality of epistemological issues since Descartes, I also included the next two articles on St. Thomas' notion of cognition, especially, his understanding of the judgment of existence. It is here that limitations of space were felt most heavily. To compensate I would suggest that the articles numbered 18, 22, 23, and 25 in the selected bibliography (pp. 307–308 *below*) be consulted by those who would like a more rounded treatment. The next two articles provide the general background within the context of St. Thomas' doctrine of being, without which the first proof of the *Five Ways* will not be fully appreciated. The last six articles take up the first proof as found in the *Summa of Theology* in its systematic and historical detail. Together, these articles present the rich and profound thought of St. Thomas Aquinas through the interpretative skills of one of the foremost interpreters of Thomistic thought of this and perhaps any century.

At this point it is my duty and pleasure to thank Father Owens for permission to put together this volume of his previously published papers. I am sure that I echo the gratitude of many of his students (including myself) at the University of Toronto as well as at the Pontifical Institute of Medieval Studies in the University of Toronto to whom his life and scholarship have been a beacon. This volume is respectfully dedicated to him with the hope that the wisdom of St. Thomas will continue to illumine the spirit of a new generation of 'lovers of wisdom.'

I would also like to thank the members of my department at Brockport, especially Dr. Joseph Gilbert for his vibrant leadership as well as Dr. and Mrs. Greenstein, and Dr. George Stack for their philosophical companionship. Finally a word of gratitude to the Editorial Board of the State University of New York Press, its current Director, Mr. William Eastman, and its previous Director, Mr. Norman Mangouni for their dedication to disseminating the products of the highest scholarship without deviation from that goal of excellence.

John R. Catan

Brockport, New York

ACKNOWLEDGEMENTS

The editor wishes to gratefully acknowledge the people and publishers who graciously cooperated in making this volume a reality. A special word of thanks to Professor Virginia Brown, Editor of *Mediaeval Studies,* and Father William Hayes, S.J., in charge of publications, as well as Father Edward Synan, President of the *Pontifical Institute of Mediaeval Studies* at the University of Toronto who encouraged me in the initial stages of the project. The various editors of the journals and books from which the final selection was made including: Father Armand Maurer, C.S.B., Editor of *St. Thomas Aquinas 1274-1974:Commemorative Studies* (Toronto,P.I.M.S.1974); Dr. Jude Dougherty, Editor of the *Review of Metaphysics;* Father John L. Treloar, S.J., Editor of *The Modern Schoolman;* Professor Eugene Freeman, Editor of *The Monist;* Father Conrad L. Harkins, O.F.M., Editor of *Franciscan Studies;* and Professor D.W. Hamlyn, Editor of *Mind.*

The following is a list in order of appearance of the articles included in this volume with the original publication information.

1. "Aquinas as Aristotelian Commentator," *St. Thomas Aquinas 1274-1974: Commemorative Studies,* ed. Armand Maurer, C.S.B. (Toronto:Pontifical Institute of Mediaeval Studies, 1974, Vol.1,213-38).

2. "Aquinas on Knowing Existence," *The Review of Metaphysics,* 29(1976)670-90.

3. "Judgment and Truth in Aquinas," *Mediaeval Studies,* 32(1970)138-58.

4. "The Accidental and Essential Character of Being in the Doctrine of St. Thomas Aquinas" *Mediaeval Studies,* 20(1958)1-40.

5. "Diversity and Community of Being in St. Thomas Aquinas," *Mediaeval Studies*, 22(1960)257-302.

6. "Aquinas and the Five Ways," *The Monist*, 58(1974)16-35.

7. "The Conclusion of the *Prima Via*," *The Modern Schoolman*, 30(1952/53)33-53;109-121;203-215.

8. "The Starting Point of the *Prima Via*," *Franciscan Studies*, 5(1967)249-294.

9. "Actuality in the *Prima Via* of St. Thomas," *Mediaeval Studies*, 29(1967)26-64.

10. "Immobility and Existence for Aquinas," *Mediaeval Studies*, 30(1968)22-46.

11. "Aquinas on Infinite Regress," *Mind*, N.S.71(1962)244-46.

AQUINAS AS ARISTOTELIAN COMMENTATOR

I

The role of St. Thomas Aquinas as an Aristotelian commentator still proves puzzling. Certainly his work in this respect is not the detached and theologically neutral understanding that is found in the moderns such as Bonitz, J.A. Stewart, or Sir David Ross. No matter how closely his attitude is concerned with explaining the Aristotelian text just as the text stands, it is consistently sensitive to any deviations of the teaching from the integrity of Christian faith and of orthodox theology. In fact, it does not at all give the impression that it is going out of its normal way when it corrects the Aristotelian tenets in the light of revealed doctrine. Rather, it proceeds as though correction of this type is a legitimate and integral part of its overall method.[1]

Does not this savor strongly of an out and out theological method? Should it not mean that the Aristotelian commentaries of Aquinas are to be classed as works of sacred theology rather than of philosophy? Is not the procedure in them theological through and through, in contrast to a genuinely philosophical treatment of the Aristotelian text? Does not this mean theology only?

However, hesitation arises at once in confrontation with this apparently extreme stand. The overwhelming predominance of the discussion in the commentaries deals with the Aristotelian thought and not with professedly theological issues. Moreover, on the supposition of outside interference the theological interest is not the only observable intrusion into the commentaries. A partly new conception of the sciences seems to dominate the whole discussion.[2] Metaphysics seems placed in an Avicennian framework, ethics and politics in traditional Christian grooves, and logic in the setting of the three Scholastically accepted intellectual activities. Would not this new philosophical coloring have to be regarded as changing the character of the commentaries just

as much as the theological concern? Or is it to be viewed as in some way connected with, and subsumed under, the theological orientation?

The above observations suggest at least that in these writings of Aquinas the
task of a commentator was not understood to be a disinterested and historically
exact explanation of Aristotelian views. It was not a function to be detached
from concern for revealed Christian truth. There can be little doubt that St.
Thomas grasped in large part the true import and thrust of the Stagirite's
tenets. He did not hesitate for a moment to acknowledge that Aristotle accepted the eternity of the world and the actuation of the heavenly bodies by
spiritual souls in the sense that these tenets were strictly essential to the
Aristotelian metaphysics.[3] He was continually aware that Aristotle in the *Ethics*
was concerned only with this-worldly contentment. Yet he undertakes to show
how the Aristotelian teachings blossom out into thoroughly Christian flora.
Does not this procedure mean much more than that in the commentaries
"theological considerations color his interpretations"?[4] Will it anywhere allow
one to view the Aristotelian commentaries as articulating "positions which are
rejected in his basically theological writings"?[5]

One may sharpen the question still further. Can the procedure in the
Aristotelian commentaries be regarded as in *any* way basically philosophical, in
contrast to that of the "basically theological writings"? Are the theological coloring and additions and reservations merely intruded from outside as occasion
demands, in order to make the Stagirite's doctrine palatable in a Christian
milieu and safeguard it from censure-prone ecclesiastical authority? Or must
these commentaries be classed as authentically theological documents? In a
word, is Aquinas as an Aristotelian commentator writing as a philosopher or as
a theologian?

The tendency to view the Aristotelian commentaries as basically
philosophical writings is of course deep-seated. Allegedly according to the
mind of St. Thomas they fill the role of a *Summa Philosophica* for beginners,[6]
providing students with a complete and suitable course of philosophy,[7] presenting Thomistic philosophy in words of the Angelic Doctor himself.[8] The
hermeneutical principle would be: "For Thomas interpreted Aristotle's
thought not only in the light of its inner consistency, but also by taking into account the results of subsequent philosophical research."[9] Seen from this standpoint, the work is properly philosophical.

There is obviously a problem, then, in regard to the nature of the Thomistic
commentaries on Aristotle. In its broadest framework, the issue is whether
these commentaries are essentially philosophical or theological documents.
Within the procedure proper to the one or the other discipline, as the case may
be, the question has to be faced how Aquinas can so patently understand the
real meaning of the Aristotelian text and yet explain it in a way that is not
Aristotle's, or even opposed to Aristotle's conception of its implications. Com-

paratively little work has as yet been devoted to this problem. At a Scholastic congress in 1950 it was noted that the number of studies published on these commentaries was minimal, totaling less than fifty, and almost exclusively mere articles.[10] The situation has not improved notably in the intervening years. The topic is still wide open for investigation.

The meaning of the word"commentary" is practically of no help in regard to the issue. It is wide enough to cover explanation of the basic document, notes on it, reflections on it, development of questions arising from it. In the last sense it became regularly applied to works on the *Sentences* of Peter Lombard, in which the basic text served merely as a springboard for wide-ranging articles on subjects of current interest. But the word did not enter into the titles of these writings of Aquinas in their original form. Rather, they were called *Expositiones*. They were presented as explanations of the Aristotelian works. This throws the problem back to the kind of explanation found in the Thomistic undertaking. Is it philosophical or theological in character? Does it respect the original meaning scrupulously, or merely use that meaning as a springboard for its own new interests? Basically, is it explaining Aristotle or is it doing something else? Or is it in some way an amorphous combination of these possibilities?

The last suggestion does not seem to be at all acceptable, for the inspiration of the Thomistic commentaries on Aristotle seems to be unitary throughout. They do not give the impression of an amalgam of disparate elements. Rather, their procedure appears to be a self-consistent enterprise, constituting an authentic literary genre. No impression of anything amorphous or fragmentary is given in the course of these writings. The command of the situation seems firm from start to finish. The attitude shown in them is that of a man engaged in a thoroughly coherent task. He is apparently doing his work in a manner recognized and accepted in his milieu. He may embody in his technique of literal commentary a distinct improvement over his predecessors in handling the Aristotelian doctrine, but in his use of pagan thought in a Christian atmosphere he appears to be carrying on a unity of method that had been achieved through a long history of intellectual effort. The procedure has the marks of something undertaken with a well thought out and consciously adopted purpose. Prima facie, accordingly, it has every right to be approached with this assumption. It is not to be dismissed lightly on the strength of present-day formal and stereotyped norms. Rather, grass roots investigations in the commentaries themselves is indicated in order to see whether or not the above assumption will be borne out.

A close scrutiny of the commentaries, then, is the way to obtain correct answers about their nature. The Aristotelian commentaries of Aquinas are twelve in number. The earliest chronological indication for any of them is the reign of Pope Urban IV (1261–1264). This is for the commentary on the

Metaphysics, a commentary that was not finished before 1272. The other Aristotelian commentaries are dated variously between 1266 and 1273.[11] The commentary on the *Metaphysics*, consequently, would seem to stretch in one way or another through the whole chronological period in which Aquinas was engaged in producing these writings on Aristotle. It may therefore quite safely be approached as the proper commentary in which to begin an investigation of the procedure of Aquinas. Later the results can be tested in briefer fashion against the method shown in the other Aristotelian commentaries.

II

The commentary of Aquinas on the *Metaphysics* covers the first twelve of the fourteen books traditionally grouped under the title.[12] A short Proem introduces the study that is to be dealt with, locating it in the science that naturally dominates all others. The Proem uses as its springboard some observations from Aristotle's *Politics*, with two explicit references. It also draws upon, but without express references, a number of characteristic Aristotelian teachings from the *De Anima*, the *Analytics*, and the *Metaphysics* itself. These various tenets are brought to bear upon the one notion "intellectual in the highest degree" (*maxime intellectualis*)[13] as the distinguishing feature of the science that is being introduced. The assembling of so many roving tenets under the one unifying principle shows a thorough mastery of the philosophical materials, and an innate ability to organize them successfully from a new and personal viewpoint. It marks Aquinas himself as the "author" of the work about to be undertaken, in the medieval sense of the *auctor*. He is the one who will be doing the thinking and passing the judgments and presenting the work as his own, no matter how liberally he is drawing upon someone else for material, help, and inspiration. Such at least is the function of the commenting writer as suggested by this Proem.

Further, there is divergence in some details from the strict Aristotelian description of the philosophical notions involved. Actuality and potentiality, for instance, are presented as consequent upon being, just as are unity and multiplicity—"ea quae consequuntur ens, ut unum et multa, potentia et actus" (*In Metaph.*, Proem.). In this regard Aristotle himself gives details about the way the most general "forms" follow upon being.[14] He regards unity and multiplicity as basic, but does not mention actuality and potentiality. Rather, actuality and potentiality name original instances of being, not subsequent properties.[15]

Somewhat similarly the formal substances that in Aristotle were described as "absolutely separate" (*Metaph.*, H 1, 1042a29–31) are designated in this Proem as separate "secundum esse," in contrast to the mathematicals, which are separate "secundum rationem." This places the division in an obviously remodeled cast, for in Aristotle the mathematicals were described as things not separate, though taken in abstraction and separated by thought from movement.[16] Against an Arabian background the things that are separate "secundum esse" are distinguished as "Deus et intelligentiae," quite apparently understood in the biblical sense of God and angels. Together these separate substances are looked upon as the common and universal causes of common being—"ens commune, quod est genus, cuius sunt praedictae substantiae communes et universales causae" (*In Metaph.*, Proem).

What has happened here? There is an unmistakable effort to keep God and the angels from playing the role of subject to the science of metaphysics. Sacred theology had already appropriated God as its specifying subject.[17] This subject accordingly had to be different from the subject of any of the other sciences. The Avicennian framework was at hand to exclude God and the highest causes from the subject of metaphysics, and substitute instead the common aspect of being.[18] It safeguarded the distinction between metaphysics and sacred theology. But why did not God but also the "intellectual substances" (*Deus et intellectuales substantiae*) have to be left outside the subject of metaphysics? Surely the exclusion of God alone would have been enough to provide for the specification of sacred theology. Why, moreover, the interest in showing that in this context metaphysics bears entirely upon things separate from matter "secundum esse et rationem," not only things that can never be in matter, but also aspects that are able to be found without matter, such as common being?[19]

These preoccupations suppose a conception of metaphysics in which separate substances, apart from distinction into God and angels, functioned as the subject of metaphysics. This conception was well enough known at the time through the position of Averroes.[20] But there was enough in the Aristotelian text to substantiate it in the description of metaphysics as "theoretical science."[21] The title "theology" had to be accorded it, and was allowed it by Aquinas on the ground that it dealt with the separate substances in the way already explained, namely as the causes of common being.[22] The alternate Aristotelian title "first philosophy" was similarly admitted for the same reason, namely that it treated of these first causes of things.[23] Both these ways of expressing the nature of the science had accordingly to be accepted and the infection localized. The new standpoint would leave the divine as the specifying subject of only sacred theology, and yet acknowledge that it was studied, though in a different way, by the philosophical pursuit. This made the traditional title "metaphysics" free to designate the science from the viewpoint of its specification by its own subject, common being, which is "transphysical" insofar as it is common to material and immaterial things alike: "*Metaphysica,* inquantum considerat ens et ea quae consequuntur ipsum. Haec enim transphysica inveniuntur in via resolutionis, sicut magis communia post minus communia" (Proem). The term "metaphysics," consequently, can still imply a science of what is separate from matter, though at the cost of introducing a technical notion of "separate" that is not to be found in the Aristotelian treatises. How could any common notions be regarded in the Aristotelian context as "separata a materia secundum esse"? To be separate in the sense contrasted with "separate in notion," they would have to be substances, and for Aristotle nothing common or universal can be a substance in the setting of the Metaphysics (Z 13, 1038b8–35).

What is the significance of this change in location for the subject of metaphysics? If for Aristotle primary philosophy or theological science dealt with the separate substances in the sense of the divine beings, and with all other things on account of their reference to this primary instance of being, does not the change become a complete reversal in perspective?[24] For Aquinas common being, from which the divine is excluded, becomes the subject of metaphysics. The divine is treated by the science only because of the reference it has to common being. Yet the one formula "separata a materia secundum esse et rationem" serves for Aquinas as the means of expressing his own conception of the subject of metaphysics in words that would apply equally well to the subject of the Aristotelian theological science.

How has this change come about? In his commentary on Boethius' De Trinitate, Aquinas had occasion to deal with the notion of theology against both the Aristotelian and the Christian backgrounds. Boethius, following Aristotle, had written that while natural philosophy and mathematics are types of non-abstract science (inabstracta), theology is in contrast to them abstract and separable (abstracta atque separabilis), since there is no matter nor movement in the substance of God.[25] In Aristotelian fashion Aquinas takes up the consideration of this subject in the plural as res divinae—divine things (V, 4, resp. 3; p. 194.14). The use of the plural, though taken from Aristotle, is supported by the Scriptural way of referring to the "invisible things of God" (ibid., line 22—from Rom., I, 20) and "the things that are of God" (p. 195.1—from I Cor., II, 11). In this way the Aristotelian plural in referring to the divine is made to bear upon the unique Christian God.

So understood these divine things can be considered in two ways, as far as the specification of theology for Aquinas is concerned. They can be considered in their role of the common principles of all things. In this way alone can they be treated by the philosophers in the science that has as its subject being qua being and which is called by them divine science. In the second way the divine things are considered insofar as they are things that subsist in themselves, and not as manifested through effects. Procedure in the first of these two ways gives rise to philosophical theology or metaphysics. Procedure in the second way is that of the theology of sacred scripture. Both deal with things separate from matter *secundum esse*, though separate respectively in two different ways, namely as things that can never be in matter, such as God and the angels, or as things that can be without matter though sometimes found in matter. Objects separate in the first way constitute the subject of sacred theology, while they function only as the principles of the subject of philosophical theology (pp. 194.14-195.27).

This conception of the science of metaphysics is merely repeated in the Proem to the commentary on the *Metaphysics*, without any significant addition or change. But the chronologically prior development of the doctrine, in the course of the commentary on Boethius, shows clearly enough the issue that is at stake. If God as he exists in himself is allowed to function as the subject of metaphysics, no room will be left for a further science about God arising from divine revelation.[26] The preoccupation is to make the intellectual world safe for sacred theology. The concern of the Christian theologian is crystal clear. It is allayed by making a new type of separate objects specify metaphysics, while the divine is left free to specify sacred theology.

The task was rendered comparatively easy and the results readily acceptable in the framework already established by Avicenna. But is the key feature in the new notion of separate object, namely separate in being (*secundum esse*), characteristically Avicennian? It is hardly Aristotelian. In the "Proem" to the commentary on the *Metaphysics* the topic is introduced through contrast with the separation of the mathematicals: "Et non solum secundum rationem, sicut mathematica, sed etiam secundum esse, sicut Deus et intelligentiae." In this contrast, *esse* can scarcely mean anything other than existence. If it had the formal sense that it would have in its regular Aristotelian use in a setting like this, it would not set up a contrast. In the Aristotelian use of the infinitive verb "to be" in similar contexts, the formal aspects of a thing were signified. For instance, the dividing and uniting by a point or instant are the same thing but differ in εἶναι (*Ph.*, IV 13, 222a16-20). Here and elsewhere in Aristotle[27] the infinitive is used synonomously with *logos*, in the sense of a formal aspect. Used with "separate," it would accordingly mean separate in notion, and not separate *secundum esse* in the additional meaning desired here by Aquinas. *Esse* would have to retain the Boethian meaning of *definition*.[28] The force of the *secundum esse* in its present use by St. Thomas calls for considerably more, then, than the formal Aristotelian meaning. Nor can the Boethian text that provides the take-off point for the discussion be expected to furnish metaphysical basis for the new concept of separation *secundum esse et rationem*.

What new factor, then, is at work in the development of the formula "separata a materia secundum esse et rationem" (*In Metaph.*, Proem.) to describe the subject of metaphysics? The context strongly suggests the meaning of existence: "...non solum illa quae numquam in materia esse possunt, sicut

Deus et intellectuales substantiae, sed etiam illa quae possunt sine materia esse, sicut ens commune." The prima facie meaning suggested by these words is that objects like God and the intellectual substances can never *exist* in matter, and that an object like common being is able to occur without matter. The reference seems clearly enough to bear on existential status, rather than on anything pertaining to the notions themselves. The verb is accordingly translated as "exist" without any hesitation in the English renditions "those things which can never exist in matter" (tr. Rowan). In the pertinent passages in the commentary on Boethius the existential bearing had been expressed so strongly as to leave it beyond doubt.[29]

In the Boethian commentary the meaning of *esse* had even in the article on the specification of divine science been clearly given its sharp Thomistic force as the actuality of essence.[30] Is this notion brought into the commentary on the *Metaphysics*? Does it bear upon the presentation of the subject of the science as common being distinct from divine being, in the recognizable Avicennian framework? If so, does it mean that the notion of separation *secundum esse* gives the subject of metaphysics a status that it could not possibly have had in Avicenna?

The rejection of the Avicennian notion of being, regarded as adding something by way of accident to the essence, is explicit in the commentary on the Aristotelian *Metaphysics*. In explaining the Aristotelian tenet that the substance of a thing is unitary and existent in virtue of its own self and not in virtue of something added, Aquinas takes the occasion to note that Avicenna's view is different. But Avicenna is wrong, for the being of a thing though other than its essence is not to be understood as something superadded in the fashion of an accident. Rather, it is as it were constituted by the principles of the essence.[31]

The characteristically Thomistic view of being pervades this passage. It means that the being of a finite thing is other than the thing itself, yet is caused by the very essence of the thing, so that nothing is more essential to a thing than its being. Not other by way of subsequent accident, the being can be other only by way of a prior actuality.[32] The disturbing feature is that this uniquely Thomistic doctrine is being used as a norm for judging in the course of a commentary on Aristotle. It is used ostensibly to defend Aristotle's tenet that the substance of a thing is existent in virtue of its own self. At the same time the tenet of the Aristotelian passage that "an existent man" (*ens homo*) is a merely verbal reduplication of what is contained in "a man" (*homo*—In IV *Metaph.*, lect.2, no. 550) is waved aside by the blunt assertion that the being of a thing is other than its essence (no. 558). The assertion is made with all assurance that it need not be defended here, and that it is accepted by the readers without argument.

This shows that the notion of being by which both Aristotle and Avicenna are being judged in the commentary is the notion developed in Aquinas' own thinking. According to that notion the nature of being is found only in a unique primary instance. It is not a nature that could be shared either univocally or in analogically ranged degrees.[33] As a nature it cannot be common. Wherever it is found outside its primary instance it is other than the nature it actuates. In consequence the nature of being cannot function as common being nor be ranged as an instance under the notion of common being. Rather, as the cause of all the things that exhibit common being it is to be regarded in this respect as the cause of common being. With the subject of metaphysics in the wake of Avicenna distinguished from God and the highest causes, and now with Aquinas designated as common being, the kind of metaphysics introduced in the Proem to the Aristotelian commentary of Aquinas becomes clear. The notion of metaphysics presented as the entry into the Aristotelian thought is that of Aquinas himself. In its light, then one need not be surprised to find judgment passed on Aristotle and Avicenna, as well as on Averroes and any other thinker.

The frequently made assertion that Aquinas was interested only in truth and not in the author making the statements now comes into focus as regards the Aristotelian *Metaphysics*. For St. Thomas human truth consisted in the correspondence of intellect with things,[34] and his own metaphysics was the way in which his own thinking corresponded to things on the metaphysical level. It was accordingly the one truth in which he could present metaphysical tenets, no matter whose words he was using.

Viewed in this light, then, the kind of philosophical truth being propounded in the commentary on the *Metaphysics* should be the truth developed and expressed in the metaphysical thinking of Aquinas himself, to the extent the text of the *Metaphysics* gives occasion to do so. The care to safeguard the interests of sacred theology in the delineation of the subject of metaphysics has already shown the dominant thinking of the Christian theologian. The particular metaphysical cast into which the Proem throws the discussion that is to ensue, now indicates further the intention to present the meaning of the Aristotelian treatises in a general framework that cannot be that of Aristotle himself. How this complicated orientation works out in practice may best be seen from a study of the details that emerge as the commentary pursues its course.

The opening paragraphs (nos. 1-4) add to the thought three well-developed philosophical reasons, not found in the present passage but taken from authentic Aristotelian reasoning in other works. They substantiate the opening sentence of the *Metaphysics*, which Aristotle himself presents merely as a readily acceptable observation. This procedure does not differ in any essential way from a modern commentator's use of Aristotelian tenets from other treatises or from fragments to explain a doctrine stated succinctly in a particular sentence. In the paragraphs that follow, other Aristotelian works such as *De Anima* and the

Ethics continue to be drawn upon to explain tenets of the present treatise, and an outside author, Cicero (no. 11) is called upon for help. All this is still standard practice among commentators today. By and large the commentary continues this presentation of the meaning found in the text, adding information judged relevant such as the names of the seven sages of ancient Greece, and representing Thales as "committing his 'disputationes' to writing" (no. 77) quite as any eminent medieval Master would do. So far things proceed as in the usual understanding of a commentary, with the virtues and the faults of its epoch.

Only at rare intervals does the alien framework imposed by the Proem make itself apparent. In this, Aquinas seems to feel himself fully in accord with Aristotle, who could make what was obscure in a preceding philosopher appear as something admirable. That was achieved by articulating "distinctly and manifestly" what the earlier philosopher wanted to say, that is, "what his intellect was tending towards, but which he was unable to express" (no. 196). In corresponding fashion Aquinas, as has just been seen (supra, nn. 31-34), explains the Aristotelian identity of being and thing in the light of his own tenet that a thing is other than its being, even though being is essential to the thing. In a severe criticism of Averroes he seems nevertheless to acquiesce in the position that knowledge of the separate substances (plural) is the goal of human intellection,[35] and in the context of the distinction of the primary philosophy from both mathematics and the philosophy of nature he continues to speak of these substances in the plural (nos. 1163-1164; 2263-2267), although apparently equating them with God as the subject matter of theological science.[36] In this setting he feels obliged to go out of the text's way to note that the primary philosophy is not concerned with separate things only, but also with sensible things. Then comes the revealing concession: "unless perhaps we may say, as Avicenna says, that these common objects of which this science treats are called separate *secundum esse* ... because they do not of necessity have their existence in matter, as do the mathematicals."[37]

This last text can leave little doubt that Aquinas is well aware of the plain meaning of the Aristotelian passages. Separate substances, namely divine things, are the subject treated of by the primary philosophy, which is on that account theological science. One has therefore to add sensible substances, *unless* one wishes to use the Avicennian framework in which notions like common being are called separate *secundum esse*.

This conclusion is confirmed by the reference to the beginning of Book Γ for the way in which the science of the primary being is the science of common being.[38] The Aristotelian framework is clearly recognized. In it the nature of the primary instance specifies the science. The secondary instances are treated of by the science in virtue of their reference to the primary instance. In the Avicennian framework, on the contrary, the common aspect specifies the science, and the divine is treated of in the science only because of reference to the common aspect, namely as its cause.

The Thomistic metaphysics of existence, however, requires that the reference to common being be explained in terms of efficient causality. The differences of the Thomistic commentary from the original Aristotelian meaning become especially apparent when details of this reference are under consideration. Aquinas acknowledges without hesitation that in Aristotle's view the first principles in the genus of substances, the heavenly bodies are besouled (nos. 2476 and 2536), and that the eternity of motion and time is essential in Aristotle's own procedure regarding the immaterial substances (no. 2496). These two tenets he himself rejects. Aristotle's reasons accordingly are not regarded as cogent for establising his conclusions. Nevertheless the conclusions themselves follow with necessity when the bringing of the world into existence is the operative factor in the reasoning (no. 2499). What can this mean if not that the Aristotelian conclusions, in order to be cogent, have to be based upon the existential actuality uppermost in Aquinas own metaphysical thinking? The shying away from the Aristotelian eternity of the world, a possible philosophical alternative, indicates also the dominance of theological motivation in this problem.

Correspondingly the *necessary* perpetuity of cosmic motion, based by Aristotle on final causality, is explained as depending in its totality upon the *will* of God. The illustration used is that artifacts are assimilated to the artisan insofar as in them the artisan's will is fulfilled.[39] The nature of the Aristotelian reference to the first causes by way of assimilation seems clearly enough recognized, but it is explained in terms of efficient causality originating from will. Further, an Avicennian and ultimately Neoplatonic consideration that a unique first principle can cause only a unitary effect is dealt with in terms of existence as an acquired actuality. It is set aside on the ground that the one efficient cause can understand a multiplicity of things and cause them accordingly (no. 2559). In the same setting the Aristotelian doctrine that a separate substance has only itself as its intelligible object is explained as meaning that God "by understanding himself understands all other things" (no. 2614) and "by knowing himself knows all things" (no. 2615). The reason given is that as first principle he contains all things in his power. Further, the order of the universe is a working out of what is in the intellect and the will of the primary movent (no. 2631), and all natural things obtain their inclinations towards their goal from the primary intelligent being (no. 2634). Against this clearly etched background of Thomistic metaphysics the explicit assertions about divine providence made in the course of the commentary (nos. 1215–1222) fall into place. The overall theological interest also comes to the fore in this regard with the statement that on account of the philosophical conclusions all things may be said according to the Catholic faith to be subject to divine providence.[40]

With the foregoing data from the survey of the commentary on the *Metaphysics*, one is in a position to formulate the questions about the kind of procedure the work involves. Quantitatively, the overwhelming percentage of the book confines itself to explanation of the Aristotelian text just as the text stands, with recourse to other Aristotelian treatises and to other writers for elucidation as the occasion demands. Taken apart as just in itself, this almost total extent of the commentary does not prima facie differ in spirit from what is understood today as a philosophical commentary or interpretation. It can accordingly be cited and used to advantage by modern commentaries on Aristotle as though it were exactly of the same literary genre as they. Any noticeable divergences can be accounted for in terms of the different literary style and approach and background of the two epochs, medieval and modern. The treatment in the Aristotelian text would from this perspective be thoroughly philosophical in character.

Even within the strictly philosophical explanation, however, at times the judgments are made and the decisions are given on the strength of the Thomistic metaphysics of existence. These occasions are few, comparatively, but they are concerned with philosophically important issues. They are not marked off by any indications that they are intrusions from the outside. Rather, they seem part of the normal flow of thought. Do they show that the whole thrust of the commentary is to propound Thomistic thought, into which the great body of Aristotelian philosophy is skilfully absorbed? Is this the bearing given it by the Proem in making common being rather than separate substance the subject of the metaphysics about to be explained?

Further, does the theological concern that is implicit in the Proem affect the general character of the treatment throughout the commentary? Does it effectively alter the rank of the Aristotelian primary philosophy as supreme among the sciences? Is it the source of the assertions about the negotiable status of the Aristotelian reasons for the eternity of the world and the besouled nature of the heavenly bodies, and of those positive claims about divine providence? Is it all-pervasive enough to change the totality of the *philosophy* in the commentary, both Aristotelian and Thomistic, into the wine of theology? Or may it be dismissed as an over-scrupulous and unjustifiable propensity of a Christian theologian to go out of his way in order to insert corrections of doctrinal error and unorthodox tendencies piecemeal wherever he finds these aberrations, no matter what happens to be the real nature of the materials with which he is dealing?

With the questions already formulated, a brief glance at the other Aristotelian commentaries of ·Aquinas is now in order before attempting the answers.

III

In the commentary on the *Ethics*, the subject of moral philosophy is discussed not in a Proem but at the beginning of the commentary proper. It is located
in human activity directed towards a purpose. On the basis of man acting first
as an individual, secondly as a member of a family or household, and thirdly as
a citizen, it allows moral philosophy to be divided into three parts (no. 6). The
first part is treated of in the *Ethics* (no. 7). Aristotle's concern with political
philosophy in the ethical treatises is explained away by stating that "the doctrine of this book contains the first elements of political science" (no. 31), and
"the reflections of the present science pertain to political science, because in
this science the principles of political science are given" (no. 225). The
philosophy in the Aristotelian *Ethics* is accordingly regarded as a science in
some way different from the Aristotelian political science. It is placed in a
framework in which a general moral science is divided into three parts, of which
the first is concerned with the activities of the individual man, and the third
with those of civil society. The second is left for economics, understood as the
science of running a household or estate.

Can any preoccupation be recognized behind this refusal to accept Aristotle's
political science as the *whole* of moral philosophy?[41] The threefold division of
moral philosophy has a deep background in Christian tradition, through Albert
the Great and Hugh of St. Victor to Cassiodorus and Boethius.[42] In spite of the
very notion of "moral," implying as it does the basis of *mores*, i.e. customs
developed in a common culture, this division allows a morality to a man just as
an individual. With Aquinas, moreover, care is taken to restrict the absolute
dominance of political science as described in Aristotle. Political science is
dominant "not absolutely but in the order of active sciences that are concerned
with things human" (no. 31). Above them all is the divine science, which envisages the ultimate end of the whole universe. The Aristotelian *Ethics*, on the
other hand, deals only with the imperfect happiness attainable in the present
life on earth.[43]

The preoccupation, accordingly, seems to be to safeguard the supernatural
happiness of the beatific vision as the ultimate end of man. This supreme goal
is something to be attained by each man as an individual. Hence there can be a
morality that applies to each man as an individual, and not just as a member of
political society. The Aristotelian *Ethics*, in finding that human happiness consisted essentially in intellectual activity, offered a welcome means to express the
theological doctrine of the beatific vision. But what was said in the *Ethics* about
the requirements for the contemplative happiness, namely, friends, good
looks, affluence, full life span on earth, and so on, did not apply in any obvious

sense to the Christian ultimate end. The whole of the Aristotelian happiness had therefore to be located in the imperfect happiness of the present life, subordinated entirely to a higher happiness even in its role of end for human activity. With this framework of Christian tradition made manifest, the commentary of Aquinas on the *Ethics* is able to proceed in the same way as the one on the *Metaphysics*. It occupies itself with explaining the text just as the text stands, with only the occasional indication in passing that it is placing the whole consideration in a Christian setting.[44]

The commentary on the *Physics* experiences no special difficulty in accepting mobile being as the subject for natural philosophy. It places the topic, however, in the framework of abstraction from matter, contrasting definition with existence: "...there are some things whose being depends on matter, and that cannot be defined without matter."[45] In that framework a creationist metaphysics is presupposed and freely used (nos. 2001-2008). The first cause is the efficient cause of the whole being, both matter and form.[46] Movement can accordingly be regarded as beginning in an indivisible moment, not requiring any prior movement (no. 2054).

The problem in which the creationist metaphysics surfaces so clearly is admittedly theological. It is the frankly acknowledged (nos. 2041, 2043) conflict of the Aristotelian eternal world with the Christian belief that the world began in time. The Aristotelian reasons are recognized as valid where movement has to originate through another movement, but not where things begin to exist through the production of their whole being by the first cause of being (nos. 2044-2045). The truth here held on faith cannot in consequence be efficaciously attacked by the Aristotelian arguments (no. 2044). Averroes is blamed for making occasion of these arguments to attack the faith (no. 1996), and the reader's confidence in him is softened by showing how the Arabian commentator's understanding of Aristotle's method is "ridiculous" (no.1970). It makes everything appear confused and without order, and his basic reason is "entirely frivolous" (no.1972).

The genre of theological polemic is unmistakable in this manner of handling the problem of the world's eternity. Nevertheless, just as in the commentaries on the *Metaphysics* and on the *Ethics*, the manifestations of sacred theology and existential metaphysics are very rare.[47] The procedure in its near entirety consists in explanation of the text just as the text stands, quite in accord with the procedure in the other two commentaries. Yet it can bring in the theological and existential considerations without any indications or feeling of an alleged change to a different type of treatment. They all seem to be integral parts of the enterprise, rather than intrusions from outside.

The Proem to the commentary on *Perihermeneias* (*De Interpretatione*) divides the science of logic according to the three activities of the intellect, namely simple apprehension, enunciation ("judgment"—nos. 31-32), and reasoning. The first two of these activities are expressly taken from an Aristotelian division, and the third is regarded as added (no. 1). Logic is without hesitation projected as a science.[48] Mention of essence or quiddity as understood "absolutely" through simple apprehension seems to presuppose the metaphysical doctrine of existence as grasped through judgment. Existence as the specifying object of judgment seems likewise understood in the explanation of truth (no. 31). Existence is explicitly presented as the actuality of every form, either substantial or accidental (nos. 71-73). Likewise unmistakable is the existential dependence of all effects on the divine will, in the explanation of God's knowledge of future contingents (nos. 195-197), and the theological motif of safeguarding the Christian notion of providence.

In the commentary on the *Posterior Analytics*[49] the theological concern does not appear, but the existential metaphysics seems back of the contrast of definition with being (nos. 15-16) and of the distinction between being and substance in all things except in God (nos. 462-463), as well as of the requirement of a cause for the existence of all necessary beings except the one first principle (no. 480). Undoubtedly a theological interest can be detected behind this last requirement, but the language remains strictly philosophical and does not allow any theological motif to appear openly. Logic is presented as a science in the Proem (no. 2), and the Aristotelian treatises on it are located in the framework of the three activities of the human intellect (nos. 4-6).

The commentary on the *De Anima* locates its study in the framework of the sciences in which first philosophy deals with things that either are or can be without matter.[50] The existential setting is still clearer in the explanation of cognition through spiritual existence in contrast to natural existence (nos. 43, 159, 282-284, 553), and in the twofold existence to which the common nature is in this way open (nos. 378-380). Theological interests are evident in the distinction of God from the other separate substances, from the viewpoint of intellection (no. 726), and in the explanation of the two intellects as powers of the soul (734-745). On the other hand, no existential stress is here laid on the Aristotelian dictum that for living things to live is to be.[51]

The commentary on *De Sensu et Sensato* likewise uses the framework of separation *secundum esse et rationem* (no. 1), and of the twofold existence of the natures of things (nos. 213, 291). The commentaries on *De Memoria et Reminiscentia* and *Meteorologica* seem occupied solely with the explanation of the Aristotelian text. That on *De Caelo et de Mundo* invokes the Catholic faith for the creation of the world in time (nos. 64-66, 287), and in these passages and elsewhere (no. 91) repeats that God causes the heavens as an intelligent agent. The reasons given by Aristotle hold only against an original production of things by way of motion, and in no way militate against the teaching of the Catholic faith. The supreme God is distinguished from the other separate substances (nos. 295, 334), and is viewed as conserving a nature (no. 295), and as the cause that imparts existence and motion (nos. 291, 295, 299, 334). Aristotle is asserted to have regarded God as the maker, and not only the final cause of the heavenly bodies (no. 91). The commentary on *De Generatione et Corruptione* (Proem, no. 2) uses the framework in which as in metaphysics the common genus considered by a science is contradistinguished from the cause of that genus. In the commentary on the *Politics* (Proem, no. 6) the subject matter is regarded as contained under that of the moral sciences in general, and as the culminating point of the philosophy that is concerned with things human (no. 7). The doctrine, including the discussion on slavery (nos. 47–96), is explained just as it stands in the text. The error of the Gentiles in anthropomorphizing the separate substances created by the one supreme God (no. 30; cf. no. 154) and similarly in calling great rulers gods (no. 84), is noted. The same overwhelming quantitative predominance of explanation of the text as it stands, with occasional appearance of the already noted theological and existential considerations, is accordingly observable in these commentaries.[52]

On the whole, then, one may say that the other commentaries continue to manifest the pattern shown in the commentary on the *Metaphysics*. The sciences are made to fit into the framework in which metaphysics deals with common being as subject and separate substance as cause of the subject. The recognition of a moral science for individual actions, distinct from political philosophy, is added. The theological interests of creation, of the supremacy of God over the other separate substances, and of universal divine providence, are safeguarded wherever occasion demands. Polytheism is branded an error. Finally, the Thomistic metaphysics of existence, in the relation of existence to common nature and in the undertstanding of efficient causality as the bestowal of existence, seems taken for granted throughout.

IV

The above survey makes it clear that, except for quantitatively minimal proportions, the Aristotelian commentaries of Aquinas are made up of explanations of the text just as it stands, with discussions of its background and of the various opinions of others about it. In all this the Aquinas commentaries do not range outside the limits of the modern notion about what a commentary should be. But in two-thirds of these commentaries on Aristotle there are passages that show an overriding theological concern. In two-thirds of them there are likewise passages that reveal a definitely existential metaphysics, something not found in the Aristotelian texts. Finally, three-quarters of the commentaries have passages that locate their subject matter in a framework of the sciences rather different from that of Aristotle.

How is this situation to be assessed? May one close one's eyes to the comparatively small number of passages that introduce theological and existential considerations, as well within the percentage limit to be expected in any commentator with strong religious convictions and definite metaphysical tendencies of his own? May one regard the passages that locate the Aristotelian treatises within the then contemporary classification of the sciences as a quite normal failure to see outside the perspective of the times, much as a modern commentator is hardly blamed for putting Aristotle into frameworks like those of ontology, psychology, or philosophy of science? May all these passages as it were be mentally excised and the other ten commentaries be allowed to join the two in which no indication of theological or existential interest appears, and in which no attempt is made at science classification? In this case the Aristotelian commentaries of Aquinas would be straight philosophical explanations of the text, with all the restrictions and merits and faults of their times.

Can one, though, legimately make this mental excision of the passages that jar with the interpretation? Do not these passages, relatively few in number as they are, set rather the whole tone of the commentaries? Certainly in their own settings they show no signs of being intrusions into the general procedure of the thought. They read as though they belong to the same original inspiration, and unable to be regarded as alien incursions except on norms that were not those of the writer. They flow forcefully from what seems to be a unitary source.

If so, what is that source? It could hardly be the metaphysical or epistemological interest. These could not be for Aquinas the inspiration of the overriding theological concern. Sacred theology, on the contrary, could be and normally would be the source of existential and epistemological inquiries for him. His most penetrating metaphysical thought is found in the commentary on the *Sentences* and other professedly theological works. His most extensive study of the classification of the sciences is in his commentary on Boethius' *De Trinitate*. For him sacred theology, as the absolutely highest wisdom, has the office of judging and orienting the results of all the other sciences.[53] It has every right, accordingly, to survey their results as occasion demands. Exactly that, it seems, has been done in the Aquinas commentaries on Aristotle. In these commentaries, then, may one say that Aquinas continues his dedication to the work of theological wisdom,[54] and that in them he continues to change what was water in the other sciences into the wine of theology?[55] The use of a new existential metaphysics may be taken as established. But that is still on the philosophical level. It does not just in itself prove theological motivation. Its structure is thoroughly philosophical. May the philosophical structure be regarded as remaining intact while its content functions as a part, in fact by far the greatest part quantitatively, of a colloidal theological enterprise?

The colloidal nature of wine allows the water to be extracted from it and replaced without too much difficulty. The overwhelming preponderant part of the commentaries may be extracted in similar fashion from the theological setting given it by the comparatively few theological passages. Extraction of philosophical statements from professed theological works such as the *Summa Theologiae* and the commentary on the *Sentences* has been standard practice for centuries. Likewise the four Aristotelian commentaries in which no theological assertions occur may be viewed in isolation from the whole work of Aquinas and be regarded as merely philosophical commentaries. But in doing so is one encountering the real St. Thomas? Is one understanding what he is doing? Is one at all in tune with the spirit of faith endeavoring to understand all the things with which it comes in contact?

A more vivid objection arises from the quantitative proportions of the theological and philosophical passages. Can a few drops of wine be expected to change into itself a chain of rather large lakes? Here the metaphor seems to break down. The biological simile of a few clusters of living cells affecting the whole medium would be more in order. At any rate, the medieval mind experienced no difficulty in seeing an author express as his own the material taken nearly one hundred per cent from other writers. Peter Lombard, for instance, could be regarded as the author of everything in his four books of *Sentences*, even though practically all the material was taken from others.[56] As long as the writer was asserting mastery over material used and was organizing and directing it towards his own purpose, he was expressing it as his own. There is accordingly not too much difficulty in regarding St. Thomas, in taking on the duties of the wise man (*CG*, I, 2), as considering himself to be pursuing the work of sacred theology throughout the whole course of his commentaries on the Aristotelian text.

It is, of course, much easier to apply this conception of philosophy changed into theology to a work like the *Contra Gentiles*,[57] than to writings that are professedly commentaries on a pagan philosopher. Yet is the difference that crucial? The theologian is writing in the service of faith (supra, n. 55). He sees a wealth of rationally developed truth in the pagan source. What better way to bring it into the service of faith than by exploring it painstakingly word for word, presenting it as a whole, and allowing it thereby to further the understanding of the Christian conception of things? Does not this accomplish the purpose much better than a piecemeal citation of convenient passages? And will not this perspective allow the four commentaries in which there is no express mention of theological interests to be viewed as an integral part of the whole enterprise? Will they be any less theological in character than the long passages within the other commentaries in which no explicit mention of theological concern is found?

But may not the Thomistic commentaries on Aristotle be regarded as Christian philosophy, genuinely philosophical in character yet brought under Christian goals? The notion of Christian philosophy is a difficult one. It has received many interpretations in recent years.[58] If it is to be kept strictly on the philosophical level, however, it cannot use revealed truths as principles for its reasoning.[59] It cannot give them a probative function. Yet the Thomistic commentaries on Aristotle are dominated by this properly theological direction. The creation of the world in time is taught as the way the case actually is. The besouled nature of the heavenly bodies is rejected. Perfect human happiness, the first principle of ethics, is located definitely in the beatific vision. Divine providence is a "must". These considerations dominate the Thomistic interpretation of Aristotle in the commentaries. They seem to generate theology, not philosophy. The purpose is to defend revealed truth, not just Christian philosophical truth.

The distinction between "personal" works of Aquinas and commentaries is obvious and has to remain. In the "personal" works he sets his own order of discussion. In the commentaries he is bound by the order in the text before him. Correspondingly, the theological character of the works will vary. Aristotelian commentary on a philosophical study will not be theological in the same way and to the same extent that the *Summae* and the *Quaestiones Disputatae* are theological. The material that is brought into theological service will manifest at far greater length its philosophical structure. The question therefore is not "theology *or* philosophy?" It concerns theology *and* philosophy found together. The question is whether the theology or the philosophy gives the work as a whole its characteristic specification. Here, just as in a colloidal, the issue of degrees enters. The *Summa Theologiae* is more manifestly theological than the *Summa contra Gentiles*, and both are more so than the Aristotelian commentaries. But the best philosophy in Aquinas is to be found in the most theological of his writings. Its cogency and its worth as philosophy are not at all diminished. Yet the anvil on which it was hammered into shape was theology.

This limited and selective participation in philosophy by the theologian is still a problem today. Aquinas at the height of his theological career devoted a decade to the interpretation of Aristotle. There is no indication that this was a side interest or a hobby. Rather, the theologian seemed to feel the need of philosophical guidance from Aristotle for his own theological work. Was this guidance, with all its prudential selection and its specially directed development, not incorporated into the theological enterprise? And may it not remain genuinely philosophy as material used by a theologian, while functioning on the theological level as the most apt medium for developing and expressing an overall theological conception of things?

AQUINAS ON KNOWING EXISTENCE

I

Difficulties about existence have plagued Western thought since the time of Parmenides. The Eleatic sage had concentrated on what was most obvious and most incontrovertible to him, namely, that something exists ($\overset{\prime}{o}\pi\omega s \ \overset{\prime\prime}{\epsilon}\sigma\tau\iota\nu$—DK, *Fr.* 2.3). He made that tenet the way (*Fr.* 2.4) and the test (*Fr.* 7.5-8.2) of truth. From it he drew consequences that succeeding Greek thinkers from Empedocles to Plotinus accepted in part and rejected in part, intrigued by much of what he had stated but repelled by seeming enormities in some of his conclusions. Later, the patristic acceptation of being as the most appropriate name for God gave additional complication to the issue.[1] In modern times the Kantian and linguistic approaches have raised the questions how existence is a predicate and whether there is a concept of it, and if so, what kind of a concept. On the other hand, the impact of Heidegger has inspired renewed and often enthusiastic absorption in the important role played by existence in philosophical thought, and current contacts with Hindu philosophies are furthering this interest.

This modern existentialist thrust, as is well enough known, prompted Thomistic writers, notably Etienne Gilson and the late Jacques Maritain, to focus attention on the basic function of existence in the metaphysical thinking of Aquinas. But on the way existence is known for him these writers, as well as their colleagues who interpret him in a participationist or transcendental framework, profess overt disagreement among themselves. The fact is highlighted in Gilson's most recently published article, as it had been in Maritain's post-humous book and in an article that had appeared a few years earlier.[2] Divergencies just as profound and just as incisive are explicitly acknowledged in the other two trends.[3]

These deep-seated differences among leading interpreters suggest the need for a close examination of the way existence is grasped by human cognition in the epistemology of Aquinas. Fortunately, an article in one of his earliest and most comprehensive works outlines his tenets on this question with remarkable clarity. The identical stand is repeated in later writings. There is no reason to think that Aquinas ever changed these views, even though the issues in which he was engaged in subsequent years did not bring him into immediate contact with the problem. The tenets belong rather to the genetic fiber of his thinking.

The one preliminary hindrance to approaching Aquinas and his interpreters in this way might be the Aristotelian dictum (*De An.*, II 4, 415a16-22; cf. I 1,402b14-16) that the nature of cognitive acts and faculties is known only through their objects. Yet equally true is the consideration that the human mind can reflect upon its own activities. From the way in which it shows itself to be functioning when it grasps existence, some needed light may be thrown upon the kind of object immediately attained in the cognition. While not at all replacing the more fundamental role of existence itself for revealing the nature of the cognitive activity that knows it, the reflexive focus on the way existence is known respectively for these writers can hardly help but bring out the kind of object isolated by each of them as existence.

In the Parmenides fragments the vision that "something exists" seems meant clearly enough as a direct *intuition* of being, in the way the term "intuition" is commonly used today.[4] Be that as it may, Maritain in the article just mentioned (supra, n, 2) used "intuition" to designate one way being is known by the intellect, *"in and through* an affirmative judgment of existing" (p.17). This is a judgment different in kind from the type in which a predicate is joined to a subject by the copula "is," even though in the predicative judgment the verb itself has the existential import required for the intuition (p. 25, n. 1). The intuition gives rise to a subsequent and reflexive *concept* of existence, found for instance in the tenet that the soul gives its own existence to the body (pp. 17-18). But there are two other concepts of existence. Both are independent of the intuition. One is abstracted in the way any common notion is abstracted from a sensible thing, as with the existence of a rose or a visitor in front of you. The other is abstracted in a way that frees it from restriction to sensible things, as in Aristotle's metaphysics, even though it is due solely to abstraction (pp. 18-32). For Maritain, accordinly, existence is known in four different ways. Three of them give original knowledge of it, while the other is a reflexive concept of what is originally intuited in judgment.[5]

In the article referred to (supra, n.2), Gilson replies to Maritain's (p. 18) charge that fascination with the *intuition* of being causes him to reject the *concept* of existence.[5] Gilson (p. 8) notes that in Aquinas there are no corresponding expressions for "concepts of being" or "concept of existence." So he has to explain what he himself understands by the terms used. "Concept" today in the exegesis of Aquinas is to be applied only to things that have being (*étants*). "Concept of existence" would be just the concept of an "*étant* avec connotation d'origine" (p. 9). Similarly we have sensible *intuitions* of things that have being, but existence as we know it is not a thing. Moreover, to be the object of an intellectual intuition, it would have to be known apart from any phantasm. But that is impossible in the present state of human nature (pp. 9–16). Gilson, however, would allow the use of "intuition" for knowledge of first principles, in contrast to knowledge of conclusions (p. 11). Existence itself, though, is grasped neither through intuition nor conceptualization, but a type of intellections in which it is asserted, posited, affirmed, and is thereby "implicitly conceived" in every *étant* that comes under our experience (p. 16).

In the participationist interpretation, Cornelio Fabro finds that the relevant texts of Aquinas "deal with the characteristic function of the two operations of the mind which divide the two-fold content of the notion of *ens,* essence and the *actus essendi.* Therefore, the *notio entis* precedes them both, just as, in fact, *ens* precedes *res* and *verum* in the grouping of the transcendentals.'"At its face value this tenet would make the notion of "a being" prior to the grasp of existence and the grasp of essence, just as the notion of "a being" is prior to the other transcendentals. It will have to be examined vis-a-vis the primacy accorded by Aquinas to existence. Against the transcendental Thomists, moreover, Fabro expressly rejects the stand that existence is originally and solely known through judgment.

Finally, in the words of the writer credited with coining the designation "transcendental Thomism," abstraction is explained by its adherents in a way "diametrically opposed" to Neo-Thomism. For them "there existed in the thought of Aquinas a deeper transcendental conception of it, where 'being' and 'something which' are considered as a priori contributions of man's intellect, conditions of the possibility of every known knowledge" and are known in sense cognition, for "man discovers 'being' only in the data of experience, he can never see or intuit it, in its purity, in his own intellect. He naturally projects it outwards, into his sense experience, and he becomes explicitly aware of it only in his sense knowledge."[8] This description is crystal clear, against the Kantian background. With it there can be no intellectual intuition of being in Aquinas, quite as there could not be in Kant. Does this mean precisely no intuition of existence? In the context, the answer can be only affirmative. "Being," contrasted expressly with "something which," has to mean "existence" for Aquinas (see infra, nn. 9–12; 15). Accordingly, the origin of the notion "existence" will lie for transcendental Thomism in the mind's own a priori structure.

The results of this survey may be summed up briefly. For Gilson and the transcendental Thomists there can be no intellectual intuition of existence in Aquinas. For Gilson there is a sense intuition of things that have existence, and for the transcendental Thomists it has an a priori source for its presence in sense cognition. For Fabro there is a notion of it, consequent upon the notion of a being and described as comparable to the Scholastic transcendental notions in its sequence upon that basic notion. For Maritain, in contrast to these interpreters, there is in judgment an intellectual intuition of existence, and there are three concepts of it, two of them independent of the intuition.

How do these various interpretations compare with what is found in the text of Aquinas himself?

II

The viewpoint presumably fundamental in this question is stated clearly and concisely by Aquinas in his commentary on the *Sentences* of Peter Lombard.[9] There the human intellect's basic awareness of a thing is described as twofold, because of the two ways in which everything presents itself to its gaze. These two are the thing's nature and its being. The well-known text may be translated in painfully literal fashion:

> Since in a thing there are two considerations, the thing's quiddity and its being, to these two there corresponds a twofold activity of the intellect. One is called by philosophers "formation," in which it (i.e., the intellect) apprehends the quiddities of things. This is also called "the thinking of indivisibles," by the Philosopher in the third book of the *De Anima*. The other comprehends the thing's being by composing an affirmation, because also the being of a thing composed of matter and form, from which it (i.e., the intellect) gets the cognition, consists in a composition of form with matter or of accident with subject (*In I Sent.*, d.38, q.1, a.3, Solut.; ed. Mandonnet, I, 903).

Later the same article, in speaking of both being and not-being, reaffirms the tenet that the human intellect *apprehends* this only by synthesizing and dividing:

> But our intellect, whose cognition takes its rise from things that have composite being, apprehends that being only by composing and dividing (ibid., ad 2m; I, 904).

The reasoning in this passage proceeds in orthodox Aristotelian fashion from objects to their corresponding activities. It uses a complicated vocabulary that calls for close scrutiny yet need not cause special irritation once its historical origins have been noted. So at the risk of some weariness its technical expressions may be submitted to the appropriate queries. What is their exact force?

How may their meaning be best rendered in English? How useful are they today?

First, the term "formation" is taken directly from the Latin translation of an Arabic word that has the basic sense of "image." It accordingly conveys a meaning that is modeled on the notion of a picture-like knowledge of the thing, and that may be rendered in English today by the word "concept."[10] The corresponding verb can be considered later.

Secondly, the term "quiddities" indicates unmistakably the object of which the "picture" is made. The term stands for that which is given "form" in the mind by the cognitional activity. Unlike "formation," "quiddity" was already entrenched in Scholastic vocabulary, and it survived the epoch. It meant the answer to the question "What (*quid*) is the thing?" In ancient times the question had been formulated philosophically by Socrates. It ran through the dialogues of Plato and the treatises of Aristotle. In the immediate background of Aquinas it had come to be placed in direct contrast to the question of "Does the thing exist?"[11] With both questions so understood in medieval times, the first could be answered positively while the second was answered negatively. You could know what a phoenix (i.e., a bird that arises from its own ashes) is without knowing that is really existed (*In II Sent.*, d.3, q.1, a.1, Solut.; II, 87). The second question was taken quite differently from its Aristotelian meaning, even though Aristotle's example of an eclipse (A*Po.*, II 8,93b2–3) was coupled with that of the phoenix. Aristotle (ibid., a20; cf. 7,92b17–18) meant that you could not know what a thing is without thereby knowing it under the general aspect of being. But by the time of Aquinas the contrast was between the thing and its existence. In the commentary (*In I Sent.*, d.33, q.1, a.1, ad 1m; I, 766) he had already explained what he understood by the Latin infinitive *esse* when it is contrasted with the quiddity or essence or nature of the thing. It meant the actuality of the essence, an actuality that explicitly was not an activity but rather a perfection that preceded the whole order of activity. This was something very new in the history of Western philosophy, but it is Aquinas' notion of *existence* from first to last. In a context like the present the infinitive *esse* should therefore be translated as "existence" or "to exist," in the way English idiom demands. *Quidditas*, in contrast, will be rendered "nature" or "essence." In the Latin text no noun had to be used to refer commonly to the two. But in English idiom a noun is obligatory. "Considerations," in the sense in which the verb was used earlier in a similar context by Aquinas,[12] seems the vaguest and consequently the most satisfactory word for the purpose.

Thirdly, and thorniest of all, there is the problem of the names for the twofold activity of the human intellect. An Aristotelian background in the *De Anima* (III 6,430a26-b6) is explicitly indicated. There one type of intellectual activity bears on "indivisibles," which are explained as objects about which there cannot be falsehood. Examples given are "incommensurable" and "diagonal," "pale," "not-pale" and "Cleon." They are obviously the subject and predicate members of a proposition, each taken separately in itself and from this standpoint regarded as neither divided nor synthesized by a copula. The other intellectual activity is the synthesizing or dividing of these articles of thought, with accompanying truth or falsity. In a synthesis like "Cleon is pale" the truth or falsity will depend upon the time to which the reference is made.

These two intellectual activities are each called "apprehension" in the text of Aquinas, with "comprehension" also used for the synthesizing activity. No difference in meaning between the two terms would have likely origin in the nonextant Arabic source.[13] Both the activities may therefore be safely regarded as apprehension. But what is apprehended in the synthesizing cognition, unlike what is known after the manner of a simple image or picture, consists, according to the text of Aquinas, in a synthesis. It consists in the composition of a form with matter or of an accident with subject.[14]

Here suspicions begin to arise. The difference from the Aristotelian source has become significant. What is emphasized by Aquinas is that the synthesis is an "apprehension" or a "comprehension." It is a type of cognition. What is known is correspondingly a synthesis, namely the thing's existence. No examples are given, but they may be readily supplied. The point is seen more easily in the synthesis of accident with subject in a case where the accident is both predicamental ("in a subject"—Aristotle, *Cat.*, 1, 1a24-25) and predicable (*Top.*, I 5, 102b4-9). "Cleon is pale" follows neither from the nature of Cleon as a man nor from the nature of the accident "pale." It is a synthesis in existence at the moment. Nothing in the nature of a man requires that he should look pale here and now, when he might just as readily be suntanned. Nothing in the nature of the color "pale" demands that it be found in Cleon. Yet the intellect knows that Cleon is pale. It knows the existential synthesis, which is the existence in this case. It has a distinctive object, existence, which differs radically from "indivisibles" insofar as it *consists in* a synthesis.

The difference from the Aristotelian viewpoint becomes still more noticeable in "composition of form with matter." Again an example has to be supplied. Nothing in a physical form, say the soul of a man, requires the matter it is here and now actuating, nor does the matter demand that particular soul. The matter is continually transferred through metabolism, the soul remains substantially the same. The two are joined together in the existence of the man at the moment. The apprehension that the man exists has for its object that factual synthesis. This is certainly a novelty in Western metaphysics, but the import is clear. For Aquinas the object of the synthesizing intellectual activity is in every case existence, whether the synthesis is of accident with subject or of form with matter.

How may this synthesizing activity be best designated in English? The intellectual cognition of things from the standpoint of their natures takes place through concepts, as has been seen (supra, n. 10), and may be appropriately called "conceptualization." But is there any corresponding facile term for the knowledge that the thing exists? The designation in the Aristotelian source was "synthesis of objects of thought" (*De An.*, III 6,430a27-28). This expresses rather the relational synthesis of predicate with subject in frozen fashion, as in the fixed propositions "It is raining" or "Inflation is non-existent." These propositions can be compared with the beautiful sunny weather at the moment and the shrinking purchasing power of the dollar, and found false. The actual existence in reality at the moment, with which they are compared, is what is meant by the object of the synthesizing intellectual activity. The synthesis seen in the proposition is a relation of the subject to the predicate. It pertains to the category of relation and is accordingly an object of conceptualization, and not an object of the synthesizing type of intellection

Elsewhere (references supra, n. 9) Aquinas uses expressions taken from the Arabic, and also "second operation" of the intellect. Those of Arabic origin did not survive as technical terms for the knowledge of existence. "Second operation" is misleading, because the two activities always occur simultaneously. Metaphysically, moreover, existence is prior for Aquinas. If any priority is to be reflected in the designation of the act that knows it, the priority of existence in regard to essence should be the one expected. Only from the viewpoint of logic, where the terms are considered in priority to the proposition, do the indivisibles precede the synthesis. But metaphysically the strict correspondence of the synthetic type of cognition with the existential synthesis in the thing should indicate that the synthesizing cognition is, as in Kant (KRV, B130; 134, note), prior from this viewpoint to the conceptualization.

"Apprehension" and "comprehension" are used by Aquinas in the text. But these, along with "knowledge" and the like, would have to be specified as "apprehension that something exists," "knowledge that something exists," and so on. By themselves the terms are too general to bear distinctively upon existence. Terms like "awareness" or "cognition" would have to be still further specified as "intellectual," to express distinction from the sensible cognition or awareness that something exists. The required specification results in expressions too awkward for ordinary use.

Traditionally, the term "judgment" has become in Thomistic literature the standard way to designate the mind's synthesizing activity. On account of its courtroom connotations it gives overtones of a decision arrived at after careful consideration of the evidence, instead of the immediate apprehension that something exists. It is understood more readily as a decision on alternatives already known than as just the original knowledge that they exist. But in lieu of a better term, of which there is no sign on the horizon, it can hardly be disturbed in its status of the established designation.

May not the difficulty in finding a suitable term arise from the inadequacy of any one word or "indivisible" expression to convey the notion at issue? The cognitional activity in question is the knowledge that something exists. Just "knowledge of existence" or "apprehension of existence" will not do, since the term "existence" taken by itself does not say that anything exists. Here the object has to be expressed in a proposition, not by noun alone. If "judgment" be understood as a shorthand symbol for "knowledge that something exists," it seems a viable term. It can be qualified as "sense judgment" whenever it is used specifically to designate the sensible perception that a thing exists. The term "judgment," then, may for present purposes be retained to signify the knowledge that something exists, or, in the case of composition with accidents, that is so and so.

Corresponding difficulties will hold inevitably in regard to the "object" of judgment. Can the notion be expressed at all adequately by a noun? "Existence," as just noted, does not convey the information that something exists. "Object" seems to imply something as it were flat and stable, held before the eye in frozen fashion. So understood it would be attained by conceptualization rather than judgment, as in the case with the set copula of a proposition that is compared with actual existence to assess its truth value. "Fact" comes closer to what is required. Yet it too carries the notion of something fixed and complete, that has to be established by comparison with what actually exists or did exist. These are all translations into the language of conceptualization, necessary as they are for study and discussion. The answers to the question "Does the Loch Ness monster exist?", "Is it large?", "Is it a reptile?" are "Yes" or "No," standing for "It is" or "It is not." No nature originally known through conceptualization can by itself convey the answer. But to become a subject for protracted scrutiny, memory, and conversation, what is known through judgment is naturally conceptualized as "existence," an "object," an "aspect," and a "fact," and may be referred to by indefinite pronouns. There is no way of dispensing with nouns in discussion of existence.

III

This safari through a terminology jungle should emerge, hopefully, into a clearing in which the relevant philosophical issues take definite shape. First, the text examined shows beyond doubt that for Aquinas the intellectual activity specifically adapted to knowing existence is judgment. The contrasted activity, conceptualization, is specifically adapted to knowing essences. These latter, even when expanded to the infinite, do not tell whether the thing exists or does not exist. That is why the the Anselmian argument cannot show for Aquinas

whether God exists or does not. The two types of knowledge stem from radically different sources. Even existence, when conceptualized, does not contain the
type of knowledge attained by judgment. The concept "the existence of the
Napoleonic empire"does not mean that the empire actually exists.

What is to be thought of this Thomistic view today? It makes the predicative
sense of "is" always existential. Aquinas is alert to the distinction between
predication of existence alone and predication of something else as principal
predicate. But in both cases the "is" expresses for him first and foremost the
"actuality of every form" (*In I Periherm.*, lect. 5, Spiazzi no. 73). The fact that
something either exists or is so and so is in every case an existential actuality of
the thing. It actualizes a nature, either substantial or accidental, in a peculiarly
Thomistic way that does not coincide with activity and that as yet had not been
noticed in philosophy.[15]

The view entails reciprocal causality of the nature and the existence. In synthesizing and actualizing, the existence is obviously exercising causality on the
nature. Yet Aquinas tends to emphasize in this context rather the determining
and specifying causality of the essence upon the existence.[16] Accordingly, the
existence "results" (*In III Sent.*, d.6, q.2, a.2, Resp.; ed. Moos, III, 238) from
the essence, and elsewhere, essence is described as that in which and through
which an existent has being. But the essence exercises this causality only under
the activity of the cause that bestows the existence.[17] In any case, the reciprocal
causality requires the presence of both existence and nature in a cognitive grasp
of either. Through sense cognition the cognitive agent is apprehending intellectually both the existence and the nature. The two have to be known
together. A nature without existence, at least cognitional existence, would not
be there to be an object, and existence as a synthesis could not be there without
what it actualizes.[18] Rather, the distinction of them into two separate objects,
like Aristotle's (*Ph.*, I 1) distinction of form and matter, is the result of subsequent thinking and is achieved in philosophy. But to apprehend anything in
either way, the two different types of intellection have to be at work
simultaneously. This takes away the strangeness of the tenet that the actual existence known in sensible things consists in a synthesis. It comes into the mind
first of all as actuality, without qualification, i.e., "absolutely" (*In I
Periherm.*, lect. 5, no. 73). Only subsequent philosophical study shows that it
consists in a composition.[19]

Since nature and existence are always known together, the question might
arise whether conceptualization and judgment are two really different intellectual activities or are merely two aspects of the same activity. The question does
not seem relevant in Aquinas. His metaphysical reasoning establishes real
distinction between faculties and substance only.[20] Just as for Aristotle (*De
An.*, III 1, 425a13-b11) the concomitant color and size are attained by the same
sensation, even though one can vary without change in the other, variation in

existence without change in nature need not indicate two really distinct cognitional activities. In any case, because of their necessarily concomitant objects, conceptualization can never occur without concomitant judgment, nor judgment without concomitant conceptualization.

Finally, existence as grasped through judgment is highly individual and non-repetitive. Not only does everything have "existence and individuation in the same respect" (*Q. de An.*, a.1, ad 2m), but also the existence has its actuality only in a "now" and is variable from instant to instant in time (*In I Sent.*, d.19, q.2, a.2, Solut.; I, 470-471). Judgment accordingly apprehends existence as an individual actuality at a definite moment in time. As the conclusion of reasoning to existence at other moments, a judgment is of course no longer immediate but is inferential and open to the errors to which reasoning is subject.

Judgment, in consequence, is "the apprehension, in the cognitive power, proportioned to the existence of the thing" (*In I Sent.*, d.19, q.5, a.2, Solut.; I, 491). Is is specifically adapted to the highly individual and temporally located existential synthesis. But is it the only way in which the human intellect knows existence? Is not existence known also in a universal and non-temporal manner? Does it not, as has already been noted, function as a stable object of human thought and not merely as a staccato collection of highly individual and incessantly varying objects of judgment?

IV

Aquinas of course does more than judge that things exist. He thinks about and writes about existence as a topic. He is thereby conceptualizing what was originally known though judgment. He conceptualizes it as an actuality and a perfection, both of which are originally objects of conceptualization, and he refers to it by indefinite pronouns as though it were a "something." He speaks of the existence of God, the existence of man, the existence of a stone, regarding existence as a single notion undiversified in itself (*CG*, II, 52, *Si enim*). He takes it as a notion common to all its instances "insofar as it abstracts from all these" (*In I Sent.*, d.36, q.1, a.3, ad 2m; I, 836). Yet he shows no interest in calling it a concept, even though he had the abstract noun *existentia* at his disposal from his earliest writing[21] and regarded the infinitive *esse* as expressing the characteristic in virtue of which a thing is called "a being."[22]

The formation of the concept is not hard to see. Existence as grasped through judgment is diverse in each individual and varies from moment to moment in time. Yet in every instance it is actuating a nature. Accordingly, on the analogy of form with matter in Aristotle, it may be conceptualized as the actuality of every form or nature.[23] But here the actuality is diverse in each instance, caus-ing diversity in the relation each time and giving rise to an object that is analagous both in notion and in existence.[24] There is but the one concept, though it reaches all its instances analogously.

To mention analogy in a Thomistic context is to stir up a vipers' nest. Yet the squirming of terms and notions can be controlled sufficiently for the present discussion. Basic is the diversity of the existential actuality, as grasped by judg-ment, in each instance. Aquinas, in context, focuses on the diversity between God and creatures, and between substance and accident. But the reason given is unrestricted. It is that the diversity in the primary instance of being requires diversity in the other instances. This implies the full meaning of diversity, namely distinction not through differentiae but by the object itself.[25] It will mean that the concept of existence will be analogous from the start, and never univocal to any two of its instances. In this regard it will not come under the Aristotelian focal meaning, in which the univocal notion "healthy" is found in plants, animals, and men, and predicated only through focal reference of food, exercise, and color. The notion itself is not found in these secondary instances—cooked spinach, though healthy, has anything but the proper func-tional disposition of the plant's bodily organism. The bodily disposition does not exist in the secondary instances, but has reference to them in various ways. Nor is existence analogous in the way a logically univocal notion has different existence, as substance in a separate form or a house in the mind of a designer. Nor is it metaphorically common, in the way evening is predicated univocally of the time between afternoon and night in any twenty-four hour cycle, though metaphorically of the declining years in a man's lifetime. None of these types and examples taken from Aristotle is meant here. The analogy in question is analogy both in notion and in existence. It is not the analogy of a univocal no-tion taken also in the ways in which it is variously referred to in other univocal notions, nor in its various ways of existing, nor in an "extended" sense given it in metaphor. It is the analogy of a notion found as a nature in only a unique primary instance, God. In the rest of the instances existence diversely actuates a nature other than itself, constituting an object that is common to the Aristotelian categories in various grades, and common to God and creatures through the exemplar causality of the primary instance.[26]

The diversity of the instances, then, does not permit the common concept in "actuality of every form or nature" or "that by which a thing exists" to be ap-plied to any two in exactly the same way. Here *existence* is the common *notion*. In it analogy in notion and analogy in existence accordingly coincide. As a result it is an analogous concept from the very first instance known.[27] In conse-quence existence and the notions based on it never carry with them the restric-tions of the instance in which they are first encountered. There is no "leap" from accident (phenomenon) to substance (noumenon) or from finite to infinite. There is but the one notion throughout. So much is this so that Aquinas can deftly call the divine existence the existence of all things, i.e., by way of efficient and exemplar causality.[28] The only instance in which existence is found to be a nature is God, with the result that the answer to the question *"What"* is existence?" can only be that primary instance. In the others, existence is not a "what."

Conversely, the current objection that existence because known originally as a characteristic can never be regarded as a substance, does not touch this type of notion. Rather, the presence of existence as accidental in things requires that it subsist in a unique primary instance.[29] There never was, in fact, a non-analogous sense that could be termed the "ordinary meaning" of existence. The ordinary meaning here is the analogous meaning. There is extension from instance to instance, just as with any common concept, but not "extension" from ordinary to analogous sense. When existence is attributed to autumn colors and to trees, the meaning is ordinary in both cases. Even in attributing existence to God, the non-philosophical person means the ordinary notion of actual presence in the universe. Only in philosophy is existence shown to be a nature in God and other than the nature elsewhere, with derivation through efficient and exemplar causality.[30] It remains always the one concept, analogously common to all its instances.

V

How do the recent interpretations accord with the way existence is known in the Aquinas article just examined?

Certainly if intuition is taken in its widest sense of "immediate apprehension"[31] the term may be applied to the original apprehension of existence through immediate judgment. But for Aquinas (see supra, n.12) what is attained in judgment is the existence known in everything called a being. The intuition, that should mean, is had by everyone who knows anything at all. For Maritain (p.19), however, there are apparently people, some of them great metaphysicians, who have not had the intuition of being. It is not made use of, moreover, in "the conversations of everyday life" (p.20). Does not this introduce into the interpretation of Aquinas a type of intuition different from everyday judgment? In fact, it makes this new type of intuition nowhere signalized in the text of Aquinas. It places his metaphysical thinking in a new framework.

Likewise in the text of Aquinas only one *ratio entis*, an analogous object, is mentioned. There should accordingly be but one analogous concept of existence. Like Maritain's concept that follows upon the intuition of being, it should be a "reflexive *re*presentation" (p.18) of what is grasped though judgment. But of Maritain's other two concepts of existence, which are of abstractive and not judicative origin, and which *precede* the intuition of being (pp.18-19), there seems no trace in the text of Aquinas. Rather, the tenet that quiddities yield no knowledge of existence should preclude the possibility of any original cognition of it through concepts. Not only the framework of a special intuition but also that of an alien "three degrees of abstraction" would seem required for viewing the Thomistic knowledge of existence in this complicated way.

Gilson's requirements for intellectual intuition of existence quite obviously ban the expression from the Thomistic context. For him the object of an intuition has to be a thing, and existence in sensible objects is definitely not a thing. Further, it would have to be known apart from a phantasm. Yet Gilson clearly attributes the cognitive grasp of existence to judgment, even though he signalizes the asserting, positing, affirming character of the act rather than the apprehending and comprehending aspect used to describe it in the text of Aquinas.[32] The conclusion that there can be no *concept* of existence is readily understandable when this is taken to mean that no new quidditative object is introduced in the conceptual representation of existence—all that happens is that other quidditative concepts such as that of actuality or perfection, are made to represent what is "implicitly conceived" (Gilson, art. cit. p.16) in judgment. Gilson (p.9) has no objection to the use of "concept" in the meaning of any object of thought, but claims that this does not touch the present question. Its bearing here has to be quidditative. However, the difference from Maritain's approach is far from a matter of words, as Gilson (pp.10; 16-17) recognizes, or of the meanings assigned to the words. The difference quite evidently is that in the interpretation of Thomistic thought Gilson refuses to accept the frameworks of a special intuition of existence, and of abstractive origins for knowledge of it.

Fabro's stand that the notion of being (*notio entis*) precedes both the notion of essence and the notion of existence as separate objects of human though is undoubtedly correct. Essence and existence, when represented separately, are each conceived as a being, just as the Aristotelian matter and form, when represented separately, are each conceived as a body. Therapeutic judgment of separation is required for the correct understanding of them as objects. Metaphysical therapy shows that the existent is originally grasped through a twofold activity of the intellect, namely judgment and conceptualization combined, and that the existence so important for the Thomistic metaphysician and conceptualized by him as actuality is the existence conceptualized in "the fact" that something exists. But Fabro concludes that Thomistic participation distinguishes existence as actuality from its *result*, the existence as fact.[33] Apparently the participationist model of an object shared by way of formal causality allows existence to be known basically in the concept of the actuality of being, with its *result* that a thing thereby exists. The texts of Aquinas seem rather to make what is grasped through judgment basic, allowing the existence thereby known to be conceptualized subsequently as the actuality of an essence. Where the notion of resulting is introduced in this context,[34] the existence is regarded as resulting from the principles of the thing's essence, and as actuality seems in no way distinguished from the fact that the thing exists. At any rate Fabro ("Intensive hermeneutics," pp. 470-471) sets the participationist interpretation in radical opposition both to transcendental Thomism and to all who speak in terms of a "Thomistic existentialism," with express reference to Gilson.

Donceel's lucid account of transcendental Thomism, the way of thinking introduced hypothetically by Maréchal, likewise emphasizes (p.76) radical opposition to the approaches of Maritain and Gilson. But the one point at issue here is whether in any authentic Thomism the human intellect can be allowed an a priori structure, or whether in Aristotelian (*De An.*, III 4, 429b30-430a2) fashion it has to be regarded as merely potential in the cognitive order, without any formal structure whatever of its own.

At the very least, this survey is sufficient to make plain that the current approaches to Aquinas on the knowledge of existence are at radical variance with one another. The divergencies cannot be explained away by patient comparison of the different ways in which each uses the same terms. They lie rather at the roots of the vital metaphysical thinking in each interpreter. This may be vivid testimony to the inherent richness and depth of Aquinas' thought, capable like the Mona Lisa of evoking surprisingly varied understanding of its meaning. It may be too that like nitrogen liquified for transport, the thought of Aquinas has to be allowed continued escape in part from the interpretation that would convey it, under penalty of bursting the container. In any case, the situation highlights a need today for further study and discussion of the original Thomistic texts. The immediate knowledge of existence in external things through judgment is indeed given high visibility in Maritain and Gilson. The reflexive nature of the concept of existence that follows upon judgment is emphasized in Maritain, and seems latent in Gilson's tenet that existence is "implicitly conceived" (p.16) in knowledge of anything that exists. The crucial function of existence as a participated actuality is brought to the fore by Fabro, and the priority of existential synthesis to conceptual objects by the transcendental Thomists. These modern insights are signal gains for the tradition of Thomistic studies. But for dissipating the real oppositions they have engendered when developed separately, direct immersion in the text itself of Aquinas seems indispensable.

JUDGEMENT AND TRUTH IN AQUINAS

I

It is well enough known that on a number of occasions St. Thomas Aquinas speaks of a sense judgment. This has seemed a scandal to some commentators. It has been explained away by saying that really it is not a judgment at all, in the proper sense of the word.[1] Yet the ancestry of the term in this setting seems unquestionable. *Krisis* (judgment) and its derivatives are used by Aristotle just as readily and just as easily for sense judgments as they are for intellectual judgments.[2] In application to animals "this at least is an obvious characteristic of all animals, for they possess a congenital discriminitive capacity which is called sense-perception" (*APo.* II 19, 99b34-35; Oxford tr.). "Discriminitive" translates κριτική. The same use of the adjective may be seen in *De Sensu*, where the sense of taste would have to possess "the most perfect power of discerning figures in general" (4,442b17; Oxford tr.) if it could "discern the common sensibles" better than sight. The verb "to judge" (κρινεῖν) is similarly used: "Each sense... discriminates the differences which exist within the group; e.g. sight discriminates white and black, taste sweet and bitter, and so in all cases. Since we also discriminate white from sweet... It must be by sense" (*De An.* III 2, 426b8-15; Oxford tr.). The verb continues to be applied in the same way at b17 and b23. Pleasure in food is judged by animals, at *PA* IV 5, 678b8-9. Likewise the noun is used for the sense of touch,[3] and (*EN* III 10, 1118a27-28) the judgment about flavors is attributed to taste.

The lineage of notion "sense judgment" is accordingly above suspicion. But can it have the same philosophical meaning in the Thomistic context that intellectual judgment has? It will have to mean an apprehension of existence, or cognition of existence, if it is to satisfy the requirements of the Thomistic notion of judgment. Judgment consists in "the cognitive power's apprehension proportionate to the thing's existence.''[4] It means in this sense the cognitive grasp of existence. Do the sensory powers grasp the existence of sensible things?

A negative reply is at least strongly suggested by the commentator already mentioned.[5] But a little reflection on Aquinas' overall doctrine of existence and nature should make one hesitant about accepting too easily the negative answer. A nature apart from existence cannot be grasped by any cognitive power. It is neither singular nor plural, neither existent nor non-existent.[6] It is merely a consideration, the absolute consideration of the nature apart from either real or cognitional or divine existence.[7] It is a conclusion reached from a comparison of the same thing in both real and cognitional existence, and the inference that the thing's nature abstracts from all existence if it is able to enjoy the ways of existing. The nature in its absolute consideration, or the common nature as common, can therefore be reasoned to, but it cannot be intuited or grasped immediately by any cognitive power. The object of any immediate cognition is something actuated by existence, real existence in the case of an object external to the world of cognition, and cognitional existence if it is something within the cognitional world. But in no case can anything be intuited without its existence being thereby grasped by the cognitive power.

This means that every act of sensation grasps both thing and existence. It could not be aware of one without the other. Its object necessarily includes both. It cannot of course separate one from the other. It cannot represent them as distinct objects, as in the intellect's abstraction.[8] But it does grasp both from the start. In a word, its object is a composite of thing and existence, an object that could not present itself to sensation except under both aspects.

The issue here at stake is of crucial importance for the Thomistic noetic. Sense experience is the origin of all further human cognition. This Aristotelian epistemological principle holds equally well for St. Thomas in regard to all naturally acquired knowledge. If the real existence of things were not grasped from the start in all sensible cognition, it could not be grasped at all in the natural course of human cognition. Since in its origins this cognition means becoming and being another thing intentionally, the existence later represented as a distinct object in intellection can be none other than the existence grasped concretely in sensation. All sensation, accordingly, apprehends the existence in its object. The existence is actuating its object, and is grasped as exercising this function. In this way it is apprehended[9] by the sense.

That the issue is timely may be seen from the efforts of transcendental Thomism to require an apriori for the Thomistic noetic, even in regard to a judgment about sensible existence, e.g.: ''However, the formal structure of this judgment—and with more reason the structure and the content of universal judgments and especially of metaphysical judgments—cannot be grounded in the evidence of sense perception.''[10]

It is hard to see how this interpretation does not give a formal and therefore an actual structure to the human intellect in its role of a cognitive power. In the Aristotelian tradition all intelligible content is located in the form, in marked difference from the Kantian notion of form as empty. Matter as matter is unknowable, from the Aristotelian viewpoint. Apriori structure would accordingly mean knowable content, against this background. St. Thomas himself seems rather to acquiesce in the Aristotelian conception implying that nothing whatsoever of the objects known lies in a prior constitution of the intellect. As compared by Aristotle (*De An.* III 4, 429b30-430a2) to a blank writing tablet the intellect can hardly be interpreted as already having any of the structure of what is to be traced upon it. At any rate, the interpretation of St. Thomas emphasized the purely potential nature of the intellect in regard to its objects:

> Intellectus ... nihil est actu eorum antequam intelligat. Oportet autem hoc sic esse, sicut contingit in tabula, in qua nihil est actu scriptum, sed plura possunt in ea scribi. Et hoc etiam accidit intellectui possibili, quia nihil intelligibilium est in eo actu, sed potentia tantum (*In III de An.*, lect. 9, Pirotta no. 722).

Even the agent intellect seems to lack for him any formal structure, for it has no determination of its own in respect of the objects known:

> Est enim intellectus possibilis in potentia ad intelligibilia, sicut indeterminatum ad determinatum. ... Quantum autem ad hoc, intellectus agens non est in actu. Si enim intellectus agens haberet in se determinationem omnium intelligibilium, non indigeret intellectus possibilis phantasmatibus,... (*ibid.*, lect. 10, nos. 738-739).

All cognitional determination seems to come originally from the sensible thing for St. Thomas, quite in accord with the Aristotelian tenet that the form of the sensible thing is its intelligible content and in this perspective its intelligible determination. How, then, is the apriori assigned to the Thomistic epistemology, and in what does it consist? The article just quoted goes on to explain: "St. Thomas does not see such a principle, in the line of Plato, Plotinus, Augustine, Bonaventure, Malebranche, in an objective *a priori*,... but in the line of Aristotle, Kant, and Hegel, he sees it in a formal *a priori* of the spontaneous spirit itself. ... its basis, speaking in the manner of St. Thomas, is the light of the intelligence itself, which informs, objectifies, conceptualizes, and judges the data from sense cognition."[11] The light of the intelligence, which in the texts just quoted from St. Thomas is described as lacking all cognitional determination, is seen as the basis of a formal apriori. It seems accordingly understood as the basis for the formal structure given the object. How this can be reconciled with the conception of the intellect as merely potential in regard to the determination it has when actually knowing, seems impossible to understand. The intellect universalizes and synthesizes, but all the determination seems to come originally from the common nature and existential synthesis already present in the sensible thing itself.

However, these are questions far wider than the scope of the present article. They do show the importance of understanding correctly what St. Thomas understands by a sense judgment. If in the object of sense judgment the structure subsequently seen in intellection is already present, there should be no reason for claiming that the formal structure of intellectual judgment "cannot be grounded in the evidence of sense perception" and in the real structure of the sensible existent itself.

One difficulty here of course in this technical use of the word "judgment" to mean the apprehension of existence. It is not an ordinary language use of the term. The technical meaning here is an awareness or knowledge or understanding that a thing exists.[12] Apprehension by the senses gives the awareness that the sensible thing exists either really or cognitionally. Sense apprehension accordingly comes under the meaning of the word "judgment" in this technical Thomistic signification. It makes one aware one that the sensible object exists.[13] It makes the sentient subject become and be cognitionally the composite of thing and existence, the composite of the two factors by which any sensible object is constituted. While sense cognition does not represent the two in separate concepts, as intellection does in the concepts of universalized nature and existential actuality, it brings into the cognitive agent's awareness an object that is already structured through an existential synthesis. This structure is what informs the intellect in the intellect's act of judgment.

With these considerations in regard to the bearing of the question and issues at stake, one may approach the texts themselves in which the "sense judgment" is discussed or at least mentioned by Aquinas. The texts have been gathered and reproduced before,[14] and there is no need to transcribe them all again. For present purposes the ones that have immediate bearing upon the above issues should provide the required enlightenment.

II

Perhaps the first point demanding clarification is the distinction between the passive role of the sense in receiving its impresssed species from the sensible thing, and its role as an agent informed by this species and thereby able to perform its characteristic activity of sensation:

> Sensus autem exteriores suscipiunt tantum a rebus per modum patiendi, sine hoc quod aliquid cooperentur ad sui formationem; quamvis iam formati habeant propriam operationem, quae est iudicium de propriis obiectis (*Quodl.*, VIII, 2, 3c).

The external senses have their own activity, but to exercise it they have to be informed, in an entirely passive way, by the activity of the external things. So informed, they issue into their "judgment about their proper objects."

Against the background of Aquinas' overall doctrine of cognition, the meaning of this text should be clear enough. The whole cognitional content is impressed upon the senses without their contributing anything to it. The form so given it enables the sentient subject to become the sensible thing intentionally. No formal element or structure or any content whatsoever is added by the sense. As the sensible awareness includes the awareness that the sensible object exists, no reason emerges for refusing the term "judgment" to this awareness, once "judgment" is understood in the technical sense of an apprehension that something exists. In contrast to the passive reception of the species, from without, the activity in which the awareness consists is an activity of the cognitive agent. In this sense it is just as much from within as is the intellectual judgment, in which "quamvis autem receptio sit ab exteriori, iudicium tamen ab interiori procedit" (*De Ver.*, XX, 1, arg. 4).

The point established, then, is that for St. Thomas cognitive action is entirely from within, even though its cognitional content and formal structure are received passively from without through the species (*formatio*) impressed upon the sentient power. With agreement on this, one can go on to consider texts from the article in the *De Veritate* in which the most frequent mention of sense judgment occurs. In the article a distinction is made between two aspects of sense cognition that parallel respectively the two acts of conceptualization and judgment in intellectual awareness:

> In intellectu autem primo et principaliter inveniuntur falsitas et veritas in iudicio componentis et dividentis; sed in formatione quidditatum non nisi per ordinem ad iudicium quod ex formatione praedicta consequitur; unde et in sensu proprie veritas et falsitas dicitur secundum hoc quod iudicat de sensibilibus; sed secundum hoc quod sensibile apprehendit, non est ibi veritas et falsitas proprie, sed solum secundum ordinem ad iudicium quod ex formatione praedicta consequitur; prout scilicet ex apprehensione tali natum est sequi tale iudicium (*De Ver.*, I, 11c).

The article as a whole is dealing with the problem of falsity in sensation. Just as in intellection truth and falsity pertain to the judgment, and not to conceptualization except insofar as a judgment springs from the conceptualizing, so in sensation truth and falsity apply to the sense judgment about sensible things.

From the viewpoint of the mere apprehension of the sensible thing there is properly no truth or falsehood but only a relation to the judgment that naturally follows from this apprehension.

The text is by no means easy to understand. The use of the term "apprehension" calls for a bit of study. A judgment, in the sense of an awareness of existence, comes under the general notion of apprehension for St. Thomas.[15] But on occasion "apprehension" may be contrasted with "judgment" and used for merely quidditative as opposed to existential cognition, quite as in the later and finally established Scholastic contrast between "simple apprehension" and judgment. In the present text it is clearly used in this way.

A second difficulty arises from the expression *formatio quidditatum*. In expressing the species in which it knows the quiddities of things, the human intellect gives them separate cognitional existence. The judgment that they so exist arises spontaneously from and accompanies this *formatio*. Is that the judgment to which the text refers? The context seems to require something more. The lines immediately preceding the above quotation direct it rather to external things: "Si autem consideretur sensus secundum quod comparatur ad res, tunc in sensu est falsitas et veritas per modum quo est in intellectu." The *res* had just been contrasted with the sense's own disposition. The meaning seems accordingly to go further and involve existential implications in any *formatio* of a quiddity, not only in regard to its cognitional existence but also in regard to the real existence in the thing from which it is abstracted. In the intellect the grasp of the existence will be a distinct act that necessarily accompanies, and in this sense arises from, the *formatio* of the quiddity, just as I cannot intellectually apprehend the desk in front of me without thereby knowing that it really exists. In regard to sense cognition a corresponding grasp of existence arises naturally from the awareness of the object as a thing, and is correspondingly named a judgment.

There is no need, therefore, to see in this passage a loose use of terms.[16] Their application seems as firm and definite here as anywhere in Aquinas. The use of "apprehension" in its restricted application to the quidditative order seems sufficiently explained by making *apprehensione tali* bear expressly upon the *formatio*. Once the general use of the terms by St. Thomas has been studied the passage may still remain difficult, but its use of the terms is seen to be technical and clearcut.

The passage goes on immediately to distinguish the areas in which the sense judgment is always true from those in which it may be false:

> Sensus autem iudicium de quibusdam est naturale, sicut de propriis sensibilibus; de quibusdam autem quasi per quamdam collationem, quam facit in homine vis cogitativa, quae est potentia sensitivae partis, loco cuius in aliis

> animalibus est existimatio naturalis; et sic iudicat vis sensitiva de sensibilibus com-
> munibus et de sensibilibus per accidens....unde sensu iudicium de sensibilibus
> propriis semper est verum, nisi sit impedimento in organo vel in medio; sed in
> sensibilibus communibus et per accidens interdum iudicium sensus fallitur
> (ibid.).

As the *sensus communis* does not express a species in its cognitive act, it may
be placed with the external senses as regards the truth of its judgment. The
term has a different meaning when Aristotle (*De An.* III, 1, 425a27; cf.
*Sens.*4,442b4-13) uses it to refer to the capability common to the external
senses for grasping the common sensibles. Accordingly "the object of the common sense is not the common sensibles, *communia sensibilia.*"[17] *To occasion
falsehood as envisaged in the above text the bringing together (collatio) of different objects by the instinctive powers is required.* The terms therefore are not
being used loosely.[18]

This text of the *De Veritate* is accordingly clear enough. Against its
background the statements about the certainty or falsity of sense judgments in
later Thomistic works can be readily understood. Sense apprehension extends
to existence and thereby is open to truth and falsity:

> Quod quidem contingit eo quod apprehendit res ut sunt. Unde contingit
> falsitatem esse in sensu ex hoc quod apprehendit vel iudicat res aliter quam sint
> (*ST*, I, 17, 2c).

That one thing *is* not another is apprehended by the judgment. This existential actuality is attained by the senses and is described under the alternate term
for judging, namely "discerning":

> Dicendum quod sensus proprius iudicate de sensibili proprio, discernendo ip-
> sum ab aliis quae cadunt sub eodem sensu, sicut discernendo album a nigro vel a
> viridi. Sed discernere album a dulci non potest neque visus neque gustus; quia
> oportet quod qui inter aliqua discernit, utrumque cognoscat. Unde oportet ad
> sensum communem pertinere discretionis iudicium ad quem referantur, sicut ad
> communem terminum, omnes apprehensiones sensuum (*ST*, I, 78, 4, ad 2m).

The two aspects of awareness of a thing (*cognoscat*) and judgment that it *is*
not something else (*discernit*) continue therefore to be distinguished in the
Summa Theologiae.

The certainty of sense judgments regarding their own sensibles is likewise
repeated: "Unusquisque autem horum sensuum iudicat de propriis sensibilibus, et non decipitur in eis" (*In II de An.*, lect. 13, no. 384). Conversely,
their admitted openness to error is used to bolster the views of Democritus:

"Iudicium autem senus non est certum, cum non semper eodem modo iudicet" (In IV Metaph., lect. 11, Cathala-Spiazzi no. 670). Degrees of truth in sense judgments are noted: "Et propter hoc verius est iudicium sensus de coloribus sensibilibus in propinquo quam in remoto."[19]

These texts imply clearly enough that for Aquinas the variable sense judgments bear upon external and distant things. How is this possible? The answer seems to lie in the work of the instinctive powers as outlined in the above text from De Veritate (I, 11c). The sheep presumably judges that the wolf in the distance in a predator, the fish that the artificial fly on the hook is food. This should serve to explain an early text in which the denial of efficient causality to creatures is said to destroy a sense judgment—"destruit iudicium sensus" (In II Sent., d.1, q.1, a.4, Solut.; ed. Manndonnet, II, 24). The examples given are that with this denial of efficient causality fire does not give out heat nor is the hand in motion—"nec manus movetur." The latter phrase seems clearly enough to be using the verb movere in a passive reflexive meaning, a use that is permissible. In the context it means clearly that God would be causing the motion of the hand, and that the hand itself would not be causing its own movement. The sentence is elliptic, but understandable with the notion of the hand as something living, and life as self-motion. The awareness of bodily self-motion is through kinesthetic sensations and internal sensation. In this restricted scope the sense judgment about the self-motion may be certain, and a definite refutation of Occasionalism. But this would not apply to the other example, fire giving out heat. The work of the instinctive powers for the assurance that the tree grows, the horse gallops, the fire burns, seems necessary to explain the sense judgment here. The judgment accordingly may be wrong. St. Thomas is not faced with the Humean problem. But in the general setting of his notions regarding the variable sense judgment, there is nothing that runs counter to the facts to which Hume drew attention.

What conclusions are to be drawn from these texts on sense judgment? They seem to be clear enough in maintaining that both sensation and intellection are somehow structured in a parallel way, in regard to the apprehension of existence: "...sensus et intellectus non solum recipiunt formas rerum, sed etiam habent judicare" (In De Sensu et Sensato, lect. 19; ed. Parma, XX, 196a). Both judge that the object is what it is and that it is not something else. Both give awareness that the object is a thing and that it exists. To this extent both have quidditative and existential aspects in the way in which they are the cognition of an object. Sensation of course does not abstract or universalize its object. Its object is always individual. There is no question of its knowing the ratio entis or any other ratio as something abstract.

Real existence is always individual. Sensation judges it just that way, as individual. Sensation cannot represent existence in any abstract concept or in any way separate it cognitionally from the thing it actuates. But it does give awareness of the totality of an entitative composite, a composite of existence and thing. It cannot grasp the thing in any other way. Its object is the concrete existent. In that object there are the quidditative and the existential factors. As impressed passively on the sentient power both those aspects enter into the actuation of the faculty, which remains in an entirely potential role in receiving the quidditatively and existentially structured object. The sense faculty accordingly contributes nothing to the content or structure of the object sensed. It does not provide any basis for an apriori element in sense cognition, as it issues into the actual awareness of the sensible thing.

III

In sensation, accordingly, the human cognitive agent becomes and is cognitively the whole sensible thing, insofar as the singular sensible object is already provided with a common nature and with an existential structure. The cognitive agent furnishes neither of these aspects. In becoming the object more deeply and on a more manageable level, the intellect first grasps it under the widest aspect of all, that of a being:

> Primum enim quod cadit in imaginatione intellectus, est ens, sine quo nihil potest apprehendi ab intellectu; sicut primum quod cadit in credulitate intellectus, sunt dignitates, et praecipue ista, contradictoria non esse simul vera (In I Sent., d.8, q.1, a.3, Solut.; I, 200).

In the ''image-forming'' or ''picture-forming'' of the intellect, the most basic picture or image through which the awareness of the object takes place is the representation of it as a being. Without the basic representation of the object as a being, nothing can be apprehended by the intellect.[20] This means quite plainly that the existent thing, the whole composite of thing and existence, is what is grasped by the intellect in its conceptualizing activity. No conceptual image or picture could be formed of the nature in its absolute consideration, for no such nature ever presents itself directly for apprehension. Only an existent thing, a being, can be conceptualized as an object in itself by the intellect. Only a being can find a place in the immediate ''image-forming'' of the mind.[21]

The point is illustrated by a corresponding order in belief. Most basic in the intellect's belief are the axioms, and notably the first principle of demonstration, the principle that contradictories cannot simultaneously be true. This of course is the principle that immediately follows upon a thing's being. The thing cannot both be and not be in the same respect. Being contradicts non-being. That is its character. The first principle of demonstration is accordingly the intellect's most fundamental belief.

All this is intelligible enough, in spite of the technical terminology taken from the Arabians and the Greeks. In the epistemological order, the basic object of human conceptualization is a being. In the logical order, the fundamental principle is the principle now called the principle of contradiction. Further on in the commentary on the *Sentences*, the penetration becomes sharper and more complicated:

> ...cum sit duplex operatio intellectus una quarum dictur a quibusdam imaginatio intellectus, quam Philosophus, III *De anima* nominat intelligentiam indivisibilium, quae consistit in apprehensione quidditatis simplicis, quae alio etiam nomine formatio dicitur; alia est quam dicunt fidem, quae consistit in compositione vel divisione propositionis: prima operatio respicit quidditatem rei; secunda respicit esse ipsius (*In I Sent.*, d.19, q.5, a.1, ad 7m; I, 489).

This text occurs in a discussion on the nature of truth. It is explaining the activity of the human intellect as the required means for understanding what truth is. Its interest consequently coincides with the aim of the present investigation. However, it still does not use the technical term "judgment." Rather, "belief" continues to appear, and the Arabian notion rendered by the term "imaginatio intellectus" is presented as a synonym of another term of similar origin, *formatio*. The deeper penetration occasioned by the study of truth, though, focuses attention on the twofold activity (*duplex operatio*) of the intellect. Whereas in sensation both the thing and its existence were grasped together in a single cognitive activity, in intellection they are also grasped together, but in double activity. One intellectual activity consists in the grasp of the simple quiddity, the other consists in the composition or division of the proposition. The first activity, accordingly, bears upon the thing's quiddity, the second upon its existence.

What does this mean? Certainaly the order of first and second in the two kinds of activity is not temporal. What is grasped first of all, as just seen, is a being. This is a composite of thing and existence. Only in function of it can anything, including quiddity and existence, be known. The two are therefore grasped simultaneously, from the temporal viewpoint. The order of first and second quite obviously comes from logic, in which the simple terms are regarded as primary and the proposition as something subsequent and including the terms as parts. The reference in the text to the composition or division of the proposition points convincingly enough to this logical background. From the Thomistic metaphysical viewpoint the priority of existence to thing might suggest a priority of judgment over conceptualization, but the priority will not in any way be temporal. The two will always be grasped simultaneously.

The activity that bears upon the thing's being or existence is described as consisting in the composition or division of the proposition. It is accordingly viewed as a synthesizing activity, in contrast to the grasp of a simple object like a quiddity. This seems to imply a complex structure in the object corresponding to the structure of the proposition. Later, in dealing with the divine knowledge of these complex objects (*complexorum vel enuntiabilium*—arg. 1, p. 902), the commentary makes this explicit:

> Cum in re duo sint, quidditas rei, et esse ejus, his duobus respondet duplex operatio intellectus. Una quae dicitur a philosophis formatio, qua apprehendit quidditates rerum, quae etiam a Philosopho, in III *De anima*, dicitur indivisibilium intelligentia. Alia autem comprehendit esse rei, componendo affirmationem, quia etiam esse rei ex materia et forma compositae, a qua cognitionem accipit, consistit in quadam compositione formae ad materiam, vel accidentis ad subjectum (*In I Sent.*, d.38, q.1 a.3, Solut.; I, 903).

Because there are the two factors, quiddity and existence, in the thing itself, there are the two corresponding activities in the intellect, the structure of the sensible thing, accordingly, is given as the reason for the twofold intellectual activity. All reads as though nothing of the structure in the object known is traceable ultimately to the intellect. No room seems allowed for an apriori arising from it to aid in structuring the object. The reason why the activity that grasps the thing's existence has to do so by composing an affirmative assertion is that the existence of a thing composed of matter and form *consists* in the composition of form and matter or of accident and subject. Since the material thing is the source of the intellect's cognition, it seems clearly represented as providing the whole structure of the object known to the intellect, the structure that is mirrored in the synthesizing activity of the intellect's grasp of existence.

Later writings of Aquinas repeat this view.[22] Perhaps the addition most worthy of note for present purposes is the inclusion of the composition of a specific differentia's nature with the generic as similarly the cause of the corresponding composition in the intellectual activity:

> Et ideo, si talis operatio intellectus ad rem debeat reduci sicut ad causam, oportet quod in compositis substantiis ipsa compositio formae ad materiam, aut eius quod se habet per modum formae et materiae, vel etiam compositio accidentis ad subiectum, respondeat quasi fundamentum et causa veritatis, compositioni, quam intellectus interius format et exprimit voce. Sicut cum dico, Socrates est homo, veritas huius enunciationis causatur ex compositione formae humanae ad materiam individualem, per quam Socrates est hic homo: et cum dico, homo est albus, causa veritatis est compositio albedinis ad subiectum: et similiter est in aliis (*In IX Metaph.*, lect. 11, no. 1898).

Just as in the commentary on the *Sentences* the composition of form with matter and accident with subject was presented as the cause of the composition in the intellect's activity, so here these compositions in the thing are offered as the foundation and cause of the truth in the composition formed in the intellect. No apriori seems required as a contribution. But the composition of "that which is related in the manner of form and matter" is added. What can this mean? Earlier in the commentary on the *Metaphysics* the relation of a specific differentia's nature to the generic nature had been described in that manner:

> Licet enim genus praedicabile non sit materia, sumitur tamen a materia, sicut differentia a forma. Dicitur enim aliquid animal ex eo quod habet naturam sensitivam. Rationale vero ex eo, quod habet rationalem naturam, quae se habet ad sensitivam sicut forma ad materiam (*In V Metaph.*, lect. 22, no. 1123).

The composition between these abstract natures is accordingly looked upon by Aquinas as a composition after the manner of form and matter in physical composites. It can therefore be ranged under the existential compositions that correspond to the composition found in the intellectual synthesizing, and that are the ground and cause of the latter's truth. This should mean that a definition like "rational animal" depends upon an existential synthesis for whatever truth it may claim. In the commentary on the *Sentences* this point had been noted:

> Et quia ratio veritas fundatur in esse, et non in quidditate, ut dictum est, ideo veritas falsitas proprie invenitur in secunda operatione, et in signo ejus quod est enuntiatio, et non in prima, vel signo ejus est definitio, nisi secundum quid; sicut etiam quidditatis esse est quoddam esse rationis, et secundum istud esse dicitur veritas in prima operatione intellectus per quem etiam modum dicitur definitio vera (*In I Sent.*, d. 19, q. 5, a. 1, ad 7m; I, 489).

This reasoning presupposes that cognitional existence is a synthesis that can ground and cause truth in the judgment that corresponds to it, just as much as does real existence. The tenet had just been stated explicitly:

> ...de eo quod nullo modo est, non potest aliquid enuntiari; ad minus enim oportet quod illud de quo aliquid enuntiatur, sit apprehensum; et ita habet aliquod esse ad minus in intellectu apprehendente; et ita constat quod semper veritati respondet aliquod esse; nec oportet quod semper respondeat sibi esse in re extra animam, cum ratio veritatis compleatur in ratione animae (*ibid.*, ad 5m).

Accordingly the "second operation" of the intellect, the judgment, is always an apprehension or knowing of existence. More exactly, it is the intellective grasp of the thing from the side of the thing's existence. It is a synthesizing grasp of a synthesizing actuality already present in the object. The structure in the object is the ground and cause of the corresponding structure in the intellectual activity, and is therefore the ground and cause of its truth. This brings the discussion to the problem of truth.

The point already established, however, is that the sensible thing contains the structure that is mirrored and known in intellection. The sensible thing is composed of nature and existence. In it the physical matter and form, and the specific and generic natures, are synthesized into a whole by the existence. The natures are common, but synthesized by real existence into an individual. But because they are already common, they are universals when given cognitional existence in the intellect's grasp of quiddities. No apriori structure of the intellect is necessary for this, since the natures are of themselves common. When they receive existence in the intellect instead of in individuating matter they have their proper existence as quiddities. Freed from the individuating matter, they are thereby universal in regard to all their instances. The nature itself, not the intellect, is the basic ground for this universality. The intellect merely gives the nature an existence in which its common aspect reigns. By that very fact, and not by any apriori structure in the intellect, the nature becomes a universal. Correspondingly, because the existential sythesizing is already present in the real or cognitional object, it is mirrored in the synthesizing structure of the judgment.

IV

The act of judgment, then, is an act of apprehending or knowing. But like any cognitive act, it has a form. The use of the term *formatio* has already been noted for the impression of the form or species of the sensible thing upon the sentient power. Determination by this form enables the sentient power to issue into the sensation of the determined sensible thing. The term was likewise used for the conceptualization by which the intellect grasps objects from the standpoint of their determined quiddities. But the requirement of form extends to all intellective acts:

> Cum autem omnis res sit vera secundum quod habet propriam formam naturae suae, necesse est quod intellectus, inquantum est cognoscens, sit verus inquantum habet similitudinem rei cognitae, quae est forma ejus inquantum est cognoscens. Et propter hoc per conformitatem intellectus et rei veritas definitur (*ST*, I, 16, 2c).

The form of the intellectual activity of judgment should therefore be the synthesis that corresponds to the existential synthesizing in its object. By reflection, the intellect can know this form and express it in what the texts just cited from the commentary on the *Sentences* called the *enunciatio*. This is what is expressed verbally in a sentence. It is a synthesis that the intellect, in the words quoted above from the commentary on the ninth book of the *Metaphysics* (lect. 11, no. 1898), forms and utters—"interius forat et exprimit voce."

The notion is not so easy to express in English. It may be called a proposition, if the word is limited to the mental construct and contradistinguished from a sentence. But "proposition" is a technical term in logic, and means an element in a reasoning process. For this reason the more suitable word in English is "judgment." The mental construct, used as a proposition in logical contexts, may readily be called a "judgment."[23] The term has the initial disadvantage, though this may turn out in the end to be a notable advantage, of being the same word already used for the intellectual activity of judgment, the "second operation" of the human mind. Now it is being use for a static proposition, in rather sharp contrast to the dynamic character of the intellectual activity. But there seems to be no reason why the form of the dynamic activity should not be known through an act of reflexive simple apprehension and grasped after the manner of form or quiddity. It would thereby be frozen in the way illustrated by Bergson's cinematographic simile, as a single slide. That is the way real forms, though they have an ever flowing existence in the real sensible thing, are grasped by the intellect's simple apprehension.[24] They are then an object that is expressed by a concept as in a sign internal to cognition, and by a spoken word as in an external sign. So the cognitive form of the intellect as it performs the act of judgment is expressed internally in a static sign or representation called a judgment, and externally in a sentence. The frozen or static nature of this judgment is readily apparent when it is held before the mind's reflexive gaze for study long after the act of judgment has taken place. "The Titanic is sinking" can still be held before the mind's eye, even though decades have gone by since the judgment was actually being made on that fatal April night in 1912.

In this context of truth, then, "judgment" has two meanings that require careful distinction. In one meaning it is the dynamic intellective act by which synthesizing existence is being grasped. In the other meaning, it is the static, frozen representation of that action's cognitional form. In the first meaning, it denotes the "second operation" of the intellect. In the second meaning, it denotes something that is known through a "first operation" of the intellect, through simple reflexive apprehension. In the first meaning, the object of the cognition is an actual existential synthesizing that is taking place before its gaze. In the other meaning, the object is a static representation of that synthesizing, even though the synthesizing is no longer taking place. In the first sense, the judgment is a cognitive activity, in the second sense a cognitional object.

What bearing does this twofold sense of judgment have on the definition of truth given in the text just cited from the *Summa Theologiae*? If truth belongs in the realm of existence and the synthesizing activity of the intellect, what meaning is to be given the term *intellectus* in the definition "per conformitatem intellectus et rei" ? Does *intellectus* mean the activity of judgment or the representation of the activity's form?

The term *intellectus* can have the sense of the representation, just as it can signify the concept engendered in the "first operation" of the mind, the action of simple apprehension.[25] But in this text from the *Summa Theologiae* (I, 16, 2c), the term had just been used for the faculty—"intellectus, inquantum est cognoscens." Shortly after it is also used for the power —" intellectus autem conformitatem sui ad rem intelligibilem cognoscere potest." One would hardly expect a change in meaning in the word as it occurs between these two instances.

It may be objected that St. Thomas passes very easily without warning from one sense of *intellectus* to the other, e.g.:

> ...per esse suum simplex cognoscit sine compositione intellectuum vel divisione omne esse vel non esse quod rei convenit. Sed intellectus noster, cujus cognitione a rebus oritur, quae esse compositum habent, non apprehendit illud esse nisi componendo et dividendo (*In I Sent.*, d. 38, q. 1, a. 3, ad 2m; I, 904).

However, the point is not too important in the text under consideration from the *Summa Theologiae*.The intellect is being regarded as having its proper form. This form as known through simple reflection becomes an object in itself. It is the knowable content of the intellect as object. Viewed as an object of cognition, *intellectus* in this context may stand indifferently for the power or for the form that is mirrored in a proposition.[26]

In reflexion the intellect can hold before its glance both the existence apprehended through the act of judgment, and the existence represented in the act and apprehended by an act of simple reflexive apprehension. They are objects of two different acts of cognition, one of an act of judgment, the other an act of simple apprehension. The intellect can compare the two objects. If in the mental representation it sees correspondence or conformity or equation with the object grasped through the act of judgment, it sees the truth of the representation. Truth accordingly is the relation of conformity or equation or correspondence[27] of the judgment (in the sense of the representation) with what the judgment (in the sense of the activity) knows.

Because the intellect can know this conformity through an act of judgment, it can know the truth:

> Unde conformitatem istam cognoscere, est cognoscere veritatem. Hanc autem nullo modo sensus cognoscit... Intellectus autem conformitatem sui ad rem in-

telligibilem cognoscere potest; sed tamen non apprehendit eam secundum quod cognoscit de aliquo quod quid est; sed quando iudicat rem ita se habere sicut est forma quam de re apprehendit, tunc primo cognoscit et dicit verum. Et hoc facit componendo et dividendo (*ST*, I, 16, 2c).

The senses cannot know truth, because they do not have this kind of reflection. Nor can the simple apprehension of the intellect know truth, since it grasps things only under the aspect of quiddity. But quiddity is the same, as quiddity, no matter which existence is actuating it. Only where different existential actuations provide two objects that can be compared, is there room for knowledge of truth. There can accordingly be truth in sensation and in simple apprehension, but in neither of these activities can it be known as truth.

These conclusions in the *Summa Theologiae* had been approached in a slightly different way in the *De Veritate*. The notion of truth requires something new and characteristic, which can be found only in the intellect:

> ... ibi primo invenitur ratio veritatis in intellectu ubi primo intellectus incipit aliquid proprium habere quod res extra animam non habet, sed aliquid ei correspondens, inter quae adaequatio attendi potest (*De Ver.*, I, 3c).

Truth requires the two objects for comparison. Only when these two objects are known can the relation of correspondence, in which formal truth consists, be seen. Two instances of being are necessary. The aspect of quiddity alone, or of what the sensible species achieves, is not sufficient. The altogether special factor is encountered in judgment:

> Intellectus autem formans quidditates, non habet nisi similitudinem rei existentis extra animam, sicut et sensus in quantum accipit speciem rei sensibilis; sed quando incipit iudicare de re apprehensa, tunc ipsum iudicium intellectus est quoddam proprium ei, quod non invenitur extra in re. Sed quando adaequatur ei quod est extra in re, dicitur iudicium verum esse (*ibid.*).

The judgment, held before the reflecting intellect as an object, is what is called true. It is compared with and seen to correspond with what is grasped in the outside thing by the act of judgment. But in this text the emphasis is on the new dimension introduced through judgment—"ipsum iudicium intellectus est quoddam proprium ei, quod non invenitur extra in re." Does not this mean that the intellect is introducing something new into cognition, perhaps an apriori that is necessary for truth?

For knowing truth, the separate cognition of the two objects is required. The one object is the existence actually synthesizing the components in the thing that is being apprehended. The other object is the judgment in the sense of the proposition that represents this synthesizing. When asked if it is true that the cat is on the mat, you see that the two objects are the judgment "The cat is on the mat" and the actual presence of the cat on the mat at the moment.[28] You compare the two objects, and if they correspond you see that the judgment is true.

This judgment, in the sense of a representation, is certainly something that is not found in the thing outside the mind. It is a construct in which the concepts corresponding to subject, copula, and predicate may be distinguished. The distinction is possible only where existence is known in a special way that allows it to be regarded as a distinct object and to be represented in the concept that is expressed by the copula. In this way the existence is represented in the judgment and able to be compared with the existence known in the thing. This is something new and altogether distinctive in the human intellect's activity. It is different from sensation, and different from the simple formation of quiddities, and it makes the knowledge of truth possible.

But it can be regarded as an apriori? As the texts already considered make clear, the synthesizing that takes place in the intellect has as the cause and ground of its truth the existential synthesizing already there in the object known. The synthesizing is presented in the object, and does not originate in any intellectual apriori. But in the act of judgment the intellect attains the synthesizing in a special act, and accordingly is able to represent it as a special object. With the distinct object that is expressed by the copula now represented before its gaze, the intellect can make the comparison with the original existence itself and know the truth or falsity of the judgment. All this does not bring in any need for an apriori. It merely means that the intellect is able to represent existence as a distinct object, just as it is able to represent the various specific and generic natures as distinct objects of its simple apprehension even though they are not really distinct in the thing outside the mind.

V

These considerations raise a number of problems that require long and careful consideration. They involve the traditional Aristotelian view that the cognitive agent itself becomes and is the thing known. This alone is a difficult topic. But it becomes more involved when it is studied against the medieval background in which a common nature received different types of existence, and still more involved when in St. Thomas the only existence immediately known for individuals is the fleeting, temporal, synthesizing existence of sensible things. The problems of truth arising in this setting are complicated, and varying approaches in numbers of different texts make an overall picture difficult to attain. But the above considerations seem sufficient to show that for St. Thomas the knowledge acquired in the judgment and able to be seen as true comes entirely from sensible things, including oneself as a sensible object.

The cognitive activity, of course, comes from oneself as agent. It is an action that one performs. But the object that it attains, the object of which it makes one aware, is entirely there in priority to the cognitive act. Its structure comes from the thing known, and not from any apriori in the intellect. In the cognitional order, consequently, the human intellect is something purely potential. In the real order it is a power of the soul, a faculty, and accordingly something actual. But from the viewpoint of providing anything in the constitution of its object, it is but a potency to be actuated by what comes from the existent thing before it.

In this conception of judgment and truth further problems regarding the possibility of error and the possibility of rational discourse have to be faced. But for the present purpose the paramount consideration is the understanding that the existential synthesis, the existential actuality, is grasped from the first sense cognition. That is required and that is sufficient to make the cognitive agent of an existential composite that can be penetrated more deeply in intellectual cognition and represented in a way that distinguishes its quidditative and existential factors. When these have been represented as distinct objects they can be compared with the original existent and the truth or falsity of the judgment can be known. The way then lies open to the unlimited vistas of reasoning.

The basic considerations, then, is that the real existential synthesis be grasped from the start in sensible cognition. With this the case, no intellectual apriori will be required or will be possible for structuring the object. The entire structure will come from the sensible thing. Sense and intellect will mirror the structure in their respective ways, without adding to it. The term and notion "sense judgment" can be an apt means for bringing out and emphasizing the initial grasp of the whole existential composite in sensation. It will show that human cognition is grounded solidly in the real existence of external sensible things. This existence is temporal, ever flowing onward. It provides the setting for the historicity of human existence and human life. Yet in every instance it has the fixity and the security that grounds the first principle of demonstration, the principle of contradiction. From this viewpoint it is in every instance "aliquid fixum et quietum in ente." (*CG*, I, 20, Procedit). It causes truth in a way that is above human manipulation and is able to offer a secure basis for reasoning in philosophy and science, as well as common considerations for the individual deliberative procedure that leads up to moral decisions. It is the guarantee of a stable as opposed to a changing truth in the historicity of human experience.

THE ACCIDENTAL AND ESSENTIAL CHARACTER OF BEING
IN THE DOCTRINE OF ST. THOMAS AQUINAS

Already within his own lifetime the doctrine of St. Thomas Aquinas on being was criticized as openly contradictory.[1] It maintained at the same time that
being was essential to created natures, and that a thing's being was constituted
by the thing's essential principles, and yet was not the essence of that thing. To
Siger of Brabant these assertions bore the earmarks of a quite apparent contradiction, even though he seems to have suspected in them the presence of
something that he did not understand.[2]

Are these apparently contradictory tenets actually present in the text of St.
Thomas? An examination of his statements on the essential and the accidental
character of being in created things can yield, as will be seen, only an affirmative answer. St. Thomas expresses this twofold character of created being
too often and in too many different ways to allow it to be attributed to
carelessness or to be explained away by any semantic considerations. He teaches
that being is accidental to created things, and that it is essential to them. The
problem is not so much to investigate the presence of these *prima facie* opposite
assertions in the writings of St. Thomas, but rather to inquire whether they are
at all contradictory in his own doctrine of being. Are they but two different
aspects that created being necessarily presents in his metaphysical analysis? Are
both required for an adequate understanding of his teaching? Will the neglect
of either one lead to a basic misunderstanding of his metaphysical notions in
regard to the being of creatures?

There is even more at stake, however, than the aim to get back of the controversies to which the Thomistic doctrine of being has given rise, in particular
on the distinction between essence and existence. That purpose, of course,
would more than justify an intensive inquiry into the problem. Yet of still

greater importance is the bearing of the question on the general nature of metaphysical knowledge and of all human knowledge taken as a whole. If the metaphysical procedure of St. Thomas establishes successfully that being is both accidental and essential to creatures, will it not be discovering a radical ambiguity or equivocity at the very base of human knowledge? Being is what is first conceived by the human intellect, and into the concept of being all other concepts are resolved. If being then, is in itself ambiguous, there will be no possibility and no need of reducing the processes of human thought to any fundamental notion that is absolutely simple. A monolithic conception of human thinking will be rendered inadequate, the ideal of a universal science will be shown to be impossible of attainment, and the way will be left open, as far as metaphysics is concerned, for the autonomy of the various sciences within their own special fields. The problem, therefore, has importance of its own apart from its relation to historic controversies. There is good reason for investigating the ambiguity of being as it is made apparent through these texts of St. Thomas.

The Equivocity of Being (*Ens*)

In the *Contra Gentiles* St. Thomas states that God alone is essential to being: "...solus Deus est essentialiter ens" (*CG*, II, 53; ed. Leonine, XII, 391b 9-10). He means evidently enough that all other things are not essentially being. The essential possesion of being is reserved to God alone. Yet in *De Veritate* he asserts just as plainly that every nature whatsover is essentially being: "...quaelibet natura essentialiter est ens;..."[3] Every nature, every thing, is accordingly by its very essence denominated "being". It is of its very self a being. Unless it were a being it could not be a nature or a reality or a thing. By virtue of its own essence, then, every created thing is a being.

Each of these statements of St. Thomas, taken just in itself, is at first sight clear enough. Only when they are confronted with each other do they indicate their difficulties. No nature except God alone is essentially *ens*. Every nature whatsoever is essentially *ens*. Only a radical equivocity in what is meant by *ens* could save these assertions from directly contradicting each other. Is such an ambiguity actually intended by St. Thomas when he speaks about being? A grammatical indication in the translation of the two sentences into English may point in that direction. In the first case, *ens* is translated without the indefinite article:"...God alone is essentially being"(English Dominican tr.). In the second case it is translated with the article "...every reality is essentially a being" (tr. R. W. Mulligan). Yet of itself this grammatical difference need not imply equivocity. In instances other than being the omission of the indefinite article in English would hardly affect the meaning. The statements "Every man is essentially an animal" and "Every man is essentially animal" differ only in niceties of grammar. The inclusion or omission of the article does not seem to indicate any diversity of meaning. Where the predicate is univocal it remains univocal in spite of the difference in grammatical expression. If in the case of being, then, there is ambiguity, the ambiguity will lie much deeper than in the grammatical form. If there is a radical difference of meaning as signified by the one term in these statements of St. Thomas, will not that difference have to emerge from the very notion of being itself? Being, apparently, will have to have one sense in which it can be predicated essentially of every nature whatsoever, and another sense in which it can be predicated essentially of God alone.

In point of fact, St. Thomas does maintain this radical equivocity of being. He sees in it the occasion of Avicenna's deception in regard to the nature of created being. Criticizing the Persian's stand that being (ens) is an accident following upon the essence of a created thing, St. Thomas writes:

> Similiter etiam deceptus est ex aequivocatione entis. Nam ens quod significat compositionem propositionis est praedicatum accidentale, quia compositio fit per intellectum secundum determinatum tempus. Esse autem in hoc tempore vel in illo, est accidentale praedicatum. Sed ens quod dividitur per decem praedicamenta, significat ipsas naturas decem generum secundum quod sunt actu vel potentia (*In X Metaph.*, lect. 3; ed. Cathala-Spiazzi, no. 1982).

The notion of being, as expressed by the Latin participle *ens*, is therefore admittedly equivocal for St. Thomas. "Equivocal", of course, was a respectable term in the philosophical tradition in which St. Thomas was writing. Aristotle in *Categories* (1, 1a1-12) had used the word "equivocal" or "homonym" to denote things of which the name is identical but whose definitions, as denoted by the name, are different. The word remained the same throughout its different usages, the definitions of the various things as denoted equivocally by the word were different, and the things themselves were "equivocal". In Latin the force of the term "equivocal" lay in the fact that the same word (*vox*) was applied *equally* to things that had different definitions as denoted by that one word, just as in Greek the etymology of "homonym" meant that one and the same (*homos*) word was used in these different cases. In Aristotle's examples, a man and an ox, as denoted by the one term "animal", were univocal; but a man and a painting, as denoted by the same Greek word (*Zôion*), were equivocal. In the first case the definitions as denoted by the word are the same; in the second case they are different.

The use of the term "equivocal" in this philosophic tradition denotes, accordingly, that the objects signified by one and the same word have different definitions, and that they are signified by that word according to one or the other of the different definitions. They have different meanings, and according to one or the other of those meanings they are designated in their respective instances by the same word. This usage evidently includes under the term "equivocal" all things that are not strictly univocal. It was continued through Boethius and so passed over into the early Scholastic vocabulary. For Boethius equivocals were of five kinds. There were equivocals by chance, as for instance the son of Priam in the Homeric epic and the son of Philip of Macedon were both called by the same name Alexander. Both are considered to have the same name entirely by chance. Then there were equivocals by resemblance, as a man and a painting were called equivocals in the Aristotelian *Categories*; equivocals by proportion or analogy; equivocals by common origin, as in Aristotle's example "medical" and finally equivocals by reference, as in the Stagirite's example "health". These four latter types were called equivocals by design, as opposed to equivocals by mere chance.[4]

"Equivocal," then, in the Scholastic vocabulary to which St. Thomas was heir, did not necessarily mean equivocal by chance. In various ways the reason for the equivocity could be found in the things themselves, and it could even be required by the very natures of the things. "Being," for instance, is of such a character that it can be either substantial or accidental. There is something about a substance that calls for the designation "being"; and there is likewise something about an accident that demands the same designation. Yet in so far as being is capable of definition, the definition or meaning in these two instances is different. One may show that this use of a common term is required on account of the reference of secondary instances to a primary instance, as in Aristotle, or by the proportionality of the respective natures to their corresponding being, as in St. Thomas. In either case the equivocity or use of the same name is not by chance. It is required by the natures of the things themselves.

In the present case, St. Thomas is asserting that being (*ens*) may signify, equivocally, either the composition of a proposition or a nature that goes in a category. In the first case it is an accidental predicate: "Nam ens quod significat compositionem propositionis est praedicatum accidentale,..." The reason given is that the composition is made by the intellect according to a determined time. To be (*esse*) in any particular time, however, is an accidental predicate: "...quia compositio fit per intellectum secundum determinatum tempus. Esse autem in hoc tempore vel in illo, est accidentale praedicatum." The sense of being that the intellect expresses when it joins subject and predicate by means of the verb "is" depends upon something accidental. It depends upon a definite time. But to be in this or that period of time is certainly something accidental to created nature as such. In this sense being is accidental to a created thing.

According to this text, then, being is an accidental predicate when it expresses existence in a particular time. It denotes such existence when it signifies the composition between predicate and subject in a proposition. Whether it is expressed by the participial form *ens* or the infinitive form *esse*, it designates in this case something that is accidental to the nature of which it is predicated. Indifferently as participle or infinitive it is an accidental predicate. The particular grammatical form, apparently, has of itself little or nothing to do with the accidental or essential character of the predication.

What is the philosophical background against which this doctrine is being sketched? To some extent at least, it is quite evidently Aristotelian. The notion of the verb in a proposition as a speech form dependent upon time for its signification is Aristotelian teaching, as is likewise the description of the verb "to be" as the expression of the composition in a proposition. But does this Thomistic way of distinguishing two equivocal significations of being fit in with the various ways in which being is expressed for the Stagirite? Aristotle's doctrine was that being is expressed in four different ways.[5] Of these first two ways listed in Book E of the *Metaphysics* were being *per accidens* and being in the sense of the true. Being *per accidens* meant that something happens to be found with something else, as for instance in the statement "The carpenter *is* a musician." There is nothing in the nature of the carpenter as such that requires him to be a musician. That he is a musician is entirely accidental to the fact that he is a carpenter. The verb "is," accordingly, expresses in this case something accidental to the nature of the subject as such. It expresses being *per accidens*. It of course presupposes being *per se*[6], for it is concerned with the principal type of being, namely being as found in the categories.[7] It is concerned with a carpenter and with music, both of which are types of being that are found in the predicaments. But the being expressed by the verb in this proposition is not a type of being found in any of the categories. It is something over and above any predicamental being. It is *per accidens* in regard to the principal type of being, that is, the being that is limited to the necessary grooves of the categories. For Aristotle the *per accidens* kind of being was as it were only a name[8], and seemed rather akin to not-being[9].

Like being *per accidens*, so for Aristotle the second way in which being is expressed, being as true, is also concerned with the principal type of being, being as in the categories. Being as true is not found in things, but in the intellect or the mind. It is in fact caused by the operation of the intellect.[10] It is viewed accordingly as presupposing predicamental being, just as being *per accidens* presupposes the *per se* being of the categories. What is found in the things according to the necessary requirements of the categories seems to be looked upon as the basic and permanent type of being, while chance associations like those expressed in being *per accidens*, or the composition that the intellect makes when in its own activity it relates different categories as subject and predicate, are regarded as subsequent ways in which the things that are in the categories may be.

Is St. Thomas, then, grouping under one head the first two Aristotelian ways of expressing being? Is he ranging both under the notion of being as an accidental predicate? If so, just how is he connecting the two? In the second *Quodlibetum*, the same twofold signification of the participle *ens* is described against the background of the two questions taken from the *Posterior Analytics* (II, 1-10, 89b23-94a19) of Aristotle, the *an est* and the *quid est*. St. Thomas states:

> Ens autem non ponitur in definitione creaturae, quia nec est genus nec differentia; et ideo alia quaestio est *an est* et *quid est*. Unde, cum omne quod est praeter essentiam rei, dicatur accidens; esse quod pertinet ad quaestionem *an est*, est accidens; et ideo Commentator dicit in V Metaphysic., quod ista propositio, *Socrates est*, est de accidentali praedicato, secundum quod importat entitatem rei, vel veritatem propositionis. Sed verum est quod hoc nomen *ens*, secundum quod importat rem cui competit huiusmodi esse, sic significat essentiam rei, et dividitur per decem genera;... (*Quodl.*, II, 3c; ed. Mandonnet, Paris, 1926, p. 43).

Here again St. Thomas is dealing with the same ambiguity of being, as expressed by the participle *ens*. *Ens* can mean being as an accidental predicate, or it can mean something essential, in fact the essence of the thing as found in one of the categories. The division is obviously the same as the one found in the *Commentary on the Metaphysics*.[11] As in that text, the being that is an accidental predicate is expressed indifferently by the participial form *ens* and the infinitive form *esse*. The *ens* that does not enter the definition of the thing is the *esse* that is an accident. It is the *esse* that goes with or belongs to (*competit*) the essence of the thing. *Ens* and *esse*, accordingly, are used synonymously to denote being in the sense of an accidental predicate. This predicate, St. Thomas says expressly, is an accident because it is apart from or over and beyond (*praeter*) the things's essence. When it is expressed by a finite form of the verb like ''is,'' as in the proposition ''Socrates is'' or ''Socrates exists,'' the situation is still the same. Being in this case is an accidental predicate, no matter what grammatical form of the verb is used to express it. It is accidental, moreover, whether it is taken to imply the being of the thing or the truth of the proposition: ''secundum quod importat entitatem rei, vel veritatem propositionis.''

St. Thomas, therefore, is quite clearly grouping under the one head the first two Aristotelian ways of expressing being. Being *per accidens* and being as the true are regarded as coming under the common caption of being as an accidental predicate. The being of the thing, in so far as it answers to the question *an est* or does the thing exist, and the being that is signified by the composition in a proposition, seem looked upon as the same way of expressing being. At least, both are implied when being is predicated of a thing in an accidental way. Does St. Thomas then understand that the verb, which according to Aristotelian doctrine expresses being according to a particular time, signifies both the being that is actually exercised by the thing and the composition that is found in the judgment?

St. Thomas does interpret Aristotle in exactly that way:

> Ideo autem dicit quod hoc verbum EST consignificat compositionem, quia non eam principaliter significat, sed ex consequenti; significat enim primo illud quod cadit in intellectu per modum actualitatis absolute: nam EST, simpliciter dictum, significat *in actu esse*: et ideo significat per modum verbi. Quia vero actualitas, quam principaliter significat hoc verbum EST, est communiter actualitas omnis formae, vel actus substantialis vel accidentalis, inde est quod cum volumus significare quamcumque formam vel actum actualiter inesse alicui subiecto, significamus illud per hoc verbum EST, vel *simpliciter* vel *secundum quid*: simpliciter quidem secundum praesens tempus, secundum quid autem secundum alia tempora (*In I Periherm.*, lect. 5; ed. Leonine, no. 22).

When being is signified in verbal form, and so according to conditions of time, it expresses principally, according to this interpretation, the actuality that the intellect understands as basic in the thing. It presents itself to the intellect by way of actuality in an absolute manner, and not hypothetically or conditionally. It means that the thing actually is or actually exists, according to the time in question. That actuality, signified in this way by the verb, is however the actuality of every form whatsoever. Such being is the actuality of every substantial form or act, and also is the actuality of every accidental form. Substance and accidents have in common the requirement of being actuated by the further actuality that is expressed in the verb "to be." When one wishes to express in a proposition, then, that any form or act whatsoever is actually present in a subject, one uses the verb "to be."

The being that is expressed by the truth in a proposition is accordingly viewed by St. Thomas as consequent upon the actual exercise of being in the thing. The proposition is true because the thing happens to be or is that way. Being as the true follows upon actuality that is the common requirement of every substance and every accident. If this requirement is something accidental to the thing, what follows it will likewise be accidental. There is no difficulty in ranging both under the heading of being as an accidental predicate.

Can this interpretation, however, be called in any sense genuine Aristotelianism? At least there is no hint in the text of Aristotle that being *per accidens* and being as the true express basically but one way of being. Nor is there any notion in the Stagirite's doctrine that a further actuality is required for all forms, substantial as well as accidental. Still less is there any teaching in

Aristotle that the being that answers the question *an est* is accidental to a thing. Rather, it is the general aspect of being that necessarily accompanies every definable thing. The definition gives the answer to the question *quid est*. But you cannot know the *quid est* without thereby knowing the *an est*. If a thing can be defined it is by that very fact known as a being in the sense corresponding to the *an est* for Aristotle. His principal example is the lunar eclipse. An observer on the moon, he claims, would know immediately that it is, but would have to reason to find out what it is. The definition would not be immediately known, but only mediately as the result of a reasoning process. So where the defining elements are not immediately known as such, the being that corresponds to the *an est* has to be known as such, the being that corresponds to the *an est* has to be known before the answer to the *quid est* can be attained (*APo.*, II 8, 93a16-b3). In no case, then, can the *quid est* be known before the *an est*.

For Aristotle, consequently, the *an est* does not signify any accidental or contingent existence. For St. Thomas, on the other hand, it denotes an accidental predicate. For Aristotle, the answer to the question *quid est* necessarily includes the answer to the question *an est*. If you know what an eclipse is you thereby know that it is. The question *an est* inquires merely if something is able to have the general character of being, and so does not indicate a combination of mutually exclusive notions, like a centaur or a goat-stag. If, like a centaur or a goat-stag, it is not even a being, there is no possibility of asking the further question "What is it?" One cannot know what it is unless one knows simultaneously or previously that it is something contained within the range of the notion "being." For St. Thomas, on the other hand, one can know what a thing is without knowing that it is in reality. The question *an est* refers here to the real existence of the thing. One can know what a phoenix is, or a mountain of gold is, or what an eclipse is, without knowing whether any of these actually exist in the real world.[13] For Aristotle, the *an est* is not at all asking if the thing exists in reality, but only if it is free from internal contradiction, if it is a being in the most general sense of the word. The answer to *an est* is for him a partial, inchoative cognition of the thing, sufficient to establish it as a being. After that one can go on to acquire the further knowledge that gives its definite nature, that tells *what* it *is*. For St. Thomas, on the contrary, the *an est* is asking precisely "Does the thing exist?" The being that answers such a question is accordingly an accidental predicate, whether it is the existence actually exercised by the thing in reality or whether it is the composition made by the intellect in forming a proposition.

That, then, is the first sense of being for St. Thomas. It is being in the sense of actually exercised existence. As such it is described as accidental to the thing. The other sense of being, however, signifies the very natures of the things found in the categories: "Sed ens quod dividitur per decem praedicamenta, significat ipsas naturas decem generum secundum quod sunt actu vel potentia'' (*In X Metaph.*, lect. 3; ed. Cathala-Spiazzi, no. 1982). In designating the natures of created things, the participle *ens* is signifying their essences. What it is expressing is essential to the things in question. Just as the predicates man, animal, living thing, body, and substance give essential characteristics of the human individual, so the further predicate ''being'' denotes his essence in a still vaguer way. Though strictly neither genus nor difference, it functions in this manner as a sort of super-generic predicate. Just as a man is an animal or a body, so also is he a being.

This description of the second sense of being seems meant to cover the third and fourth Aristotelian ways of being, just as being in the sense of an accidental predicate included the Stagirite's first two ways. The third way for Aristotle was being as in the categories, and the fourth way was being as act and potency. St. Thomas is joining these two under the one caption "the natures of the ten genera according as they are actually or potential." In the light of his doctrine just considered about existence as the actuality of every substantial form and every accidental form, any predicamental form may be considered either as actuated by its existence. In the former case it denotes the nature or the essence of the thing and belongs to one of the categories. In both senses, therefore, it comes under the one head of predicamental being and is expressed by the participle *ens* when *ens* means that which is divided into the ten categories.

In denoting the essence, *ens* in this second sense involves the thing itself to which existence, as an accidental predicate, belongs: "Sed verum est quod hoc nomen *ens*, secundum quod importat rem cui competit hujusmodi esse, sic significat essentiam rei, et dividitur per decem genera;..." (*Quodl.*, II, 3c; ed. Mandonnet, p.43). In this sense *ens* designates the thing that exists. It means a being. It is an essential predicate, not an accidental one. It includes all the being that is divided into the ten categories. When *ens* in the other sense is said to be an accident, it cannot, therefore, be an accident in the meaning of something *praeter essentiam rei* and *aliquid non existens de essentia rei* (*ibid.*). It is something over and above the essence, something that does not appear in the essence of the thing. In this way St. Thomas interprets Aristotle's (*Metaph.*, B. 3,998b17-27) dictum that being is not a genus. It is not a genus because it lies outside the ten supreme genera of things. The genera are concerned with natures or essences, and existence lies outside the whole order of finite essence.

The equivocity of the participle *ens* for St. Thomas consists then in the twofold usage of the term to denote on the one hand the very essence or nature of a created thing, and on the other hand to denote an actuality that lies outside the essence. In the former case it is an essential predicate, in the latter case an accidental one. It means on the one hand any nature or thing that goes in a category, on the other hand the existence that lies outside all categories.

Because he can understand *ens* in the former sense, St. Thomas is able to consider himself the defender of the Aristotelian teaching that every nature is essentially a being (*Metaph.*, Γ 2, 1003b26-33) and that being adds nothing over and above the nature, so that "a man and a 'being' man are the same" (b26-27). *Ens* designates the nature of the thing, and not something accidentally added to that nature. Without further explanation St. Thomas can simply deny the Avicennian tenet that being is an accident, and can say that Avicenna was deceived by the equivocity of being. He can for the purposes of the question under consideration restrict the meaning of *ens* to one of its senses and ignore for the moment the other.

In the commentary on Boethius' *De Hebdomadibus*, for instance, St. Thomas just as sharply contrasts the meaning of the participle *ens* with the actuality that is expressed by the infinitive *esse*: "Aliud autem significamus per hoc quod dicimus esse, et aliud per hoc quod dicimus id quod est; sicut et aliud significamus cum dicimus currere, et aliud per hoc quod dicitur currens. Nam currere et esse significantur in abstracto, sicut et albedo; sed quod est, id est ens et currens, significantur in concreto, velut album." The *quod est* or *ens* is contrasted with the *esse* in the same way in which a runner is contrasted with the act of running. *Ens*, like "runner", signifies *in concreto*. It signifies the subject as possessing the act of being or the act in question, abstracting from the subject that is or the person who runs. Accordingly, they signify *in abstracto*, that is, in abstraction from their subject. Like the noun "whiteness," they denote their act abstractly. *Ens* and "runner," however, signify the subject concretely with the act, just as the neuter of the Latin adjective "album," meaning "a white thing," expresses the subject as qualified by the color white.

In this usage, therefore, St. Thomas restricts the participial form *ens* to the one sense of the "thing that is," and the infinitive form *esse* to the sense of the actuality of being. They are compared as subject and form, against the Boethian background of the *quod est* and *quo*. For the most part throughout his works, the participle *ens* is in fact used by St. Thomas in the sense of "that which is." Yet at times he does not hesitate to use it without explanation, solely in the other sense of the actuality of being. He may even say that *ens* does not express the essence or quiddity: "...in quolibet genere oportet significare quidditatem aliquam, ut dictum est, de cujus intellectu non est esse. Ens autem non dicit quidditatem, sed solum actum essendi..." (*In I Sent.*, d. 8, q. 4,a.2, ad 2m; ad. Mandonnet, I, 222-223). Emphasizing the fact that the notion of a thing does not involve the thing's real existence, St. Thomas can state bluntly in this way that *ens* does not mean the quiddity, but only the act of being. It signifies the act in abstraction from the concretion with the essence. The participle *ens* is here expressing the act *in abstracto*, just as definitely as does the infinitive form *esse* in this text and in the text already quoted from the *Commentary on the De Hebdomadibus*. Just as St. Thomas in the present text resumes the notion *esse* by means of the participle *ens*, so in fairly numerous other instances[15] does he use *ens* as a substitute for *esse* in expressing the act of being. He feels free to use *ens* as a substitute for *esse* in expressing the act of being. He feels free to use it in either sense, and may on occasion restrict it to just one of its two senses and deny it the other sense. This is quite in accord with the Aristotelian usage of equivocals.[16]

One may be tempted to ask if this equivocity of the participle *ens* is really required by the nature of being, or if it is merely an accident of usage. If subject and act are different, why not consistently use one term to denote the subject, and another term to denote the act? St. Thomas implies clearly enough that they are different objects of signification: "Aliud autem significamus per hoc quod dicimus esse, et aliud per hoc quod dicimus id quod est;..."(*In De Hebd.*, c. II). One object is signified by the Latin infinitive form of the verb, namely the act *in abstracto*, like "being" or "running." Another object is signified by the Latin participles, namely the concretion of subject and act, like "that which is" or "a runner." Why not, then, use the infinitive *esse* consistently to mean the act of being, and the participle *ens* just as consistently to denote that subject that exercises the act? Is there anything in the nature of being that would militate against such a consistent usage?

There is a grammatical peculiarity that makes itself felt at once in attempting to answer these questions. In Latin, for all other verbs than "to be" the participial form signifies *in concreto* only, and not *in abstracto*. "Currens" and all other such participles denote the one who exercises the act. They denote the concretion of subject and act, and not the act taken by itself. "Currens" means "a runner", and not the act of running. Only the participle *ens* can signify both the act of being and the subject that exercises the act. In English, for all verbs other than "to be" the participial form designates the act and not the subject. The participle signifies only *in abstracto*, according to St. Thomas' terminology, and not *in concreto*. "Running," for example, means the act taken by itself, and not the one who runs. "Being," however, just as in Latin, can have both significations. One may speak of "a human being" in the sense of the subject that is human, and one may likewise say that a man possesses being. In both languages the participle can denote either the act alone or the subject concretely with the act. Does this hint that in the case of being, language is not able to restrict the notion to just one signification, as with other verbs? Is there something about being that renders equivocity indispensable?

One may expect readily enough a difference between verbs that signify an act belonging to one of the categories of accidents, and a verb signifying an act that is beyond all the categories. It is easy enough to compare the act of running, as is done in the text of St. Thomas, with the act of whiteness. Both belong in the categories. It is easy enough to consider the act and the subject as separate objects of consideration in each case. One can think of the subject whiteness, a body, in complete isolation from that particular color. Whiteness is merely accidental to the body, in the full predicamental sense of accident. Similarly one can think of the subject of running, an animal, apart from the act of running. No animal necessarily has to be thought of as always running. Running is a predicamental accident. But can one ever think of the subject of being in complete isolation from all being? No matter how one tries to conceive it, it is always represented as a being. If it is not represented as a being, it is not represented at all. It would be nothing. There would be nothing there to represent.

This super-universal or transcendent character of being prevents the consideration of any subject whatsoever in precision from being. No subject can prescind from being in the way that a body can prescind from whiteness or an animal from running. Being is a necessary aspect of everything whatsoever. It is somehow essential to every nature. It seems like an act that is wrapped in its own subject. There can hardly be any question here of two realities, one of which is subject and the other is the act, as there are in the instances of the body that is white and the animal that is running. The ambiguity cannot be explained by saying that the same term *ens* is used on some occasions to denote the subject of being and so signifies something essential to every nature; while on other occasions it is used to mean the act of being and so designates something accidental to all created natures. The difficulty is that the subject in this case cannot be considered as prescinding from the act. The subject necessarily is a being, and yet its being is accidental to it. In what sense, then, is the act of being accidental to a created nature, and in what sense is it not accidental? The root of the equivocity seems to lie not in the distinction between subject and act, but in the very relation of the act of being to its proper subject. Being appears as *both* accidental and essential to any created nature.

ESSE—An Accident and Not an Accident

In the fifth article of the twelfth *Quodlibetum* St. Thomas notes, on the one hand, that an accident is conceived as belonging to a pre-existing subject (*accidens intelligitur inesse alicui praeexistenti*—ed. Spiazzi, p. 226b). On the other hand, he recalls the well-known dictum of St. Hilary that regarding God "*esse enim non est accidens nomen*" ("Being is not an accidental name,..."—*De Trin.*, VII, 11; tr. McKenna). This saying implies that in all creatures being is an accident. According to the conception of accident that has just been noted, being should therefore require in creatures a pre-existing subject. Yet, St. Thomas insists, being is the first act of all. Even an angel cannot be pre-existent to its own being. No form whatsoever can be except through its *esse* (*nulla forma est nisi per esse*). Substantial being (*esse*), then, is not proper-ly an accident in created things, even though it is an accident in the sense that it is not part of their essence: "Et sic dico quod esse substantiale rei non est ac-cidens, sed actualitas cuiuslibet formae existentis,...et sic proprie loquendo, non est accidens. Et quod Hilarius dicit, dico quod accidens dicitur large omne quod non est pars essentiae; et sic est esse in rebus creatis,..." (*Quodl.*, XII, 5; ed. Mandonnet, p. 430).

This text recognizes two senses of the term "accident." There is a wider sense, in which everything that is not a part of the essence may be called an ac-cident. In this sense of something over and above (*praeter*) the essence, being, whether expressed by the participle *ens* or the infinitive *esse*, has been called an accident in the passage already quoted from the *Quodlibeta* (II, 3c; ed. Man-donnet, p.43). In the same sense, presumably, being (expressed by both *ens* and *esse*) was named an accidental predicate in the text from the commentary on the tenth Book of the *Metaphysics* (lect. 3; ed. Cathala-Spiazzi no. 1982), since the two passages are quite closely parallel. In the wide sense, then, everything outside the essence is an accident, whether or not it is a form answer-ing to the conditions necessary for the accepted categories of accidents. Against the background of the mediaeval controversies,[17] this can only mean that the notion "accident" is wider than the nine Aristotelian predicaments. There is a sense of the term that does not fit in with the concept of a predicamental acci-dent. In this wider sense, being is in created things an accident: "...et sic est esse in rebus creatis,..."

In the proper sense of the word accident, however, the being of created things is not an accident: " ...proprie loquendo, non est accidens." The proper sense of accident, in the tradition that lay behind the mediaeval metaphysics controversies, would be understood as denoting the accepted Aristotelian meaning of a predicamental accident. But the substantial being of a thing can hardly be a predicamental accident. A predicamental accident supposes its substance already complete as substance, and is added to a so completed sub-ject. Without substantial being, however, there is simply no subject to which an accident could be added. Substantial being, therefore, cannot function as a predicamental accident, as an accident in the proper sense of the Aristotelian tradition: "Et sic dico quod esse substantiale rei non est accidens, sed actualitas cujuslibet formae existentis,..."

The notion expressed by the infinitive *esse* in this text is clearly the actuality of every form. As seen in the preceding section of the present article, this is the actuality upon which the composition in a proposition is grounded, and is be-ing in the sense of an accidental predicate.   The whole question of whether be-ing is an accident in a wide or in a proper sense, accordingly, is concerned with being that is taken *in abstracto*. It is a question that is asked about the act of be-

ing, and not about the subject of being. The sense in which *esse* is not accidental is not, at least as far as the position of the question envisages it, the same
sense in which *ens* is essential to every nature. The two meanings of accident in
the present question bear directly upon the sense in which *ens* was called an accidental predicate. Being, as expressed by the participle *ens*, has already been
shown to mean both subject and act. As subject it was essential to all natures, as
act it was accidental. Now, being in the sense of act is declared to be one way an
accident, and in another way not an accident. It is an accident in a wide sense,
but not in a proper sense. In the proper sense of the word "accident," the act
of being is not accidental to its subject.

Is this distinction of a proper and a wide sense of accident merely an *ad hoc*
invention? It hardly can claim any sanction in Scholastic tradition. That being
was neither substance nor accident but something better than either, had
already been taught by William of Auvergne.[18] But that it did not come under
any of the predicamental accidents and still had to be called an accident, in a
different sense of the term "accident," was something new. The doctrine that
being is accidental to things was also familiar enough.[19] But that this doctrine
required a notion of accident that was not contained within the proper sense of
the word in the Aristotelian tradition, had not been brought forward. True, accident had been contrasted with property in the traditional scheme of the
predicables.[20] But this distinction did not go outside the orbit of the categories.
Rather, it narrowed the concept of accident instead of widening it. It was entirely concerned with the way in which one category was predicated of another.
It was not at all a widening of the notion "accident" outside the sphere of the
predicamental accidents. The wider sense that allowed being to be called an accident without making it a predicamental accident seems to arise only from the
consideration of the present question. If the distinction between the wide and
the proper senses of accident is valid, it will have to have its foundation in the
peculiar way in which the act of being is accidental to a creature. The distinction does not help to discover the accidentality of being. Rather, it is first
revealed by the study of the way in which one category is accidental to another.
Therefore it is accidental in a wider sense.

There is nothing in the traditional doctrine of accidents, then, that will be of
positive aid in investigating the accidental character of being in the doctrine of
St. Thomas. Negatively, the study of the traditional notions makes clear that
being is not an accident in the Aristotelian sense of the term. It is not related to
its subject in the way that a predicamental accident is related to its substance:
"...esse est accidens, non quasi per accidens se habens, sed quasi actualitas cujuslibet substantiae;..." (*Quodl.*, II, 3, ad 2m; ed. Mandonnet, p. 43). It cannot be described as just *per accidens* to its subject. It is rather the actuality of
every substance, as though necessary for the constitution of every substance
even though it is an accident. The vocabulary becomes difficult, and seems to

throw but little light on the doctrine. The solution will have to emerge from a deeper study of the Thomistic notion of being, and not from any definitions of the term "accident" or *per accidens*. The negative consideration that being is not a predicamental accident, however, is sufficient to indicate that substantial being somehow enters into the very constitution of the substance itself. Not being a predicamental accident, it must be prior to the whole order of predicamental accidents, and so contained somehow within the order of substance. Yet it is always outside the essence. In that sense it is always accidental. These considerations point in the direction of a notion of accident that is prior to, and not subsequent to, the notion of substance. This implication will have to be carefully investigated in the texts of St. Thomas that give being a priority to essence in created things. There may well be a close connection between the assertions that being is not a predicamental accident, and the tenet that every nature is essentially a being.

As they stand, however, these statements regarding *esse* as an accident or not an accident bear directly upon being as the act of a subject and not as the subject itself. In fact, in all the texts considered so far, the infinitive *esse* has been used only to denote the subject of being. The participle *ens* is used in both senses, but the infinitive *esse* has been restricted to one sense, that of the act. This usage of *esse* in the one sense only is regular throughout the texts of St. Thomas. True, he recognizes the current, and in point of fact traditional, use of the infinitive to signify also the essence or nature:

> Sed sciendum, quod esse dicitur tripliciter. Uno modo dicitur esse quidditas vel natura rei, sicut dicitur quod definitio est oratio significans quid est esse; definitio enim quidditatem rei significat. Alio modo dicitur esse ipse actus essentiae; sicut vivere, quod est esse viventibus, est animae actus; non actus secundus, qui est operatio, sed actus primus. Tertio modo dicitur esse quod significat veritatem compositionis in propositionibus, secundum quod 'est' dicitur copula: et secundum hoc est in intellectu componente et dividente quantum ad sui complementum; sed fundatur in esse rei, quod est actus essentiae (*In I Sent.*, d.33, q.1, a.1, ad 1m; ed. Mandonnet, I, 766).

In this passage the senses of being are basically the same as those expressed by the participle *ens* in the texts already analyzed. True, there are three senses mentioned now instead of the two previously used to embrace the four ways in which being was expressed to Aristotle. However, one sees readily enough that the second and third senses are joined together here as closely as they were in the other texts. The being that signifies truth in the composition of a proposition is ranged with the being that is the act of essence. It is grounded upon that actually exercised being, even more explicitly in this text than in the ones previously considered. The being that is expressed by the copula "is" is indeed found in the intellect in so far as the completion of the proposition is concerned; but it is based upon the being that is the act of the essence and that is found in the thing. The second and third senses, accordingly, are concerned with being as act, and not with being as subject. They denote being as taken *in abstracto*.

The first sense listed is being as quiddity or nature. It means the nature that is or exists. It seems to correspond to what was expressed by the participle *ens* in the sense in which being is wrapped in nature, the sense in which every nature is essentially a being. It denotes the form or nature, whether substantial or accidental, that is actuated by the act of being. It signifies the subject of being, being as taken *in concreto*. But here, instead of being designated by the participial form, the subject of being is expressed by the infinitive *esse*.

The same usage is reported in the third book of the commentary on the *Sentences* as follows:

> "...*esse duobus* modis dicitur. *Uno modo*, secundum quod significat *veritatem propositionis* secundum quod est copula; et sic, ut Commentator ibidem dicit, *ens* est *praedicatum accidentale*. Et hoc esse non est in re, sed in mente quae conjugit subjectum cum praedicato, ut dicit Philosophus in VI *Meta*....*Alio modo* dicitur *esse quod pertinet ad naturam rei*, secundum quod dividitur secundum decem genera. Et hoc quidem esse in re est, et est actus entis resultans ex principiis rei, sicut lucere est actus lucentis. *Aliquando* tamen *esse* sumitur *pro essentia*, secundum quam res est; quia per actus consueverunt significari eorum principia, ut potentia vel habitus" (*In III Sent.*, 6, 2, 2, Resp.; ed. Moos, III, 238).

In the first sense mentioned in this text, *esse* is described synonymously with *ens* as an accidental predicate, and in the second sense it is the act of a being (*actus entis*). These senses, accordingly, express being as taken *in abstracto*, and not as the subject of the act. The third sense reported is that of essence. The reason given for the legitimacy of using the infinitive *esse* to signify essence is that by custom the potency may be designated by the act. This would mean that being primarily denotes act, but secondarily may denote the potency to that act. The potency or subject of being may therefore be called a being, an *esse*. Just as the thing that is may be called an *ens*, so may it also be called an *esse*.

St. Thomas seems merely to be reporting this usage of the infinitive *esse* to denote the essence or nature. In expressing his own thought he appears to avoid very carefully any use of the term *esse* in this sense of the subject of being. It is difficult, though perhaps not impossible, to indicate texts where he takes advantage of this custom of using *esse* to signify essence. Yet there need be no doubt about the usage that he reports. William of Auvergne, in the immediate philosophical background at Paris, carefully explained the twofold sense of *esse*:

Oportet autem te scire, quia esse duas habet intentiones, et una earum est residuum a circumvestione et varietate accidentium, et hoc est proprie quod nominatur essentia, sive substantia,…et significat illud solum quod diffinitiva oratione significatur sive nomine speciei. Hoc igitur est quod dicitur substantia rei, et ejus esse, et ejus quidditas: et hoc est esse, quod diffinitio significat, et explicat, et hoc ipsum dicitur rei essentia. Secunda autem intentio hujus quod est esse, est illud quod dicitur per hoc verbum est de unoquoque, et est praeter uniuscujusque rationem. In nullius autem ratione accipitur esse, quidquid imaginati fuerimus, sive hominem, sive asinum, sive aliud, ut in ratione ejus esse intelligamus, eo solo excepto de quo essentialiter dicitur; ejus namque essentia nisi per ipsum esse intelligi non potest, cum ipsa, et ejus esse omnimodo sint una re." (*De Trin.*, c. II; ed. Paris, 1674, Supplementum, p. 2b).

The infinitive *esse*, as William explains it, has accordingly two senses. In one sense it expresses only what is signified by the definition of the thing, that is, it denotes the essence or substance or quiddity of the thing. William's tendency to use three different expressions where one would do, serves in this case at least to make his meaning triply clear. The second sense of the infinitive *esse*, he continues, is found in what the verb "is" denotes when it is predicated of anything whatsoever. This is something not contained within the essence of anything except God. It is outside (*praeter*) the essence of every other thing. Imagine anything you wish, a man, a donkey, or anything else, and examine its notion or essence. You will not find that being in this second sense is contained within any such essence. The only exception is God. Of Him it is predicated essentially, for His essence and His being are entirely one in reality. His essence can be understood only as being in this second sense of the term.

William, accordingly had no difficulty in accepting the infinitive *esse* in a sense that definitely meant essence, along with the other sense in which it meant something outside the essence. He sees nothing strange in the use of *esse* to denote just what is expressed in the definition of a thing. Boethius, whose writings served to fix so much of the Scholastic vocabulary, had identified the *esse* of a thing with its definition: "Quod est autem, esse rei? Nihil aliud est nisi definitio" (*In Isog. Porphys.*, editio secunda, IV, 14; ed. Brandt, p. 273.13). The definition signifies what the thing is, and so its essence or nature. In the *De Hebdomadibus* Boethius uses the term *esse* consistently to denote natures, substantial and accidental: "Diversum est, tantum esse aliquid, et esse aliquid in eo quod est; illic enim accidens, hic substantia significatur" (*PL*, LXIV, 1311C). He distinguishes these natures, under the designation of *esse*, from the *quod est* or composite that is the creature: "Diversum est esse, et id quod est: ipsum enim esse nondum est. At vero id quod est, accepta essendi forma, est, atque consistit." (1311B). *Esse* is understood as having a formal sense.

The use of the infinitive of the verb "to be" to denote a form or formal aspect of a thing goes back, in point of fact, to Aristotle. The infinitive was regularly used by the Stagirite with a possessive dative to designate the form of a thing as distinguished from the matter and the composite in instances like "the being of man" or "the being of blood." In such expressions the Greek infinitive "to be" means the form of man or the form of blood. It designates only the form. This use of the infinitive seems to have originated from the technical Aristotelian phrase το τι ην ειναι. Literally translated, the phrase would read in English "the what-was-being,"[21] although the imperfect tense of the Greek verb ("was") has to be understood as signifying not past being but timeless being. The infinitive of the verb "to be" in this formal sense was extended in Aristotle to express any formal aspect of the thing, even though that formal aspect did not involve a real difference. The "now" of time, for instance, both divides and joins past and different formal aspects of it; they differ from each other in "being" (*Ph.*, IV 13, 222a19–20).

That St. Thomas has the Aristotelian formula in mind as he reports the usage of the infinitive *esse* in the sense of essence, appears from the way in which he introduces that meaning of the term: "Uno modo dicitur esse ipsa quidditas vel natura rei, sicut dicitur quod definitio est oratio significans quid est esse;…" (*In I Sent.*, d.33, q.1, a.1, ad 1m; ed. Mandonnet, I, 766). He is reporting the tradition that uses *esse* to signify what is expressed in the definition of a thing. The definition gives formal characteristics, the proximate genus and the specific differentia. The phrase "quid est esse" has its unmistakable Aristotelian background.

The use of the infinitive *esse* to signify the essence of a thing was therefore quite traditional. Nor was there any grammatical reason why the Latin infinitive of the verb "to be" could not have continued to express this meaning. As it developed into the Italian form *essere* it retained such usage. One says in Italian "un essere umano" in the sense of a man, just as in French one speaks of "un être humain." The infinitive of the verb "to be" in these languages derived from Latin may readily denote the thing itself, and not directly the act or characteristic of being. It can signify the nature or essence, which is the subject of being. In St. Thomas' phrase, it can signify *in concreto*.

There is no compelling historical reason, then, either in philosophical or in grammatical tradition, why St. Thomas himself should not have used the infinitive *esse* to express both subject of being and act of being, just as he uses the participle *ens* in both senses. Philosophically as well as grammatically both forms of the verb are open to the same ambiguity. Both may be equally translated by "being" and "a being" in English, and express in the former way the act of being, and in the latter way the nature that exists. Both grammatical forms may signify either *in abstracto* or *in concreto*. Yet St. Thomas uses the infinitive *esse* to signify only *in abstracto*. That is his regular custom. Why? No compelling reason is forthcoming. It looks as though he is arbitrarily restricting the infinitive in his own vocabulary to just one of its two possible usages. Yet in the whole history of philosophy it would be hard to find a first-rate thinker who resisted better than St. Thomas the temptation to coin his own philosophical vocabulary. He employed the traditional terminology in current use at the time, no matter how difficult it was for that old terminology to express radically new thought. For posterity, this practice of St. Thomas has perhaps been singularly unfortunate. It has made his thought difficult to grasp, and has rendered the astonishing freshness and newness of his metaphysical procedure and its deep-rooted separation from that of his contemporaries and predecessors imperceptible at first glance. In the particular case of the infinitive *esse*, however, there seems to be not the coining of a new philosophical term, but the arbitrary restriction of an old one to just one of its current philosophical meanings.

Does this restriction indicate a new and vitally important role of the actuality of being in the metaphysical thought of St. Thomas? If the act of being is to have an altogether distinctive and unprecedented function in his thinking, it could be expected to give rise to a more or less unconscious tendency to reserve one particular term for its expression. The usage would be formed of denoting this function regularly by the same term. So in the texts of St. Thomas, while the participle *ens* is used in both its senses, the infinitive *esse* seems arbitrarily confined to signifying the act of being. Such a departure from current usage calls for special attention from the student of St. Thomas, and is sufficient ground for a presumption that the act of being will be a focal point of metaphysical interest as Thomistic thought unfolds its innermost meaning.

What St. Thomas, in fact, has been saying in the texts just quoted from the commentary on the *Sentences* is, that being in the sense of a thing's actuality is the very act of the essence just as living is the act of the soul (sicut vivere, quod est esse viventibus,[22] est animae actus) and illuminating is the act of a thing that gives light (sicut lucere est actus lucentis). Just as operation is recognized as the act of any nature, so being, in the sense of actuality, is likewise the act of all such natures. There is an important difference, however. Living and illuminating and all such activities are predicamental accidents. They are secondary acts. They presume and require the primary act of the thing. That primary act of the thing, according to this doctrine of St. Thomas, is being. Being in this particular sense is the act of the essence or nature, and not a secondary act but the primary act: "non actus secundus, qui est operatio, sed actus primus" (*In I Sent.*, d.33, q.1, a.1, ad 1m; ed. Mandonnet, I, 766).

Every created nature or essence, according to this doctrine, will have two kinds of act. It will have its own activities or operations. These are added to it as predicamental accidents. They presuppose the essence complete in its substantial being. The actuality expressed by *esse* is not an act of this kind. It actuates the essence within the order of substance, and not in the order of predicamental accidents. It is properly the act of essence as such, and not, as are the operations, an act of the essence's powers: "Actio enim est proprie actualitas virtutis; sicut esse est actualitas substantiae vel essentiae" (*ST*, I, 54, 1c; cf. 79, 1c).

Any created nature, then, has to be actuated in two different ways, namely by its being and by its operation. The teaching that a thing has to be before it can operate would be a more or less commonplace observation, and need not carry any special metaphysical implications. But the insistence that the actuality of being has, without being a predicamental accident, correspondingly the same relation to the nature that operations have, points to a new metaphysical approach. It suggests that the nature is something different from its own being just as it is something different from its own operations. This is quite at variance with traditional Aristotelian teaching. But it differs also from Avicenna, for it maintains that being is not a predicamental accident and so is not something that is subsequent to essence. It indicates a new metaphysical conception of being.

Upon being as the act of essence, then, the interest of the present study will have to centre. In what sense is this act required by created essence, and so will be called necessary or essential to it? In what sense is it outside the essence, different from and accidental to the essence? In what sense does it flow from the essence, as do the operations, and in what sense is it something that does not flow from the essence but comes from outside? There are sufficiently numerous texts in St. Thomas that assert both of these latter possibilities, contradictory as they seem at first sight. These texts will have to be examined before proceeding to a study of the doctrine in itself. As regards St. Thomas' use of the infinitive *esse*, however, the texts already seen show that in the presentation of his own doctrine it is regularly used to denote only the act of being, and not the subject of being. Yet St. Thomas records the traditional use of *esse* to signify the nature or essence that is the subject of being, and thereby acknowledges that the infinitive form carries in itself the same equivocity as the participle *ens*. There is no real advantage, then, in attempting to preserve the infinitive form in English translation. Of its nature the infinitive does not necessarily mean the act as distinct from the subject. The participial form expresses the notion correctly and idiomatically. "The being of a thing" is normal English and carries all the force of the Latin *esse rei* just as well as does the unidiomatic phrase "the 'to be' of a thing." There is very rarely any danger of confusion with the English use of "being" in sense of a subject, like "a human being." The indefinite article makes the sense abundantly clear. It is of course possible to think up instances where the sense is not clear once the phrase has been detached from its context. "The being to which I just referred" could mean either the act of being with which I was dealing in a philosophical lecture, or it could mean the thing about which I was talking. But when read in its context the phrase should not occasion any misunderstanding. The English language is supple enough to express these meanings of being without having to be twisted or strained. "Being," then, is the correct translation of both *ens* and *esse* when they signify the act of being. In English it signifies *in abstracto*, just as the participle "running" expresses the act of running that in Latin is signified by the infinitive *currere*.

The word "entity" has also been used by St. Thomas to denote being in the sense of act—"secundum quod importat entitatem rei, vel veritatem propositionis" (*Quodl.*, II, 3c; ed. Mandonnet, p.43). The abstract form of this term satisfies the one condition that he has laid down for expressing the act of being, namely that it signify *in abstracto*. Similarly "natura entitatis" is used synonymously with *esse* in this sense: "Invenitur enim in omnibus rebus natura entitatis,...ita tamen quod ipsarum rerum naturae non sunt hoc ipsum esse quod habent: alias esse esset de intellectu cujuslibet quidditatis" (*In II Sent.*, d.1, q.1, a.1, Solut.; ed. Mandonnet, II, 12). In the same synonymous way "natura essendi" is found: "...quodcumque ens creatum participat, ut ita dixerim, naturam essendi: quia solus Deus est suum esse" (*ST*, I, 45, 5, ad 1m). "Natura essendi" is used here somewhat apologetically for the act of being that all creatures participate and that is predicated as a nature of God alone. In St. Thomas' regular usage "nature" in creatures means essence as contrasted with being (*esse*). Yet being may from one point of view be referred to as a nature that is participated by all things just as human nature is participated by all men. It may accordingly be termed the *ratio essendi* or the *ratio entis*: "...natura essendi convenit Deo absque omni limitatione et contractione; unde ejus virtus activa se extendit...ad omne id quod potest habere rationem entis."[23] However, St. Thomas does not ordinarily speak of being as a nature or an aspect (*ratio*) or a form. He usually reserves such terms for the order of essence as contrasted with being. Being itself is referred to as an act, an actuality, a perfection, and is usually expressed by the infinitive *esse*.

Existentia is also found at times,[24] though rarely, to denote the actuality of being. It satisfies the condition of signifying *in abstracto*. Though from its etymology it has more the meaning of "appearing" or "standing out" and may be found used in that sense by St. Thomas (e.g., sicut aliquid non existens de essentia rei—*Quodl.*, II, 3c; ed. Mandonnet, p. 43), it had already taken on the modern sense of "existence." However, like the abstract forms just noted, it is not his regular way of signifying the act of being. This point of form is worth keeping in mind. It seems to indicate that though there is one viewpoint from which the act of being may be thought of as nature that is participated, the preponderant way in which it has to be treated requires that it be kept in contrast to nature and regarded as an act that is not a nature. In other words, the act of being, though a nature in God, is spoken of by St. Thomas as though it is not a nature in creatures.

These considerations are sufficient to establish being as an equivocal that can be taken either as the subject that is or as the act that makes the subject be. In either sense it can be expressed by both the Latin participle *ens* and the Latin infinitive *esse*. St. Thomas ordinarily uses *ens* to signify the subject of being, though often enough he uses it to signify the act. *Esse* he uses regularly to signify the act, though acknowledging that it may be used also to signify the subject. This infinitive *esse* is his preferred form for denoting the act of being, though on occasion he may refer to the act of being in terms or phrases that signify a nature participated. The order of this act to its subject has already been seen described as both accidental and not accidental. A further aspect of the same question is whether or not the act of being is caused by the principles of the thing's essence. Under this aspect the texts show the same ambiguity. According to some, being is a consequence of the thing's essential principles. According to others, being does not follow from the principles of the essence. These texts have to be examined to see what light they throw upon the general problem of the accidental and essential character of being in the metaphysical doctrine of St. Thomas.

ESSE—A Result and Not a Result of Essence

On the one hand, being is for St. Thomas the terminus of efficient causality.[25] Without being, a thing cannot exercise any efficient causality at all, and so cannot be the cause of its own being: "Non autem potest esse quod ipsum esse sit causatum ab ipsa forma uel quiditate rei, causatum dico sicut a causa efficiente,..." (*De Ente et Essentia*, c. IV; ed. Roland-Gosselin, p. 35.6-8). Accordingly, the essential principles of a thing are not sufficient to give rise to its being: "Impossibile est autem quod esse sit causatum tantum ex principiis essentialibus rei, quia nulla res sufficit quod sit sibi causa essendi,..." (*ST*, I, 3, 4c). This way of thinking is developed at sufficient length by St. Thomas[26] and is too clear to require comment. Being (*esse*) has to come to a thing by way of efficient causality, which a thing cannot exercise until it has being. The being of a thing, then, cannot be caused by the principles of its essence.

On the other hand, in a considerable number of texts the opposite seems stated just as clearly. The doctrine may be summed up in the formula "esse per se consequitur formam creaturae,..." (*ST*, I, 104, 1, ad 1m). This is reminiscent of the Aristotelian doctrine that form is the cause of being. For Aristotle it meant that the form was the primary instance of being in the thing, and that from the form being was derived to the matter and to the composite.[27] In the Thomistic doctrine, where form is one of the constituents of essence while being lies outside (*praeter*) the essence, the Aristotelian formula will have to take on a considerably different meaning. It is in fact used with a certain reservation by St. Thomas. It is allowed to state that the form is indeed the cause of being, but only in its own way, as though, absolutely speaking, the formula needs restriction: "...quamuis huius esse suo modo forma sit causa" (*De Ente*, c. II; ed. Roland-Gosselin, p. 10.7). It looks as though the form in its own way or its own order, that is, in the order of formal causality, may be a cause of the thing's being, but not in the order of efficient causality, of which being is the proper terminus. This is brought out more clearly in other pasages. St. Thomas speaks of God as the immediate efficient cause of natural being, but of the form of the creature as the immediate formal cause and principle: "...esse naturale per creationem Deus facit in nobis, nulla causa agente mediante, sed tamen mediante aliqua causa formali; forma enim naturalis principium est esse naturalis: ..." (*De Ver.*, XXVII, 1, ad 3m; ed. Mandonnet, I, 693a). As formal cause, therefore, the form is an immediate principle of the thing's being. It is through its form that the thing has being: "Deus...unicuique dedit formam per quam esset" (*De Car.*, 1, ad 13m; ed. Mandonnet, III, 272b).

Is it in this formal sense that St. Thomas can speak of the thing's being as a result of the principles of the thing? He states without reservation that the being (*esse*) results from these principles: "Et hoc quidem esse in re est, et est actus entis resultans ex principiis rei, sicut lucere est actus lucentis" (*In III Sent.*, d.6, q.2, a.2, Resp.; ed. Moos, III, 238). The thing's being is described as though it followed from the principles that make up the nature or essence. This is brought out more forcefully in the best-known text of all:

> Esse enim rei quamvis sit aliud ab ejus essentia, non tamen est intelligendum quod sit aliquod superadditum ad modum accidentis, sed quasi constituitur per principia essentiae (*In IV Metaph.*, lect. 2; ed. Cathala, no. 558).

The being that is meant here is clearly the being that is other than the essence, and so the act of being that lies outside the essence. It is different from the essence. Yet it is not something superadded by way of accident to the essence. It is not an accident added to an already complete essence, as a predicamental accident would be. It is as it were constituted by the very principles of the essence. Once the principles of the essence are there, the being of the thing is also there. They do not then require anything superadded to make them be.

What can this doctrine mean? It is intended as as defence of the Aristotelian teaching that the addition of the participle "being" does not denote anything new in the thing, and that every substance is of its very nature a being. It is meant as a refutation of the Avicennian tenet that being is something accidental and subsequent to created essences. It understands being as a principle that is indeed other than the essence, yet not an accident in the sense of a predicamental accident, as the Avicennian doctrine had been represented in Averroes' critique. Being is not subsequent to the essence, even though it is other than the essence. It is something different from the essence, yet is as it were constituted by the same substantial principles that make up the essence.

To Siger of Brabant this formulation of the Thomistic doctrine appeared as an open contradiction. Siger regarded it as an attempt at a middle of the road position between the Aristotelian teaching that being was essential to everything, and the Avicennian tenet that being was a superadded accident in created things:

> Ponunt autem quidam modo medio, quod esse est aliquid additum essentiae rei, non pertinens ad essentiam rei, nec quod sit accidens, sed est aliquid additum quasi per essentiam consitutum sive ex principiis essentiae.[28]

This sketch of Siger's presents clearly enough the Thomistic doctrine in its main outlines. It uses St. Thomas' own expressions, though contrasting them in a sharp way calculated to emphasize their apparently contradictory character. With the final statement considered as the conclusion, Siger has no quarrel. That the being of a thing is constituted by its essence is correct Aristotelian doctrine. Since this is the ultimate conclusion of the Thomistic treatment, it can render the main burden of the teaching acceptable. But the way of expressing it seems incomprehensible: "Etsi conclusio vera sit, modum tamen ponendi non intelligo" (*Metaph.*, Introd., q. VII; ed. Graiff, p. 16.25). As he is reported by Godfrey of Fontaines, Siger regards the statement of the doctrine as self-contradictory. What is constituted by the principles of the essence is nothing other than the essence itself. To say that it is not the essence, yet is constituted by the principles of the essence, is to affirm and to deny the same thing: "Dicere quod esse non est essentiae rei, sed aliquid constitutum per essentiae principia, est idem affirmare et negare: cum constitutum per essentiae principia nihil aliud sit quam ipsa res ex illis constituta (Ibid., p. 16 [14]-[17]). What is constituted by the principles of the essence is the thing itself. The thing is therefore its own being. Being is of its very essence. One cannot say without contradiction that being is not of its essence.

Siger, however, is sufficiently intrigued to speculate on what such an addition to the essence would have to be. It would not be of the essence of the thing, yet it would not be one of the accidents. It could not be the thing itself, nor could it be either of the parts of the thing's essence, matter or form. It is an entirely new notion, and fits under none of traditionally accepted constituents of reality. It would not have the character of matter, or of form, or of the accidents. It would have the nature of none of those three, but would constitute a different and fourth nature in reality: "Sed dicere quod esse sit aliquid additum essentiae rei, ita quod non sit res ipsa, neque pars essentiae ut materia vel forma, et dicere quod non sit accidens, est ponere quartam naturam in entibus" (Ibid., p. 16.29-32).

Siger is undoubtedly putting his finger on a sensitive spot in this new notion of being. It is described as something that cannot be ranged under the traditional Aristotelian classifications of matter, form and accidents. It is a notion that places being before any of the predicamental accidents. In that sense being is not accidental to a thing's nature. Yet it is not the thing nor any of its essential parts. But it is as it were constituted by those essential principles. Once those principles are there, it also is there, without having to wait for any further addition. The only conceivable way in which this doctrine can make sense is to regard being as somehow prior to essence. If being were subsequent to the essence it would be a predicamental accident. If it were simultaneous, it would be the essence or part of the essence. It is none of these, yet it is other than the essence. It must therefore be prior to the essence. Such a possibility does not occur to Siger. Yet, if such be the relation envisaged in the Thomistic texts, it does not in the least attenuate Siger's observation that a fourth nature is being added to the traditional classifications. There is nothing in the Aristotelian background to account for any real principle prior to the substantial form.

This suggestion that being is understood as somehow prior to essence is, however, not without its *prima facie* difficulties as one reads the texts. If St. Thomas actually means that being is prior to nature, how can he speak of being as at all constituted by the thing's essential principles? If those principles in any way constitute the thing's being, are they not envisaged precisely from that point of view as prior to the being? How can St. Thomas say without any reservation that being (*esse*) is an act resulting from the principles of the thing? He speaks of it plainly as "actus entis resultans ex principiis rei" (*In III Sent.*, d.6, q.2, a.2, Resp.; ed. Moos, III, 238). If the act of being is looked upon as a *result* of the thing's essential principles, it is hardly taken as prior to the essence.

Could the difficulty here lie in the two types of causality that are involved in the production of being? As already noted, being for St. Thomas is the terminus of efficient causality,[29] but always by means of a formal cause. The form is in this way the cause of the thing's being. It is the formal cause of being, just as the agent is the efficient cause of being. Is the whole problem, then, merely a question of the reciprocal relations of the different types of causality? Does it hinge on the doctrine that *causae sunt invicem causae*? Is the act of being a result or effect of the thing's essence in the line of formal causality, even though it is a prior effect of the efficient cause?

Should this turn out in fact to be the meaning of St. Thomas' teaching, it will nevertheless be an innovation in the bearing of the maxim *causae sunt invicem causae*. As applied to formal cause, that saying ascribed reciprocal causality to form and matter only. Form exercised its proper causality on matter by informing and specifying it, and thereby underwent the proper causality of matter by being sustained and multiplied. They were reciprocally cause and effect, each in its own order. If the maxim is extended to the reciprocal relations of form and being, it will mean that form is specifying being and is thereby in some way actuated by that being. But this would mean a radical change from the Aristotelian notion of act. For the Stagirite form and act coincided. To actuate and to inform and to specify were the same. In this new instance, however, the potency, that is, the essence, would do the specifying. The essence would specify as potency, not as act.[30] The being would actuate, but would not specify, and could hardly be described as informing. The form would be thrown into the role of potency or matter, from the Aristotelian point of view, and yet would thereby be exercising formal causality. A profoundly new explanation of act and of formal causality would be required.

Does the Thomistic doctrine of being make essence in this way a potency to the act of being without giving it the role of matter? Does it make being an act without allowing it to specify or determine in a formal manner? If it succeeds in establishing these points, will it not provide a ready framework in which being may appear as both essential and accidental to created natures, according to the texts already considered? If the form is the cause of being in its own special way, that is, as formal cause, it will in its own order necessarily determine the essence to being. Formal causality is a necessary type of causality. All formal results follow necessarily from their formal causes, as may be seen in the procedures of mathematics. If its form determines every nature to be a being, then every nature is essentially a being. There is nothing in the form itself, however, that requires its submission to any efficient causality. That it is acted upon by another efficient cause does not follow with necessity from its own formal nature. If its act of being has to be given in this way by an external efficient cause, that act can only be accidental to it in this order of causality.

There is a possibility, therefore, that from the viewpoint of formal causality every nature is necessarily determined by its form in the direction of being, and so, as far as its essence is concerned, is essentially stamped as a being. Yet if the nature has to be produced through efficient causality, that formal determination will not be actual by itself, but only through the work of an agent other than itself. Its actuality will be other than itself, and so will lie outside its essence or nature. Its act of being will from this point of view be accidental to it. From different standpoints, then every created nature will be essentially being. It will be other than essence, and nevertheless will result from and so be constituted by the principles of the essence. Such seems to be the framework indicated by the foregoing texts for the solution of this Thomistic problem. Does the general doctrine of being found in the works of St. Thomas allow one to proceed along these lines and to establish successfully both the accidental and the essential character of created being? An examination of the Thomistic notion of essence and the Thomistic notion of being may be expected to yield the answer to this question.

ESSENCE

The texts already considered use the term "essence" to denote what is expressed by the definition of a thing. They make it signify consistently the subject of being, in contrast to the act of being. Etymologically there is no reason why "essentia" should not mean the act of being, just as *esse* and *ens* may designate it. It is an abstractive form derived from the same root as they. It is apparently formed from a supposed participle *essens*, which would add the participial ending to the infinitive *esse* somewhat as *patiens* does to *pati.*[31] It was coined, according to Quintilian (*Inst. Or.*, II, 14, 2; III, 6, 23) to translate the Greek philosophical term *ousia*. There is nothing, then, in its morphology or its original historical background to prevent it from signifying *in abstracto*. Morphologically, in fact, it is better adapted to express the act of being than the subject of the act. St. Augustine claimed that the Latin *essentia* should properly be reserved to God alone, signifying as it did the being that had no subject, no mutable *substantia*: "Res ergo mutabiles neque simplices, proprie dicuntur substantiae....ita ut fortasse solum Deum dici oporteat essentiam. Est enim vere solus, quia incommutabilis est,... (*De Trin.*, VII, 5, 10; PL, XLII, 942). Yet the Greek term that *essentia* was coined to translate, *ousia*, could be used to express the subject. It was regularly translated *substantia* by Boethius, and *substantia* accordingly became its Latin equivalent. In this way *essentia* became in actual philosophical usage a synonym for *substantia* in expressing one of the meanings of the Greek *ousia*, namely the subject of accidents.

One need not be surprised, therefore, to find that in spite of its morphology the term *essentia* is restricted in the usage of St. Thomas to denote the subject of being, and does not occur in the sense of the act of being. Unlike the apparently arbitrary restriction of *esse* to just one of its two current philosophical meanings, this reservation of *essentia* to the opposite meaning has the full sanction of centuries-old tradition. However, the general conformity with its current usage as a subject of accidents and as expressing the content of the definition need not at all imply that St. Thomas' notion of essence adds nothing new to the traditional conception. He has left a work on the subject entitled *De Ente et Essentia*. It is an early work, being dated some time between the years 1254-1256, when he was little more than thirty years old. Yet it is a treatise that is surprisingly rich in its doctrine of being, and it explains the notion of essence so carefully and so explicitly that comparatively few texts from the later works are required to supplement its teachings as far as essence is concerned. It has to be considered, of course, as an early expression of St. Thomas' doctrine on the relations of essence and being. It leaves open the question of whether or not that doctrine was developed further or even changed in the later phases of his teaching. A radical change in the Thomistic notion of essence between the time of the *De Ente et Essentia* and the more mature periods has in fact been proposed,[32] but is not supported directly by any texts describing essence in these later years. It is based rather upon a special interpretation of texts concerning being in the later works, an interpretation that involves a fundamental change in the notion of essence as set forth so clearly an unambiguously in the *De Ente et Essentia*. The description of essence in this earlier work may therefore safely be studied for what it is in itself and as supported by later texts that deal with essence. Whether or not the doctrine of being that is found in the more mature works is consistent with this notion of essence is a further and different question.

In the short Proem of the *De Ente et Essentia*, St. Thomas quotes Avicenna[33] for the assertion that being and essence (*ens autem et essentia*) are what the intellect first conceives. He proposes to treat of what is meant by the term "essence and being" (*quid nomine essentie et entis significetur*—ed. Roland-Gosselin, p. 1.7-8). He is evidently considering these two notions as closely bound up with each other. In which of the two senses is he understanding the participle *ens*? Does he mean it to signify *in abstracto* or *in concreto*? At first sight he would appear to be taking it *in concreto*. In the opening lines of the first chapter of the work he proceeds as though *ens* denotes a composite and essence one of its components. In conformity with the method of analysis, which takes the composite and divides it in order to reach its components, he proposes to take first the composite *ens* and examine it with a view towards isolating the notion of essence (c.I; p. 2.4-7).

This procedure would indicate that *ens* is being taken *in concreto*, as a composite of essence and the act of being. It is to be analyzed into these two components, and from that starting point essence is to be considered as far as possible in isolation. Yet St. Thomas at once goes on to state that *ens per se* has a twofold meaning. It can signify the being that is divided into the ten categories, or the being that is expressed in the truth of propositions (c. I; p. 2.8-11). These two senses of being are immediately recognizable as those already considered in other texts of St. Thomas. They are sketched against the Aristotelian background of the four ways in which being is expressed.[34] Here, however, being *per se* is understood as excluding the first Aristotelian sense, being *per accidens*, but as including the second sense, being as the true. The other two Aristotelian senses are grouped as before under being as in the categories. The division, then, has the same general background as in the previously considered texts.

Does this mean that *ens* in the opening lines of the first chapter of *De Ente et Essentia* signifies equivocally both *in concreto* and *in abstracto*? Does it have to be taken ambiguously as both the subject of being and the act of being? But as the act of being, how could it be considered as a composite that includes essence as one of its components? When it signifies the act of being it does not signify *in concreto* but only *in abstracto*. It does not denote a composite. Yet the procedure of St. Thomas in this chapter requires that it designate a composite. It has to express a composite notion that includes the notion of essence. Accordingly, the difference between the two meanings of being is here described in a somewhat different way than in the other texts. It leads up to the special purpose now in mind, namely that essence has to express something positive. The being that signifies the truth of propositions is presented as anything about which an affirmative proposition can be formed, even though it expresses nothing positive in reality. In this way even privations and negations are called beings or are said to be (*entia dicuntur*—c.I, p. 3.3-4). One says, for instance, that blindness is in the eye.[35] In the other sense, however, namely as in the categories, being (*ens*) means something positive in reality (*aliquid in re ponit*—c. I, p.3.6). In this sense blindness and the like are not beings (*entia*—p. 3.7).

The force of the distiction here is that true propositions can be formed even about things that have not any positive status in reality. True propositions can be formed about negations and privations. In this way negations and privations are spoken of as being, as blindness for instance is said to *be* in the eye, and accordingly they are called beings. But such things have no essence. A necessary requirement for essence is a positive status in reality. Only in being as divided in the ten categories is essence to be found. Only beings of the latter kind are composites that have essence as one of their constituents.

According to this reasoning, however, negations and privations seem also to be looked upon as beings, in the sense of composites of a subject and its act. Of what, then, are they composed, if essence is not one of their constituents? In the *Commentary on the Sentences*, a work that originates from the same period as the *De Ente et Essentia*, a clearer explanation is given. In answer to the argument "de quocumque vere potest dici quod est, ipsum est ens", St. Thomas states:

> ...ens dicitur dupliciter. Uno modo quod significat essentiam rei extra animam existentis: et hoc modo non potest dici ens deformitas peccati, quae privatio quaedam est: privationes enim essentiam non habent in rerum natura. Alio modo secundum quod significat veritatem propositionis; et sic deformitas dicitur esse, non propter hoc quod in re esse habeat, sed quia intellectus componit privationem cum subjecto, sicut formam quamdam. . . . Sed hoc esse non est nisi rationis, cum in re potius sit non esse, et secundum hoc quod in ratione esse habet, constat quod a Deo est (*In II Sent.* d. 37, q.1, a.2, ad 3m; ed. Mandonnet. II, 947).

This parallel passage describes clearly enough the constitution of a privation. The intellect takes the privation as though it were a form and combines it with a subject. In doing so it gives a type of being that is found only in itself (*esse rationis*). This type of being is not being in the world of external reality (*in re potius sit non esse*). Considered as a being (*ens*), then, a privation or a negation is taken by the intellect as though it were a form and is composed with a subject; and this composite of quasi-form and subject is given being of reason (*esse rationis*) in the intellect but not in external reality. Quite evidently *ens* in this sense means a composite of being and subject of being. But that subject of being is not an essence, because it is not a positive reality.

The Aristotelian divisions of the way in which *ens per se* is expressed are invoked in the present context, therefore, not in order to establish the distinction between being as act and being as subject of that act, but to show that being as the true has an extension beyond being as found in the categories. In that further extension it does not enter into composition with an essence, because it is not composed with something positive, that is capable of existence outside the mind. In this case *ens* does not signify an essence. When one speaks of privations and negations as beings, one is not thereby implying that they have an essence. But *ens* in the other sense signifies an essence (*significat essentiam extra animam existentis*). Essence, accordingly, is something positive that can exist in reality. It is something expressed affirmatively: "Non autem inventur aliquid affirmative dictum absolute quod possit accipi omni ente, nisi essentia ejus, . . ." (*De Ver.*, I, 1c; ed. Mandonnet, p. 3b). To this extent St. Thomas is following the Avicennian description of essence as the notion of affirmative being (*intentionem esse affirmativi*).[36]

With the positive status of essence made clear, St. Thomas gathers the different descriptions of it that were current at the time, and the terms used to designate it. It is considered to be what is expressed by the definition of the thing. It is therefore *what* the thing is, and so may be called the quiddity. Since it is the being that is divided into the ten categories, it has to signify something common to all the natures by which the different beings are placed in the predicaments. Just as humanity, for instance, is the essence of man and places man in his proper genus and species in the category of substance, so essence in general will be that which places anything whatsoever in a category. It is identified by St. Thomas with the Aristotelian what-is-being (*hoc per quod aliquid habet esse quid*), which for the Stagirite meant form alone. St. Thomas accordingly states that essence is also called form in so far as "form" signifies the certitude" of anything, in the Avicennian sense of the term "certitude." He is making no special effort to distinguish very clearly the form from the essence. He speaks as though he is concerned for the moment only with what is conceptually intelligible in the thing; and the matter in itself is unintelligible. So essence may be called "nature" in the Boethian sense of what is intelligible through the definition of the thing (c. I, p. 4.6-9). But the reason why it is called "essence" is that *through* it and *in* it the being in question has its proper act—*per eam et in ea ens habet esse* (p. 4.15-16). In conformity with it does the thing have being—*essentia autem est secundum quam res esse dicitur* (p. 10.4-5).

St. Thomas, then, understands by essence something of positive meaning like the nature of a man or a horse or a tree. It is something that is expressed in the definition of the thing by means of genus and specific differentia. It is the content of the definition, when that content is positive. Anything outside the content of the definition will be outside the essence. The essence, accordingly, is what can be conceptualized in the manner of a definition. It is *what* the thing is. It is able to be in reality. In fact, through that order to being it is called essence, which is a term formed, as has been seen, from the Latin infinitive of the verb "to be." Its order to being is described as twofold. It is that *in* which a thing has being, and so is the subject of being. It is also that *through* which a thing has being, and so is a principle or cause of being. Since it is something according to which a thing has being (*secundum quam res esse dicitur*), it will apparently function as a sort of formal cause of being.

In this description essence is represented both as identified with the concrete being and as one constituent of it. *Ens* as found in the categories is spoken of as though it were the same as essence,[37] and yet is considered as a composite of which essence is but one of the constituents. What does this imply? Is essence, like being, of its very nature an ambiguous term? Does it have to denote in one sense the whole composite being, and in another sense only one constituent of that being? When you speak of an essence can you mean a man or a tree that actually exists in reality and is endowed with the act of being, although it is something other than that act? If so, you are designating a composite, and you are having essence signify *in concreto*. Can you also abstract the essence from the concrete being and represent it by itself in abstraction? This would seem to be making it signify *in abstracto*, even though it is in this case the subject rather than the act. Or is it the subject of being so wrapped in its proper act that it cannot be represented apart from the act? If it is represented as without any being at all, how can there be anything to represent? Or can it in some way abstract from being without entirely disassociating itself from that act? The answers to these questions will have to be sought through the text of St. Thomas. But from the start it seems clear that as a matter of fact he is representing essence in both these ways. The Aristotelian background against which he has made his divisions of being should keep this from causing surprise. The Aristotelian senses of being as in the categories and being as act and potency were combined, as has been seen, in the one classification of predicamental being whether actual or potential (...ipsas naturas decem generum secundum quod sunt actu vel potentia—*In X Metaph.*, lect. 3; ed. Cathala-Spiazzi, no. 1982). A nature or essence, accordingly, is placed in the categories whether it is considered as actual or as potential. When considered as actual, the essence would be considered along with its proper act of being, and so would denote the concrete being. When considered as potential, it would be taken without that act, and so as just one constituent of the composite. This way of speaking, then, fits in with the manner in which St. Thomas combines the Aristotelian senses of being. Can it be justified by his doctrine of essence?

In examining the notion of essence, St. Thomas shows that in material things the essence itself is composite. It consists of matter and form. This was accepted Aristotelian doctrine, and called for no further explanation as long as essence was considered merely as a nature. But when taken as a principle of being it gives rise to a more complicated situation. One of the elements, matter, was in itself something that had the function of subject, and so could without difficulty be looked upon as combining with form in the role of the subject of being. But from the viewpoint of essence as the formal principle or cause of being, how could matter play any part? Of itself it has nothing formal in its nature, and so could hardly be conceived as exercising any formal casuality. St. Thomas, accordingly, gives the form a special role in this respect. Essence is that by which a thing is denominated a being (*essentia qua res denominatur ens*—p. 10.5-6), and so presents as it were the formal pattern of being. That essence is neither form alone nor matter alone, but both. Yet a restriction has to be made—the form is in its own way the cause of this being (*quamuis huius esse suo modo forma sit causa*—p. 10.7). Although the two principles constitute the essence, only one of them functions as the formal cause and the denominating principle. The same doctrine is stated (...*quamvis forma sit principium esse*) and illustrated in the same way in the *Commentary on the First Book of the Sentences* (d.23, q.1, a.1, Solut.; ed. Mandonnet, I, 555).

Matter, then, is part of the essence in material things, even though it has no formal function in regard to being. But if the essence is what is signified by the definition, how can it contain matter? The definition is of the universal, and matter is considered to individuate. St. Thomas answers this objection by distinguishing matter just in general from designated matter (*materia signata*—p. 11.1-3). Designated matter is matter considered under determined dimension of length, breadth, and thickness, as though it is something that can be "pointed out" or designated with the finger.[38] The notion is quite clear. If you consider any matter as under this particular length and breadth and thickness that you indicate with your finger, such matter is individuated and is limited to the one particular thing. If on the other hand you consider matter in general, without indicating particular dimensions, you are considering matter universally, and nothing hinders it from forming part of a universal notion.

In it essential points this doctrine had been outlined by Aristotle. The same notions, like man or horse, could be taken either universally or singularly. They remained the same notions, composed of the same genus and specific differentia. " 'Man' and 'horse' and the like applied to singulars, but universally, are not *ousia* but something composed of this particular formula and this particular matter, as taken universally; but as taken singularly, it is from the ultimate matter that 'Socrates' has already been constituted'' (*Metaph.*, Z 10,1035b27-31). What is expressed by the definition—i.e. in Scholastic language the essence—can be taken singularly or universally. It contains both matter and form in either case, and so is the same notion, regardless of the individuation.

From this doctrine St. Thomas concludes that the essence of Socrates and the essence of man differ on accordingly to the designation or non-designation of the matter. The essence of man as such contains matter, but non-designated matter. To change that essence into the essence of Socrates, you do not add anything at all to the essence except the designation of the matter to certain determined dimensions. Socrates is ''rational animal,'' not just ''rational animal'' in general, but this particular rational animal that you point out with your finger. By so doing you are adding nothing to what was already contained in the essence ''rational animal.'' You are merely pointing it out in a particular instance.

From this consideration St. Thomas draws a general, and for the present problem an extremely important, conclusion. As individual and species differ only according to designation and non-designation, so also do species and genus. The species adds nothing that is not already contained in the genus, but merely designates something already there. The type of designation, however, is different in each of these two cases. The designation of the individual is through matter when considered under determined dimensions. The designation of the species in the genus, on the other hand, is through the constitutive differentia, which is taken from the form. The designation of the species, then, takes place through the expressing of a new formal characteristic; while no new formal element is expressed in the designation of the singular individual. Yet the parallelism evidently means that the species, in spite of the new formal designation, contain nothing that was not already contained in the genus.

From this doctrine of the knowledge of species and individuals through designation, St. Thomas develops a teaching that has been strangely neglected or forgotten in later Scholasticism, including Neoscholasticism. It is the doctrine of abstraction with precision and without precision. From the time of Suarez the notions of abstraction and of precision have been regarded as the same.[39] It is difficult today to realize how vital is the notion of abstraction without precision for understanding the Thomastic doctrine of essence and being. It means that something can be contained within a notion and yet not be expressed by that notion. What limits a generic notion to a specific one, for instance, is already contained within the generic notion: ''Hec autem determinatio uel designatio que est in specie respectu generis, non est per aliquid in essentia speciei existens, quod nullo modo in essentia generis sit''—p. 11.19-21). It is in the genus as something that is not determined. It needs only the designation or determination by the differentia, in order to constitute the species. St. Thomas' point is that this designation or formal determination does not add any content to the genus. It does not make the genus contain anything that was not contained in it before. All that happens is that what is in the genus becomes limited or determined to just one of its species.

This doctrine, of course, leaves all Thomistic generic and specific concepts confused concepts, taking the full weight of the Cartesian attack upon such concepts. They all confuse many different things or objects within the same concept, and leave the task of sorting out to the specific differentiae or the individual designations. Yet in that very confusion lies the key to their serviceability and their power to ward off any wedge of Nominalism. After several centuries of thinking, consciously or unconsciously, against the background of clear and distinct ideas, it is hard to realize that metaphysical thought and in fact all scientific thought is rendered possible only because these concepts are able to confuse many objects into one and so provide the framework for predication. Aristotle had long before shown, in arguing against the Platonic Ideas, the impossibility of a self-contained generic notion that had the status of a unit in itself: "Now, if the 'animal' in "'the horse' and in 'man' is one and the same, as you are with yourself, how will the one in the things that exist 'apart' be one, and how will this 'animal' escape being divided even from itself?" (*Metaph.*, Z 14,1039a33-b2; Oxford tr.).

St. Thomas explains this doctrine with the example of "body." It can be taken either as a part of an animal or as a genus. As a part of an animal it is contrasted with soul. In this sense it cannot be predicated of a man, for a part cannot be predicated of the whole. You cannot say that a man is his body. You have to say, in this meaning of the word, that a man has a body, just as he has a soul. Any composite has its integral parts. They are not predicated of it, for it is not completely identical with any one of them. On the other hand, "body" can be taken as meaning corporeal substance. In this case it has living and non-living corporeal things as its species. In this sense "body" is predicated of its inferiors as a genus. You can say that a man is a body, just as a stone is a body, or a plant or a horse is a body. In this way "body" signifies everything in a man, including his substantial form or soul. It is not at all contrasted with soul, but signifies a whole of which the soul is a part. Because it signifies the whole thing, it is completely identified with the thing and so can be predicated of it.

How are these two so different notions of "body" formed? They are both formed by abstraction. In each case th notion of a nature in which three dimensions can be designated is abstracted. The dimensions themselves, of course, pertain to the category of quantity.[40] Body, in the sense of a substance, has to be defined in terms of the possibility of having the three dimensions. This notion of a substance capable of the three dimensions is abstracted from the individual sensible things. But it can be abstracted in two different ways. It can be abstracted in such a manner that it does not exclude the addition of further perfections, that is, the perfections of animate, sensitive, and rational nature. One can say that man is a body, and still be able to see in him those further perfections. One is not excluding them from the notion "body." One is not prescinding from them. In this way one is taking body as a genus. It excludes nothing that is in a man, not even the individual designation, and so it can be predicated of a man, as for instance when one says "A man is a body." As a genus, "body" does not indeed express the further perfections of living, animal, and rational nature. It contains them, however, implicitly: "Et sic forma animalis in forma corporis continetur implicite, prout corpus est genus eius" (*De Ente*, c.II; p. 14.10-11).

In this way a genus implicitly contains its inferiors. It signifies indifferently any form whatsoever that can be denoted by the names of its species: "...et ideo, cum dicebatur corpus est quod habet talem formam ex qua possunt designari tres dimensiones in eo, intelligebatur quecumque forma esset, siue animalitas siue quecumque forma alia."—p. 14.6-10). The genus contains implicitly everything that these more specific natures express. It denotes the whole thing, and not just a part of it. "Body" as a genus signifies any substance in which three dimensions can be designated, whether it be a stone or a horse or a man or any other corporeal thing. Because it excludes nothing in the individual and so is completely identified with that individual, it can be predicated of every individual to which its generic character extends. It signifies everything that is contained in its species and their individuals. It denotes the *totum* of which it is predicated, and not just a part of that *totum*. It includes all its inferiors in a unit that is based upon the very indifference by which it signifies them (*unitas generis ex ipsa indeterminatione uel indifferentia procedit*—p. 19.16-17). A genus, then, cannot be conceived as a self-contained nature to which something outside itself is added to constitute the species, as form, for instance, would be added to matter. Rather, it signifies a plurality of forms and individuals, indifferently, and can be applied in predication as completely identical with any one of them. Genera and species, accordingly, abstract from their inferiors without prescinding from them.

On the other hand, the notion "body" may be abstracted in such a way that it does not signify the whole nature or individual, but only an integral part. In this sense a man is said to be composed of body and soul. Body is regarded as excluding from its own content the higher aspects of the soul. The composition of the two constitutes the nature of man. How does the abstraction now take place? The notion of a substance capable of the three dimensions is abstracted as before, but now the addition of further perfections is expressly excluded. If something else is later added, it is understood as something outside (*praeter*) the signification of body in this sense (p. 13.5-10). The notion is closed off at the stage of corporeal substance capable of the three dimensions, and is represented as a complete and finished nature. Whatever else may be added lies outside that notion. In this sense, soul is not contained in the notion of body, whereas it was contained, though implicitly, in the notion of body as genus.

In this second and non-generic sense, then, body excludes or prescinds from soul. It is a notion obtained by abstraction with precision, in contrast to the generic and specific notions that were obtained by abstractions without precision. The difference is that abstraction with precision excludes the residue from which it abstracts, while abstraction without precision does not exclude that residue but continues to keep it within the notion abstracted, though implicitly. The essence or nature of a thing can be abstracted in either of these two ways. The nature "man" can be abstracted without precision, and so will exclude nothing that is found in any individual man. On account of this complete identity it can be predicated of any individual, as when one says "Socrates is a man." It signifies in this way the *totum* that is Socrates. On the other hand, it can be abstracted with precision. It can be abstracted in such a way as to exclude the individual designation. In this way it is expressed by the word "humanity," and cannot be predicated of the individual man. One cannot say "Socrates is humanity." Rather, it functions as an integral part, and so one says that Socrates has humanity or human nature, just as one says that he has a body and has a soul. Taken with precision, the essence has the role of a part. It is looked upon as combining with the individuation to compose the singular. In this case it is not complete identically with the thing, as it was when abstracted without precision.

This means that for St. Thomas "essence" can have a twofold sense. Essence may be abstracted without precision. It then means the thing itself. It is that which is. In this sense, to speak of a distinction between essence and being is the same as to speak of a distinction between a thing and its being. Essence so taken includes implicitly everything that is in the thing itself, even the individual designation. An animal is an essence, a man is an essence, Socrates is an essence, when "essence" is understood as abstracted without precision. Essence in this sense is predicated of all its individuals, and is completely identified with every one of them.[41]

On the other hand, essence for St. Thomas can be abstracted with precision. Taken in this way it excludes the individuating principles and so is represented as a part of the thing even though it includes the whole of the nature, both material and formal principles. It conceives these principles as functioning in a formal way with regard to the individual subject: "Et ideo humanitas significatur ut forma quedam, et dicitur quod est forma tocius; non quidem quasi superaddita partibus essentialibus, scilicet forme et materie, sicut forma domus superaddita partibus eius integralibus; set magis est forma que est totum, scilicet formam complectens et materiam, tamen cum precisione eorum per que nata est materia designari" (*De Ente*, c. II; p. 22.12-18). When abstracted in this way the essence is not completely identified with the individual but functions as a part of the individual. One says that a thing has an essence, that Socrates has human nature. In this sense it is strictly not the essence that exists. Rather, the existing thing is such and such a kind through its essence, or because of its essence.

When the essence is abstracted without precision, therefore, essence and thing are identical. One may say indifferently that Socrates exists or that a man exists. In this case it is the essence that exists. On the other hand, when the essence is abstracted with precision, it is not the individual:

> Sic igitur patet quod essentiam hominus significat hoc nomen homo et hoc nomen humanitas sed diuersimode, ut dictum est,...Et propter hoc eciam nomen essentie quandoque invenitur predicatum de re, dicitur enim Socratem esse essentiam, et quandoque negatur, sicut dicitur quod essentia Socrates non est Socrates" (*De Ente*, c.II; pp. 22.18-23.7).

The essence abstracted with precision, then, does not exist as such. Only the individuals exist properly speaking. When one speaks of humanity (i.e. human nature) as existing, one means that it exists in individuals. Avicenna, for instance, distinguishes humanity and equinity from the being that either has in reality or in the mind. St. Thomas also, in places where his language reflects the Latin translation of Avicenna, will speak in the same way; e.g. "humanitati enim ex hoc quod est humanitas, non debetur esse in actu; potest enim cogitari humanitas et tamen ignorari an aliquis homo sit" (*In I Sent.*, d.8, q.4, a.2; ed. Mandonnet, I,222). It is always the individual (*aliquis homo*) that is represented as existing, when one is speaking of the relation between humanity and being. When it is predicated, however, the essence has to be taken as abstracted without precision, and so as containing implicitly and confusedly all that is in the individual: "Et ideo relinquitur quod ratio generis uel speciei conueniat essentie secundum quod significatur per modum tocius, ut nomine hominis uel animalis, prout implicite et indistincte continet totum quod in indiuiduo est" (*De Ente*, c. III; p. 23.25-28).

Taken in this way, that is, as abstracted without precision and so as containing everything that is in the individual, the essence can be considered in two ways. It can be considered either just in itself, or as existing. Considered in the first way, it is not able to receive the predication of anything accidental to it: "Uno modo secundum rationem propriam, et hec est absoluta consideratio ipsius, et hoc modo nichil est uerum de ea nisi quod convenit sibi secundum quod huiusmodi, ..." (*De Ente*, c. III; p. 24.2-5). Considered in the second way, it has a twofold existence, that is, in reality and in the mind: "Hec autem natura habet duplex esse: unum in singularibus et aliud in anima; ... (p. 25.9-

10). Neither existence, however, belongs to the nature in its absolute consideration: "Et tamen ipsi naturae secundum primam considerationem suam, scilicet absolutam, nullum istorum esse debetur."[42] Of itself the essence does not require either type of existence. The reason is that if existence in this particular individual was of the essence of man, it would limit man to the one individual. If it were essential to human nature to exist in Socrates, then it could never be found anywhere else. It could never be in any other individual or in the mind. Conversely, if it were of the essence of human nature not to be in Socrates, it could never be found in him. In its absolute consideration it simply abstracts from being in Socrates or in any other individual or in the mind. It can be in any of these, it need not be in any of them. No such being is required by it in its absolute consideration: "Set uerum est dicere quod homo in quantum est homo non habet quod sit in hoc singulari uel in illo uel in anima" (De Ente, c. III; p. 26.6-8).

The abstraction in which this absolute consideration of the essence takes place is abstraction without precision. It does not prescind from being in any individual or in the mind "Ergo patet quod natura hominis absolute considerata abstrahit a quolibet esse, ita tamen quod non fiat precisio alicuius eorum" (p. 26.8-10). St. Thomas mentions this as though it is entirely evident. If a nature had to be conceived as excluding all being by way of precision, it just would not be at all. There would be nothing there to be conceived. To think of something and prescind from all being would be impossible. Being, therefore, is not excluded from the essence in its absolute consideration. It is included implicitly in it. In fact, none of the ways in which the essence can be is prescinded from in its absolute consideration. Under that consideration it is able to be in this individual or in that individual or in the mind. But it thereby abstracts from all those existences. If any being whatsoever were of its essence absolutely considered, it would be bound to that being and so could never be completely identified with anything else.[43] Predication would be rendered impossible. In its absolute consideration, consequently, essence abstracts from all being—a quolibet esse.[44] Yet it prescinds from none of the existences that are possible to it. It remains open to them all.

Naturally, such a way of conceiving essence is only a "consideration." Essence is never a direct object of the intellect as absolute. The intellect always sees it either in an individual or as intentionally existent in the mind. It never sees it without some existence. But it can reason that the same essence is found in all those existences and so absolutely in itself it is bound to none of them. In that way, it is considered absolutely, as the conclusion of a reasoning process. But directly it is always perceived in some existence. From such being it can never prescind, no matter how much it abstracts from it.

Since essence can never prescind from or exclude being, but has to include it implicitly while abstracting from it, every nature is therefore essentially a being. In its very essence it has to include being implicitly and so of its very essence it is a being. Through this doctrine one side of the equivocity of being, namely that every nature is essentially a being, is justified by the very process in which the notion of essence is obtained, that is, by abstraction from being without precision from being.

BEING

That, however, is only one side of the problem. On the other side, abstraction from being involves a peculiar consequence. Since the essence abstracts from being, it of course does not express anything about the particular existence the essence may happen to have: "Omnis autem essentia uel quiditas potest intelligi sine hoc quod aliquid intelligatur de esse suo; possum enim intelligere quid est homo uel fenix et tamen ignorare an esse habeat in rerum natura. Ergo patet quod esse est aliud ab essentia uel quiditate" (*De Ente*, c. IV; p. 34.10-15). Naturally, when you are thinking about the man or the phoenix, the essence has existence in your mind. But if it also can have existence in a real individual instance or in another mind, it is not bound to any one existence and so abstracts from all being, accordingly to the principles just considered. So far there is nothing peculiar. The argument would apply equally well to any characteristic. But St. Thomas goes on to show that this reasoning in the case of being applies to all things with one possible exception. If there is a thing whose very nature is its being, it would be a unique nature. It could not coalesce with any other nature in reality as generic or specific aspect does: "Si autem ponatur aliqua res que sit esse tantum ita ut ipsum esse sit subsistans, hoc esse non recipiet additionem differentie quia iam non esset esse tantum set esse et preter hoc forma aliqua" (*De Ente*, c.IV; p. 34.24-27). If being is a nature, it cannot be differentiated either formally or materially, and so cannot be either a generic or specific aspect of any other nature. If being is found multiplied, it has to be first of all in itself as a unique and primary instance. In all other instances it will be found outside the natures of things and merely participated by them (—*non potest esse nisi una et prima*—p. 34.16).

The reasoning then goes on to show that there is such a nature in reality. It finds that the being of creatures is not caused by the principles of their natures but from an extrinsic principle as does light from the influx of the sun—*aduenit ab aliquo principio extrinsico sicut lumen in aere ex influentia solis* (*De Ente*, c. IV; p.35.4-6). Ultimately such being has to come from subsistent being. Being is in this way established as a subsistent nature in reality.[45] It is a real nature, and so, as the foregoing reasoning has demonstrated, it will never coalesce in reality with the natures that participate it. Unlike the generic and specific perfections it will not be absorbed in reality with the essence, but will remain really other than the essence and in that sense outside (*praeter*) the essence. Since it is in this way outside the essence of the thing, it will belong to the thing only accidentally:" ... quidquid est in aliquo praeter essentiam ejus, inest ei accidentaliter" (*Comp. Theol.*, c. LXVI). The being of creatures is therefore an accident.

The being from which essence cannot prescind is in this way accidental to the essence. It is an act that is received into the essence as into a potency, and that remains really distinct from the potency in all real created things.[46] Even in the angels there will be this composition[47] of act and potency of being (*esse*) and subject of being (*quod est*):

> Omne autem quod recipit aliquid ab aliquo est in potentia respectu illius, et hoc quod receptum in eo est est actus ejus. Ergo oportet quod ipsa quiditas uel forma que est intelligencia sit in potencia respectu esse quod a Deo recipit, el illud esse receptum est per modum actus" (*De Ente*, c.IV; p. 35.19-23).

In so far as abstraction without precision means that the being is implicitly contained in the essence, it does not at all imply that being is actually contained. The essence absolutely considered is entirely potential in regard to being, and so can be thought of as containing being only in the sense that potency involves act. It is potential towards being, of its very notion it is a potency to being, even when in its absolute consideration it abstracts from all being. Its very name "essence" implies its order to being. It can never prescind from being, even though the act of being always remains outside it and other than it. The act of being inheres[48] in it and adheres[49] to it, in the manner of an accident.

It is however, an accident that is not subsequent to the essence, but prior to it. What has to be regarded as the first effect produced is the very being of the thing: "Primus autem effectus est ipsum esse, quod omnibus aliis effectibus praesupponitur et ipsum non praesupponit aliquem alium effectum" (*De Pot.*, III,4c; ed. Mandonnet, II, 52a). Unless the being is regarded as first produced, no other effect or aspect of the thing can be there. Every other aspect presupposes being. Being itself comes first, it presupposes no other effect in the thing. It has therefore priority over all else that is produced. All other effects or aspects are grounded upon being: "...ipsum esse, quod omnes alii effectus praesupponunt, et supra quod fundantur" (*Comp. Theol.* c. LXVIII). Being is what is most basic in anything. In this sense St. Thomas interprets the saying of the *Liber de Causis* "prima rerum creatarum est esse" (*In Lib. de Causis*, lect. IV, init.; ed. H.D. Saffrey, pp. 27 ff.). To produce the being of the thing, however, is thereby to produce the thing itself or its essence. Speaking of creation, St. Thomas states: "...ex hoc ipso quod quidditati esse attribuitur, non

solum esse, sed ipsa quidditas creari dicitur" (*De Pot.*, III, 5 ad 2m; ed. Mandonnet, II, 56b). By the very fact that being is given to a thing, the thing itself
is produced: "...Deus simul dans esse, producit id quod esse recipit" (Ibid.,
a.1, ad 17m; p.45a). To give it being, then, is to produce the essence and the
thing. Even though the act of being has always the priority, it and the essence
are not represented by St. Thomas as though they were two realities, but rather
as two distinct constituents of the one and the same reality or thing. In order to
have any created reality whatsoever, the two constituents have to be presupposed.

In this quite unparalled way, then, the act of being is accidental to every
created thing. It is accidental, not as an accidental reality subsequent to the
essence, but as a prior constituent necessary to make the essence a reality.
Without it the essence is not a reality but only a consideration that abstracts
from it but cannot prescind from it. Such is the doctrine in the Thomistic texts.
But how can any nature have an essential order to an act that is so accidental to
it?

EFFICIENT AND FORMAL CAUSES OF BEING

St. Thomas does not seem to feel any contradiction in these apparently opposite assertions. Rather, he speaks as though the formal casuality of the
essence, in essentially requiring being, thereby presupposes the extrinsic efficient causality that produces an act over and above the essence:"...esse per se
consequitur formam creaturae, supposito tamen influxo Dei: sicut lumen sequitur diaphanum aeris, supposito tamen influxu solis." (*ST*, I, 104, 1, ad
1m). The *diaphanum* was understood as a quality that enabled the air to
receive the illumination of the sun. It was the proximate or immediate potency
to light.[50] Its whole purpose was to be a potency to light. In this way it was the
proper subject of light.[51] *Per se*, or of its very nature, it was meant to be the
cause of light. Of its very nature it was what enabled the air to become
luminous. It was conceived as a form, an accidental form, that constituted the
air immediately in potency to light and made it the proper subject of light. It
was therefore the formal cause of light in the air, presupposing, however, the
influx of the sun as the efficient cause. In a word, it could not actually exercise
its formal casuality unless the sun were exercising efficient causality upon the
same effect, namely upon the light in the air.

In a corresponding way, St. Thomas teaches, being follows upon the form
per se. The form is of its very nature a potency to being. Its direction is essentially towards being. Of itself it therefore determines the creature to being. It is
accordingly the formal cause of its own being, and so determines the kind of

being that the thing possesses. That is not some accidental function of the form, that is its very nature as essence. *Per se* it is the cause of being in the creature, in its own line of casuality, namely, formal casuality. So much is this so, the text just quoted goes on to say, that the form taken just in itself is directed to being only, and not to non-being. In incorruptible creatures like the angels any order to non-being is from the side of the existential act that is accidental to the form: "Unde potentia ad non esse in spiritualibus creaturis et corporibus caelestibus, magis est in Deo, qui potest subtrahere suum influxum, quam in forma vel in materia talium creaturarum."[52]

The form, however, cannot exercise its determining function in the line of formal causality, it has to be, to exist, for of itself it is actually nothing and cannot exercise any causality whatsoever. Yet in being made to exist it thereby determines that being: "...quia tamen qualibet forma est determinativa ipsius esse, nulla earum est ipsum esse, sed est habens esse" (*In de Hebd.*, c. II; ed. Mandonnet, I, 176). As essentially the determinative principle of being, it exercises this formal casuality upon an act that is added to it and is other than it. "...esse enim quod hujusmodi est, est aliud secundum essentiam ab eo cui additur determinandum" (*De Pot.*, VII, 2, ad 9m; ed. Mandonnet, II, 254a).

In determining the being of a thing, nevertheless, the form does not function as an act. It determines the matter as act and accordingly form and act coincided for Aristotle. But in the Thomistic doctrine the form of itself, independently of its being, is not actual. Without that being, it is actually just nothing, and could not do any determining whatsoever. So in determining its act of being, it does not function as act. Rather, it functions as potency. The text last quoted continues: "Unde non sic determinatur *esse* per aliud sicut potentia per actum, sed magis sicut actus per potentiam" (p. 254a). No actuality, then, need be considered as functioning in the form in its priority to being, that is, in the priority in which it determines the being by way of formal causality. In that priority it is functioning as potency, and not as act. It is made actual only by its being, and cannot function as an actuality in any priority whatsoever to that being. In determining and limiting that being it functions only as potency. Any actuality that it has comes from that being and has to be considered as subsequent to that being. In this way being is the effect upon which all other effects are based, as the texts have stated. In giving a metaphysical account of a thing, one cannot think of the essence as something already constituted by its form and matter and then having the act of being added to it. Rather, from a metaphysical viewpoint, one has to start with the act of being that the primary efficient cause gives by participation, and consider that in being participated it has to be limited and thereby gives rise to the essence that determines it. The act of being is accordingly not a thing that is produced, but is the constituent that exercises the most fundamental priority in the thing that is produced.

The form is indeed the act and the complement of its matter, though it is made actual only through its being. It makes the essence something definite and something positive, something that is placed in one of the ten categories of being. It constitutes the essence, for instance, a man or a tree or a metal or some other definite type of thing that presents a positive object to the intellect's conceptualization. The positive character of the essence, however, is actually positive only through the being that actualizes the essence. Considered in priority to that actualization by being, the form can function only as potency. It determines being in its role as the subject of being, and in that role it is not exercising any actuality whatsoever. Rather, it is *receiving* its actuality. Its role is receptivity and potency. But in receiving being, an act that of itself is absolutely unlimited, it necessarily limits being to its own capacity and thereby determines formally the act of being.

The determining or limiting principle of a created being, then, is something positive even though everything positive about it actually comes from the act of being that it receives. Without that act it is just nothing, it is not actually anything positive but only potentially so. Such potentiality is sufficient to make it a positive limitation of being. It is the thing that is, the man or the tree or the metal—all positive enough notions. The being of a created thing cannot be considered as though it were a thing in its own right and then limited by having something of itself cut off, as a board is limited to the size of a table. Once being is posited as a thing, all the Parmenidean consequences follow—it is unique, all-embracing, and immutable. Being, therefore, cannot be considered as limited in any privative or negative way.[53] It can be limited only by a positive thing. What exists in creatures is properly speaking not the act of being, but the created thing: "Unde in compositis ex materia et forma nec materia nec forma potest dici ipsum quod est, nec etiam ipsum esse" (*CG*, II, 54; ed. Leonine, XIII, 39a26-28).

In its very functioning as potency to being, therefore, the form is in its own way the principle and cause of being, and in so functioning it is made actual. From the viewpoint of the subject of being it is the ultimate determination of the thing to being: "Per hoc enim in compositis ex materia et forma dicitur forma esse principium essendi, quia est complementum substantiae cuius actus est ipsum esse: sicut diaphanum est aeri principium lucendi quia facit eum proprium subiectum luminis" (*CG*, II, 54; XIII, 39a20-25). As subject and as potency the form is a principle of being. Considered just in itself, it determines the thing to being and not to not-being. In this way being follows from the principles of a thing's essence, in the line of formal causality, presupposing, of course, the influx of an efficient cause: "...esse per se consequitur formam creaturae, supposito tamen influxu Dei" (*ST*, I, 104, 1, ad 1m). The order to being is of the very essence of the thing. The essence is *per se* a potency to being, and *per se* a subject of being. In this way being is not something accidental to it, but is required by its very nature. When ascending through the widening predicates man, animal, living thing, body, substance, one finally comes to "being", one is not thereby passing over to an accidental category. One is remaining within the same category, even though the act that makes the thing a being is other than the thing's essence.

CONCLUSION

With these considerations in mind, one is in a position to bring together what may have seemed so many loose ends in the Thomistic texts on being. Being in creatures is neither just accidental nor just essential. It is both. It has to be viewed from both standpoints, if the doctrine of St. Thomas is to be understood. Created essence is of its own nature an order to being, and so far as it itself is concerned being is essential to it. But "as far as it itself is concerned" is not enough. In order to be, it also has to be produced efficiently by something other than itself, and from that viewpoint its being is accidental to it. Neither of these viewpoints can be dispensed with, and neither can be reduced to the other. They stand as ultimate, irreducible ways in which finite being is caused. Human intellection in spite of all its wishes and efforts cannot reduce its object to any one simple principle. The basis to which all thoughts and conceptions and principles are ultimately reduced is being (ens).[54] But being as originally known by the human intellect is not something simple. It is being as found in sensible things, and so is an object that is equivocal. Yet in its light the simpler components, essence and existence, have to be understood. The result is that the equivocity cannot be entirely eliminated in human thought. It can only be carefully recognized, and so kept from being a cause of deception. One always has to think in terms of things and realities, even when reducing these to principles neither of which is in itself a reality.

The ambiguities that follow from the consideration of being, therefore, cannot be done away with by human cognition. They are too fundamentally rooted in the first notion of being that is directly attained by the human intellect and to which all other conceptions have to be reduced, even the notions of the principles of created beings, essence and existence. If either side of the equivocity is left out of consideration, the doctrine of St. Thomas will be misunderstood and will be ranged with some other metaphysical tradition. If only his teaching that being results from the principles of the essence and so is as it were constituted by those principles is taken seriously, his doctrine of being will be judged orthodox Aristotelianism, as it appeared to Siger of Brabant, and his statements that being is an accident in creatures will be set aside as inexplicable or inconsistent. His assertions, however, that being in creatures is other than their essence, are too frequent and too sharply phrased to be dismissed today without serious consideration. In another and different background that arose within two or three years after his death, and appears sketched in the controversies of Giles of Rome and Henry of Ghent, the two phases of his doctrine have been taken as applying respectively to different realities. There is a being that is essential to the thing, the *esse essentiae*; it is a reality constituted by the essence and identical with the essence. There is another really distinct being, the *esse existentiae*, that is accidental to the thing and that is the result not of the principles of the essence but of the activity of an external efficient cause. Yet in the doctrine of St. Thomas the being (*esse*) that is other than the essence is the being that results from and is as it were constituted by the principles of the essence. It is the same *being* that is caused formally by the essence and efficiently by the external cause. As Suarez proved so convincingly, the *esse existentiae* is the *esse essentiae*.[55]

It is the same being, in a word, that is both accidental and essential to creatures. It is the act of being that results from the principles of the essence by way of formal causality, yet only when it is caused efficiently by a different and external agent. It is the act in regard to which every nature is essentially a being, and yet it is identified as a nature only with the divine essence. In all other natures it is an accident, though it is not subsequent to the essence like predicamental accidents, but prior to it. It is accordingly both accidental and essential. The composition of essence and being in every created reality leaves a fundamental equivocity in the basic notion of being as it is originally attained by the human mind, and that ambiguity may be expected to follow through in all subsequent metaphysical thinking.

DIVERSITY AND COMMUNITY OF BEING
IN ST. THOMAS AQUINAS

I

According to numerous texts in the writings of St. Thomas Aquinas, being is different, or more properly diverse, in its manifold instances. While a specific or generic nature remains identical as a nature in all its particular occurrences, being varies radically in every individual case. That doctrine was formulated definitely in the earliest period of St. Thomas' literary activity: "...omne quod est in genere oportet quod habeat quiditatem preter esse suum, cum quiditas uel natura generis aut speciei non distinguatur secundum rationem nature in illis quorum est genus uel species, set esse diuersum est in diuersis.''[1] The quidditative nature expressed in the species or genera, according to this text, remains the same nature in all its instances. It is a common nature in which the different species or the many individuals coincide. Whether generic or specific, it is always other than the being (*preter esse*) of anything that belongs to a class. In sharp contrast to this communizing function of any quidditative nature, being is represented as everywhere diverse (*diuersum in diuersis*). No two things, apparently, can ever coincide in their being, as they do in their specific and generic natures. Two men, to supply an example, coincide in their human nature, and a man and an ape coincide in their animality; but they never coincide in their being. The one never *is* the other. In their being they remain diverse. Being seems regarded as an inevitably diversifying principle. In groups of things, abstraction leaves out of consideration the differentiating traits and retains only the common. In this way it sets up the specific and generic natures. The higher the genus the more common is its range, extension increasing as content lessens. But the reciprocally inverse ratio of content and extension does not seem to hold for the highest grouping of all, that of things under being.[2] Something new happens when the quidditative order is left and the thing's being is considered. Rather than communication in any one common nature, according to the *prima facie* meaning of the above text, there appears a diversity of being in every individual instance. The one thing simply *is* not the other.

Against the same background of the distinction between being and essence, the community in nature with difference in being continues into the subsequent years of St. Thomas' work. The *Conta Gentiles* states the same doctrine: "Quicquid est in genere secundum esse differt ab aliis quae in eodem genere sunt: alias genus de pluribus non predicaretur. Oportet autem omnia quae sunt in eodem genere, in quidditate generis convenire..." (*CG*, I, 25; ed. Leonine, XIII, 76a19-b2). Things that coincide in a genus differ from one another in being. By differing in being they provide the necessary condition for predication. If the inferiors of the genus were not given each its own being, they would not constitute a plurality of subjects with which the genus could be contrasted and of which it could be predicated. Rather, they would merge indiscernibly in a single quiddity. They seem to require difference in being in order to protect them from complete absorption in the generic nature. Each of the many different inferiors has to *be* the common nature[3] in its own diverse way. Without difference in being they could not retain their own identity when they communicate in a species or genus. They are described, therefore, as differing in being (*secundum esse*), quite apparently in the same sense as the diversity of being that was noted in the *De Ente et Essentia*. Being continues to be regarded as the diversifying principle. According to this doctrine, it remains immune to all generic unification. No matter how much things may be united generically, they will always differ from one another in being. The unifying elements seem exhausted when one has completed the analysis of the thing's nature. When one passes over to its being, which is other than its nature, one finds a diversifying rather than a unifying principle, according to the obvious sense of this text from the *Contra Gentiles*.

Likewise, the contrast between community in genus and species on the one hand, and difference in being on the other hand, is carried over into the *Summa Theologiae*. If anything, it is expressed even more pointedly: "Tertio, quia omnia quae sunt in genere uno, communicant in quidditate vel essentia generis,... Differunt autem secundum esse: non enim idem est esse hominis et esse equi, nec huius et illius hominis" (*ST*, I, 3, 5c; ed. Leonine). The context is still the distinction between being and essence in creatures though not in God. The generic essence or quiddity unites things. It is a common feature in which differing things communicate. It is contrasted in clearcut fashion with the principle in which things differ, namely being. Things that coincide in essence differ in being (*secundum esse*). The reasoning is applied to both species and individuals. Each species has its own being. This is cognitional being, for the species as such exist only in intellectual cognition.[4] The species "man," accordingly, differs in being from the species "horse," though the two species coincide in the genus "animal." The nature of man has its own cognitional being as a species. In that being it does not coincide with "horse," though "man" and "horse" coincide in the generic "animal." In the real world, of course, only individuals exist,[5] and every individual, even though it coincides in specific and generic nature with other things, remains radically different from them all in being.

According to these texts, then, St. Thomas from the earliest through the mature periods of his writing maintained that being is always a diversifying principle of things. He speaks as though in the ascent of the Porphyrian tree with its ever widening branches the unifying features end with the highest genus, in which the thing is located according to its essence. When the thing's being is reached, it appears as other than the essence[6] and so as not subject to the norms that govern generic and specific characteristics. In opposite fashion it is an aspect that diversifies things. In contrast to quidditative features, the act that lies outside the quidditative natures does not make things coalesce in any new genus. By its touch, rather, it renders them diverse or different from one another.

Being, accordingly, is diverse in every case. It does not function in the fashion of a genus or common nature. Nor is there anything very surprising in this teaching of St. Thomas. No matter how much one shares one's human nature and animal nature with others of the same species or genus, one's being remains inalienably one's own. No matter how much one communicates in activities or purposes or specific similarities with others, one's being stays proper[7] to one's self. Others may resemble you, see you, know you, help you, harm you, but none of them *is* yourself. You alone *are* yourself. In your being you differ radically from all others. Your being is diverse from all other instances of being. This seems nothing more than an example of the first principle of demonstration, the principle of contradiction. A thing *is* itself and is not what is other than itself and is diverse from all other things. It differs from all else in its being (*secundum esse*). Being, consequently, has to be diverse in every instance. A little reflection on the first principle of demonstration seems to bear out amply the significance of these texts in St. Thomas regarding the inescapable diversity of being.

***

In the contexts from which the above statements of St. Thomas are taken, however, there occur assertions that are of apparently opposite meaning. In the same passage in which the lines quoted from *De Ente et Essentia* are found, the being of creatures is regarded as universal being (*esse universale*—c. V; p. 38.1) and as common. It is described almost as though it were abstracted without precision, after the fashion of a genus, even though the term "abstraction" is not used: "Esse autem commune sicut in intellectu suo non includit additionem, ita non includit in intellectu suo aliquam precisionem additionis, quia si hoc esset, nichil posset intelligi esse in quo super esse aliquid adderetur."[8] In this continuation of the discussion in which, on the basis of its diversifying character, it was so sharply distinguished from specific or generic nature, being is now described as "common." The community is at least modeled on generic and specific community, for the description is based upon the way in which specific and generic concepts abstract from without prescinding from their inferiors. In isolating the "universal being by which everything formally is,"[9] it would seem as though one ascended the Porphyrian tree in an every widening series of universals, abstracting successively without precision from individuals, man, animal, living thing, body, and then somehow rising from "substance" to the notion of "common being" (*esse commune*), a notion that does not prescind from the addition of restricting traits. The description seems to parallel closely enough the account given by St. Thomas of the way in which specific and generic notions are abstracted without precision.[10] The species does not explicitly include the addition of individual designations, but it does not exclude them. The genus does not expressly include the addition of specific differentiae, yet it does not exclude them when it is abstracted without precision. So in the notion (*intellectus*) of common being, the text states, no addition of further characteristics is included, but the addition of such traits is not at all excluded. Being (*esse*) seems regarded in this text as the most basic of all notions in a thing, open to the ever narrowing addition of the generic and specific divisions. Being appears conceived as the most common and most fundamental aspect of things, upon which the restrictive generic and specific aspects may be imposed. Yet the being that is under consideration in the context is expressly regarded as other than the nature of anything that belongs to a genus.

Similarly in the chapter immediately following that of the text quoted above from the *Contra Gentiles* on things coinciding (*convenire*) in generic nature though differing in being, the apparently opposite doctrine in regard to being is clearly stated: "Res ad invicem non distinguuntur secundum quod habent esse: quia in hoc omnia conveniunt" (*CG*, I, 26; ed. Leonine, XIII, 81a9-11). According to these lines, being is not a distinguishing characteristic. It does not render anything distinct from anything else. It is the trait, rather, in which all things coincide. The term that was used to state how things coincide in a genus is here used to describe how all things coincide in being.

Likewise in the *Summa Theologiae*, in the same context of the distinction of being from essence in creatures but not in God, being is regarded as common because it does not exclude the addition of further determinations, just as the generic nature "animal" does not exclude them:

> Alio modo intelligtur aliquid cui non fit additio, quia non est de ratione eius quod sibi fiat additio: sicut animal commune est sine ratione, quia non est de ratione animalis communis ut habeat rationem: sed nec de ratione eius ut careat ratione...secundo modo, esse sine additione, est esse commune (*ST*, I, 3, 4, ad 1m).

The being that is caused efficently by the first principle of all being (*esse*), in a context in which the essence of creatures is distinguished from their being (arg. 3), is described as common to all: "...non...secundum eandem rationem speciei aut generis, sed secundum aliqualem analogiam, sicut ipsum esse est commune omnibus" (*ST*, I, 4, 3c).

Being, then, though not a specific nor generic characteristic, is nevertheless common according to the type of community that in the Aristotelian classifications is still wider than the generic, namely the analogous.[11] It is not a genus, but appears rather as a sort of super-genus, embracing everything whatsoever. One seems to mount through the species and the intermediate and highest genera, and continue on to the widest aspect of all, being. This, in fact, is exactly the way St. Thomas describes the process in *De Substantiis Separatis*, an unfinished work that is accordingly dated in the closing years of his life. It states:

> Nihil enim per se subsistens, quod sit ipsum esse, poterit inveniri nisi unum solum; sicut nec aliqua forma, si separata consideretur, potest esse nisi una. Inde est enim quod ea quae sunt diversa numero sunt unum specie, quia natura speciei secundum se considerata est una. Sicut igitur est una secundum considerationem dum per se consideratur, ita esset una secundum esse si per se existeret. Eademque ratio est de genere per comparationem ad species, quousque perveniatur ad ipsum esse quod est communissimum. Ipsum igitur esse secundum se subsistens est unum tantum.[12]

Just as individuals coincide in the one species, and the species coincide in the one genus, so finally do the genera coincide in the most common feature of all, which is being.

Again, there seems to be nothing very surprising in this view, taken by itself. "Being" is predicated of everything that is. It is therefore the widest predicate of all. It is a transcendent[13] characteristic of things. It functions quite readily as a sort of super-genus, extending over all the categories as the most common of predicates. It is the most common aspect that can be found. Everything has the aspect of being, just as every individual man has human nature. All things without exception, therefore, should easily coincide in the notion of being, just as all individual men coincide in the notion of man.

II

Both viewpoints, then, are explicit in the texts of St. Thomas. Both appear to be in accord with ordinary linguistic usage. Each thing's being is radically different from any other's being, and in that way is *diverse*. Yet being is the most *common* of all predicates. No discrepancy seems felt by St. Thomas in sponsoring each of these views, even in the same context. No difficulty is experienced today in using either apart from the other in everyday language. Yet each of the two views seems in definite contradiction to the other. If being is a characteristic common to all things, how can it conceivably be diverse in every individual instance? If it is radically diverse in each new case, how can it be a trait in which all things coincide.?

Can any help be given by the fairly well-known statement of St. Thomas that being is not diverse in itself, but is diversified by the different subjects that share it? The statement is: "Esse autem, inquantum est esse, non potest esse diversum: potest autem diversificari per aliquid quod est praeter esse; sicut esse lapidis est aliud ab esse hominis."[14] Being, considered just as being, cannot be diverse. It can be diversified, however, by things other than itself. The being in a stone, for instance, is quite apparently not the same as the being in a man, for to be a stone is certainly not to be a man. Inanimate being seems decidedly different from human being. The being of one individual is not the being of another. Being is multiplied in the subjects that partake of it. Just in itself, according to this text, being exhibits no ground for diversification. But it can be shared by different subjects, each having its own being, and in this way it becomes diversified.

But could not the same be said, in a proportional way, of any common nature? No common nature varies in itself. It is pluralized only by the species or the subjects that share it. From that viewpoint, being and quidditative common nature stand on identical footing. The following paragraph, from the same chapter of the *Contra Gentiles* as the text just quoted, does in fact compare them exactly on the basis of multiplication through the things that share them:

> Natura communis, si separata intelligatur, non potest esse nisi una: quamvis habentes naturam illam plures possint inveniri. Si enim natura *animalis* per se subsisteret, non haberet ea quae sunt hominis vel quae sunt bovis: iam enim non esset *animal* tantum, sed homo vel bos. ... Sic igitur, si hoc ipsum quod est esse sit commune sicut genus, esse separatum per se subsistens non potest esse nisi unum. Si vero non dividatur differentiis, sicut genus, sed per hoc quod est huius vel illius esse, ut veritas habet; magis est manifestum quod non potest esse per se existens nisi unum (*CG*, II, 52; XIII, 387a31-43).

If a common generic nature, like the nature "animal," could subsist as a nature in itself and not just in singulars, it would have to be unique as subsistent animality. There could be no more than one such subsistent animal nature. There might still be many individuals possessing the nature, but as subsisting in itself it would have one instance only. It can be divided and multiplied, therefore, only by the species and individuals that share it. This is the same argument that had been advanced for the diversification of being, and here it is straightway applied from the common nature to the case of being. Taken just in itself, being, like a quidditative common nature, could furnish no ground for diversity. It could be pluralized, however, in becoming the being of this or that individual. The consideration that being cannot be divided by specific differentiae like a genus merely adds to the force of the argument. A genus, in so far as it is predicable, that is, in so far as it is abstracted without precision, implicitly contains its differentiae,[15] and of its nature is meant to be divided by them. When actually differentiated it is no longer the generic nature along, but is a specific nature like man or ox. From that viewpoint, it is differentiated by what is implicitly contained in it. An act that is received into a subject other than itself, however, does not contain that subject, any more than a form contains its matter before being joined to it by an efficient cause.

All the more manifest, then, is the argument when applied to being. It has the same weight as it had when it was seen in the case of a quidditative common nature, and makes itself felt all the more through the elimination of a possible distraction from the way in which a genus implicitly contains its differentiae. The generic nature coalesces in reality with its differentiae, yet it is divided by them. It can of course be prescinded from them in such a way that they lie outside its own proper nature.[16] Much more obviously, however, do the divisors of being lie outside the nature of being, for being can be pluralized only by subjects that are other than its own nature, in reality.

The argument, therefore, is fundamentally the same when applied to a quidditative common nature and when applied to being. Accordingly, it does not show how being is itself a diversifying principle. It establishes only that all things communicate in being as all species communicate in their genera and all sungular things communicate in their species. It *allows* the diversification of their being by things that are other than being; but it does not show that they differ through their being. Yet the texts of St. Thomas quoted above state clearly: "secundum esse differt ab aliis" (CG, I, 259; "differunt autem secundum esse."[17] The question is not merely of a common aspect becoming diversified by individuals that remain the same according to the common trait in which they participate, as all individual men remain specifically the same in their common humanity. It is a question *also* of their diversificaion by that common trait in which they share. One cannot say that men differ according to their animality or are diverse according to their humanity. Yet they are diverse according to their being, the being that they share in common. Being functions not only in the manner of a super-genus that is most common to all things, but at the same time parallels somehow the thing's individuation: "...unumquodque secundum idem habet esse et individuationem."[28] Being, in fact, is not placed in a common definition any more than are the individuating notes. Why is being not placed in the definition of any finite thing? At least one reason is the non-identity of the individuals in being even though they are united in species and genera:

> Ad secundum dicendum quod secundum Avicennam in sua *Metaph.*, esse non potest poni in definitione alicuius generis et speciei, quia omnia particularia uniuntur in definitione generis vel speciei, cum tamen genus vel species non sint secundum unum *esse* in omnibus (*Quodl.*, IX, 3, 1, ad 2m; ed. Spiazzi, 183b).

To urge that being is not diversified in itself but only through its recipients, consequently, explains merely the super-generic role of being. It does not at all explain how being has a diversifying function in its own right, and how being is most proper to everything as well as most common to all. Rather, it accentuates the seeming contradiction instead of solving it.

But is not the reception of being by a subject other than itself considerably different not only from tthe specificaion of a genus by differentiae but also from the reception of a common nature by an individual or even of a form by matter? Genus, species, and form are all involved in a thing's nature. But being does not at all enter into the nature of any finite thing. The nature remains the same whether the thing has real or cognitional being.[19] the thing can acquire or lose either real being or cognitional being without undergoing any change whatsoever in nature. A tree has the nature of a tree whether it exists in reality or in someone's thought. In the example used by St. Thomas one can know what a man is or what a phoenix is, without knowing whether, either exists in reality.[20]

This difference between the way quidditative predicates belong to a thing and the way being belongs to it is brought out clearly enough in the logical structure of predication. That a thing has being, is expressed when the verb that otherwise functions as the copula is used alone. "A tree is" or "there is a tree," means that the tree has being. It does not say anything about *what* the tree is, either substantially or accidentally. It asserts only that the tree exists.[21] Quidditative predicates, on the other hand, have to be expressed by some notion added to the copula, as in "a man is an animal." Even when other verbs are used to express predicamental accidents, they can also be construed with the copula and the participial form. "A man is running" can stand for "a man runs." But one cannot say, without repeating the meaning, that "a tree is being" with the same force as "a tree is growing." The English idiom prefers "exists" for "is" in the simple assertion of being. But even when one says "a thing is existing," no further notion of the essential order, either of substance or of accident, is signified. "A thing is existing" has the same meaning as "a thing is." Both mean that being is enjoyed by the thing. When any other characteristic is shared, a further notion has to be added to the copula. But the being that is both common and proper is expressed by the verb "is" used alone. It does not tell anything about what the thing is, but simply asserts that the thing exists.

What is the reason for this difference between the predication of being and the predication of quidditative characteristics? The difference seems to lie in the way in which a common nature is received by a subject and the way in which being is received by it. A common nature is received as the thing's essence and is expressed by a notion, therefore, that declares *what* the thing is—body, living thing, animal, man. It is absorbed in reality into the individual thing's nature. Being, on the other hand, is received as an actuality that remains other than the essence in reality, and cannot be expressed by any notion that helps show what the thing is. It is expressed by the verb "is" used alone, for what the verb "is" signifies does not pertain to the nature of the thing. Being is not received as a generic or even as an accidental nature. It is not received as a nature at all, for it in no way adds to what the thing is. It is not received, therefore, as a form is received by matter or as a generic or specific nature is received by an individual.

The difference is emphasized through a consideration of the types of causality by which being and common natures or forms are participated. A specific or generic nature is shared by way of formal causality. It is as it were a set knowable form in which different subjects participate, as for instance humanity is shared by all men, whiteness by all things white, baldness by all heads without hair. An efficient cause may be required to join the form to the subject, as a painter is required to paint a house white. But the joining of the form to the subject is by no means the whiteness of the house. Its whiteness consists in its sharing in the color white in an abiding way, as matter in general partakes of form. This is formal causality, even though a prior efficient cause is required to join form to subject.

Being, however, when it is participated, does not add any new formal characteristic to the thing. It leaves the thing's formal nature, both substantial and accidental, entirely unchanged as nature. There is no participation in any new form. No new formal causality is exercized. The thing is merely made to be. The only causality by which being is shared is efficient causality. The being of man or the being of tree does not add any new formal note or trait. Even when forms are predicated of their subject, the verb "is" does not at all increase the formal content of the predication, as in the example, "a tree is green." The "is" merely signifies the union of form and subject in being. This total failure to manifest any new formal effect in the thing's nature has occasioned the denial that being is a predicate at all.[22] It is obviously not a predicate of the essential or quidditative order. It does not make the thing participate in any new form. But it does make the thing be, and that is more important than any formal effect, for without being the thing would be simply nothing. From that viewpoint, being may be regarded as exercising the most formal role of all in the thing, in the sense in which "formal" is equated with actual.[23] But this does not mean that being exercises any formal causality in the thing, in the sense in which formal is contrasted with efficient causality. Being is participated as a result of the efficient causality of an agent without thereby exercising any formal causality in the thing. It may make a form be in the thing, but all the formal causality involved is exercised by that form and not in any way by the being.

This means that being in its highest instance is an efficient cause and not a formal cause of things. To exercise efficient causality, being has to subsist in its primary instance. The real subsistence of being is in fact shown by tracing to its source the being found in observable things and participated by them through efficient causality. If being did not subsist, there could not be efficient causality and so no participation of being. On the other hand, a common nature, which shares itself with subjects through formal causality, cannot subsist in itself. In the case of a generic or specific characteristic, there is no subsistent nature. There is no really existent primary instance. The really existent instances are only the individuals that partake of the nature. From them the nature is abstracted. It can exist as a specific or generic nature only in the abstraction of the intellect. The common nature itself is just reached as the result of a consideration that abstracts and compares the nature existent in different instances and sees thereby that it is common to all the instances. There is no really existent *common* nature to be participated.[24] It is only an abstraction, and when it is abstracted without precision it does not exclude the addition of further perfections. When it is explicitly determined to those perfections, it absorbs them into its nature, as when animal nature for instance is human and individual in the one man Socrates. It includes them in the one real nature, and thereby renders them identical in reality with itself and with one another.

When things participate being, on the other hand, they are participating a nature that is found as such in reality. They are sharing in a nature that cannot itself become identical with any specific nature, as "animal" becomes "man" by making one of its differentiae explicit. If the nature of being were set up as an essential predicate of any individual or of any finite nature, it would at once absorb that individual or nature into itself.[25] The conclusions of Parmenides would inevitably follow. Being, therefore, cannot be participated in the status of a nature or a form. It can be shared only by making things be, without adding any feature whatsoever within their natures. Unlike a genus, it cannot be regarded as forming part of the thing's nature. It cannot be absorbed into that nature. When it is participated by way of efficient causality, it can no longer have the status of a nature. It cannot be part of anything's nature. It can just actuate a nature into which it itself does not enter. In this way it is predicated of things without requiring that the things be identical within itself, as things are identical in reality with their generic natures. The Parmenidean consequences, accordingly, do not follow upon the predication of being.

However, if subsistent being is the efficient cause of all things, it must somehow contain all things within itself. The nature of being has to contain all perfections within itself, as even the Parmenidean reasoning shows. Far from a so-called "Eleatic monotone," being necessarily involves all other perfections: "Omnium autem perfectiones pertinent ad perfectionem essendi:…"[26] There is a sense in which they all may be predicated of subsistent being, though with the necessary reservation that subsistent being does not become anything pertaining to them, but remains above them all.[27] In this sense being is the richest of notions. All other perfections may be predicated of it and are contained within it. It has the greatest content of all notions, as well as the widest extension. But this means that it contains within itself its own diversifying principles. Generic and specific determinations are perfections, and all perfections are contained in the nature of being. There can be no perfection, no actuality outside being that might determine it.

But will this hold for the individual determinations of things? Why cannot being be diversified by reception into purely potential subjects, as form is individuated by reception into matter? Cannot an act be diversified by something that functions merely as potency, without the introduction of any actual determining characteristic at all?

There is indeed a sense in which matter individuates form and essences diversify being. But that is hardly the whole story. Matter and essence are subsequent to being, absolutely speaking. The being of the thing is simply prior to either. Where things are individuated through reception in matter, they inevitably require matter for their diversification; nevertheless they have in their being a prior cause of the diversification:

> …causa diversitatis in rebus non est materiae diversitas. Ostensum est enim, quod materia non praesupponitur actioni divinae, qua res in esse producit. Causa autem diversitatis rerum productionem praeexigitur, ut scilicet secundum diversitatem materiae diversae inducantur formae.[28]

Unity and plurality, in fact, follow upon being. The unit by which the individual is a unit in itself and diverse from all other individuals in a multitude will therefore follow upon the thing's being.[29] Any being that is participated thereby involves its own determination,[30] otherwise it would not be participated, but would be subsistent being. In this way it determines itself by its essence, and in the case of material things by its matter. But the actuality of all such determination comes from the being. The subjects that lie outside being and receive being can play the role only of potency in diversifying being. Of themselves they are not, and so cannot provide any of the actual determinations of being. Prior to any individuating role of essence or matter is the actual diversifying function of being as it is participated. No determination can be added to it from outside its own nature:

> Nihil autem potest addi ad *esse* quod sit extraneum ab ipso, cum ab eo nihil sit extraneum nisi *non-ens*, quod non potest esse nec forma nec materia. Unde non sic determinatur *esse* per aliud sicut potentia per actum, sed magis sicut actus per potentiam. Nam et in definitione formarum ponuntur propriae materiae loco differentiae, sicut cum dicitur quod anima est actus corporis physici organici. Et per hunc modum, hoc *esse* ab illo *esse* distinguitur, in quantum est talis et talis naturae (*De Pot.*, VII, 2, ad 9m; ed. Pession, II, 192b).

The actuality of the determination by which one individual is not another, then, will have to have its origin in the thing's being. Being has to provide its own differences, even though it requires a potency other than itself in which to actualize them.

From a logical viewpoint, this difference between being and any generic nature may be expressed in the traditional Aristotelian dictum that being is predicated of all differentiae while no genus can be predicated of its own differentiae. In regard to the subject constituted by being (*to on*), Aristotle formulates this principle very clearly:

> But it is not possible that either unity or being should be a single genus of things; for the differentiae of any genus must each of them both have being (*einai*) and be one, but it is not possible for the genus taken apart from its species.... to be predicated of its proper differentiae; so that if unity or being is a genus, no differentia will either have being or be one.[31]

The differentia, to function as a differentia, just has to be. If it did not have being, it would be nothing and could not exercise any differentiating function. It could not make itself felt in any way in the constitution of the thing. It would be simply nothing.

The reasons why a genus cannot be predicated of its differentiae are given by Aristotle in the *Topics*:

> For if "animal" is predicated of each of its differentiae, then "animal" would be predicated of the species several times over; for the differentiae are predicates of the species. Moreover, the differentiae will be all either species or individuals, if

they are animals; for every animal is either a species or an individual (*Top.*, VI 6, 144a36-b3; Oxford tr.).

If the genus were predicated of its differentiae, it would be contained in each differentia and so would be predicated of the species separately with the predication of the differentiae. For example, if "animal" were predicated of "two-footed," then "two-footed" would be animal or an animal, in its very nature as a differentia. So when you say "Man is two-footed," you would be saying that man is an animal, since "two-footed" includes "animal" as one of its predicates. You would be repeating the predication of the genus, namely "man is an animal."

Such is the first Aristotelian argument why a genus cannot be predicated of its differentiae. But how can the Aristotle who argues in this way be the same man who maintains that the ultimate differentia includes the first genus and all the intermediate differentiae?[32] From the logical viewpoint of the *Topics*, the differentia does not include the genus, since the genus cannot be predicated of it. The differentia does not partake of the genus, nor does the genus partake of its differentiae.[33] Yet from the viewpoint of the function of form in the *Metaphysics*, the ultimate differentia, expressing as it does the form, does include the genus. Why are the results so different when the topic is approached from these two different standpoints? The Aristotelian text does not give any express answer. In the *Metaphysics*, Aristotle is concerned with safeguarding the unity of substances in spite of of the plurality of generic and specific forms to which they give rise in human cognition. He allows a sense in which the genus does participate its differences: "And even if the genus does share in them" (*Metaph.*, Z 12, 1037b21; Oxford tr.). But even in this case the same difficulty holds. Genus and differentia still set up a plurality. The solution offered is the way in which the Aristotelian form is a principle of unity for all that it actuates; and in this case the ultimate differentiae. The metaphysical unity of a nature is thereby safeguarded, in spite of its logical divisions.

All this, however, does not explain very thoroughly why the genus in one sense contains its differentiae and in another sense it does not. St. Thomas is much more explicit. In one and the same passage he repeats the Aristotelian doctrine that the ultimate differentia signifies the whole subject: "differentia significat totum; sed non significat tantum formam,"[34] and yet goes on to say that the differentia in its primary concept does not determine what its genus is: "Differentia uero e contra, sicut quedam determinatio a forma determinate sumpta, propter hoc quod de primo intellectu eius sit determinata materia, ut patet cum dicitur animatum, sive illud quod habet animam; non enim determinatur quid sit, utrum sit corpus uel aliquid aliud" (*De Ente*, c. II; p. 17.7-11). Genus and differentia are but determinations of the thing. The genus gives a determination that is material in regard to the differentia: "...genus significat totum ut quedam determinatio determinans id quod est materiale in re" (p. 17.1-2). The differentia is a further determination; but in its primary notion, according to this doctrine of St. Thomas, it expresses merely a determination of something, leaving that "something" in its vague and indefinite transcendental sense. The genus consists in a determination and that determination does not belong to the primary notion of the differentia. How, then, can the genus signify the whole, and not just its own determination?

Moreover, the whole essence of the definition is somehow contained in the differentia, and correspondingly, the differentia is contained in the genus:

> ...ita quod tota essentia definitionis, in differentia quodammodo comprehenditur. Ex hoc enim animal, quod est genus, non potest esse absque speciebus, quia formae specierum quae sunt differentiae, non sunt aliae formae a forma generis, sed sunt formae generis cum determinatione. ...Unde cum differentia additur generi, non additur quasi aliqua diversa essentia a genere, sed quasi in genere implicite contenta, sicut determinatum continetur in indeterminato, ut album in colorato.[35]

The differentia, accordingly, includes the whole essence of the definition. It includes all the parts of the definition. It includes the genus. The differentia is not as essence apart from the essence of the genus. Yet St. Thomas can also say that the genus is not a part of the essence of the differentia, but is something outside its essence: "Vnde dicit Auicenna quod genus non intelligitur in differentia sicut pars essentie, set solum sicut ens extra essentiam" (De Ente, c. II; p. 17.11-13). He states frequently that the genus does not enter the definition of the differentia, nor does the differentia enter the definition of the genus.[36] The genus, therefore, is not predicated in strict identity of its differentiae.[37] Nevertheless, in so far as the differentia signifies the whole essence, the genus can be predicated of it.[38]

Can these two conflicting sides of the question be reconciled? One side makes the genus so coincide with the differentia in essence as to be predicable of it. The other side places the genus outside the essence of the differentia in a way that prevents such predication through identity. The difficulty seems to lie in the twofold character of the differentia. It is both qualitative and substantive, as Aristotle had noted: "...for the general view is that the differentia always expresses a quality"; yet "the differentia is never an accidental attribute, any more than the genus is:..."[39] It is a *quale quid*, a substantial quality:

> ...secundum quod qualitas dicitur "differentia substantiae," idest differentia, per quam aliquid ab altero substantialiter differt, quae intrat in definitionem substantiae. Et propter hoc dicitur, quod differentia praedicatur in quale quid. ...ac si ipsa differentiae qualitas sit. Uno igitur modo ipsa differentia substantiae qualitas dicitur.[40]

Because of this twofold character, the genus is both a predicate and a subject. As a predicate, it is the substance of the thing and so is a whole that contains the differentia implicitly. Correspondingly, the differentia is the substance of the thing and so is a whole that contains the basic genus and all the intermediate differentiae. When it is added to the genus it is added not as a part to a part, but as a whole to a whole: "Differentia vero additur generi non quasi pars parti, sed quasi totum toti" (*In X Metaph.*, lect. 10, no. 2114). It is the one and the same substance as the genus. But even though it is a whole, and identical as such with the genus, it nevertheless qualifies or determines the genus. As a quality or determination *of* the genus, it enters into new relation with it. It sets off the genus as the subject that is qualified:

> Hoc enim modo se habet genus ad differentiam, sicut subiectum ad qualitatem. Et ideo patet quod genus praedicabile, et genus subiectum, quasi sub uno modo comprehendentur, et utrumque se habet per modum materiae. Licet enim genus praedicabile non sit materia, sumitur tamen a materia, sicut differentia a forma. Dicitur enim aliquid animal ex eo quod habet naturam sensitivam. Rationalem vero ex eo, quod habet rationalem naturam, quae se habet ad sensitivam sicut forma ad materiam.[41]

In this new relation, however, the genus and the differentia are related to each other as *parts* of the species, just as any matter and form are parts of their composite: "... unde quodammodo et genus et differentia dicuntur esse in specie, sicut partes in toto."[42] Considered as qualitative or determining, the differentia functions as form, and so only a part of the specific nature. Viewed in this way, it lies outside the essence of the genus. So regarded, it is taken according to its primary notion, for its primary function is to qualify. It is primarily a quality, even though a substantial quality. Distinguished from the genus as formal part of the species from material part, it does not show the identity necessary to receive the predication of the genus, since part is not identical with part in the way required by predication. Considered as substantial, however, it comprises the whole specific nature. It is added to the genus not as part to part, but as whole to whole. It contains the generic nature within itself, and is contained implicitly in the genus. It is the same in essence as the genus. Regarded in this way it has all the identity with the genus that is necessary for predication.[43]

How can that be? Genus and differentia, of course, are merely notions formed by the human intellect of the one real thing, say a man. In reality they are the one human nature. In their status of genus and differentia they exist only in the mind.[44] In a particular man the individuating traits are left out of consideration by the intellect, and only those in which he coincides with all other men are retained. In this way the man is conceived according to his specific nature, and the notion of the species "man" is set up. The same man can be conceived according to the aspects that he has in common with all sensitive beings, with the traits that distinguish him from brute animals left out of consideration. In that way the same individual man is conceived according to his generic nature "animal," and the genus is set up. In each of these cases the same thing, the same individual nature is being conceived, but in different ways. Both specific and generic notions signify the same whole. Moreover, what determines the generic nature to the specific is likewise the same whole. It is the human nature that is found in the individual man, now conceived as determining "animal" to "man." It is the same human nature that was represented as a whole in the species and in the genus, and now represented as a whole under its qualifying aspect in the differentia.

Since the function under which the whole nature is conceived in the differentia is that of qualifying or determining, it makes the differentia in its primary notion a quality, even though in the category of substance. The natural differentiae of substances remain unknown to the human intellect. But they can be represented through accidental differences, and so "rational" from the activity of reasoning, or "two-footed" from the number of feet, have been used to stand for the substantial differentia of man. Whatever term is used, it signifies the whole substance of man as determining him to a definite species and not leaving him merely in the generic consideration of "animal." But in conceiving that whole substance first as genus and then as differentia, the intellect has set up two separate notions, each of which has its own separate being in the mind. It has to represent those two notions as combining to constitute a third notion, that of the species. It represents them as the two *parts* of the whole specific nature, the one as the material and the other as the formal or determining part, even though it is conceiving the same whole nature in all three cases:

> ...neque genus est materia, set a materia sumptum ut significans totum; nec differentia forma, set a forma sumpta ut significans totum. Vnde dicimus hominem animal rationale, non ex animali et rationali, sicut dicimus eum esse ex anima et corpore; ex anima enim et corpore dicitur esse homo, sicut ex duabus rebus tercia uero res constituta, que nulla illarum est; homo enim neque est anima neque corpus; set si homo aliquo modo ex animali et rationali esse dicatur, non est sicut res tercia ex duabus rebus, set sicut intellectus tercius ex duobus intellectibus; intellectus enim animalis est sine determinatione specialis forme exprimens naturam rei ab eo quod est materiale respectu ultime perfectionis; intellectus autem huius differentie rationalis consistit in determinatione forme specialis; ex quibus duobus intellectibus constituitur intellectus speciei uel diffinitionis (*De Ente*, c. II; p. 18.9-19.9.).

A third thing constituted out of two other things is neither of them, as for instance man is neither body nor soul. It is identified with neither of them, and so neither can be predicated of it; nor can either be predicated of the other, on account of their lack of identity as different parts of the same whole. When differentia and genus are set up as separate notions combining to form a third notion, the species, neither can be predicated of the other, according to this reasoning. The notion "rational" is not the notion "animal," and to together they constitute the notion "man."The notion "animal" expresses the nature of man, it signifies the whole nature, but from the viewpoint of his sensitive life. It does not express the special determination contained in the form of man, that of human sensitivity. As sensitivity can be either human or non-human, it is left undetermined in its generic notion and as the subject or the matter for qualification by "rational" or "irrational." The notion "rational" consists in the special determination that the form of man contains. The *raison d'être* for its abstraction as a distinct notion is to express that special determination. In its primary notion, therefore, it expresses only that determination, and not the generically determined type of matter that it qualifies. "Rational" as a differentia means "rational something" and so signifies the whole nature, and can be predicated of the species and individuals. But in its primary notion it does not determine that the "something" it qualified is "animal." In its primary notion, accordingly, even though it signifies the whole nature, it leaves the genus out of what it expresses, and from that viewpoint leaves the genus out of its essence and definition. As qualifying the genus, it is set up by the intellect as something outside the content of the genus, something of which the genus is the subject and to which that genus is related as matter to form. As denoting the whole substance, however, it signifies the same thing as the genus. The genus is identical with it as a whole, though distinct from it as a part:

> Si ergo consideretur in genere et differentia id a quo utrumque sumitur, hoc modo genus se habet ad differentias sicut materia ad formas. Si autem consideretur secundum quod nominant totum, sic aliter se habent. ...Sed hoc utrobique distat, quia materia est in utroque divisorum, non tamen est utrumque eorum; genus autem utrumque corum est; quia materia nominat partem, genus autem totum.[45]

The genus when considered as a whole is each of its divisors, each of its differentiae. It is predicable of them. A "rational something" is an animal. In so far as it is a substance, the differentia signifies the whole, and the genus may be predicated of it.[46] In so far as it is a quality, however, the differentia in its primary notion sets off the genus as a subject distinct from itself and outside its essence, and so does away with the identity necessary for predication: "Et ideo eciam genus non predicatur de differentia per se loquendo, ut dicit Philosophus in tertio *Metaphysice* et in quarto *Topicorum,* nisi forte sicut subiectum de passione predicatur" (*De Ente*, c. II; p. 17.14-18.2). As a quality, even though a substantial quality, "rational" is not "animal." As substance, then, the differentia is identical with the genus as subject, and so is distinct from the genus in essence, as part from part in the species; for the genus in its role of subject is not qualitative. The twofold character of the differentia as a *quale quid* places it respectively in relation to its genus as whole to whole and as part to part. Correspondingly, the *genus praedicabile* functions as the whole, the *genus subiectum* as a part.

The intellect's way of abstracting without precision, consequently, allows the natures of things to be considered in specific and generic fashions in such a manner that while expressing only the specific or generic traits they exclude none of the other determinations. As common natures they have no being of their own that would set the one up in exclusion of the other, according to the principle that follows upon being, the principle of contradiction. The one can be the other, whole can coincide completely with whole, predication through identity is possible. There is here no "Platonic Fallacy" that would establish the generic and specific natures as separate beings, for in their consideration as common or absolute natures they abstract from all being and have no being whatsoever of their own. But genus and species receive each its own being in the intellect, and the thing's nature can likewise be conceived as determining its generic aspect to the specific, that is, the nature can be conceived as the differentia. In this way the differentia has its own cognitional being apart from that of species and genus, and when considered as qualitative can be viewed as combining with the genus in the role of a part to form a third notion, the species. The Thomistic doctrine of abstraction without precision, accordingly, shows how Aristotle's metaphysical teaching that the ultimate difference includes the genus is actually in full accord with his apparently opposite logical statement: "Nor is the differentia generally thought to partake of the genus; for what partakes of the genus is always either a species or an individual, whereas the differentia is neither a species nor an individual. Clearly, therefore, the differentia does not partake of the genus" (*Top.*, IV 2, 122b20-23; Oxford tr.).

As qualitative, however, the differentia has to have its own being. As a determination of the genus it is set apart from the genus in the being that is given it in the intellect. In order to have that separate status as a differentia it has to *be* in this way. It can be placed outside the essence of its genus and still remain a differentia, but it cannot be placed outside being without ceasing to be a differentia. A common nature implicitly contains all its determinations as substantive, but does not include them as qualitative. Being, on the other hand includes all its determinations as qualitative. Where it is subsistent, in God, being as a substance includes in its own unity all the perfections of things. As a predicate, being extends in analogous ways to all things, even to all differentiae in their qualitative function. Its all-embracing extension does not allow it to taper off into the undiluted sameness of a genus. Because it extends to all possible differences, even as differences, it has to include them all in their differentiating function. Paradoxically, because it is most common it has to be all its own differences. The logic of predication shows that being has to be all its own differences. The logic of predication shows that being has to be most diverse because it is most common. Community, when pushed here to the furthest extreme, involves the greatest diversity. Being is so common that it has to be diverse in every instance. It requires reception in a subject other than itself in order to be diversified. But that subject is nothing in itself apart from being, and of itself can provide no actual diversification. It can function only as potency.[47] All the actuality of the diversification has to come from the new being that it participates.

As a predicate, then, being is at the same time the most common and the most diverse. But how is this possible from a metaphysical standpoint? Will it not make being a self-contradictory notion, like the notion of a square circle? Will it not give being the status of a meaningless frame of reference, to which nothing can conceivably correspond in reality? Could not this be an excellent case of a problem rising from the necessary use of language, and not from any distinct feature in reality?[48] Does it not make being rather an ultra-equivocal word that can be used indiscriminately for anything and everything, but has no meaning that could spark any legitimate metaphysical investigation? Or is there something peculiar about the way in which the notion "being" is obtained? It does not pertain to the natures of sensible things. It cannot be grasped, therefore, through a consideration of any of those natures in abstraction, in the way specific and generic notions are isolated. How, then, is the notion of being obtained by the human intellect? What is the doctrine of St. Thomas in this regard?

III

From his earliest writings on, St. Thomas makes very clear the location of being in sensible things, the things in which all human cognition takes its origins. Their being, he emphasizes, is not the being of form, nor of matter, but of the composite. This holds true even though, according to the traditional Aristotelian dictum, the form is in its own way the cause of the thing's being:

> ...esse substantie composite non est tantum esse forme nec tantum esse materiae sed ipsius compositi; essentia autem est secundum quam res esse dicitur. Vnde oportet ut essentia qua res denominatur ens non tantum sit forma nec tantum

materia sed utrumque, quamuis huius esse suo modo forma sit causa (De Ente, c. II; p. 10.2-7).

However, the De Ente et Essentia does not develop the theme that being pertains to the composite. It shows that being is other than the things's nature, is received by the thing as into a potency (C. IV; pp. 34.4-36.3), and is diverse in its various instances, while a specific or generic nature does not vary as nature in its different subjects (c. V; p. 37.18-21). The being that is always diverse is nevertheless regarded as universal— "illud esse uniuersale quo quelibet res formaliter est" (p. 38.1)—and as common (esse commune), though without any further explanation.

In the human soul, this being is sufficiently diverse to ensure individuation even after the soul is separated from matter:

> Et licet indiuiduatio ejus ex corpore occasionaliter dependeat quantum ad sui inchoationem, quia non acquiritur sibi esse individuatum nisi in corpore cuius est actus, non tamen oportet quod, subtracto corpore, indiuiduatio pereat quia cum habeat esse absolutum ex quo acquisitum est sibi esse indiuiduatum ex hoc quod facta est forma huius corporis, illud esse semper remanet indiuiduatum; et ideo dicit Auicenna quod indiuiduatio animarum et multitudo dependet ex corpore quantum ad sui principium set non quantum ad sui finem (c. V; p. 39.17-40.2).

The human soul enters into immediate composition with its being, though in the case of all other corporeal forms the being pertains not immediately to the form but to the composite.[49] The human soul's absolute being is such that it guarantees individuality even when the principle that is said to individuate the form, namely designated matter, has gone. In its inception that being may depend upon the occasion of the body, but it survives the union with matter and in surviving remains individual. Its individuality and so its diversity must therefore come principally from itself, rather than from the composite nature that receives it. But no further explanation is given in the De Ente et Essentia of the role played by the composite as such in accounting for the diversity of being.

In his commentary on the Sentences, however, the explanation is quite detailed. The aspect of being (ratio entis)[50] constitutes the subject of a single science metaphysics, yet it is diversified in diverse things:

> ...in communi sicut metaphysica, quae considerate omnia inquantum sunt entia, non descendens ad propriam cognitionem moralium, vel naturalium. Ratio enim entis, cum sit diversificata in diversis, non est sufficiens ad specialem rerum cognitionem (In I Sent., Prol., q.1, a.2, Solut,; ed. Mandonnet, I, 10).

As in the De Ente et Essentia, the community and the diversity of being are stated side by side without any embarrassment. The doctrine is likewise firmly set in the distinction between essence and being:

> ...cum enim in omni creatura differat essentia et esse, non potest essentia communicari alteri supposito, nisi secundum aliud esse, quod est actus essentiae, et ideo oportet essentiam creatam communicatione dividi (*In I Sent.*, d.4, q.1, a.1, ad 2m; I, 132).

When the essence or common nature is shared by several supposits, it has to participated according to other and other being. Because it has different being in every case, it is divided as often as it is participated. The difference or otherness of being in every instance becomes the reason for the division of the common essence among different supposits. Essence is regarded as the principle of unity, being is viewed as the principle of otherness or division.[51] The unifying principle, essence, and the diversifying principle, being, are known through two different intellectual operations. What is (*ens*) is grasped in the manner of a picture (*imaginatio intellectus*). As such it may well be complex in the way of a still life painting that consists of different and related elements; but it is not complex in the sense of exercising any engagement or variation in motion and time. It is regarded as though it were something steadily looked at, fixed in itself before the mind's eye as somehow a still and permanent unit. What is known through the other operation of the intellect however, is attained in the complex and dynamic fashion of a proposition in which something is declared to be or not to be, to be what it is nor not to be what it is not:

> Primum enim quod cadit in imaginatione intellectus, est ens, sine quod nihil potest apprehendi ab intellectu; sicut primum quod cadit in credulitate intellectus, sunt dignitates, et praecipue ista, contradictoria non esse simul vera: unde omni alia includuntur quodammodo in ente unite et distincte, sicut in principio (*In I Sent.*, d.8, q.1, a.3, Solut.; I, 200).

The notion of "what is" (*ens*) includes all things. It is therefore a unifying notion. Yet in it, to judge from the above reading of the text, all things remain distinct from one another. Each of them, according to what is attained in the other operation of the intellect, is what it is and is not what it is not. In its being each is diverse from all the others. In so far as they participate being, things are set apart from one another, even though in another way they are united through that participation.

The twofold operation of the intellect in attaining things is described in greater detail later in the same work:

> ...cum sit duplex operatio intellectus: una quarum dicitur a quibusdam imaginatio intellectus, quam Philosophus, III *De anima*, text. 21, nominat intelligen-

tiam indivisibilium, quae consistit in apprehensione quidditatis simplicis, quae alio etiam nomine formatio dicitur; alia est quam dicunt fidem, quae consistit in compositione vel divisione propositionis: prima operatio respicit quidditatem rei; secunda respicit esse ipsius (*In I Sent.*, d. 19, q. 5, a. 1, ad 7m; I, 489).

What is attained through the first-mentioned operation of the intellect (*imaginatio intellectus*) is now determined as the quiddity. This is obviously what was expressed by the term *ens* in the previous text. It continues to be regarded as something simple in the manner of a picture or intelligible form, something as it were flat and self-contained. It appears all together as a unit. It remains steady before the intellect's gaze. In that way it is considered indivisible, and so not as something complex. The thing's being, on the other hand, is grasped in more active fashion. It is not something presented in itself as a picture or form before the mind's eye. It is grasped rather by the actual joining or separating that is expressed by a proposition. From this viewpoint the quiddity as such is not something complex, but presents all its elements in the unity of a single stabilized picture or form. Yet the being that it enjoys can be known only by way of a complexity: "...quaelibet res incomplexa habet esse suum, quod non accipitur ab intellectu nisi per modum complexionis" (*ibid*)., p. 490). The thing's being, accordingly, presents itself to the intellect in the manner of a complexity.

In fact, as had been mentioned in the *De Ente et Essentia* (c. II; p. 10.2-4), a thing's being, at least in the sensible things from which human cognition takes its rise, is the being of a composite. It follows upon the composition of the matter and the form: "...esse consequitur compositionem materiae et formae."[53] "Composition" here seems meant in a rather dynamic sense. The essence with its various elements may be regarded as forming the one flat picture and from this viewpoint may be considered as incomplex in a way that allows it to be grasped by the first operation of the intellect; but the being that arises from the very composing of these elements cannot be grasped in that way. The being can be attained only as a conplexity. It is not the finished product of the composition, the already accomplished union of matter and form, or of subject and natures. That relation between them would be something fixed and settled. It would be attained by the first operation of the intellect. Rather, the second operation of the intellect grasps the existential uniting of the matter and form, or subject and nature, into the one single unit. The uniting lies in the being of the thing. In that sense it is dynamic, not flat like an image or picture. The radically different character of the two components of a thing, essence and being, requires accordingly the twofold operation of the intellect for knowledge of it:

> Cum in re duo sint, quidditas rei, et esse ejus, his duobus respondet duplex operatio intellectus. Una quae dicitur a philosophis formatio, qua apprehendit

quidditates rerum, quae etiam a Philosopho, in *III De anima*, dicitur indivisibilium intelligentia. Alia autem comprehendit esse rei, componendo affirmationem, quia etiam esse rei ex materia et forma compositae, a qua cognitionem accipit, consistit in quadam compositione formae ad materiam, vel accidentis ad subjectum.[54]

The compositions of matter and form, substance and accident, take place in being. So much is this so, that the being of these things, according to the above text, *consists* in such compositions, at least when the compositions are understood in a certain way. That way, as can be gathered from the text lies in the active uniting that corresponds in the thing to the dynamic composing in the intellect's act of affirmation. Such is the only type of being originally attained by the human intellect, and even the simplicity of the divine being has to be understood by it in the manner of a complexity: "Sed intellectus noster, cujus cognitio a rebus oritur, quae esse compositum habent, non apprehendit illud esse nisi componendo et dividendo" (*In I Sent.*, d. 38. q. 1, a. 3, ad 2m; I, 904).

Since in the real world the composition of matter and form always takes place in designated dimensions,[55] the composition will always be that of an individual. The being that follows upon that composition and consists in that composition will likewise have to be individual. The real being of sensible things, therefore, will be individual because it is a composition that is individual. It will have to be new in every separate case. As a finished product, as a set and established relation of union between the components, the completed composition of essential elements may be regarded as a state in the essential order and so may be conceptualized after the fashion of an essence. But the actual joining or composing of the two elements is not an essence at all. It is something that takes place in being. In the real order this is obvious enough. If the death of an animal is understood as substantial change, it means that the matter in the animal acquires a new substantial form. Of itself, that matter was not determined to either form, the one lost or the one newly acquired. The composition of this particular form with this particular matter does not follow from the nature of either, but is in the order of being. In fact, the presence of primary matter is known through the requirement of an enduring subject for the change from one substantial form to another. The very way in which primary matter is attained by the intellect shows that of its nature it is not determined to the form it actually posesses; and reciprocally, the form is not of its nature determined to that matter, else it could never lose that particular matter. Moreover, the same form acquires new matter in the phenomena of nutrition and growth.

The composition between matter and form in the real world, accordingly, is in the order of being. It is always between form and designated matter, and so

is always individual—"unumquidque secundum idem habet esse et individuationem" (Q. de An., I, 1, ad 2m; ed. Calcaterra-Centi, II, 284a). As a universal in the mind, human nature still consists of matter and form but not of
designated matter. There it will have the being that follows upon this composition, the being of a universal, that is, cognitional being. Such universal matter
can be joined to any specific form—man, horse, tree, stone, and so on. Of itself
it is determined to none of them specifically. It is composed with any one of
them in the cognitional being it acquires in the intellect. Similarly the specific
nature is not composed of itself with any particular individual, not the genus
with any definite species. That composing takes place in the intellect when it
grasps the being of the thing.

Since the being of each thing follows upon and consists in the composition of
its elements, the being of a man will be different from the being of a horse, and
the being of this individual man will differ from that being of that individual
man, as St. Thomas has stated in the Summa Theologiae (I, 3, 5c). The being
in each case is diversified according to the composition. Where the composition
is individual, as in the case of the sensible things in which human cognition
begins, the being is individual. Each new composing of the elements is not the
other, and so no one individual is the other. Being is diverse in every individual
instance.

Besides the terms already seen in the texts from the commentary on
Sentences describing the second operation of the intellect, namely credulitas
intellectus and fides, the word "judgement" is also used in this context to
denote the intellect's grasp of the thing's being.[56] The use of the term
"judgement" and the frequent occurrence of "enuntiatio" and "nuntiabile"
in these passages, show clearly enough that the problem in being discussed
against the background of Aristotle's De Interpretatione. There "truth and
falsity imply combination and separation" (Int., 1, 16a12-13; Oxford tr.); but
"there is no truth or falsity... unless 'is' or 'is not' is added, either in the present or in some other tense" (a17-18). This attaining of truth or falsity by the
affirmation or denial of being is still expressed in English translation by the
term "judgement": "spoken affirmations and denials are judgements expressed in words" (Int., 14, 24b1-2; Oxford tr.). Judicium was the Latin translation
used by St. Thomas. It was understood by him explicitly in the sense of an act
of cognition, an intellective act of apprehension by which the being of a thing
was known.[57] For Aristotle, such judgments were wrapped in the notion of
time. They involved a verb, and a verb by definition (Int., 3, 16b6) carried the
connotation of time: "There can be no affirmation or denial without a verb; for
the expressions 'is,' 'will be,' 'was,' 'is coming to be' and the like are verbs according to our definition, since besides their specific meaning they convey the
notion of time" (Int., 10, 19b12-14; Oxford tr.). It need hardly be surprising,
then, to find that time enters deeply into St. Thomas' discussion of the com-

position of a thing's elements in being.

In the commentary on the first book of the *Sentences*, the being of sensible things, in spite of its unity,[58] is described as intimately involving the divisive consequences of time: "Esse autem nostrum habet aliquid sui extra se: deest enim aliquid quod jam de ipso praeteriit, et quod futurum est" (*In I Sent.*, d.8, q.1, a.1, Solut.; 1, 195). Being as encountered in the sensible world, even though it is one, never brings itself together in time. At any given moment throughout the main part of its course, some of itself has already perished in the past, while more of itself is yet to be in the future. Some of it is definitely outside itself. It may in fact be called imperfect if it does not complete its full course in time: "... et sic dicitur esse imperfectum sui deest aliquid de spatio durationis debitae; sicut dicimus vitam hominis qui moritur in pueritia, imperfectam vitam" (ibid., q.2, a.1, ad 5m; p. 203).

In strict speech, of course, it is not the being of the thing that endures or is imperfect, but rather the thing itself on account of its being. Being in sensible things is never a subject, yet to be spoken about it has to be represented as subject. Continual therapy is necessary to prevent deception by the necessities of language and of logic. With the regular practice of such therapy, however, metaphysical discussion can be carried on, and being can be thought about and spoken about. Logic requires that being, when reasoned about or discussed, receive the status of a subject. So regarded, the being of material things may be said to be measured by time:

> Illud enim quod habet potentiam non recipientem actum totum simul, mensuratur tempore: hujusmodi enim habet esse terminatum et quantum ad modum participandi, quia esse recipitur in aliqua potentia, et non est absolutum quantum ad partes durationis, quia habet prius et posterius (*In I Sent.*, d.8, q.2, a.2, Solut.; I, 205).

Such being has durational parts before and after any given moment. It is not absolutely in itself as regards duration. It has parts spread out before and after its actuality, an actuality that occurs only in the present moment. It is far from all together, but rather is spread out according to the measure of time. As a result, all of it except the present is non-existent, is not. The being of material things is only in the present instance of time. Not only is it restricted to an individual composing of matter and form, but also it is doing that composing in a particular moment of time.

Indivisible in itself, then, a thing's being is spread out according to the measure of time. But what does this mean? Upon what is the spread in time really founded? The spread and the measure are based on cosmic motion. To the argument that the indivisibility of being requires an indivisible measure like eternity,[59] St. Thomas answers that the spread arises not from the nature of being but rather from the cosmic motion to which the being of material things is subject:

> ...esse rerum temporalium non mensuratur tempore nisi prout subjacet varia-tioni ex motu caeli. ...Et inde est quod omnia quae ordinatur ad motum caeli sicut ad causam, cujus primo mensura est tempus, mensurantur tempore (*In I Sent.*, d.19, q.2, a.1, ad 4; I, 469).

The being of temporal things, accordingly, is subject to continual change *(variatio)* along with the regular motion of the heavens. The substance of a sen-sible thing remains the same throughout all this motion, but its being is con-tinually changing. Its being is continually perishing in successive parts. It re-mains only in the present, which in turn is giving way for the immediately future part:

> Unde sicut est idem mobile secundum substantiam in toto motu, variatur tamen secundum esse, sicut dicitur quod Socrates in foro est alter a seipso in domo; ita nunc est etiam secundum substantiam in tota successione temporis, variatum tan-tum secundum esse, scilicet secundum rationem quam accepit prioris et posterioris. Sicut autem motus est actus ipsius mobilis inquantum mobile est; ita esse est actus existentis, inquantum ens est. Unde quacumque mensura mensuretur esse alicujus rei, ipsi rei existenti respondet nunc ipsius durationis, quasi mensura (*In I Sent.*, d.19, q.2, a.2, Solut.; I, 470-471.

The thing remains the same in substance throughout all the motion, but continually changes in being. In being it varies from instant to instant, while remaining all the while the same thing. A man like Socrates stays the same in-dividual, though he changes in being during the time he moves from place to place. His being is continually changing with the motion in which it is involv-ed. In the constitution of time, of course, the motion is what is real. The formal character of time comes only from the work of the intellect: "...et similiter est de tempore, quod habet fundamentum in motu, scilicet prius et posterius ip-sius motus; sed quantum ad id quod est formale in tempore, scilicet numeratio, completur per operationem intellectus numerantis."[60]

Sensible things, then, including men, have their being dependent upon con-tinued motion. Matter is the principle of mobility as well as of individuality—"omne quod habet materiam mobile est" (*In I Phys.*, lect. 1, 3). The being that you had one minute age is gone, though you remain the same person. The being that you will have an hour from now has not yet come, does not yet exist, if one may speak subject to the required therapy. As a result of this inevitable commitment to time, to know any individual thing properly as individual is to know its being in time:

...secundum opinionem Avicennae et ex dictis Algazelis, videtur sequi quod Deus enuntiabilia nesciat, et praecipue in rebus singularibus; quia ponunt quod scit singulatia tantum universaliter, id est in natura particularitatis suae. Unde concedunt quod scit hoc individuum et illud; sed non scit hoc individuum nunc esse et postmodum non esse; sicut si aliquis sciret eclipsim quae futura est cras in suis causis universalibus, non tamen sciret an modo esset vel non esset, nisi sensibiliter videret (*In I Sent.*, d.38, q.1, a.3, Solut.; I, 903).

To know any singular thing properly as singular (*in natura particularitatis suae*) you have to know its being in time (*nunc esse et postmodum non esse*). If you did not grasp its being in time, through sensation, you might know this or that individual, but only according to universal knowledge. Its being at any given moment is conditioned by time, and to know it as properly individual is to know it as existing in that particular time. Time so enters the individuality of every sensible thing that to grasp it as individual is to grasp it as in a definite instant of time. The divine mind knows all individuals not just in a causality that abstracts from time, but in their temporal conditions here and now. In consequence the divine intelligence knows all the conditions that pertain to the thing through both matter and form:

...forma quae est in mente artificis non est causa totius quod est in artificatio, sed tantum formae; et idea esse hanc domum, et caetera quae consequuntur naturam per formam artis, nescit artifex nisi sensibiliter accipiat: sed ideo quae est in mente divina, est causa omnis ejus quod in re est; unde per ideam non tantum cognoscit naturam rei, sed etiam hanc rem esse in tali tempore, et omnes conditiones quae consequuntur rem vel ex parte materiae vel ex parte formae (*In I Sent.*, d.38, q.1, a.3, ad 1m; I, 904).

The being of a thing, therefore, has to be grasped in all the complexity of its present circumstances. In a sensible thing it is strictly limited to the here and now,[61] as far as its actuality is concerned. It is limited to the "here," because it consists in the existential uniting of individuated components. It is restricted to the "now," because that uniting is taking place in the present instant of time; as it was in the past it no longer is, and as it will be in the future it does not yet exist.

The same doctrine regarding the being of sensible things continues through the later period of St. Thomas' writings. In the commentary on Aristotle's *Metaphysics*, the being that is other than the essence of a thing is as it were constituted by the principles of the essence—"quasi constituitur per principia essentiae" (*In IV Metaph.*, lect. 2, no. 558). This being is known by way of an intellectual composition that is conditioned by time, for it is being that occurs in a determined time:

Nam ens quod significat compositionem propositionis est praedicatum accidentale, quia compositio fit per intellectum secundum determinatum tempus. Esse
autem in hoc tempore vel in illo, est accidentale praedicatum (*In X Metaph.*, lect.
3, no. 1982).

The being that is expressed in a proposition is seen as occurring in a definite instant of time. From this occurrence in a particular point of time, the accidental
character of that being is established.

The composition in which the being itself consists had already been emphasized: "Esse autem, in quo consistit compositio intellectus, ut affirmatio,
compositionem quamdam et unionem indicat" (*In IX Metaph.*, lect. 11, no.
1900). As had been mentioned in the commentary on the *Sentences*, being
consists in a composition of a certain kind. Since being is other than essence,
the composition in which it consists will have to be outside the essential order
and so will not be a predicamental relation of union or anything else in the
manner of essence. In sensible things, which are composites of matter and
form, the being arises from the composing parts: "Sed esse compositorum
surgit ex componentibus" (ibid., no. 1903). This was explained as holding for
both substantial and accidental being (n. 1896-1902). In the substance of sensible things there is the physical composition of form with matter, and a logical
composition that resembles it, the composition of nature with individual:

Cum autem intellectus compositionem format, accipit duo, quarum unum se
habet ut formale respectu alterius: unde accipit id ut in alio existens, propter quod
praedicata tenentur formaliter. Et ideo, si talis operatio intellectus ad rem debeat
reduci sicut ad causam, oportet quod in compositis substantis ipsa compositio formae ad materiam, aut eius quod se habet per modum formae et materiae vel etiam
compositio accidentis ad subiectum, respondeat quasi fundamentum et causa
veritatis, compositioni, quam intellectus interius format et exprimit voce. Sicut
cum dico, Socrates est homo, veritas huius enunciationis causatur ex compositione
formae humanae ad materiam individualem, per quam Socrates est hic homo: et
cum dico, homo est albus, causa veritatis est compositio albedinis ad subiectum: et
similiter in aliis (*In IX Metaph.*, lect. 11, n. 1898).

This means that the composition of the substantial as well as of the accidental components of a thing takes place in being. With regard to accidents, it is
not hard to see. There is no reason in a man's nature as human nature why he
should be white. Human nature also allows the colors yellow, black, brown,
and red. That human nature and whiteness be actually joined together, is a fact
of being, not of essence. But the same holds for substantial composition. That a
particular substantial form should be joined to its matter, is a question of being. Its matter can be joined to another substantial form successively, for matter
functions as the subject that changes from one form to another. The union bet-

ween matter and form is in being. From the composition of the two the being arises, viewed from this standpoint. Neither the form is, nor the matter is, properly speaking, but the composite of both. It is the actual composition of the parts that corresponds to and causes the truth in the proposition, for that composition in the thing is composition in being. It is not a still life picture that lies all spread out at once before the mind, but the dynamic existential uniting that is the being of the thing, grasped by the act of judgment. To accept the actual composition is to accept the one as *being* in the other—*in alio existens.*

Likewise in the commentary on the *Perihermeneias,* the being that is expressed in the proposition intimately involves time. The operation by which the intellect composes and divides is distinguished as in the other works from the operation by which it grasps the essence in itself and as an indivisible.[62] The proposition signifies being.[63] But this being, in which the judgment of the intellect is expressed, is added to the subject in a definite time. Simply taken, it is restricted to the present time:

> ...quando additur *esse* vel *non esse,* per quae exprimitur iudicium intellectus. Potest autem addi *esse* vel *non esse,*vel secundum praesens tempus, quod est esse vel non esse in *actu,* et ideo hoc dicitur esse *simpliciter;* vel secundum tempus praeteritum aut futurum, quod non est esse simpliciter, sed *secundum quid;* ut cum dicitur aliquid fuisse vel futurm esse (*In I Periherm.,* lect. 3, no. 13).

The being of things in the past is only in the memory, and the being of things in the future is known only in their causes. What actually exists is in the present and is perceptible through the senses:

> ...anima in componendo et dividendo necesse habet adiungere tempus, ut dicitur in III *De anima;* consequens est quod sub eius cognitione cadant res sub ratione praesentis, praeteriti et futuri. Et ideo praesentia cognoscit tanquam actu existentia et sensu aliqualiter perceptibilia; praeterita autem cognoscit ut memorata; futura autem non cognoscit in seipsis, quia nondum sunt, sed cognoscere ea potest in causis suis (*In I Periherm.,* lect. 14, no. 19).

The being that is attained in the second operation of the intellect, accordingly, has to be grasped under the aspect of time, whether present, past or future. Actual being, or being as it is simply understood, occurs only in the present time.

Just as in the other works, being involves the composition of form and subject, whether that composition be substantial or accidental. To signify that a form is present in a subject, the verb "is" is used. It signifies according to time, as outlined in the text just quoted. Aristotle is interpreted in the sense that being is in a way the actuality of every form:

Ideo autem dicit quod hoc verbum EST consignificat compositionem, quia non eam principaliter significat, sed ex consequenti; significt enim primo illud quod cadit in intellectu per modum actualitatis absolute: nam EST, simpliciter dictum, significat *in actu esse;* et ideo significat per modum verbi. Quia vero actualitas, quam principaliter significat hoc verbum EST, est communiter actualitas omnis formae, vel actus substantialis vel accidentalis, inde est quod cum volumus significare quamcumque formam vel actum actualiter inesse alicui subiecto, significamus illud per hoc verbum EST, vel *simpliciter* vel *secundum quid:* simpliciter quidem secundum praesens tempus; secundum quid autem secundum alia tempora. Et ideo ex consequenti hoc verbum EST significat compositionem (*In I Periherm.,* lect. 5, no. 22).

This text states explicitly that the actuality signified by the verb "being" is more than just a formal union that would pertain to the essential order, whether substantial or accidental. The composing is a further actuality, over and above the whole order of form. Though the verb "is" signifies the actual composition of form with subject, the notion of "composition" is not uppermost in what it signifies, but rather accompanies the aspect that it principally signifies. What it signifies first and foremost is the most basic of all actualities in the thing. That is the being of the thing, and in sensible things it consists in an existential composition. In expressing the being of the thing, the verb "is" signifies that "composition" aspect concomitantly, and so in Aristotelian phraseology may be said to "consignify" it.

In a word, the two aspects, composition and being, are both present in any such uniting of essential components, either in reality or in cognition. They are two aspects of the same actuality in sensible things. But of the two, the priority is held by being. There is composition because there is being. The composition is existential because "being" is its absolutely prior characteristic. Without the composing, of course, there could be no sensible being, for there the being consists in the composing. In one sense, indeed, the being may be said to follow upon the composing and to arise from the composition, in correspondence with the Thomistic technique that allows being to follow upon form in one order of causality even though being is absolutely prior to form.[64] But from the viewpoint of actuality pure and simple, the being comes first.[65] The being as it proceeds from its efficient cause results thereby in its own determination, or better, if one may be permitted to use the expression, its self-determination,[66] to conditions of here and now. If it did not result in this self-determination, which is an essence other than itself, it could not proceed from an efficient cause, it would be something in its own right, it would be that which is, and so subsistent, uncaused being. Where the self-determination is the essence of a material thing, this self-determination is conditioned by matter, the principle both of individuation and of mobility. The being, in absolute priority as act, unites the matter and form in existential composition according to these conditions of place and time, and thereby is its own diversification not only in the individuality of designated matter, but also in the durational particularity of each successive and ever fleeting moment of time.

From the viewpoint of logical construction, subject and predicate are regarded as the prior elements in a proposition. They are regarded as already had by the mind through simple apprehension, and then as joined or separated through the act of judgment. In logical analysis, consequently, the incomplex notions of the subject and of the predicate are given the more basic role, and their composition or separation becomes a subsequent function. Since the two operations of the intellect have been traditionally described in logical setting of the *Perihermeneias* (1-5), with its concern for truth and falsity, they have been named according to the order in which they are viewed by the logician. The apprehension of incomplex objects or of things according to their essence is called the first operation of the intellect, and the apprehension of things in the complexity of their being is called the second operation of the intellect. From the logician's standpoint that order is correct, but in metaphysics it can be the occasion of a far-reaching illusion. In a finite thing there is no possibility of having as essence without existence or an existence without essence. The two have to go together. The acts of the intellect by which they are grasped correspond to them and likewise have to go together. There is no possibility of grasping a thing according to its essence in simple apprehension without simultaneously grasping it according to its being, either real or cognitional as the case may be. Simple apprehension and judgment, consequently, always accompany each other. But just as in the thing it is being that enjoys the absolute priority, so in the activity of the intellect it is judgment that has the priority, in its sense of the knowledge of the thing according to the thing's being. When the logician gives priority to the incomplex being enjoyed by that nature at the moment, being that he simultaneously grasps he regards it in his mind, or with its real being if he regards it in the outside world—"Logicus enim considerat modum praedicandi, et non existentiam rei."[67] He takes for granted that the subject and predicate already have being, and devotes himself to examining the function they have in his constructions. But the metaphysician, in St. Thomas' view, is primarily concerned with that being in its priority to the essence. For the metaphysician the judgment that a thing exists means that the thing has been attained according to its being and according to its essence, in their respective priorities of act and formal determination. It does not mean, for him, that he has taken two incomplex notions, namely thing and being, and then joined them together in a complex construct. In this doctrine the priority of synthesis to conceptualization is as operative as in Kant; though it corresponds to, and for truth has to be dependent upon, the synthesizing priority of being in the thing. Likewise the stability of essences is firmly placed in reality itself, not just in separate snapshots taken by the intellect; while the deepest reality in sensible things, their being, is immersed just as thoroughly as with Bergson in the ever changing flux of time.

On account of its absolute priority, then, being provides its own diversification when it actuates a mobile substance in time and place. As it has to provide its own self-determination in its particular essence, so in material things it diversifies itself in each new existential composition and at each successive moment. The matter and form that it joins together in making them be, the specific and generic natures that it unites with the individual, and even the fixed relations of one to the other, may as essences have their own universality and eternity,[68] but the actual composing takes place in a definite designation of matter and at the present moment of time. The being is diverse in every instance. The only being that is directly known by the human intellect is the being of material things. From them the intellect has to reason to the proportional diversification of being in immaterial substances through specific natures and eternity, and to the unicity and eternity of subsistent being through its pure simplicity. But from the being that it directly knows, the intellect has sufficient data to show how any act of being that proceeds from an efficient cause thereby diversifies itself from any and every other act of being.

IV

If being, though, is so radically diverse in its every instance, how can it be the most common of all predicates? "Being" is a predicate that can be applied to all things without exception, just as "corporeal" can be predicated of all sensible things. It is conceptualized after the fashion of an incomplex essence, like animality or corporeity. In this guise it is made the subject of assertions, as has been done throughout the course of this paper. It has to be so conceptualized if one is to reason about it or speak about it. How is this possible?

There are, accordingly, two parts to the problem. The more basic is that of the way in which being, attained originally through the judgment and not through simple conceptualization, can be subsequently conceptualized on the model of an incomplex nature. The second concerns how it becomes, when so conceptualized, the most common of all concepts even though it is radically diverse in every instance. The first part of the problem has to be seen against the general background of all human thought. The intellect resolves all its conceptions into "that which is," the composite in which all its cognition originates—ens. To understand anything, to reason about anything, to speak about anything, the intellect has to represent it as something that is. It has to represent it as a nature that has being. Even the two entitative principles of what is (ens), namely being and essence, have to be represented each as "something that is," as an ens. Each is simpler than the composite to which together they give rise, but each has to be represented in terms of that composite and never in terms of itself. The essence just in itself has no being, it is actually nothing. Yet to think of it in contrast to its being, the intellect has to represent it as a being. Its being (esse), likewise, is not something. Only in the unique case of subsistent being, is being a thing. Yet the intellect has to represent created being as something, as an existent, as a being, if it is to reason about it or speak about it.

Represented in this way, being is conceived as something that exists. It is represented, therefore, as an existent nature or essence. If the term "concept" may be used today to denote the grasping of a thing according to its essence,[69] one may say that being is represented in such a concept. But unlike the concept of a nature, the concept of being cannot be originally obtained through abstraction. The intellect may abstract successively from individuating notes, and from specific and generic traits up to the highest genus, but after that nothing more can be abstracted. Being, if so abstracted, would be the equivalent of nothing. As being is grasped by way of dynamic composition, any attempt to "abstract" here would actually be to separate, and so would result in a judgment of not-being instead of being.[70] The two would become confused in each other. But the judgment is an act of knowing. Through it the intellect knows the thing's being, in entitative union with the thing. To separate the two, and to represent the being, so known, in contrast to the thing, it has to represent that being as a further nature. To understand accidents in contrast to their substances, it has to represent those accidents themselves as substances. It has to think of "walking" and "talking" as though they were things in themselves, just as it represents the color "white" as "whiteness." It knows "being" as an act through judgment, and so can represent it under the general concept of an act, even though it did not originally attain it through a concept.[71] It can conceive it as the act of all acts. In analyzing for logical purposes its knowledge that Socrates exists, it can represent being as *something* that is said of or predicated of the subject Socrates, and of any other subject whasoever, even of that act itself[72] when standing as the subject of a proposition.

The other part of the problem is less difficult. No matter how individual or restricted anything is, when it is represented in a concept by the simple apprehension of the intellect it is represented as universal. Even the concept "individual" is universal, and can be predicated of any singular thing.[73] As a universal it is a concept of the second intention, while in the first intention an individual is signified by terms like "Paul." "Being," as originally known in the judgment, antecedes all such concepts of itself, and so when represented in a concept of the first intention can be common even though what was originally known is restricted to the here and now. As common, however, it can exist only in the intellect.[74] Hence the being that is isolated and represented by way of an incomplex concept is not the *esse tantum*[75] that is reached by tracing the finite act of being to its source in subsistent being. In that demonstration the starting point is the being that is actually known by judgment in a particular existent thing and that is caused efficiently by some other thing and ultimately by a cause that is *esse tantum*. Hence St. Thomas repeatedly insists that *esse commune* is not *esse divinum*. Divine being excludes all possibility of addition, but common being allows the restrictive addition of limiting essences. Even though each new act of being is diverse in itself, it is the effect of the one common cause. Moreover, it is the participation, through efficient though not through formal causality, of the one nature of being.[76] This is amply sufficient to render being analogously common to all things. Yet in its conceptualization after the fashion of an incomplex nature, being inevitably loses the complexity in which its actual force consists. The *esse tantum* that is demonstrated as the first efficient cause of the being which is actually judged in things, literally *is* existence, subsistent in itself; but the *esse commune* that is the incomplex conceptualization of all being, merely *has* existence through an act of cognitional being that is other than itself. A common nature like "animal," because originally attained as a nature through conceptualization, can retain the same force as a nature both in cognitional and in real existence. "Being," on the other hand, because grasped originally as an act other than the sensible thing's nature, cannot retain its original force of giving being when it is conceptualized after the fashion of an incomplex nature.[77] Even though it is explicitly represented as infinite in content, it cannot furnish any ground in this conceptualization for reasoning to the real existence of being as a nature in God. The ontological argument for the existence of God is not possible in the doctrine of St. Thomas.

V

The fundamental teachings of St. Thomas on being, then, amply justify the twofold series of assertions on its diversity and community. Being is diverse in every instance, yet is most common to all things. All things are diverse in being, yet they coincide in being. Being as a nature cannot be diverse. As subsistent in God, it is unique.[78] But it can be participated by other things, and diversified in them.[79] As a nature, being contains all perfections and all actual determinations in its own ineffable unity. When participated, it provides the actuality of each determination and each diversification through the particular essence that is its own self-determination. In sensible things it is the existential composing of the essential parts according to designated dimensions and at the present moment of time. It thereby diversifies itself under the conditions of here and now. Known originally through the active engagement of the judgment, it is subsequently conceptualized as the first and basic actuality of things. So conceptualized it extends analogously to all things, even to its own determinations in their very role of determining it. It is therefore of unlimited content as well as extent. But the price paid is drastic. When represented as transcendentally common in the manner of an incomplex notion, it does not convey the complexity in which the being of a thing actually consists. To signify the actual existing, it has to be referred back in every diversity. Where it cannot be referred back to such an immediate apprehension of being, for example in the case of the divine existence, being, in its simple and common conceptualization, is detached from its actual meaning. As common it presents only a pale and infecund shadow of the unfathomable act of all acts and perfection of all perfections, the act that subsists as a nature in God and is participated as an act other than a nature in everything else.

AQUINAS AND THE FIVE WAYS

I

Do the well-known "five ways" in the *Summa of Theology* represent satisfactorily the attitude of Thomas Aquinas towards the demonstration of God's existence?[1] There are reasons for doubt. In their mode of expression, the "five ways" are puzzling. They are of conflicting historical provenance. They do not make clear whether they are more than one or just one proof, whether they are entirely metaphysical in character, or whether they need to be prolonged or completed to reach the Christian God.[2] Nowhere else in Aquinas is this fivefold arrangement used. Even the fivefold grouping in the chronologically close *Summa against the Gentiles* differs significantly.[3] The early commentary on the *Sentences* groups three "ways," all attributed to the pseudo-Areopagite[4] but accepted by Aquinas as leading to God from creatures.[5] The commentary also offers the Neoplatonic argument from observed plurality to a primal One.[6] Elsewhere other groupings and other arguments are used.[7]

On the other hand, a single and differently worded demonstration from the accidental character of observed existence was presented in the early treatise *On Being and Essence*, and was used repeatedly in the commentary on the *Sentences*.[8] Yet in the late *Compendium of Theology* only the argument from motion, the first of the "five ways," is found.[9] The "ways," in fact, seem open to easy synthesis,[10] as well to the suggestion that they do not really express Aquinas's own thought.[11]

There is room, then, for an inquiry into the relation of Aquinas himself to the "five ways" of the *Summa of Theology*, quite apart from the question of their validity or nonvalidity as purely philosophical arguments.

II

First, there can be no doubt whatever that in the *Summa of Theology*, Aquina's own attitude towards the five ways is entirely positive. In answer to the formally placed question "Does God exist?" the sole and unequivocal answer given is: "That God exists can be proven in five ways" (*ST*, I, 2, 3, c). There is no hesitation or qualification of any kind. The answer to the question is affirmative, and the sole justification offered for the affirmative answer consists in the five ways of demonstration that follow. The five ways are accordingly regarded as sufficient for the demonstration in the context of Aquina's *own* thought, for the *Summa of Theology* has to be viewed as a "personal" work and in no way a commentary on somebody else's text. Moreover, the conclusions of the five ways are the basis for the cogent positive theology about the attributes and operations of God that follows. According to all criteria, the reasoning here is that of Aquinas himself. The starting points of the reasoning, namely the conclusions of the five ways, are in consequence accepted by him as adequately demonstrated by these arguments.

All this is true and incontrovertible. Yet the suspicion arises that it is giving only one side of the question. In the *Summa against the Gentiles*, close enough in time to the *Summa of Theology*, four of these same five ways are presented as "arguments by which both philosophers and Catholic teachers have proved that God exists."[12] The way by means of contingency, which is omitted in the grouping in the *Summa against the Gentiles*, is given two chapters later in language that indicates the Latin Avicenna. Elsewhere (*De Pot.*, V, 3, c) it is explicitly attributed to Avicenna by Aquinas. It refers to Aristotle for the proof that an infinite series in efficient causes is impossible, and in general shows an easily recognizable Aristotelian background, even thought its terminology and immediate formulation are Arabian in character.[13]

All the five ways of the *Summa of Theology*, then, are found introduced, in works that preceded this *Summa*, as arguments evolved by other thinkers. They are not presented as Aquinas's own formulations. This conclusion is fully as solid as the one drawn above about the personal acceptance on the part of Aquinas of the reasoning contained in those five ways. Moreover, there is not the least hint of any incompatibility in this twofold attitude. In the *Summa against the Gentiles*, just as in the *Summa of Theology*, Aquinas proceeds to use the conclusions of the ways to work out his own positive theology. The procedure is exactly the same whether the ways are labeled as those of other thinkers or simply as the five ways by which the existence of God may be proved. The external or internal provenance of the ways seems a matter of indifference as far as the points at issue for Aquinas are concerned.

This means, clearly enough, that the five ways have to be regarded both as the arguments of Aquinas himself and as the arguments of other thinkers. As in the case of motion and rest in Plato's *Sophist* (249CD), both sides of the question have to be accepted in order to save the phenomena. To see in the five ways the reasoning of other philosophers or theologians, then, is not automatically to deny them the character of Aquinas's own thought. Yet the problem that is raised by this situation becomes difficult. How can arguments that did not prove the existence of God (in the Christian sense) be seen as identical with those that do?

The "first way" stems from Aristotle, with whom it reached a multiplicity of finite movements.[14] Aquinas recognizes that the Aristotelian reasoning presupposed eternal cosmic motion and required souls in the heavenly bodies.[15] Yet without these tenets, acknowledged as essential for Aristotle, he finds the argument much stronger![16] What has happened?

The nerve of the argument in both thinkers is that potentiality is actualized only by something already in actuality. For Aristotle, to be actualized meant to acquire form. For Aquinas, it meant to be brought into existence, since for him existence is the actuality of every form of nature.[17] For Aquinas, consequently, the conclusion reached by the argument can be located only in the unique subsistent existence that is recognized at once as the God seen in the patristic interpretation of "I am who I am" (Exodus, 3:14) and described as the "unlimited and undetermined ocean of being."[18] The argument, then, remained the same in structure and procedure when used by Aristotle to reach a multiplicity of celestial souls and finite separate substances, and when used by Aquinas to prove the existence of the unique and infinite God. But the respective assessments of actuality cause radical difference in the result of the demonstration.

No incompatibility could be felt in this double bookkeeping at an epoch in which each thinker use Aristotelian texts freely to support his own individual thinking. As Aristotle did in regard to his predecessors, the medievals believed they were stating clearly the same notions that the Greeks could express only imperfectly. True, Aquinas nowhere writes that he is proceeding in this manner. He regards the "five ways" definitely both as the arguments of other thinkers and as reasoning to which he himself unhesitatingly adheres. The historian is left with the task of explaining how the same argument can reach a radically different result in Aquinas from that of its source.

One historical fact that may be documented, however, is that Aquinas can regularly see in the acquiring of existence the probative force of the arguments of other thinkers, even though they themselves make no mention of the reception of existence. He finds three ways (called both *viae* and *modi*) in the Pseudo-Dionysius (*On the Divine Names*, VII, 3; *PG*, 3 871), and in all three sees the operative reason in the reception of existence: "And the reason for that is, that the existence of a creature is from another. Hence in this manner we are led to the cause from which it comes."[19] In accordance with that norm he goes on to interpret the ways of knowing God that had been collected by Peter Lombard from Ambrose and Augustine. The same method of interpretation may be noted in a work of the middle period: "...philosophers as Plato, Aristotle and their disciples, attained to the study of universal being: and hence they alone posited a universal cause of things, from which all others came into being, as Augustine states."[20] Likewise one reads in the late period: "...and these were the Platonists...Since therefore all things that exist participate being, and are beings by way of participation, there must be at the peak of all things something that is being by its essence, that is, its essence must be its being; and this is God..."[21] These texts indicate sufficiently that Aquinas regularly sees in certain arguments of the philosophers and theologians the procedure that he himself formulates in the commentary on the *Sentences* and in *On Being and Essence.*[22] His framework is that the existence grasped in sensible things through judgment is not a constituent of the thing's nature but comes to the thing from something else and ultimately from subsistent being. He can accordingly regard these arguments as the demonstrations formed by other thinkers and at the same time, from his own and different viewpoint, as valid ways of proving God's existence.

The openness of Aristotelian procedure from motion—as taken over in the first way in the *Summa of Theology*—to this twofold interpretation is quite apparent. Sensible motion can be regarded as the acquiring of a new accident or as the acquiring of new being. Both are occurring for Aquinas in the process of movement. Both result concomitantly from the action of the efficient cause: "Further, to this genus of cause is reduced everything that makes anything to be in any manner whatsoever, not only as regards substantial being, but also as regards accidental being, which occurs in every kind of motion."[23] Approached only from the viewpoint of the new accident, as in Aristotle, the argument leads to a plurality of finite movements. Regarded from the standpoint of the new existence that keeps actuating potentiality in the thing being moved, as with Aquinas, the demonstration results in nothing less than the unique Christian God.

The "second way" in the *Summa of Theology* is explicitly based on efficient causality. A thing cannot be its own efficient cause, for in that case it would exist before itself.[24] Here as elsewhere with Aquinas, the operative notion in efficient causality is the bestowal of existence. A thing whose nature is not existence has to acquire existence from something else and ultimately from a cause that is existence. In this form the argument is obviously not Aristotelian, though it is attributed expressly to the Stagirite in the *Summa against the Gentiles* (I, 13, Procedit). The argument is found by Aquinas in the second book of Aristotle's *Metaphysics* (II, 994a5-7; 18-19). There efficient causality is explained only in terms of motion, and the requirement of a "first cause" for any series of causes is established. The argument is not directed by Aristotle towards proving the existence of God. Yet read with Aquinas's concept of efficient cause as the bestower of existence, that is exactly what it does prove.

The "third way" starts from the observable fact that some things come into being and perish. Their existence is accordingly contingent, dependent upon something that exists necessarily, and ultimately caused by something that has no cause for its own necessity. For the proof that a gradated series of necessary beings must have a first cause, it refers to the corresponding proof in the second way. The starting point of the argument is easily found in Aristotle.[25] The further development is attributed to Avicenna and is extended to meet the plurality of necessary beings as found in Averroës. The Arabian background is outlined in a work of Aquinas that may be dated after the *Summma against the Gentiles* and shortly before the first part of the *Summa of Theology*, namely *On the Power of God* (V, 3). This indicates sufficiently that the argument in the "third way" is looked upon as a proof given by other thinkers, quite as the other four ways were designated in the earlier *Summa against the Gentiles* (I, 13, init.). Yet in both these preceding works the operative force of the argument is seen in the acquiring of existence from a cause. The version expressly attributed to Avicenna states the contingency of things in the regular Thomistic observation that their existence is over and above (*praeter*) their essence: "Because seeing that being is something besides the essence of a created thing, the very nature of a creature considered in itself has a possibility of being" (*De Pot.*, v, 3,c; Dominican trans.). Similarly the *Summa against the Gentiles* states: "But what can be has a cause because, since it is equally related to two contraries, namely, being and nonbeing, it must be owing to some cause that being accrues to it" (I, 15, Amplius; trans. Pegis). Overtly, then, Aquinas in the "third way" is taking an argument that he attributes to Avicenna and is reading it in his own existential framework as outlined in *On Being and Essence*.

The argument from the grades of being, which constitutes the "fourth way" in the *Summa of the Theology*, is described in the other *Summa* as "gathered from the words of Aristotle" (*SCG*, I, 13, Potest; trans. Pegis) in the second and fourth books of the *Metaphysics*.[26] In neither place in Aristotle is there question of proving the existence of God, in the sense of the the unique Christian Deity, but rather of a plurality of principles that "themselves are the cause of the being of other things" (*Metaph.*, II, 1,993b30; Oxford trans.). Yet Aquinas reads the argument as leading to a single being, namely "something that is for all existents the cause of existence and goodness and every perfection whatsoever." This is exactly what follows when graded existence is regarded as an actuality participated by subjects other than itself, as in *On Being and Essence* and the numerous passages in the commentary on the *Sentences*.

The "fifth way" is taken from "the directing of things" to an end. The argument is attributed to John Damascene, and in some manner to Averroës.[27] The starting point is particular, not universal: "certain things lacking knowledge, namely bodies on the level of nature, act on account of a goal." The conclusion is: "There is, then, an intelligent something by which all things of nature are directed to their goal. This we call God." The argument is hardly the one from design that has been made notorious by Kant and Paley. The presence of design in the universe is not the operative feature. It is rather the *directing* according to design, for this directing has to come ultimately from an immobile and self-necessary principle. In reply to the objection that agents less than God could ultimately account for the directing, Aquinas answers: "But all things mobile and capable of failing have to be accounted for by a first principle that is immobile and that is necessary by reason of its own nature, as has been shown"(*ST*, I, 2, 3, ad 2m). The cogency of the argument is accordingly seen by Aquinas in the manner in which it falls into the framework of the first and third "ways," which in turn is that of *On Being and Essence* and the commentary on the *Sentences*. In Damascene, on the other hand, the force of the argument lay in the requirement of a omnipotent power to hold together the jarring components of the universe and perpetually keep them from dissolution, while in Averroës the argument was insinuated by the metaphysician's need for the principle of finality to prove God's solicitude for the things of this world.[28]

The "five ways," consequently, are arguments taken from other thinkers but understood by Aquinas in the framework of his own metaphysics of existence. The pattern is clearcut. Existence is not contained within the natures of sensible things, it comes to them from an efficient cause, and ultimately from subsistent existence. Ways of embodying this demonstration are seen in traditionally accepted arguments. One way is seen in the Aristotelian argument from motion. There the actuality is different from the observed potentiality. It comes from something already actual in that regard, and ultimately from something that is actuality without potentiality. Where actuating takes place through existence, this way can lead only to subsistent existence. Similarly, where the being of sensible things is found caused, contingent, or participated, as in the second, third and fourth ways, it has to come from uncaused, self-necessary, and subsistent being. Finally, where things are found directed towards an end, the directing, if mobile and contingent in its existence, requires ultimately an absolutely immobile self-necessary principle, already located in subsistent existence. All five ways are probative for Aquinas, because all five can be understood as starting from observed sensible things in which existence is other than nature, and as proceeding to existence identified with nature, which is the Judeo-Christian God as named in Exodus.

III

This understanding of the "five ways" can be tested by examining the arguments expressly rejected by Aquinas and those not included in his writings, as well as those not listed in the *Summa of Theology* but accepted by him elsewhere as valid. If those not accepted are such that they do not fit into the existential framework of *On Being and Essence*, while those accepted in other places do function in that framework, the criterion for a valid proof will appear quite convincingly to be its capability of being understood as the procedure from the accidental existence of sensible thing to the subsistent existence of God.

The most notorious instance is the rejection by Aquinas of the Anselmian argument.[29] Its starting point is the notion of something than which nothing greater can be thought. It would be acceptable to Aquinas only if the real existence of the object concerned were already contained in the starting point. As this is not granted, the argument is rejected as invalid. The reason back of the rejection seems to be that perfection known merely by concepts, even if expanded to the infinite, will never contain existence, since existence is grasped originally by judgment and not by conceptualization. The argument patently cannot fit into the framework of *On Being and Essence*, for it is not explaining accidentally possessed existence through subsistent existence.

Also rejected is the argument that the existence of God is known through some likeness of him or some transcendental notion naturally implanted in human cognition. The reason for the rejection is that the likeness does not make one aware of "God as he is in his own nature,"[30] and that a general notion does not show the existence of a designated particular (*ST*, I, 2, 1, ad 1m). This is applied explicitly to the transcendental notions of truth and goodness that are present in every mind. Likewise the argument from divine illumination, namely that God as the intelligible light in which all things are understood should be immediately known just as the corporeal light is seen along with sensible things, is set aside on the ground that all human knowledge comes naturally from sensibly perceptible things.[31] These arguments are classed as ones meant to make the existence of God self-evident to men. Aquinas regards them as *inferring* the existence of a personal God from a likeness or general notion. But they do not proceed by taking the existence of the image or the notion as something accidental and then by reasoning to subsistent existence. They could not do this without abandoning the quasi-immediate way of inferring God's existence. In consequence this way of arguing cannot be made to fit into the existential framework developed in *On Being and Essence* and in the commentary on the *Sentences*.

The present-day argument from religious experience would seem to come under this type of inference. Here the phenomena are finite manifestations. They are not to be identified with the infinite divine existence. They require some sort of inference if they are to attest the existence of a personal God. But the starting point is the nature of the phenomena, not their accidental existence.[32]

Another argument not used by Aquinas is the inference from the alleged common consent of mankind.[33] This procedure could not by any stretch of interpretation be brought under the reasoning from accidentally possessed existence to subsistent existence. Further, the moral argument, made prominent by Kant and used so powerfully by Newman, infers from one's consciousness of responsibility the God before whom one is responsible.[34] It is obviously not able to be read in the existential framework of On Being and Essence. Finally, the argument from design, in which the existence of God is inferred on the analogy of the universe with a mechanism, remains in the area of natures—as the designed mechanism of a watch requires a watchmaker, so the designed nature of the universe requires an intelligent cause.[35] The procedure is not from purposive actualization to subsistent existence. Consequently the argument cannot be brought under the existential interpretation of Aquinas. It is not the "fifth way" in which the analogy does not appear and where the example of the archer shooting the arrow is an instance of guiding that requires an immobile and self-necessary principle for its ultimate explanation.

On the other hand, there are arguments for the existence of God taken from preceding thinkers and recognized as valid by Aquinas, even though they are not listed under the "five ways" of the Summa of Theology. There is the Neoplatonic argument accredited to Pseudo-Dionysius and accepted by Aquinas as a demonstration.[36] It argues from cosmic multiplicity to a unique first principle, God. Since unity for Aquinas is a transcendental property of being, this argument is readily understood in terms of being. Being implies unity, so multiplied being means that being is participated by things other than itself. With the difference established in this manner between things and their being, the argument can easily be read in the metaphysical framework of On Being and Essence. Similarly, along with proofs from goodness and beauty, the Augustinian argument from truth is acceptable if understood in the sense that the limited truth knowable to man requires a primary and unlimited truth.[37] This regards truth as a transcendental property of being, and allows the argument to fit into the framework in which participated being grounds cogent reasoning to subsistent being.

The character of the arguments accepted by Aquinas and that of the ones rejected or unused by him, point alike to the same conclusion. Arguments taken from other thinkers are regarded as valid if they can be understood in the framework that starts with accidentally possessed existence and reasons to subsistent existence. Arguments that cannot be read in that way are not looked upon as valid. The reason, moreover, emerges clearly enough from the overall metaphysical tenets of Aquinas. For him the nature of God is existence, and the characteristic effect of God in creatures is existence.[38] Existence is consequently the one philosophical path from immediately known things to God, at least by way of cogent reasoning. Other arguments may vividly suggest the existence of God, press it home eloquently to human consideration, and for most people provide much greater spiritual and religious aid than difficult metaphysical demonstration. But on the philosophical level these arguments are open to rebuttal and refutation, for they are not philosophically cogent. Remaining on the side of the nature of any observable object or event, one reaches cogently no further than a finite nature or agent. Only from the starting point of its existence, which is not a nature in the finite thing, does the human mind encounter with Aquinas a path for cogent reasoning to existence as a nature, that is, to the existence of God.

IV

Does this conclusion mean, then, that for Aquinas every cogent philosophical argument for the existence of God has to be metaphysical in character? The answer to this question, quite obviously, will depend on the acceptation given the term "metaphysical" in the context. If "metaphysical" is to have the same connotation as "ontological" here, then the demonstration of Aquinas is definitely not the type of argument that bears this connotation when one is speaking of arguments for the existence of God. The ontological argument does not proceed from what is grasped through judgment, but only from what is known through conceptualization. The demonstration of Aquinas, on the contrary, proceeds from the existence of sensible things. If "metaphysical" is meant to exclude sensibly existent things from the starting point of Aquinas, then it does not apply to his demonstration. All five ways in the *Summa of Theology* start from things existent in the physical world.

If, on the other hand, the term "metaphysical" may be understood as referring to what is beyond the *nature* of physical things, namely their existence, the demonstration of Aquinas is genuinely metaphysical. The first and the fifth ways, in regard to those who originally used the arguments, took their start on the plane of the philosophy of nature. But they both were open to interpretation on the plane of existence as the actuality towards which things were being moved and directed. The other three ways, starting respectively from the acquisition, contingence and participation of being, lend themselves at once to metaphysical interpretation. Functioning on the plane of existence and not of nature, the five ways are exemplifications of the same metaphysical procedure from accidentally possessed existence to its ultimate source, subsistent existence. They are not cosmological reasoning.

V

According to these considerations, each of the five ways express the original thinking of Aquinas, even though the arguments were taken from other sources in which they reach conclusions philosophically different from his. In this double provenance of the thought lies the "enigma" of the five ways. Despite formulation from their historical origin, all five start in the *Summa of Theology* from existents that possess being in accidental fashion, and proceed from there to existence that subsists. All function on the "existence" side of the "essence-existence" couplet. They are accordingly five different ways of incorporating the one basic demonstration.

But that demonstration may be embodied in a number of other ways, and in arrangements of ways different from that of the *Summa of Theology*. The number or arrangement used on any given occasion seems to have been a matter of convenience for the moment.[39] There is consequently nothing sacrosanct about the number five or the particular arrangement in the *Summa*. That *Summa* may indeed represent the height of Aquinas's achievement. But the fact that in subsequent writings he drew up proofs for the existence of God without any concern for aligning them with the fivefold procedure show sufficiently that he himself did not give the five ways a privileged position. He never writes as though he had established five ways and only five for the demonstration of God's existence. Rather, the arrangement of the ways is left free, remaining flexible and open to wide change as occasion happened to demand.

THE CONCLUSION OF THE PRIMA VIA

I

THE PROBLEM OF THE *PRIMA VIA*

Of the five "ways" to prove that God exists, the one which proceeds from the movement of sensible things is called by St. Thomas Aquinas the "first and more manifest."[1] This way is described by him as having an efficacy that is irresistible.[2] It is the only way that is used in the direct treatment of the question in his last résumé of his own theological doctrine.[3]

The argument from motion, however, has had a long and varied history. In the light of that history, it would seem at first glance to be anything but an easy and manifest proof that God, as He is understood by a Christian, exists.

The external structure of the *prima via* is obviously taken by St. Thomas from Aristotle. Looked at in this light, the argument has its sources in the *Physics* and the *Metaphysics*.[4] Yet in the *Physics* the proof from motion seems to reach nothing further than a celestial soul.[5] In the *Metaphysics*, the demonstration arrives at a plurality of separate substances, each of which, although act without any admixture of potency, is nevertheless a finite entity.[6] In neither case does the result of the proof at all resemble the Christian God. Yet the immobile movent reached by the Aristotelian process is said by St. Thomas, without comment or elucidation, to be the God of whom he is treating as a Christian theologian.[7] How can this be? Certainly something that may be a celestial soul or a plurality of finite separate entities is hardly what Christians see at once to be the God of scriptural revelation, the God who had declared Himself to Moses in the words of Exodus, "I am who I am."[8]

In such a background, then, need no one be surprised to see that the conclusion of the *prima via* has been found unsatisfactory by many later writers? Leading Scholastic thinkers after the time of St. Thomas have minimized or sought to supplement or have even rejected the argument from motion. Duns

Scotus considered it to be a less perfect manner of reaching God, attaining Him in a more *per accidens* way than do the other proofs.[9] Cajetan looks upon the argument as concluding just to a first immobile movent in general, without caring for the moment whether or not that movent be merely a celestial soul; later the predicate "immobile movent" is shown to be in truth proper to God, and so the conclusion is drawn directly, but *quasi per accidens*, that God exists.[10] Suarez rejects the argument entirely maintaining that it cannot conclude even to an immaterial prime movent, let alone an uncreated one.[11] Other outstanding Scholastics may be listed as having stated that the *prima via* does not immediately and explicitly prove that God exists.[12] A recent writer, finally, insists even more strongly than Cajetan that the demonstration must be "prolonged" in order to attain its desired result.[13]

In view of this rather discouraging history, one may well ask how St. Thomas is justified in stating so abruptly of the immobile movent reached by the *prima via*, "And this all understand to be God."[14] May one still view the procedure from sensible motion as the "first and most manifest way" of showing that God exists? Can it even be considered to reach the Christian God at all satisfactorily? If so, how is it the most obvious and most evidently cogent of all the five ways?

In attempting to answer these questions, the first step, naturally, will have to be a brief glance at the *prima via*, and then a comparison with its Aristotelian sources from both structural and doctrinal viewpoints.

II

THE STRUCTURE OF THE *PRIMA VIA*

The structure of the *prima via* in the *Summa Theologiae* is remarkably clear. Its starting point is located in things of the sensible world, things which are evidently perceived through sensation to be in movement. The examples given are of fire heating wood and the hand moving the stick which pushes something else. From an analysis of this movement of sensible things two propositions successively emerge. The first is that whatever is being moved is being moved by another; the second, that an indefinite series of movents that are being moved cannot account for this motion. The conclusion from the analysis of the movement seen in sensible things is therefore that there is a first movent which is not being moved by anything, and this all understand to be God.

The argument, accordingly, is constructed as follows:

1. Starting point: Some things in the sensible world are being moved.
2. Propositions: (a) Whatever is being moved is being moved by something

else; (b) An indefinite series of moved movents cannot account for motion.
3. Conclusion: There is a first movent which is not being moved by anything at all, and this all understand to be God.[15]

The starting point—namely, that things in the sensible world are in movement—is looked upon as evident through sensation and as needing no further elucidation. That a first movent which is not being moved by anything is the Christian God does not seem to be conceived as open to challenge. Only the two propositions are considered as needing proof. These are demonstrated through an analysis of the sensible movement in terms of act and potency.

The first of the two propositions emerges from a metaphysical examination of the movement seen in sensible things. It is not accepted in any a priori way, either analytic or synthetic, but is reached frankly as a conclusion from what is seen happening in the sensible world. St. Thomas reasons with an evident example before his mind. A piece of wood which is cold is being heated by a fire. The movement in this case is alteration, change in quality. Insofar as the wood is being moved from cold to heat, it is in potency to being hot. This is at once seen to be the necessary condition for being moved. The thing that is being moved has to be in potency in the same respect. So nothing can move itself. If it is being moved, it is being moved by something else.[16]

The basis of this argument is that the act is something over and above the potency, something more than the potency, and so has to come from something which already has or is that act.

The second proposition follows from a continuation of this study of sensible movement in terms of act and potency. If that which is imparting the motion is thereby being moved itself, it also is necessarily being moved by another. If this third is also a movent that is being moved, it likewise is being moved by still another. But one cannot proceed in this way indefinitely, for there would be no first movent. Therefore there must be a first movent which is not being moved by anything; and this all understand to be God.[17]

This reasoning quite evidently derives its force from the doctrine of act and potency explained in the proof of the first proposition. Anything that is being moved does not have of itself the act towards which it is being moved. So in an indefinite series of moved movents, none would have the act of itself. Accordingly, such a series would never be able to account for the motion. Since there is sensible motion, then there must be something which of itself is act, in the sense that it is in no way being actualized by anything else. "To impart motion," the proof has stated, "is nothing else than to educe something from potency to act."[18] The first movent, accordingly, is not being moved by anything, in the sense that it is not being actuated by anything whatsoever in imparting the motion. Such a movent, St. Thomas declares without the least hesitation, is understood by all to be God.

In examining the historical genesis of this argument, then, one should carefully watch the starting point, the two propositions, and the conclusion. From such a study one may hope to find in exactly what respects the argument of St. Thomas resembles its sources in Aristotle and in exactly what respects it differs from those sources in order to arrive at such a radically different conclusion.

III

ARISTOTLE

Three presentations of the argument from motion are found in Aristotle. They are located, respectively, in the seventh book of the *Physics*, the eighth book of the *Physics*, and the Book Lambda of the *Metaphysics*.

BOOK VII OF THE *PHYSICS*

The seventh book of the *Physics* is a treatise quite detached from the main groupings.[19] It establishes in its opening paragraph the proposition that "everything that is being moved is necessarily being moved by something."[20] This "something" is understood as being in some way "other"[21] than the thing which is being moved, even though it may not be outside[22] that thing. The proposition itself is demonstrated by a proof based upon the divisibility of every mobile thing. A mobile thing has parts. If one of the parts were not in motion the whole as such, primarily and per se, would have to be at rest.[23] The mobile thing, accordingly, cannot be being moved primarily and per se; so it must be being moved by something which is in some way other than the thing itself considered primarily and per se.

This reasoning of the Stagirite has been found difficult or unacceptable by commentators throughout the ages.[24] It is regarded by St. Thomas, however, as a *propter quid* demonstration, based on the "primary and per se" character that is denied to anything mobile, as such. The argument concerns any mobile thing which has in itself the principle of its motion. If such a thing were imparting motion to itself without being moved by another, it would be being moved primarily and per se; just as if something were hot without having that heat from something else, it would have to be the primary and per se instance of heat. But the argument of the Stagarite has shown that no mobile thing can be being moved primarily and per se.[24]

This reasoning, St. Thomas argues, seems to be a *propter quid* demonstration, for it contains the cause why it is impossible for any mobile thing to be moving itself. That a thing is moving itself means nothing else than that the thing is the cause of its own motion. Now to be cause to oneself of any characteristic means to possess that characteristic *primarily*; for what is primary in any genus is the cause of what is subsequent, as fire, which is the cause of heat to itself and to others, is the primary instance of what is hot. But motion depends upon the parts of the mobile thing. So there cannot be any such thing as a *primary* mobile whose motion would be independent of its parts, any more than a divisible thing could be the primary being; for as divisible it would depend upon its parts.[26]

This explanation of St. Thomas' is in its nature highly metaphysical. Though without explicit reference here, it is evidently, from both doctrine and example, based upon a principle taken from a document which Greek tradition has rightly placed among the metaphysical treatises of Aristotle. The highest instance of any characteristic is the one which is the cause of that characteristic to the other things which are designated by the same name.[27] But mobile things are essentially imperfect; they cannot have a "highest"—that is, a perfect and primary instance in their own genus. Therefore no mobile thing can be the cause of its own motion primarily and per se.

Such an interpretation is in principle entirely Aristotelian. It makes the argument of the Stagirite convincing and satisfying. Yet it is not used in the text of the *Physics*. The Stagirite himself does not invoke the principle that is found in the *Metaphysics*. Rather, he leaves the argument on the physical plane, the plane of natural philosophy.[28] He is apparently content to have shown that "being moved" cannot pertain primarily and per se to any mobile thing. Having excluded the one alternative by this negative conclusion, he accepts the other alternative without further investigation. He continues on the same physical plane to prove his second proposition—namely, that a series of mobile things, each of which is being moved locally by another, cannot go on to infinity; there has to be a first movent.[29] In the interpretation given by St. Thomas, the way to prove the second proposition would lie wide open. Since mobile things cannot have a primary and perfect instance in their own genus, they must ultimately have that motion from something which is not mobile. But Stagirite does not proceed in this way. Instead, he enters upon a laborious argument from purely physical considerations of time and motion.

In a word, Aristotle's treatment in the seventh book of the *Physics* remains within the limits of natural philosophy. The basic argument is made clearer and more convincing by St. Thomas, but only by being raised to the metaphysical level. What was kept strictly on the physical plane for the Stagirite is treated metaphysically by St. Thomas.

The nature of the primary movent reached by the Aristotelian reasoning is not determined. It is left vaguely as the "first movent." Even the obvious conclusion that it has to be immobile is not made explicit. Whatever is being moved is being moved by something, and a series of movents that are being moved cannot extend into infinity. The only conclusion drawn by the Stagirite from these two propositions is that there must be a first movent, not as final cause, but as that from which the beginning of motion proceeds.[30] St. Thomas, entirely in accord with his interpretation of the basic argument, expressly concludes to the immobility of the first movent as its proper characteristic.[31]

This argument is not used in the *prima via* of the *Summa Theologiae*. It shows, however, that St. Thomas approaches the question from the viewpoint of the essential imperfection of motion. Such an approach, based on the relation of the imperfect to the perfect, is on the metaphysical level. Because motion is essentially imperfect, it requires something outside the order of mobile things—understood as divisible or extended things—to account for it. But St. Thomas does not say that the immobile movent attained solely by the reasoning on this basis is God. Quite obviously, any immaterial movent would satisfy the requirement of the argument as it stands. Apparently all that Aristotle intended it to show is that any series of local movements has to have as its first movent a soul, either celestial or terrestrial. Based as it is upon the extended and divisible nature of the mobile things, it can lead, even as it is here interpreted by St. Thomas, only to an unextended and indivisible nature. Proceeding from this basis alone, it does not necessarily involve God as He is understood in the Christian sense.

BOOK VIII OF THE *PHYSICS*

The eighth book of the *Physics* bases its procedure on the *eternity* of motion. It describes motion under the simile of a sort of life to physical things.[32] It envisions a treatment which will be of interest not only to natural philosophy, but also to the science which treats of the first principle;[33] namely, the primary philosophy.

Motion, the Stagirite argues, is eternal because every motion presupposes a subject which has to be generated or at least changed by a preceding motion. So every motion by its very nature presupposes a prior motion.[34] The same holds proportionally for every corruption, which by its nature similarly requires a further corruption.[35] The nature of time supports this argument. The divisible time can neither be nor be known without the indivisible "now," the medium which has to have time both before and after it. Time, therefore, has to be eternal. Accordingly, motion, of which time is but an affection, must likewise be eternal.[36]

St. Thomas accepts the validity of the Aristotelian argument that motion which has to arise through the process of nature (that is, through motion) must be eternal. This, however, leads for him to the conclusion that the original production of things was not a motion or change, but a sort of "emanation" which required no subject.[37] Contrary to Aristotle, therefore, St. Thomas can allow a first indivisible in motion, before which there was no motion, and a first indivisible in time, before which there was no time.[38]

The ability to see motion originating in an indivisible indicates quite evidently an entirely different approach to the problem. In fact, what primarily seems to interest St. Thomas in this argument is how the mobile things originally acquired their *esse*, whether it is from eternity or not, cannot be by way of motion.[39] Motion, in a word, even though it is eternal, cannot ultimately be produced through motion. The essentially imperfect nature of motion seems here, as in the commentary on Book VII, brought to the fore. Motion requires something more than motion to explain its presence.

Moreover, the eternity of motion, which is the basis laid by the Stagirite for his demonstration, is regarded by St. Thomas as irrelevant to the proof. Whether motion is eternal or not, its *esse* has to be accounted for by a sort of emanation from the cause of all *esse*.

Clearly, St. Thomas has shifted the starting point of the demonstration from the Aristotelian *eternity* of motion to the *esse* of motion.[40] The culmination of the proof, accordingly, will have to be in the cause which ultimately produces motion from the viewpoint of the *esse* of motion. What exactly is signified by *esse* in this context is for the moment not made clear.[41] But enough is evident to show that St. Thomas is proceeding from a starting point radically different from that of the Stagirite, and that his approach to the proof from motion is here, as in Book VII, highly metaphysical.

After establishing on the basis of sense evidence[42] that there are things which are sometimes being moved and sometimes at rest, the Stagirite proceeds to prove that whatever is being moved is being moved by something.[43]

The first proof is an induction of all the different types of movement. Things that are moving and being moved per accidens, are moved by belonging to, or being parts of, something else that is in movement.[44] Things being moved by violence and against their nature are clearly being moved by something else.[45] In things which by nature move themselves, as animals, there is one part which moves, distinguished from what is being moved.[46] Finally, inanimate things which are naturally in motion are moved per se by what generates their nature, per accidens by what removed the impediment.[47] In treating this last type Aristotle insists that every nature or habit will always be in action if the proper conditions are present and nothing is hindering. If a man has knowledge he will be thinking, unless something hinders him; otherwise he would be ignorant. Fire burns, if nothing is preventing it; light and heavy bodies exercise their respective activities straightway, if nothing hinders. Quantity similarly expands at once, if nothing prevents it.[48]

All that Aristotle requires is the form or nature in the agent and the presence of the *passum*; and then, if nothing hinders, the activity and motion straightway take place. The only per se cause required is that which generated the form in the matter. The thing by its very nature "energizes"[49] according to that form, without the need of any further per se cause. The only other factor ever required is a per accidens cause to remove any impediment that may be present. This is the same notion of efficient causality that is found in the *Metaphysics.*[50] Natural things always "energize," and all that is required to explain efficiency is the presence in the agent of a form that is the same as, or equipollent to, the form produced in the *passum.* No awareness of any existential problem in efficiency can be perceived in the text of the Stagirite.

St. Thomas reports this doctrine of the Stagirite faithfully and without comment.[51] For the moment, he remains strictly within the limits of the Aristotelian conception of efficiency.

Having established this first proposition on the basis of induction, Aristotle immediately goes on to show that one cannot proceed indefinitely in a series of moved movents. Since all things that are being moved are being moved by something, the first in a series of movents is in a greater sense the movent than the others. The others depend on the first in imparting motion, but not the first on the others. The movement of all the others, accordingly, depends on the first. There must therefore be a first movent which is not being moved by another. An indefinite series of moved movents would have no *first* movent and so could not account for motion. In a series of moved movents, then the first movent is necessarily being moved by the hand, the hand being in its turn moved by the man, and the man finally being moved by nothing other than himself.[52] The self-movent, accordingly, is located in animate beings.

The doctrine is further explained by showing that if everything which is being moved is being moved by a *moved* movent, this requirement (that every movent is being moved in imparting its motion) will be either per accidens or per se. If the requirement is only per accidens, motion need not be eternal.[53] If on the other hand every movent is being moved not per accidens but necessarily, then a particular movent would be giving itself, either immediately or mediately, the same type of act to which it is being moved. This would mean that one who is teaching is thereby learning what he is teaching and so would necessarily both have and not have the knowledge in question. So the first thing that is in motion in a series either will be moved by something that is at rest or else will be moving itself.[54]

The cause and first principle of motion, moreover, should be that which moves itself rather than that which is being moved by another, since that which is per se a cause is always prior as such to that which is cause only in virtue of being dependent on something else. Accordingly, a new approach to the question from the viewpoint of *how* a thing moves itself should bring out this same doctrine. For motion is a process towards act; it is an imperfect act. The mobile thing is in potency to act; it lacks the act towards which it is tending. The movent, however, already has that act, as, for instance, what is hot imparts heat and what has the form generates. If a thing as a whole could heat itself, it would be at the same time both hot and not hot in the same respect. Therefore, when a thing moves itself, one part of it is the movent and another part is being moved. The self-movent, further, cannot be conceived as having parts which reciprocally move each other. In this case there would likewise be no *first* movent, and so the arguments just considered would apply equally in this case. Nor is the primary self-movent being moved by a self-moving part, for in this case that part would be the primary self-movent.[55]

The result of this reasoning, then, is that in all instances that which primarily imparts motion is immobile.[56] This immobile movent has been located as a part of the self-movent, quite clearly in the sense of a soul. Again, in all the foregoing explanation of the reduction of potency to act, the only requirements are that the movent already have the form that is being imparted and that it be in contact with the *passum*. No existential problem seems to arise.

St. Thomas in his commentary has no disagreement with this Aristotelian reasoning[57] and is careful to point out that, although for motion in general the Stagirite had rejected any primary instance, he can nevertheless admit a primary self-movent in particular.[58]

The final step in the Aristotelian argument is to show that among such immobile movents at least one must be eternal.

In some self-movents—namely, plants and animals—the immobile movents sometimes are and sometimes are not, without any process of generation and corruption.[59] But the eternity of motion does not permit that all unmoved movents should be so. There has to be some *eternal* immobile movent to cause the *eternally continuous* motion.[60] Moreover, if the continuity of the eternal motion is to be accounted for, this eternal movent cannot be mobile even per accidens, as, for instance, are the souls of terrestrial things which move from place to place with their bodies, or those heavenly bodies which have several motions.[61] It will impart continuous motion; but the movent that it is moving mediately can impart contrary motion and so cause some things to be sometimes in motion and sometimes at rest.[62] Finally, the primary movent has no magnitude and is located at the circumference of the universe where the motion is quickest.[63]

This reasoning, evidently, leads to nothing more than the soul of the outermost heaven. Starting from the eternity of motion, it has shown by induction that whatever is being moved is being moved by something. But in a series of things that are being moved, there must be a first movent in virtue of which the others impart motion. This first movent is not being moved by anything other than itself and so has to be a self-movent; and in a self-movent the motion is caused by a part that is immobile, as in animate things.[64] The eternal continuity of motion, however, can be explained only by a celestial soul which is im-

mobile both per se and per accidens; and the sole reason why the primary movent must be immobile both per se and per accidens is this eternal continuity of
motion. Since efficient causality is explained ultimately by form as act, it requires nothing further in this order of cause. Every Aristotelian form
"energizes" of its own nature, when nothing hinders. The soul of the first
heaven in this way fully suffices to explain the primary movement of the
heavens as efficient cause. In the line of efficient causality the argument is closed. It leaves no way open to argue to any further *efficient* cause of motion.

St. Thomas, however, cannot admit a primary movent which *necessarily*
causes eternal movement.[65] But otherwise he remains quite close to the text in
his commentary on this final part of the demonstration. He speaks cautiously in
regard to the sphere movents, in such a way as not to commit himself to any
animation of the heavens.[66] Having rejected the eternity of motion as a fact, he
is not in a position to press home the force of the Stagirite's argument. At one
point he interprets the text as excluding a certain possible proof for the eternity
of the primary movent. The primary movent is immobile. Therefore it cannot
be generated or corrupted; it cannot at one time be and at another time not be;
and so it must be perpetual. But he notes that Aristotle does not bother about
this reason. The capacity to acquire or lose *esse* does not prevent a thing from
being immobile according to the Stagirite's doctrine of being. But the fact that
some souls come to be and perish is mentioned by Aristotle merely to show that
the totality of such souls cannot account for the eternal continuity of motion.
The same fact is interpreted by St. Thomas as indicating a direct argument for
the eternity of the primary movent, an argument, however, in which the
Stagirite is not interested.[67] On the basis of *esse* as an act which is acquired or
lost in generation and corruption, this argument would be conclusive; and *esse*
had as a matter of fact been substituted for the eternity of motion by St.
Thomas as the starting point of the demonstration at the beginning of his commentary.[68] But St. Thomas, remaining with the text, does not press his own
viewpoint further. Nor does he anywhere in this part of the commentary proper
expressly indentify the Aristotelian prime movent with God.[69] Only in the
solemn invocation at the conclusion of the treatise does he mention that the
Philosopher ends the study in the principle of all nature, which is the God of
Christian worship.[70]

BOOK LAMBDA OF THE *METAPHYSICS*

Book Lambda of the *Metaphysics* contains a further development of the proof from motion. This book, like the seventh book of the *Physics*, is a comparatively detached treatise. It has no certain references either to or from any of
the other metaphysical writings. It shows some dependence on Book Nu,

however, and refers back explicitly to the physical treatises.[71] It presupposes especially the doctrine of eternal motion and time, as established in the eighth book of the *Physics*. It presents itself as a treatment of entity (*ousia*).

The starting point of the demonstration is once more the eternity of motion. Motion and time are eternal, and being accidents they presuppose substance (*ousia*). There must, then, be an eternal immobile substance. This substance has not only to be in act, but its very entity (*ousia*) must be act, if it is to be the principle of eternal motion; if its nature were potency, it would be possible for it not to be, and so motion need not be eternal. This substance, accordingly, will be without matter. As the object of knowledge and love, it will impart motion to the first heaven.[72] It knows itself and nothing else.[73] To account for the other original movements in the heavens, a plurality of such separate substances is required.[74]

In this reasoning Aristotle considers the first heaven as being moved, through *final* causality, by a separate entity which is entirely without matter. Since a number of other eternal movements are observable in the heavens, these likewise require corresponding separate movents. The argument of the *Metaphysics*, accordingly, leads to a plurality of eternal, separate movents, which are final causes only and not efficient causes. As act is equated with form and finitude in the primary philosophy, each of these pure acts, including the first, has to be finite.

The treatment from the viewpoint of *ousia*, therefore, adds nothing further in the line of efficient causality to the immobile movents of the *Physics*. It shows that the movent must have an eternally unchanging object of desire, which has to be pure act. This object of desire is not required to expain efficiently any passage of the sphere soul from potency to act, but only to account for the eternally unchanging character of the motion which it causes. The further treatment in the *Metaphysics*, accordingly, adds nothing to the Aristotelian requirements for the functioning of a cause from the viewpoint of efficiency. Like the procedure in the eighth book of the *Physics*, this proof rests on the eternity of cosmic motion.

St. Thomas realizes full well that the Aristotelian argument is based on the eternity of the world.[75] Yet without the least hesitation he changes this basis to the production of *esse*, and on that new foundation he builds up the demonstration in such a way as to arrive at substance without potency. If the world is not eternal, it has to be produced in *esse* by something which preexists. This likewise, if it is not eternal, would have to be produced by something; and since one cannot proceed indefinitely, one must reach an eternal substance in which there is no potency.[76] The act in question, accordingly, seems to be that of *esse*, produced in mobile things by something which preexists. The motion of the Aristotelian argument is interpreted in terms of the production of the act which makes a thing exist. It concludes to a substance which exists per se.[77] The potency envisaged in the demonstration seems to include a potency to the act of existing per se.

St. Thomas is also careful to point out that the necessity of the primary movement is subject to the will of God, just as artifacts are to the will of the artificer[78] Likewise, a heavenly body has the potency of receiving its *esse*.[79] In this interpretation, the primary immobile movent by knowing itself knows all other things.[80] It seems to impart motion, then as the efficient cause of all things according to their act of *esse*; and hence, as their efficient cause through intelligence and will, it knows those things in itself. Since Aristotle himself uses the terms "god" and "gods" to designate separate entity in their treatise, St. Thomas has no hesitation in referring to the primary movent as God. He sees the Aristotelian argument concluding to the God of his own religious faith.[81]

IV

ST. THOMAS AQUINAS

SCRIPTUM SUPER LIBROS SENTENTIARUM

In his commentary on the first book of the *Sentences*, St. Thomas presents the arguments that proceed from creatures to God under three heads, independently of any Aristotelian schema. The procedure is threefold: through causality, through removal, and through eminence. The basis of the reasoning in all three cases is that the *esse* of creatures is from something else.[82]

The first reason, the *via* of causality, is that there must be something from which creatures derive their *esse*, since creatures have *esse ex nihilo*. This latter fact is evident "from their imperfection and potentiality." The imperfection and potentiality of creatures—the way along which the *prima via* of the *Summa Theologiae* proceeds—are made the basis for the argument from *esse*. The imperfection and potentiality of creatures, accordingly, are seen as manifesting a lack of *esse* and so from this viewpoint lead to some one thing that is primary and which is forthwith seen to be God.[83]

The second argument, based on "removal," is that the imperfect presupposes the perfect. But bodies are imperfect, because they are finite and *mobile*. Therefore there is something more perfect than bodies. But if this incorporeal being is also changeable, it is likewise imperfect. Therefore beyond souls and angels there must be an immobile and all-perfect being, which is God.[84] The angelic nature is looked upon as a *species mutabilis*. The angels, unlike the Aristotelian separate forms, are considered to be "changeable." This bears particularly upon their operation since creation and annihilation are not properly *mutatio*.[85] But the reasoning is brought under the heading that the *esse* of creatures is *ab altero*. Apparently, then, the potentiality and mutability are being conceived in relation to an ultimate act which is *esse*.

Of the three manners of reaching God in the *Sentences*, then, two proceed from the potentiality and mobility of creatures. They attain God respectively as the primary cause of the *esse* of creatures and as the immobile being which is presupposed by all mobile and changeable natures which have their *esse* from another. The operative notion in the procedure from potentiality and mobility to God seems to be that of *esse*.

THE *CONTRA GENTILES*

In the *Contra Gentiles* St. Thomas takes the material from Aristotle but builds up the demonstration along his own lines. He is laying down "the reasons by which Aristotle proceeds to prove that God exists." He finds that the Stagirite "aims to prove this from motion by two *viae*."[86]

The first of these two *viae* seems to result directly in a *first immobile movent*:

> Everything that is being moved is being moved by something else. But it is evident through sensation that something is being moved, for instance the sun. Therefore it is being moved by something else moving it. This movent will accordingly either be being moved or not. If it is not being moved, we have therefore what was proposed, that it is necessary to posit an immobile movent. And this we call God. But if it is being moved, it is being moved by something else moving it. The process will therefore either go on indefinitely, or it will arrive at some immobile movent. But it cannot go on indefinitely. Therefore it is necessary to posit a first immobile movent.
>
> But in this proof there are two propositions to be proved; namely, that *everything that is being moved is being moved by another* and that *in movents and things one cannot proceed indefinitely*.[87]

As in the *Summa Theologiae*, the fact from which this reasoning starts—namely, that something is being moved—is accepted as evident. The conclusion, that the first immobile movent is what "we call God," is likewise treated as needing no proof. Only the two propositions need to be demonstrated.

The first proposition, St. Thomas proceeds, is proved by Aristotle in three ways. The first is the proof from the seventh book of the *Physics*, from the essentially imperfect nature of motion. The second is the argument from induction given in the eighth book of the *Physics*. The third is the demonstration that the movent as such is in act, while the thing being moved is in potency in respect to that act. But nothing can be in act and potency at the same time in the same respect. This third argument is likewise taken from the eighth book of the *Physics*; but there it is used, not as a proof of the first proposition that whatever is being moved is being moved by another, but to show that motion must originate in a self-movent and that in the self-movent only a part can be the immobile movent.[88]

The first of these three arguments, as it stands, applies only to divisible—that is, extended—things.[89] The second is merely an induction. The third alone carries full probative force, and it is the only one retained in the *prima via* of the *Summa Theologiae*.

The second proposition is also established by three arguments. The first is the one taken from the seventh book of the *Physics*, that infinite things cannot be being moved in finite time. The second is the proof from the eighth book of the *Physics*, that motion has to be primarily caused by a first movent, while in an infinite series there is no first. The third is the immediately following argument of the *Physics* which presents the foregoing proof from the viewpoint of the movent and that by which it imparts motion, or, in the terminology of St. Thomas, the principal and the instrumental movents.[90]

The first of these arguments holds only for things that are subject to time; namely, corporeal things. The second and third are unrestricted in their demonstrative scope. For St. Thomas they amount to one and the same proof, which is the one used in the *prima via* of the *Summa Theologiae*.

This first *via* from motion in the *Contra Gentiles*, accordingly, seems to conclude directly to a first immobile movent, which is God. The eternity of the world and the animation of the heavens do not enter into the demonstration at all as it is here developed by St. Thomas. But that these two tenets were presupposed in the original context of the arguments is not forgotten. Their omission, however, only strengthens the proof.[91] The disregard of these two fundamental tenets and the altered order of the arguments shows clearly enough that the proofs have been taken out of their context and been developed into an independent demonstration, even though their individual structure is followed as closely as possible.

The arguments of the second *via* from motion in the *Contra Gentiles* are all taken from the eighth book of the *Physics*. The first proposition established is that not every movent is being moved. This is proved by the last of the three arguments used by Aristotle to show that one cannot proceed indefinitely in a series of moved movents. The first conclusion, accordingly, is that there must be a first movent which is not being moved by anything external to itself.

The second step is to show that this has to be either entirely immobile or else self-movent. But if it is self-movent, it is being moved by an immobile part. The Aristotelian arguments to prove this, including the impossibility of a thing's being in act and potency at the same time (already seen by St. Thomas in the first *via*), are given in their original order. In a similar way are repeated the arguments that among such self-movents there must be one which is eternal and moved by a part that is immobile both per se and per accidens. Since God is not a part of a self-movent, Aristotle in his *Metaphysics* proceeds further to the entirely immobile separate movent which is God.[92]

St. Thomas takes account of the eternity of the world and the animation of the heavens in building up these arguments into his second *via* from motion. But the demonstration is stronger without those tenets. At the basis of the proof from this new viewpoint, the notion of the passage from *non esse* to *esse* is coupled with that of the passage from potency to act.[93]Here, as in his commentary on the eighth book of the *Physics* and his other presentations of the argument, the operative notion seems for him to be the reception of *esse* as the act of a potency.[94]

In the *Contra Gentiles*, accordingly, St. Thomas has taken the arguments of the seventh and eighth books of the *Physics* and combined them in the form of two different *viae*. The first of these *viae* proceeds along the lines of the two propositions that "whatever is being moved is being moved by another" and that "one cannot proceed indefinitely in a series of moved movents." Each of the two propositions is proved by three arguments, of which the first in each case is taken from the seventh book and the others from the eighth book. The Aristotelian order is followed, except that the third and vital proof of the first proposition is taken from a later and somewhat different setting. The second *via* proceeds from the proposition that not every movent is being moved and, following the arguments of the eighth book of the *Physics* from where the first *via* ended, arrives first at a self-movent, then at an immobile part of that self-movent, and finally, with the aid of the *Metaphysics*, at an entirely immobile prime movent, which is God.

The first *via* assembles its arguments in such a way as to dispense entirely with the eternity of the world and animation of the heavens. The general structure of this first *via* and the principal proof in each case for its two propositions are retained in the construction of the *prima via* in the *Summa Theologiae*. But in this way the *via* has been completely detached from its Aristotelian basis, the eternity of cosmic motion. It reaches an entirely different conclusion; namely, the unique and creative God of Christian revelation.

THE *DE POTENTIA*

In *De Potentia* the preoccupation in the argument from motion seems clearly to be with *esse*. The later philosophers, St. Thomas states, posited some universal cause from which all other things came into *esse*. This is in accord with the Catholic faith and can be demonstrated by a threefold reason. First, *esse* is found as common to all things and so has to be given them by some one cause.

This is considered to be a Platonic reason.[95] The second reason is taken from Aristotle. There must be a most perfect being because there is an entirely immobile and most perfect movent, as the philosophers have proven. Therefore all other things, being less perfect, must receive *esse* from this immobile movent.[96]

The argument from motion is here seen to prove a being from which all other beings receive *esse*. The notions of "being moved" and of "receiving *esse*" seem to coincide, as far as the conclusion of this argument is concerned, in leading to the entirely immobile movent.

The third reason, attributed to Avicenna, reaches a being which is *ipsum suum esse* because it is pure act.[97] The notion of act, when entirely free from potency, is accordingly the very act of *esse*.

THE COMPENDIUM THEOLOGIAE

In the *Compendium Theologiae*, written after the Prima Pars of the *Summa*, the connection of motion with *esse* for St. Thomas in this demonstration is especially clear.

The one argument given to prove directly that God exists is the proof from motion. The primary movent, without further reasoning, is said to be "what we call God."[98] The immobility reached by the demonstration is such that God *necessarily* exists, for everything that is possible to be and not to be is mutable.[99] Here the notions of motion and the transition from *non esse* to *esse* are coupled together. The same immobility means that God's *esse* is eternal.[100] Moreover, the pure act reached by the argument from motion is *ipsum esse*, since all motion tends to *esse* as its ultimate act.[101] This is said after *esse* had been explained as an act different, except in God, from the essence which is signified by the definition.[102] To this ultimate act even essence is in potency.

From these passages it is clear that St. Thomas is looking upon all motion as ultimately a tendency towards *esse*. *Esse* is the act which is ultimate and to which every other act is potency. Even essence, except in God is still potency to *esse*. The demonstration from act and potency, then, has to reach a pure act which is the act of *esse* alone. The entirely immobile movent, being pure act in this sense, can for St. Thomas be only the act of *esse* reached on the basis of an act not originally attained through that cognition by which corporeal things are known according to their essences.

The starting point of St. Thomas, accordingly, is wider than that of Aristotle. It includes an act which is not attained in the cognition of things according to their form. The inclusion of this act in the starting point vitally affects the whole course of the demonstration and makes the conclusion radically different. Motion, as analyzed by Aristotle, is merely a process towards form; for

St. Thomas, it is a process towards a further and existential act. For Aristotle the act without potency, to which the argument finally concludes, can be only finite form. For St. Thomas the pure act has to be something over and beyond the order of form and finitude and is expressed by the infinitive *esse*.

The force of the Thomistic argument from motion, then, lies in its view of all movement from the standpoint of existential act. A thing cannot be being moved except through acquiring new existential act, and this ultimately can proceed only from the subsistent act of existing.

THE *SUMMA THEOLOGIAE*

The relation of the *prima via* in the *Summa Theologiae* to the Aristotelian reasoning from motion should be fairly clear from the foregoing survey. The *prima via* follows the lines of the first way from motion in the *Contra Gentiles*, restricting itself to the one essential proof given for each of the two propositions. The structure of the two propositions and their proofs, accordingly, are ultimately taken from Aristotle, as are also the examples used to illustrate them. But the eternity of the world and the animation of the heavens, essential to the Aristotelian way of reaching separate entity, do not enter into the demonstration; and the conclusion reached directly is at once seen to be the God of Christian revelation. Should not this mean that St. Thomas, here as in his other presentations of the demonstration, is looking upon the motion of sensible things as being ultimately actuated by a distinct existential *esse*? In this way the term of the procedure through act and potency will be a pure act which is the very act of existing, and not a finite form.

Does the context of the *prima via* bear out this anticipation?

In the first article of the Quaestio in which the *prima via* is located, God is said to be His own *esse*, with forward reference to the fourth article of the immediately following Quaestio.[103]There God's essence or nature or quiddity is shown to be His *esse*. The second proof given for this is from act and potency. *Esse* is the actuality of every form or nature. Goodness and humanity, for instance, are not expressed in act unless they are expressed as having *esse*. *Esse* therefore in such things is related to an essence which is other than itself as act to potency. Since in God there is nothing potential, as has been shown, He cannot have any essence different from His *esse*.[104]

The act and potency envisaged in the *prima via*, accordingly, include essence as potency to the act of *esse*. Just as goodness or humanity so the motion of sensible things seems to be looked upon as being in act through its *esse*.[105] Since every motion means a new participation in existential act, the immobile movent which is not being moved by anything can be only the subsistent act of existing. The act which is finally reached in the demonstration, then, is the act which in this sense is not being actuated by anything else, the subsistent act of *esse*.

How is this *esse* known?

The divine *esse*, St. Thomas explicitly states in this context, cannot be known by us insofar as *esse* signifies the act of being, just as the divine essence, with which it is identical, cannot be known to us. Only insofar as *esse* signifies the composition in a proposition can we know that the proposition which we form of God, when we say that God is, is true. This we know from His effects.[106]

What is meant by this twofold way of expressing *esse*? How does the way of attaining the *esse* which is the act of being differ from the way of attaining the *esse* that is signified by the composition in a proposition?

Certainly the *esse* which is the act of being is not attained by the same cognition in which a thing is known according to its essence and expressed in its definition.[107] The act of being is grasped in the second operation of the intellect, in judgment.[108] This act, it is true, can also be later expressed in an act of simple intellection, when a judgment is logically analyzed. It can be expressed by the concept of act. Just as form is to matter, so *esse* is to essence. In this way the concept of act, taken originally from form, may be extended analogously to the being which was attained originally in the judgment. In this way one may think and speak of "existence" or the "act of existing."

But this simple conception of *esse* does not permit one to affirm that the act of existing is being exercised.[109] That can only be judged. It is attained solely by the second operation of the intellect. Sensible things immediately present to the external sense are grasped in the act of judgment according to this actually exercised *esse*. The intellect irresistibly judges that they exist here and now. In this way one may be said to know their act of being, their *actus essendi*; namely, through the judgment, the second operation of the intellect. But this second operation of the intellect extends much further than the realm of things actually existing in the world. It is applied to whatever may be the object of a proposition, even regarding negations and privations where no essence is present that could be actuated by *esse* in the world of things.[110] Moreover, from any true proposition to which the intellect has assented one may proceed by reasoning, the third operation, to acquire certitude about unknown things.[111]

In the present context of the *Summa Theologiae*, the *esse* in both senses clearly refers to what is attained in the act of judgment, and not to knowledge in the order of essence. In the sense of the act of being, it is contrasted with knowlege of essence; we cannot know God's *esse* in this sense, just as we cannot know His essence. In the second sense it signifies composition, the joining together of subject and predicate, which pertains to the act of judgment. In both senses, according to the wording of the argument being answered, it must reply to the question *an sit*. The problem is to show that there is a sense in which we can know *an sit* of God without thereby knowing *quid sit*, even though God's essence is identical with His *esse*. If we could know the divine *esse* in the sense of the act of being, St. Thomas answers, we would thereby know the *quid sit*—something which in fact we do not know. But from His effects, we know that the proposition "God is" is true; and in this sense we reach the divine *esse*, without thereby knowing His act of being.

To know the divine *esse* as an act, accordingly, would seem to mean that one would grasp it immediately in the act of judgment, as one does the *esse* of sensible things. On the other hand, a reasoning from the *esse* of effects, affirmed in a true proposition, enables one to affirm with certitude the existence of the unknown cause, even though it does not give us knowledge of the essence of the cause. In the unique case of God the reasoning shows that His essence has to be identical with His *esse*; yet as an act this *esse* can remain unknown, even while being known as responding to the truth of the proposition attained with certitude; namely, that God exists.[112] But the divine *esse* attained in this way by the reasoning process is such that one has merely to proceed by the way of negation to develope the whole of one's philosophical knowledge of God.[113]

V

CAJETAN

Cajetan, writing two-and-a-half centuries after St. Thomas and in a milieu in which the Thomistic distinction between essence and existential act had long been neglected,[114] approaches the argument in the background of an Arabian controversy. Avicenna had reasoned that since no science establishes its own subject, *ens commune* and not God is the subject of metaphysics. Averroes, wishing to safeguard against this view the traditional Aristotelian conception of the science, used the same principle[115] to show that separate substance, which is indeed the subject of metaphysics, has to be established in natural philosophy.[116] The Aristotelian argument from motion, accordingly, becomes with Averroes a purely *physical* argument.

In this background Cajetan admits that the *prima via* seems to conclude directly to a movent no more than an intellective soul. In support he cites what St. Thomas says in the *Contra Gentiles*.[117] The argument, therefore, is to be looked upon as concluding immediately only to a predicate which is in truth proper to God and is later shown to be such. In this way the existence of the predicate involves the existence of God.[118] It is sufficient, then, that from the argument *ex parte motus* one infers that there is a first immobile movent, not caring for the moment if it be the soul of the heavens or of the world. That is a further question. In a word, the *prima via* for Cajetan reaches a predicate proper to God, but not the divine essence immediately.

In citing the *Contra Gentiles* to support this view, Cajetan takes no note of the division of the argument from motion in that work into two *viae*. The first of these *viae*, it will be remembered, constructs the argument from Aristotelian principles and contains the reasoning and the structure later used in the *Summa Theologiae*. In regard to this first *via* of the *Contra Gentiles*, St. Thomas, just as in the *Summa Theologiae*, states directly of the conclusion, "and this we call God." There is no question of its being a celestial soul. In the second *via* from motion, St. Thomas follows the stages of the argument as they are found in the eighth book of the *Physics*, admits that it reaches only a celestial soul, and then follows Aristotle over into the *Metaphysics* to reach an entirely separate movent. In neither case, therefore, does St. Thomas mean that God is reached by a purely physical argument or that the proof from motion belongs to natural philosophy. And in regard to the reasoning as it stands in the *Physics*, St. Thomas is at pains to make it clear that if the two Aristotelian tenets of the eternity of the world and animation of the heavens are omitted then the argument concludes directly to God.[119]

Nor is the attitude of not caring for the moment if the immobile movent is a world soul or celestial soul to be found in the text of the *Summa*. The text looks upon the reasoning as reaching an unmoved movent which all understand to be God. There is no hint of any indifference to the nature of the movent so reached. Nor does the following question of the *Summa* proceed, as Cajetan's treatment implies, to add any further *positive* determination to the nature of the immobile movent. Rather, as St. Thomas carefully points out in the introduction to that question, it proceeds in a negative way. It does not show that the immobile movent is to be further determined as the act of existing, but rather that this pure act as already established cannot be the actualization of either matter or essence.

So much for the text itself. In passing over to doctrinal criticism, the question becomes more delicate. One must be careful not to attribute to Cajetan implications of his statements which he himself would not have accepted. But this consideration does not dispense one from pointing out the consequences to which his treatment of this problem leaves an open road. Cajetan thinks that the argument reaches a predicate which can be shown to be proper to God. But, in general, an immobile movent which may apply indifferently to God and to an intellective soul is an analogous notion—or at least some type of equivocal notion in the Aristotelian sense. In its application to its different instances it will be partly the same, partly different. It is the "different" characteristic which will determine it to a particular instance. But this different element cannot be derived from the common characteristic reached by the argument. It will have to come from some further source. Suarez will later point out quite properly that the demonstration at this stage requires an entirely new process of reasoning based upon a different starting point in order that the argument reach to God.[120]

In particular, the characteristic necessary in this case stem from a different order of being. The human intellect is so constituted that it cannot completely grasp the being of anything in a single act. To know the being of any existing thing, it has first to conceive that thing according to its essence in an act of simple apprehension and then through judgment attain that thing according to its act of existing. No matter how far—even to the infinite—it extends being as grasped in the first act of apprehension, it can never reach any act of existing. A being greater than which none can be thought, when conceived by the human intellect solely on the basis of essence, does not contain any existential act whatsoever. That is a peculiarity of the human way of thinking. St. Thomas' critique of the Anselmian argument was given in the first article of the same question which contains the *prima via* and so forms part of the introduction to the problem of God's existence. That critique seems based precisely on this peculiarity of human intellection. Even though one is conceiving by the term "God" than that which nothing greater can be thought, one is not thereby understanding that what is signified by the term exists (*esse in rerum natura*), unless one first admits that it does exist in reality.[121] This reasoning is that one may conceive God as something than which nothing greater can be thought, extending this conception without limits.[122] One is not thereby compelled to think that God exists. The act of really existing is not included in such a concept of infinite being. Only when the act of existing accompanies it from the very start may one argue that it exists. But that, of course, is merely to beg the question.

This profound treatment of the Anselmian argument involves the whole Thomistic doctrine that the act of existing is other than the essence as directly attained in human knowledge and that the two types of cognition, essential and existential, stem from two different sources. No matter how far the type based on essence is extended, it can never of itself attain the least act of existence.

If, then, the *prima via* leads directly to the notion of pure act in general, of immobile movent that may be indifferently the Christian God, an angel, or an Aristotelian immobile movent, the argument is no longer that of St. Thomas. It would result in a notion of pure act based on the essence of things. That notion of act, it is true, can be extended to include the notion of existential act by way of analogy. In this way only is a *concept* of existence formed. As matter is to form, so essence is to existence. As that which actuates matter is form, so that to which essence is potency, when a thing is judged to exist, actuates the essence and so comes under the concept "act." That concept of existence is perfectly legitimate. It is in fact the only way in which the intellect can naturally form the concept of existence, and so it is indispensable if one is even to speak about existence at all. But from such a concept the conclusion that anything does exist can never follow. Only through the act of judgment can the act of existing be grasped as such. That is the peculiarity of the human intellect. If, then, the *prima via* concludes merely to immobile movent in general, pure act equally applicable to the Aristotelian movents, it has reached only a type of entity based upon the essences of finite things. It proves thereby that such a type of entity exists, but without giving the existential act the operative function peculiar to the metaphysics of St. Thomas. The process may go on further to show by various means that this immobile movent is (or happens to be) identified with God. But can it ever reach the philosophical notion of God that is proper to the metaphysics of St. Thomas? Will it ever be able to declare the divine essence in terms of genuine existential act? In reasoning from an essential predicate to the nature of God, is it not rather leaving the way open to a philosophical conception of God in which the divine essence ultimately becomes, if not the "cause" as in Descartes,[123] at least the "sufficient reason" for the divine existence?

The root of the difficulty undoubtedly lies in the ambiguous conception of "pure act". The argument from motion, by eliminating all potency, finally reaches pure act. But if with Aristotle potency is equated with matter and act with form, the pure act reached will be form only. If, on the other hand, the form toward which motion tends is treated as part of an essence in potency to existential act, then the elimination of all potency whatsoever will result immediately in a subsistent existential act. Such a pure act cannot at any stage be looked upon as indifferently an intellectual soul or a finite separate substance or as the Christian God. It is seen at once to be identified with the "I am who I am" of Exodus.

SUAREZ

Suarez, approaching the question against the background of the Arabian controversy, as Cajetan did, expressly regards the Aristotelian argument from motion as a purely *physical* proof.[124] It cannot reach any immaterial substance, being in many ways inefficacious for this purpose. The principle that whatever is being moved by something else does not take into account virtual act. By a virtual act a thing can reduce itself to formal act. So one might say that the heavens are being moved by some innate force, just as the downward motion of the stone results from its intrinsic heaviness.[125]

Moreover, the Aristotelian argument rests upon a false principle; namely, the eternity of the world. Even the power to cause motion eternally would not be sufficient to prove that the movent was immaterial. Still less need motion that is not eternal or motion as such be caused by an immaterial movent. To ask whether the first movent has the power of moving from itself or from another is to get outside the argument from motion and get into the metapysical argument based on efficient causality.[126]

What is the argument which Suarez is criticizing?

Certainly it is not the *prima via* of St. Thomas. Suarez sees in the sensible thing no further act over and above its essence. The analysis of act and potency in sensible motion cannot, therefore, lead to the subsistent act of *esse*.

But is it even the Aristotelian argument? Suarez indeed intends it, by express reference,[127] to be the proof of the *Physics* and the *Metaphysics*. Yet the basic proposition of the Stagirite in this argument seems to be undermined by the introduction of "virtual act," by which something can reduce itself to act and so dispense with the necessity of being moved by something else.

What is this virtual act?

Neither here nor elsewhere does Suarez give any further explanation than by pointing to a few examples or by citing the authority of Duns Scotus.[128]

Scotus uses both the term "virtual act" and the examples cited by Suarez. It is idle, he claims, to cite the authority of Aristotle to show universally that nothing can move itself. Sensation shows that a heavy body moves itself downward; and this is in agreement with reason since an equivocal agent can contain the action virtually and still be formally in potency to the term of that action.[129] In reply to the objection that in this case the formal act could contain nothing over and above the virtual act, Scotus admits that the virtual act precisely as such is more perfect than the formal; but where that virtual act is limited, the formal act gives a grade of perfection which is less than the virtual act, but nevertheless adds something to it.[130]

The instances of this virtual act given by Scotus are (*a*) heavy bodies moving downward of themselves, (*b*) local motion of animate things, (*c*) nutrition and augmentation, (*d*) alteration, as in water becoming cold of itself, (*e*) cognition, and (*f*) intellective appetite—that is, free will. Of these, the second, third, fifth, and sixth are vital actions and were treated by Aristotle as requiring a movent in the *generans* or the environment. The first and fourth were also considered by the Stagirite and seen as requiring a per se cause in the *generans* and a per accidens cause in the *removens prohibens*.[131]

Ultimately the reasoning of Duns Scotus in this question comes back to the inductive argument from these examples. Why is virtual act compatible with potency to formal act in the same subject and in the same respect? The ultimate answer is that we see examples of the combination; therefore, there can be nothing contradictory about the combination or we could not have those instances of it.[132]

The objection that naturally arises is faced squarely. Formal act contains something more than virtual act. Therefore virtual act cannot fully account for it.

The reply of Scotus has been that the virtual act is of itself more perfect; yet in limited agents the formal adds a less perfect grade which nevertheless is a real addition to the virtual act.

Where does this addition come from? Scotus here seems utterly unaware of any problem at all, for an equivocal agent contains the perfection of its effect in a more perfect way. He writes as though that fully accounts for all the perfection in the effect, even including the added grade.

What background of efficient causality does such reasoning imply?

In Aristotle, efficient causality was explained entirely in terms of form. All that was required to account for the new effect was equal or greater formal perfection in the source of motion. Therefore no separate (Platonic) forms were necessary to explain causality.[133] But in this reasoning of the Stagirite, no notice of any existential problem is taken. As long as the required formal perfection is found in the agent, the new effect seems to be fully explained.

The reasoning of Dun Scotus seems to be fixed in this Aristotelian background. With univocal agents, self-motion is impossible because the formal act is already present in the agent. But in equivocal agents, the act is not yet formally present, though it is virtually so. From this virtual act the agent can *reduce itself* to formal act. The perfection is already there in a more eminent way in the virtual act, and the formal act is not yet present and so can be acquired.[134] Everything that is necessary for self-motion is present.

Certainly in a background like the Aristotelian where the metaphysical explanation of new being is restricted to the realm of form or essence, such an account seems flawless. Aristotle himself required nothing more in natural things once they had been generated and the obstacle had been removed. They ''energize'' forthwith. For Scotus the new mode or grade is less perfect than the virtual act and so from the viewpoint of formal causality is fully accounted for.

But what has been neglected in both the Aristotelian and Scotistic accounts?

Neither the one nor the other seems to feel any need to explain the new act of existing that actuates a formal act which before was found only virtually in its cause. Both proceed as though there were in this regard no problem that called for a metaphysical explanation. From the viewpoint of formal causality alone the equivocal agent may be capable of accounting fully for the different effect. But what accounts for the effect as existentially different? No answer is forthcoming; no treatment even is given; no problem seems to be felt.

In the doctrine of virtual act, then, Suarez through Scotus is remaining quite within the Aristotelian explanation of being through form as act. Why, then, is the result of the proof from motion so much less in Suarez than in Aristotle? Why does the proposition that ''whatever is being moved is being moved by something else'' lose with Suarez—apparently, at least—the universality which it had in Aristotle?

The answer to both questions lies in the doctrine of creation. For Suarez, creation in time dispenses with the eternity of motion, the basis of the Aristotelian argument for reaching immaterial entity. Viewed by Suarez with

this fatal restriction, the argument naturally cannot reach an immaterial movent. Likewise the necessity of explaining the motion of natural things
ultimately through another motion, that of generation, disappears once the
ultimate origin of natural things is explained not through motion, but through
creation. The motion of the *generans*, accordingly, need not be taken into consideration in explaining the downward motion of heavy bodies, or the action of
hot water becoming cold of itself.[135] In this double background of the
Aristotelian notion of form and the Christian doctrine of creation, the argument from motion leads quite correctly to nothing further than a material first
movent. But the proof being criticized is not at all the *prima via* of St.
Thomas.[136]

VII

CONCLUSION

The *prima via* of St. Thomas, unlike the Aristotelian argument from motion,
proceeds from sensible change analyzed ultimately in terms of existential act.
From this different starting point the Thomistic *via* emerges into propositions
of act and potency taken in a wider sense than they were by the Stagirite and so
concludes immediately to a pure act in the sense of the subsistent act of existing. This conclusion is radically different from the conclusion of the
Aristotelian argument, which was a plurality of finite entities.

Why, then, does St. Thomas say so serenely that it is Aristotle who is concluding to the existence of God in a context which can refer only to the Christian God?

The answer to this question lies in the way in which St. Thomas, in general,
so bewilderingly attributes his own metaphysical doctrines to the Stagirite. Using the external structure and technique of the Aristotelian argument from motion, St. Thomas reads into its formulae his own metaphysical notions. Yet so
skillfully does he do this that never once in all his presentations of the argument does he put on the lips of Aristotle a statement to which the Stagirite
would not literally subscribe. St. Thomas says that in the *Physics* and
Metaphysics Aristotle proves by way of motion that there is a God. Aristotle
would not have the least hesitation in making this statement his own, apart
from the modern capitalization. He actually means his argument in the
Metaphysics to prove that there is a god—about fifty-five of them, in fact. For
Aristotle, the term "god" was applied to the separate entities and to the
celestial movents. St. Thomas, using the same term, understands it to mean
something quite different. Likewise, St. Thomas maintains that it is false to say
that Aristotle meant the immobile movent to be only the cause of motion, and
not the cause of being, to the world.[137] That, indeed, is just what Aristotle

meant. Separate entity is the cause of being to all other things. Yet by "cause of being" St. Thomas is understanding efficient causality. Aristotle meant final causality. Similarly, by the term "being" the two understand something which has its source in two radically different acts. For the Stagirite the source of being is form; for St. Thomas it is the act of existence. St. Thomas allows Aristotle to talk and all the while serenely understands the formulae in his own Christian and existential sense. Never once in commenting on these arguments does he say that Aristotle taught creation or that the Stagirite's separate substance was an efficient cause. Not for a moment does he allow that the eternity of the world motion is not essential to the Aristotelian argument or that the animation of the heavens is not a step in the reasoning of the eighth book of the *Physics*. Could a man who did not realize the nature of the material he was handling continually avoid such pitfalls?

The *prima via*, accordingly, is not the Aristotelian argument from motion, even though it uses the same external structure and technique. The Aristotelian proof, starting from sensible motion analyzed in terms of act that is equated with form, leads quite properly in the *Physics* to a celestial soul and in the *Metaphysics* to a plurality of finite separate substances. Such are the immobile movents reached by the Aristotelian argument.

The *prima via*, on the other hand, starts from motion analyzed in terms of act that extends beyond form into the existential order. The only absolutely immobile movent reached on such a basis can be the subsistent act of existing, infinite and unique, *esse* without addition or possibility of addition. It is seen at once, without any "prolonging," to be identical with the "I am who I am" of Exodus. St. Thomas correctly states of it without further elucidation, "And this all understand to be God." His process of reasoning in the following Quaestio is negative. It add no further determination to the immobile movent reached by the *prima via* and seems in no sense to be a "ransom"[138]that had to be paid for using an Aristotelian argument.

But why does St. Thomas maintain that this is the "more manifest" way, so efficacious that it cannot be resisted?

There is, of course, no question here of different proofs, but rather of different "ways" of expressing one and the same proof. Likewise, there is little need of comparison with the third, fourth, and fifth *viae* of the *Summa Theologiae*, which are extremely difficult arguments. But does not the second *via*, based on efficient causality, lead much more clearly to subsistent *esse*?

St. Thomas gives no explanation of why the *prima via* is more evident. The reason, however, seems to be fairly clear. The starting point of the *secunda via* is the acquisition of *esse* by things which did not have that *esse* before and so could not be efficient causes of themselves when they did not even exist. The starting point, accordingly, is substantial change—that is, generation—which is a particular type of motion. But substantial change is not so immediately evident through sensation as the change from cold to heat or the local motion of the stick that is being moved by the hand. Substantial change had been denied by more men—for example, all the early Greek natural philosophers—than had motion in general, as for instance by Parmenides. The starting point, motion in general, with the particular instances of alteration and local motion, is much more evident than is substantial change. The argument built upon it, accordingly, is "more manifest." There is, again, no question of regarding the *prima* and *secunda* or any of the other *viae* as separate proofs. They are merely diferent ways of proceeding in what is fundamentally the same argument. All five *viae* proceed by finding in various ways the existential act in sensible things and then reason to the source of that act, which is subsistent *esse*. St. Thomas had no hesitation in further dividing the argument from motion into two different ways in the *Contra Gentiles*, without at all adding a new proof.

The procedures of Aristotle and of St. Thomas are therefore quite clear, and the difference between them is manifest. They lead, without any flaw in their respective demonstrative processes, to two radically different conclusions. Similarly, the procedure of Suarez is evident, and his conclusion is correctly drawn from his premises. Starting with sensible things in which there is no act over and above the essence and which have their origin through creation in time, the argument from motion cannot lead even to a spiritual movent. An entirely material movent, given its virtualities originally through creation, is sufficient to account for the motion of the universe. Understood in this background, the argument from motion is entirely *physical*.

Difficult to understand, however, is the interpretation of Cajetan. Cajetan defends a real distinction between essence and *esse* yet takes no account of such a distinction in commenting on the *prima via*. He sees the argument leading only to a predicate, which is later shown to be proper to God. Yet how this can be done, in regard to a philosophical notion of God as subsistent existential act, without an unjustifiable passage from the realm of essences to the existential order is hard to understand. The only possible method seems to be simply to return to the argument and, by taking another look at it, to see that the immobile movent which one mistook for a predicate was all the time the divine *esse* itself. But in this case one is only confirming the procedure of St. Thomas in saying immediately, "And this all understand to be God." On the basis of an analysis of sensible motion as ultimately made actual by existential act,[139] the movent that is not being moved by anything, in the sense explained in the text of not being actuated by anything in imparting its motion, can be only the ultimate act which does not actuate an essence and so is the subsistent act of existing, *esse* without addition or possibility of addition. Evident at once to the Christian, Jew, or Moslem is the immediate identity of this act with Him who in Exodus revealed Himself as "I am who I am." Such is the immediate conclusion of the *prima via*.

THE STARTING POINT OF THE PRIMA VIA

I

In an article published some fifteen years ago,[1] I undertook to show that in the *Summa Theologiae* of St. Thomas the *prima via* for reaching God has as its immediate conclusion existential actuality. Notwithstanding the resemblance in external structure to its Aristotelian model, the Thomistic *via* does not arrive at a plurality of finite forms. Rather, it culminates in a unique actuality that all are supposed to recognize at once as the God of Scriptural revelation, the God just described solely in terms of being.[2] The argument, accordingly, seems to conclude directly to an actuality whose very nature is to be. In "a first movent that is not being moved by anything"[3] the Thomistic reasoning does, like that of Aristotle, conclude to actuality that is entirely devoid of passive potentiality. But can it, like the argument of Aristotle, see pure actuality in any finite form or plurality of finite forms? On account of St. Thomas conception of the way anything is actual, namely through existence, is not his argument bound to regard everything quidditative as potential in respect of both being and opera-tion? By "a first movent that is not being moved by anything," then, can the argument be envisaging any nature other than existence? By pure actuality must it not mean only existence, the sole actuality that is not in potency to anything further, the sole movent that in imparting motion is not being brought to actuality by anything at all?[4]

Nor may one say that the existential character of the primary movent's nature is a corollary drawn by further reasoning from an already established conclu-sion.[5] If the actuality immediately reached by the argument is not existence, how can further reasoning conclude to a nature that is existence itself? Would not the process be open to the basic objection against the ontological argu-ment? From quidditative perfection, no matter how well established, would not an existential conclusion be illegitimately drawn? The primary movent would indeed be established as an existent, but its nature would not be immediately recognized as existence itself. From the nature so known, without existence appearing as essential constituent, the conclusion that it is existence would be reached. No. In the framework in which St. Thomas has already rejected the Anselmian argument, this way of reasoning does not offer any entrance into the existential domain.[6] Rather, the alternatives are clear. On the one hand, the argument may be regarded as based upon the motion's existence that is grasped through judgment. It would then proceed directly in the line of existence to a movent identical with existence itself. On the other hand, it may be conceived as based upon a quidditative actuality in things. It would then conclude to an existent movent from whose nature neither subsistent existence nor any other existence can be deduced. Does not the case have to be either the one or the other? Pure actuality, as St. Thomas understood it, has either to be reached by a demonstration in which existence is the operative factor from the start, or else it cannot be reached at all. Therefore pure actuality cannot take on the meaning of subsistent existence by way of a corollary from the nature of a primary movent that has not already been established as existence itself.

This is what the study of the conclusion of the *prima via* showed.[7] Two objections are easily raised against so operative a role for existential actuality in the argument's procedure. They concern the starting point of the reasoning. The one is that existence is not mentioned at all in the starting point. No cognizance whatsoever is taken of it. If it has in fact so operative a role, why is it not explicitly mentioned? Why the complete silence in its respect? More generally, and more pointedly, in regard to all the *quinque viae* the claim has been made that "this explanation of the starting points of the ways is at variance with the very text it purports to interpret."[8] In its extreme form, then, this first objection maintains not only that the existential understanding of the starting point is not explicit in the text, but that it is at variance with the text itself.

A second objection is that the existential interpretation of the starting point presupposes in some way that a real distinction between the thing's essence and its existence has already been accepted. But no real distinction between a thing and its being can precede a demonstration of God's existence. Only after having proved God's existence can one know that there is a real distinction between essence and existence in all other beings. The distinction cannot be read into the starting point of any demonstration of God's existence. There can be no question, therefore, of existence as an operative factor in the starting point of the *prima via*, according to this way of setting up existence in the argument.

These objections are serious. The first admits no ready answer. Rather, it involves many questions regarding the procedure of St. Thomas in a theological work such as the *Summa*. More deeply still, it focuses attention upon the nature of metaphysical reasoning in the theology of St. Thomas, with the problem whether this metaphysical reasoning is formally philosophy or formally theology. It is the question about the way a philosophical proof should be organized in a theological work. The second objection concerns the basic problem of man's original grasp of existence as he first knows things. Has he an immediate intuition of existence upon which he can base a reasoning process? Does he have to distinguish the existence from the thing itself if he is to give existence an operative role in an argument? If so, to what extent does he have to distinguish the existence from the thing, and what means has he for making that initial distinction?

Certainly, these objections call for another and closer look at the starting point of the *prima via*, with the express purpose of seeing whether or not the operative feature in the starting point itself is motion's existential actuality. In the event of an affirmative answer, there will remain the questions, why within the text of the argument St. Thomas does not explicitly mention existence when analyzing the starting point, and to what extent, if any, existence has to be distinguished from thing in the starting point in order to play an operative role in the argument.

II

Clearly, the starting point of the *prima via* is that some things are being moved in this world. The term "moved," as the examples[9] in the argument show, is not restricted to the sense of local motion, though local motion is of course included in its scope. One example is a cane that has been moved by the hand and is itself pushing something else. This is local motion. The other example is a piece of wood being heated by a fire. From the viewpoint of change in temperature the wood is regarded as being "moved" by the fire and altered by it. In the *prima via*, accordingly, "being moved" includes alteration as well as local motion. The term quite apparently has here the wide technical sense given it in the tradition of Aristotelian natural philosophy.

In this wide sense of accidental change, then, the starting point of the *prima via* is that some things are actually being moved in the sensible world. The starting point is not restrictively the nature of motion, or the concept of motion, or the mobility of things, or anything else that can be expressed in merely quidditative terms. It is rather the fact that motion is taking place. From this point of view its contrast with the starting point of Duns Scotus' demonstration is striking, and is well enough known. For Scotus,[10] the starting point is expressly quidditative. For St. Thomas, on the contrary, the starting point is the actual motion that some things are here and now undergoing. The process of concretely observed motion is then explained in terms of actuality and potentiality.

What does this indicate? It certainly suggests that St. Thomas was accepting without qualms the Aristotelian description of motion, in the passive sense of the term, as "the fulfilment of what exists potentially, in so far as it exists potentially."[11] Against this background, motion appeared as an actuality that is there in the sensible thing, though it is functioning as actuality only insofar as the thing is potential to something further. Motion, accordingly, was something to be explained in these terms of actuality and potentiality. Into these terms, in fact, the *prima via* analyzes its starting point to show that whatever is being moved is being moved by something else: "For nothing is being moved except insofar as it is in potentiality to that towards which it is being moved; while something imparts motion insofar as it is in actuality. Indeed, to impart motion is nothing else than to bring something from potentiality to actuality."[12] Different from any conception of motion in modern physics or modern logic, the understanding of it in the *prima via* is offered in the obviously Aristotelian terms of actuality and potentiality.

What does this understanding of motion imply? It means that for St. Thomas motion is an actuality really present in sensible things, but actual only in rendering a thing potential to something further. On both these points, the presence of motion in the observed world and the analysis of its nature into actuality and potentiality, St. Thomas and Aristotle are in accord. However, in his Commentary on the *Physics* St. Thomas is careful to note that in the Aristotelian procedure the description of motion is antecedent to the question of its existence in things,[13] even though the existence of motion in general is a presupposition of natural philosophy.[14] This observation has an important bearing on the crucial difference between the two thinkers in regard to the eternity of motion.[15] It underscores the significance of the existential consideration in St. Thomas' treatment of Aristotle. But it does not at all infringe upon the general way in which the Aristotelian analysis of motion functions as the background in the starting point of the *prima via*. The description is clearly Aristotelian. For both thinkers, accordingly, motion is an "imperfect actuality,"[16] in the sense that it is tending towards further actuality that is terminal.

This conception of motion, then, involves a twofold actuality. It involves the imperfect actuality in which motion itself consists, and the further terminal actuality that the very nature of motion implies. The two kinds of actuality have to be carefully distinguished, yet the one cannot be considered in separation from the other during an explanation of motion. If the actuality in which motion consists were regarded as an actuality already *accomplished*, as an actuality there for itself, it would no longer exhibit the nature of motion. Motion is the process of *accomplishing* a further actuality. It cannot be understood except in reference to that actuality. The twofold actuality, therefore, has to be kept present in one's understanding of motion.

Perhaps this point is significant enough to merit a glance at an instance in which it is exemplified in Aristotle,[17] and at the illustration with which it is introduced in the *prima via*. The completed structure of a house, in Aristotle's example, functions as a terminal actuality in an artifact. It is an actuality that remains, that has status in itself. But the process of being built, though an actuality, is present in the materials only in the role of potency to the completed structure. The process of being built has no abiding status of its own. It is actual only insofar as it is passing into something further. It does not remain even for the smallest *part* of time in the actuality it has attained at any given instant. It is always in process to further actuality, as long as it is motion. Before the building process commences, the potentiality in regard to the completed structure is in the materials, but just as potentiality. In the finished edifice, the actuality is there functioning in its role of actuality. It is present *qua* actuality. But the actuality in which the process of being built consists is there in the role of potentiality, of potentiality to the finished structure. Similarly, in the first example of the *prima via*, being heated is an actuality in the wood, and not solely a potentiality, in regard to heat. Yet it is an actuality not in its own right, but only insofar as the wood is potential to a higher degree of heat. It cannot be or be understood except in reference to the further actuality. Both actualities are involved. If the actuality of the changing process itself were not present in the wood, how could there be any question of the wood being heated? It is only the pertinent actuality present, since the terminal actuality has not as yet been acquired. Yet the motion is but an imperfect actuality through which the further and terminal actuality is being acquired by the things in motion. It is a process through which actuality yet to come is being given by means of an imperfect actuality now present in the sensible thing.

For St. Thomas, however, nothing can be actual except through being.[18] This is the way actuality is explained in the immediately following *quaestiones* of the *Summa*.[19] It is accordingly the understanding of actuality that is evoked by the use of the term in the *prima via*. The actuality signified in the description of motion can be had for St. Thomas only through existence. Moreover, the actuality towards which motion is directed and in which it terminates is being.[20] Motion consists in a process towards the being of its term. The existence of its term is the actuality that it finally brings about. Accordingly, to be brought into actuality is to be brought into being, and a process towards actuality is a process towards being. To prescind from the existential actuality would mean doing away with the actuality of the motion and of its terminus. It would, in the context of St. Thomas, be equivalent to saying that things are not being moved in the sensible world.

In the setting of the *prima via*, then, the fact that some things are being moved in the sensible world means that they have the existential actuality of

motion and by its means are in the process towards the further existential actuality of its terminus. How else could the notion of actuality into which motion is analyzed be understood, against the metaphysical background of St.
Thomas? How could any actuality be meant, unless actual through existing? Of
course, the statement "some things are being moved in this world" may be
taken out of its own context and read against a narrowly Aristotelian
background. The sensible thing's form would then be understood as actual in
virtue of itself and as imparting actuality to the matter and the composite.[21]
Understood strictly in the Aristotelian setting, no existential actuality would be
operative in the starting point of the argument from motion. But would the
argument any longer be the *prima via* of St. Thomas?

Likewise in the other backgrounds outside that of St. Thomas the existential
feature lacks any operative role, for instance in Plato, Duns Scotus, Cajetan,
Suarez, Kant.[22] If the argument is taken out of the immediate setting it has in
St. Thomas, it does not honor the claim that the actuality of motion has to be
understood existentially. But in St. Thomas, by the same token, in what other
way can motion be actual than by existing? In what other way can a thing be
moved than by having the motion existing in it? And, conversely, what else
does the existing of motion in a thing mean than that the thing actually is being moved? Further, that the motion exists in the thing means that the terminus of the motion is being brought into existence. Existence is universally
the terminus of all the types of motion, even though these types are specifically
different. In the examples already considered, the fire causes heat, and the
builder constructs a house, but both are in accord in causing the being of these
effects; for without the primary effect of being there cannot be any effect at
all.[23]

Far from being at variance with the text, then, is not the existential explanation of the starting point the only explanation possible in the setting of St.
Thomas himself? How else, with him, can you have actuality except through
being? Only by existing is motion actual for him, and only by bringing about
the existence of its terminus does it reach the actuality for which it is meant.
The whole process in which an imperfect actuality is tending towards a terminal
actuality is existential in character. How else, then, can a de-existentialized
understanding of the actuality be obtained than by detaching the starting point
of the *prima via* from its setting in St. Thomas himself? Against the
metaphysical background of St. Thomas, the very wording of the text "some
things are being moved in this world," requires that the actuality of the motion
be understood as actual through existing. The wording, emphatically enough,
is not confined to the nature of motion, or the concept of motion. It expresses
the existence of motion in the visible world.

Has this existential understanding of the *prima via's* starting point presupposed in any way the real distinction between a thing's essence and existence?

Certainly the initial judgment that motion exists in the sensible world is made antecedently to one's knowledge of that distinction. Whether it is expressed in the wording "some things are being moved in this world," or "motion is going on in this world," or any such equivalent phrasing, the judgment that motion exists is made.[24] Existential judgments of this type are being made continually in everyone's daily experience. They do not require or presuppose any acquaintance with the philosophic tenet of a real distinction between essence and existence. The one judgment required is that the motion is really there, that it is actually taking place. In that way the motion is understood to have its own actuality and to be bringing about thereby the actuality of the terminus towards which it is tending. So understood it is analyzed in terms of actuality and potentiality, and is regarded as bringing about new actuality to the extent it brings about new existence. It results in the existence of its terminus. Existence, accordingly, is the ultimate actuality involved,[25] whether really distinct from the essence or not. Having understood actuality in this way, from the start, the argument in arriving at pure actuality arrives at existence alone.[26]

Surely no real distinction is presupposed or assumed in this reasoning. No attention, in fact, is paid to any distinction between motion and its being, even though some kind of a distinction is implicit in the judgment that motion exists. The motion itself is expressed by a simple concept, its existence by the complexity of a judgment. That distinction is implicit in every judgment, no matter how primitive. Further distinction is not required for the argument. Enough is already present to understand the motion as actual through its existence.

But if this is all that is meant by the existential feature in the starting point of the argument, one may be tempted to ask, does not the whole question become trivial? In requiring existence in the starting point, are you saying anything more than that an actuality has to be something? Unless an actuality has being of some kind, it is nothing. In dealing with an actuality, however, one is dealing with something. An article published a few years ago observed: "Before we can attach any predicate to anything..., we must presuppose that it exists. If we were not making that assumption, we could not even raise the question whether a given predicate attaches to it."[27] Accordingly, "we will always be too late either to apply or to withhold a predicate of existence" (ibid.). If nothing more than this is meant by existence, then, it can hardly be considered to offer a factor that would be operative in a demonstrative process. To stress the existential feature understood in this way, in the starting point of the *prima via*, seems merely to labor the obvious in calling attention to a universal presupposition that can have no meaning whatsoever for the argument.

Here, perhaps, one has exposed the most sensitive nerve in the whole metaphysical functioning of St. Thomas' thought. It is a nerve so thickly protected that it has not often been touched by commentators. That the argument from motion can allow the real existence of the motion in sensible things and yet proceed without giving the existence any operative role, is a commonplace, and can be seen clearly in Aristotle and in Duns Scotus and in so many others. That quiddities can be regarded as having an actuality of their own in express contrast to real existence, may be seen from the doctrine of "essential being" (*esse essentiae*) that sprang up among the scholastics in the wake of Avicenna's notion of essence.[28] But the conclusion that existence has to be regarded as merely presupposed or assumed, instead of being directly known, does not at all follow from the fact that men have been able to reason in these ways. To maintain that all one knows is expressed by the nonexistential predicates, and that existence is not directly known but just presupposed through the knowledge of these predicates, can hardly be accepted in approaching St. Thomas' tenets on actuality. Mentioned but rarely, yet asserted too plainly to leave any doubt about its meaning and its importance, is his teaching that a thing's being is known through a different operation of the mind from the one through which the thing's nature is conceived.[29] Instead of being presuppposed or assumed, the sensible thing's being is known, is apprehended, is understood, directly, through the activity of judgment.[30] The thing's being is grasped not in the manner of a simple still-life picture, but in a dynamic complexity worked out in the one-directional continuum of time.[31] This way of knowing the sensible thing's existence is a tenet peculiar to the thought of St. Thomas. It is very easily missed under all the items of the superstructure raised upon it, as the history of the commentators shows. But if it claims to give direct knowledge of sensible existence, in an operation different from yet always accompanying the knowledge of the thing's nature, is it not indicating something far from trivial for a doctrine in which nothing is actual except through existence?

Regardless, then, of any real distinction or lack of real distinction between sensible motion and its existence, the fact that they are the objects of two different though concomitant activities of the intellect is highly significant for the starting point of the *prima via*. Grasped not in the manner of a finite nature, as is everything known through the first operation of the intellect, the existence is known in a way not necessarily subject to the limitation that arises from the nature of every finite object. Accordingly it is able to remain open to a progress of demonstration that will establish its nature and primary instance in the unlimited actuality of subsistent being.

The significance of this Thomistic view about the way existence is apprehended would be hard to exaggerate. It is basic for the understanding of St. Thomas' metaphysical procedure. It is what enables him to reason so differently from his predecessors and from other metaphysicians. It is what requires his notion of actuality in the starting point of the *prima via* to be interpreted in so radically different a fashion from Aristotle and from others who begin their proof with motion. It means that every sensible thing and every sensible occurrence is known in a twofold way. From the standpoint of its nature, it is known through the first operation of the mind, called in scholastic terminology simple apprehension. From the standpoint of its being, it is known through the second operation of the mind, called in scholastic terminology judgment. One and the same thing is known in both ways, simultaneously. For convenience of expression, however, St. Thomas' own manner of saying that the first operation regards or grasps the thing's nature, and the second its being, may be followed.[32] In this twofold grasp of the sensible thing, St. Thomas is able to respect both aspects of the perceptible world, the manifestly permanent features and the basic thoroughgoing flux. Unlike Bergson he is not obliged to honor only the ever flowing duration as the sole reality in the universe, relegating the abiding features to a cinematographical activity of the intellect. Unlike Alston[33] and so many others, he is not obliged to reduce existence to the universal presupposition required by any nature expressed in a quidditative predicate. Rather, he sees both stable nature and flowing existence in the sensible thing itself. He grasps them in the thing through two different intellectual activities. His way of understanding how existence is known in the thing by a specific operation of the intellect enables him to develop an authentically existential metaphysics, different from any other. It is this metaphysics that sees nothing actual except through being.

This means, then, that the existential interpretation of the starting point in the *prima via* depends ultimately on the way existence is grasped through judgment for St. Thomas. Because the motion actually taking place in the sensible world is seen as actual through its real existence, the actuality towards which it is ultimately tending has to be existence. Regardless of the kind of distinction understood between motion and its existence, and without any attention being paid to the distinction, the different way in which the existence is directly grasped and known *allows* it to function as an intelligible factor in the ensuing demonstration. It allows existence to play an operative role in the reasoning. The function of existence as the actuality through which anything else is actual then *requires* that existence play the operative role. The starting point of the *prima via*, accordingly, is that things are being moved in the sensible world, with the motion known as actual through what is grasped by judgment.

But again, the former objection persists in this new context. If the authentic interpretation of the *prima via* in its starting point depends upon the way the fact of motion is known through judgment, why did not St. Thomas himself emphasize and clarify this tenet? Why is there no mention of it in the *prima via* or in any other version of his argument from motion? If the special grasp of the sensible world through judgment is basic in his metaphysical procedure, why is it not presented cogently in that role, instead of just being mentioned disjointedly, and only on incidental occasions? Why is the whole of the *De Ente et Essentia* developed without any explicit reference to the function of judgment? Surely the work of an historian is not to invent new metaphysical doctrine, but rather to report what is already there.

There is little need to stress the fault committed by an historian who presents his own inventions as the doctrine of the author with whom he is dealing. The fault is not justified by the fact that it has so often been committed. But in all the foregoing interpretation, has any tenet been attributed to St. Thomas that is not found explicitly stated in his writings? That a thing's existence is grasped through the second operation of the intellect, is expressly even though infrequently noted. That nothing can be actual except through existence is just as pointedly though likewise infrequently stated.[34] Those are the two Thomistic tenets that are pertinent here. They are not invented by any modern historian. They are explicit in the text of St. Thomas. They are, however, brought now into different focus. They are viewed in the role they play in St. Thomas' metaphysical thinking when that thinking is analyzed on a purely philosophical plane. The question concerns the organization of the metaphysical thinking from a viewpoint other than that of the author himself. Is not this a legitimate task for an historian? Is he not obliged to explain the past in a way required by the exigencies of the times in which he himself lives? Does he not have to present his material in a manner organized to meet the needs of contemporary thinking? If his reading public is accustomed to having metaphysics organized from a philosophical and not a theological viewpoint, can the historian exempt himself from the labor of making his author's metaphysics intelligible to a public that will assess it in a philosophical framework? He is not permitted to add any tenets of his own. But he is both permitted and required to bring the materials before him into the focus made obligatory by the new mentality of his readers.

By the same token, however, the historian is called upon to explain why St. Thomas himself did not organize his own metaphysical teachings from the philosophical viewpoint that is mandatory today. What, then, is the character of the organization they have in St. Thomas? Why is it so different from a strictly philosophical order?

III

The bearing of the question should by this time be clear enough. If the existential feature is so unavoidable in the starting point of the *prima via*, if actuality cannot be understood in any other sense against the background of St. Thomas' metaphysical thinking, why is there no mention of existence in the argument itself? Why is the argument not presented in a way that brings out its existential import, and organizes its procedure in accord with the requirements of an existential metaphysics? Why, in a word, is the organization of the argument so different from the philosophical organization that St. Thomas' tenets on existence would seem to demand?

The *prima via*, as is obvious enough, is located in a theological context. Accordingly, as found in the *Summa Theologiae*, the argument from sensible motion is developed as a formally theological item. That is sufficient to make it formally theological in character.[35] It does not call for formal organization from a philosophical viewpoint. It need not be presented as part of a philosophical synthesis, nor be developed in a way meant to satisfy the interests of philosophic inquiry. On grounds of its position in its own context, therefore, the argument requires only the development and way of presentation that meet the needs of the theological situation in the *Summa*.

Does the theological character of the *prima via*, then, account for the complete silence on the existential character that, from a philosphical viewpoint, has to be operative in the starting point and procedure of the argument? To answer this question, a confrontation with the way St. Thomas proves the existence of God in a formally philosophical context would be of great help. Do his writings offer any instance of the proof's development in a formally philosophical setting?

The *De Ente et Essentia* at once comes to mind. True, this short work was written while St. Thomas was engaged with his *Commentary* on the *Sentences* of Peter Lombard. It was the work of a theologian, of a man actually immersed in the teaching of the theology at the period in which the treatise was written. It contains nothing of note that may not also be found in the *Commentary* on the *Sentences* in formally theological guise. There is no reason to claim that its philosphical tenets were thought out in any other setting than that of the theological commentary. There is no reason, therefore, to think that they were originally developed in any other matrix than the theological. They first saw the light of day, one need not doubt, as theology. Historically there is no indication that they were first thought out as philosophy, and then used as philosophically complete materials in an ancillary role in theology. Yet with all this recognized, the *De Ente et Essentia* is admittedly[36] a philosophical work. Its statements and conclusions do not go beyond the philosophical pale. They are developed without explicit help or management on the part of theology. They are organized from a patently philosophical viewpoint, they rest on bases that are philosophical through and through, they are presented within the range of a genuinely metaphysical problem. Their express purpose is to explain what is meant by "essence and being (*ens*)," and how these are found in various types of things, and how they are related to the logical notions of genus, species, and differentia.[37] Whatever may have been the personal intention of

St. Thomas in explaining these topics to Dominican confreres, and no matter whether they were originally developed on the level of theological thinking, they are here given separate organization by St. Thomas himself and synthesized in a framework that does not go beyond the philosophical. They are dealt with in this work as "metaphysical notions."[38] There seems accordingly no reason for declining to recognize the *De Ente et Essentia* as one of the "many purely philosophical discussions"[39] produced during the middle ages.

A second difficulty is whether the *De Ente et Essentia* does in fact contain a proof God exists. The work has been regarded as a dialectical treatment of the notions mentioned in its introduction. Accordingly it should not be engaged in proving the existence of anything. Does this view of its procedure square with the text? It may be maintained without too much difficulty throughout the opening chapters of the treatise. One of the principal notions is being (*ens*), the other is essence. Being is here taken in the substantive sense of the being that is divided into the ten Aristotelian categories.[40] Taken this way, being means that which is or that which exists. It embraces the whole range of finite things. These are known through various processes of abstraction. To that extent the treatise is dealing with concepts. But to constitute a being in this sense, the essence has to exist either in reality or in the mind. Existence, however, is not part of the essence, nor is it derivable in the way one notion is derived from another. It has to be caused efficiently.[41]

At this point is it any longer possible to view procedure in terms of the derivation of one notion from another, in terms of analysis of notions, in terms of dialectical development? Rather, is not the formal sequence of one notion from another expressly set aside? The existence is not a new notion added to the essence or emerging from the essence. It is what an efficient cause achieves through real activity. It has subsistent existence, that is, something that is existence alone, as its primary cause. In this clearly non-dialectical way the reasoning concludes that there has to be a first cause, and identifies this first cause with God: "It is necessary that there be some thing that is for all things the cause of being, in that it itself is being only; ...and this is the first cause, which is God."[42] In the reasoning there is no question of the formal sequence of one notion from another. There is only question of something being by an efficient cause.

The difficulty here seems to lie in the very notion of dialectic when faced with existence. Dialectic, in keeping with its logical nature, deals with notions in abstraction from existence.[43] What happens when it encounters existence itself as an actuality of the things it is analyzing? If it tries to deal with existence as a notion on a par with characterizing predicates, it immediately becomes entangled in baffling problems.[44] It can conceptualize existence only by subsuming it under some notion taken from the quidditative order, for instance the notion of "perfection" or of "something." But the existential bearing is thereby lost. The concept of existence does not tell one that anything exists. Interpreted as a dialectic, the argument from the existence of things becomes reduced to the ontological argument.[45] To call the present argument a dialectic, one would have to extend the meaning of "dialectic" to cover all demonstrative reasoning. In denoting the quest of efficient causes, it would have to include the physicist's reasoning to elementary particles, and the detective's reasoning from the clues to the murderer.

However, the question whether the procedure in the *De Ente et Essentia* is a proof for the existence of God is not settled by the nondialectical nature of the reasoning. In point of fact, the reasoning does not commence with the assertion that something exists.[46] It is presented rather in conditionalized form—whatever things exist have their existence caused by subsistent existence. True, one's own real existence and the cognitional existence of the objects of one's thought are known in the very act of reasoning. The existential premise is implicitly given. The materials for the proof of God's existence are therefore present, but they are not formally organized into a proof. From that viewpoint one may say that the *De Ente et Essentia* does not contain a proof for the existence of God. The treatise is organized around composite beings and their essences. It needs existence only to explain the composite. It can be satisfied with the conditionalized form of the argument that establishes subsistent existence. That things exist shows that they are being made to exist by subsistent being. Nothing further is brought into the reasoning here. The minor premise "But things do exist," is not stated. The reasoning is not found organized as a demonstration of God's existence, but is developed only as needed in the process of showing the entitative composition of things.

Similarly no mention is made of the way existence is grasped through judgment, nor of the dynamic temporal composing in which it consists. This would be expected in a treatise whose set purpose was to deal with existence in its own right. But existence is not one of the announced themes for the *De Ente et Essentia*. If it had been named *De Esse et Essentia*, or *De Ente, Essentia, et Esse*, it could be expected to give a well-rounded discussion of existence. But it does not propose this theme, and it is not organized to deal with the topic for its own sake. Its purpose and its organization, accordingly, do not call for a thoroughgoing and fully developed treatment of existence. From this viewpoint even the materials in *De Ente et Essentia* for a proof of God's existence need not be expected to occur in the completely satisfying status demanded by each step in a fullfledged demonstration.

A final difficulty is whether the proof constructed from these materials in the *De Ente et Essentia* is the same demonstration as the *prima via*. Does St. Thomas' statement that "in speculative matters the middle term of a demonstration, that perfectly demonstrates the conclusion, is one only, but there are many middle terms for probable reasoning,"[47] apply in the present situation? Does it imply that though there may be a number of ways to establish God's existence with probability, there can be only one philosophically demonstrative means? In the materials offered by the *De Ente et Essentia*, this is clearly existence. If the conclusion of the *prima via* requires that existence be its operative factor, and if its starting point allows nothing to be actual except through existence, the presumption is that its reasoning in terms of actuality and potentiality is geared to existential functioning throughout. This should be sufficient to identify it at least *prima facie* with a proof constructed from the materials in *De Ente et Essentia*. In both cases the one means of demonstration is existence.

With these preliminary difficulties met, the *prima via* may be compared with the reasoning in the *De Ente et Essentia*. The latter treatise (c.IV;pp.34.7–35.10) shows that one can know what a man or a phoenix is without knowing whether the man or the phoenix has real existence. The existence is not part of the essence. Nor can existence follow upon the essence—to cause the existence is to cause the thing itself,[48] and to exercise the efficient causality that would cause the thing's own existence would be to presuppose that existence. Neither coincident with the essence nor subsequent to it, the existence when had by the essence can appear only as prior to it. This notion of the priority of existence to essence is not stated explicity here, but it is implicit in the reasoning, and is St. Thomas' explicit teaching elsewhere.[49]Nor is the word "accident" used to express the notion that existence is not part of the essence, though again the term is used elsewhere.[50] The combined accidentality and priority of the thing's existence in regard to its essence results in the conclusion that the thing "has its being from something else" (p.35.11). The reason is not given any development, just as the preceding considerations were not given development into the notions of accidentality and priority. But its cogency emerges from the dependence implied in any accident, a dependence that in this case cannot be primarily upon the thing in which the existence inheres; for unlike predicamental accidents, the existence is not subsequent to the thing itself but prior to it. In this way the reasoning of the *De Ente et Essentia* shows that the thing is dependent upon something else in line of efficient causality for its being, that is, that its being is caused efficiently by something else. The same reasoning holds till you arrive at something whose being is not accidental and prior to its essence but is identical with it.

Even though the reasoning in the *De Ente et Essentia*, then, is not organized as a proof for the existence of God, and accordingly does not make explicit some aspects required for the proof's cogency, it nevertheless reveals clearly enough the general lines of a metaphysical demonstration. The conditionalized form can be done away by perceiving the real existence, in the example given, of at least one man. That existence, actually being has by the man, is being caused by something else, and ultimately by something that is, not has, existence. Subsistent existence can then be identified with the God of Christian worship.

Does the *prima via* coincide, metaphysically, with this reasoning? It certainly starts with an actually existent occurrence—"some things are being moved in this world." "Being moved" means being brought into actuality (*reduci in actum*) by something else, since the same thing cannot simultaneously be potential and actual in the same respect. Ultimately it is being brought into actuality by something that is actual without being brought into actuality by anything, and that is straightway identified with God.

The different stages of the *prima via*, accordingly, correspond in general with those of the reasoning in the *De Ente et Essentia*. There are, however, some notable contrasts. In the *prima via* there is no explicit mention of existence. Though a thing can be brought into actuality only by being made to be, this consideration is not expressed in the *prima via*. Further, a thing is made to be in ways other that by motion, for instance by creation or conservation. Motion is only one of the ways by which something new is given being. In commenting on the Aristotelian argument from motion, St. Thomas speaks of the case in which things did not acquire being through motion,[51] as though motion were the obvious way, yet only one of the ways, in which things acquire it. The scope of the *prima via*, consequently, is narrower than that in the *De Ente et Essentia*. The reasoning in the latter is concerned universally with all the ways in which being may be had from something else and ultimately from subsistent being. The *prima via* is concerned with only one way by which actuality is achieved, namely through motion.

In detail, the *prima via* makes no attempt to prove that whatever is being moved is being moved by something. It takes that for granted, and concentrates on proving that the movent has to be something other than the thing moved. The Aristotelian argument, however, had been worded to prove that "everything being moved is necessarily being moved by something,"[52] and St. Thomas in his commentary regarded the Stagirite's proof as a *propter quid* demonstration. For St. Thomas, accordingly, this proposition was not self-evident but was a demonstrated conclusion. Yet nothing to that effect is mentioned in the *prima via*. The very wording in the passive voice "some things are being moved" suggests pointedly enough that they are being moved by something. Metaphysically, however, it cannot be taken for granted. One should not need Hume to make that clear. In understanding that motion and its terminus are made actual through being, one could thereby prove, through the accidentality and priority of being, that the actualizing mentioned in the *prima via* is being done by an efficient cause. But this consideration, though clear enough for anyone reasoning against the background that nothing is actual except through being, is not brought out in the *prima via*.

Further, the notion that an actuality had through something else is coming ultimately from a thing that is the actuality itself,[53] is contained in a negative and, even at that, hardly more than implicit way in the *prima via*. According to its phrasing, secondary movents, understood in the sense of all movents other than the primary movent, impart motion in virtue of having been moved by the primary movent: "...sic non esset aliquod primum movens; et per consequens nec aliquod aliud movens, quia moventia secunda non movent nisi per hoc quod sunt mota a primo movente (*ST,* I, 2, 3 c). The distinction between first and second movents here is evidently not one of mathematical succession. Every moved movent, whether first or second or third in mathematical order, or whether without serial number in a temporally infinite succession, is a secondary movent in the sense of *moventia secunda* in the *prima via*. Against the Aristotelian background, the primary instance of any kind of thing is the cause of the secondary instances. But this principle is not expressly invoked in the present text. Instead of asserting that the primary movent is actuality itself, or pure actuality, the argument describes it negatively as a movent that is not being moved by anything —"primum movens, quod a nullo movetur" (ibid.).

These differences of the *prima via* from the reasoning in the *De Ente et Essentia* are indeed notable. But are they any more than differences of expression? Do they continue to present the same argument in different guises? Does the same demonstration underlie the different formulae?

The answers to these questions can emerge only from a detailed comparison of the successive steps in the *prima via* with those of the demonstration indicated by the materials in the *De Ente et Essentia*. The first step indicated would be a study of existence as immediately known by men, as a dynamic composing apprehended through a specific operation of the mind called judgment, as an object of cognition radically different in character from the quidditative characteristics of things. This initially required study is not made in the *De Ente et Essentia*, a treatise not organized around an investigation of existence or around a proof for the existence of God. The reasoning in the *De Ente et Essentia* starts rather with an admittedly evident distinction between what a thing like a man or phoenix is, and the existence of the man or phoenix in reality or in the mind. One glance at the history of the controversies on essence and existence, or the modern discussions of existence as a predicate, is enough to show that the meaning of existence has to be solidly established before it can serve as the basis for a demonstrative procedure. The inital study and isolation of existence is emphatically indicated, therefore, by the materials in the *De Ente et Esentia*. The organization of the materals in this treatise, however, did not require it to be undertaken. But the *prima via* is explicitly organized as a proof for the existence of God. If existence is the operative factor in that proof, how is the *prima via* justified in leaving out the initial and thoroughgoing study of existence as an immediate object of human cognition? Here the question requires a different answer from the one in the case of the *De*

Ente et Essentia. But the two correspond in the fact that the initial and so necessary discussion of existence is omitted.

Secondly, can "be brought into actuality" (*reduci in actum*) really mean in the *prima via* "be brought to existence," just on the grounds that for St. Thomas nothing can be actual except through existence and that the terminus towards which motion tends is existence? There seems no other way of understanding a process towards actuality in his own context. But may this existential intepretation be used when it is not even alluded to in the text itself? Could the argument not be meant by St. Thomas himself to remain in a strictly Aristotelian setting, and not to be functioning in his own existential metaphysics? Read against the background of a metaphysics in which nothing is actual except through existence, the argument would mean that new actuality is being made to exist through motion, and that the actuality ultimately acquired is existence. This step of the argument would be thereby coinciding with the step in the *De Ente et Essentia* (c. IV;p.35.3-11) in which existence is had through efficient causality. It would differ only in the wider scope of the *De Ente et Essentia*, which extends to other ways of getting existence than through motion. It would give the starting point of the argument the operative existential bearing that would make it lead directly to subsistent existence as its conclusion. But if the existential bearing was really meant by St. Thomas, how can mention of it be absent in the wording of the text?

Thirdly, the understanding of motion and its terminus as actual through existence enables one to see why the passing from potentiality to actuality has to be caused[54] by something, and by something other than the effect. In the wording of the *prima via*, the necessity of having a movent is merely assumed, seemingly on the ground of acquaintance with the Aristotelian *Physics*. All that is proven is that the movent has to be something other than the mobile thing, since the one thing cannot be simultaneously actual and potential in the same respect. Is this at all identical, from a metaphysical viewpoint, with the corresponding step in the *De Ente et Essentia*? Or is there any apparent resemblance whatever? There is in fact no mention, even vaguely, of the accidentality and priority that would show the dependence of the existential actuation upon a movent. Of course; a person reading the argument from the Thomistic existential viewpoint could be aware of those two characteristics. In their light he could understand that the motion is being caused efficiently, and accordingly accept the cogency of the step in the demonstration. But is there any hint in the wording of the argument that this is meant? Rather, does not the situation indicate that the universally admitted authority of the Aristotelian *Physics* allowed the requirement of a movent to be accepted without further question? Although the step corresponds with that of the *De Ente et Essentia* when the argument is read from the existential viewpoint, does not the wording of the *prima via* itself seem to point in quite another direction?

Finally, the *prima via* reaches the negative assertion that the first movent is not being moved by anything. How can this be equated with the positive notion of the *De Ente et Essentia* (c. IV; p. 35. 18) that the first being is existence alone? Would not the corresponding step be that the first movent is actuality alone, in the meaning of actuality itself? But does this even make sense, unless the actuality is thereby understood as subsistent existence? A subsistent form (an angel) is a subsistent actuality. But could it meaningfully be identified with subsistent actuality *tout court*? Does not the experience of Aristotle indicate that any number of subsistent actualities can be reached by his own argument from motion? How can any one of them be equated with actuality itself, as something positive that would include all actuality? Subsistent existence would have to be read into the notion of the first movent, to make it coincide in its final step with the conclusion indicated by the *De Ente et Essentia*.

A confrontation with the *De Ente et Essentia*, then, shows notable lacunae in the *prima via*, when examined from the viewpoint of a complete metaphysical proof. Must one look to its theological context for explanation?

IV

Does the fact that the argument from motion in the *Summa Theologiae* is presented in a theological setting suffice to explain these omissions? Does the theological viewpoint from which the work as a whole is organized allow the suppresion of steps that metaphysically are required for the cogency of the *prima via*

Certainly the method according to which the *Summa Theologiae* is organized excludes a fulllfledged metaphysical development of the proof for God's existence. That would extend to the length of a monograph in itself. It could not be crowded into the limits of a brief item in an article. At best only a few highlights of the demonstration can be mentioned. The proof in any case has to be strongly summarized. No other course is possible in the method called for by the *Summa Theologiae*. A development of the argument that would give all the steps required for a satisfactory presentation from the metaphysical viewpoint is decidedly out of the question. All that is permitted by the situation in the *Summa Theologiae* is a very brief summary of the demonstration.[55]

This narrows the problem to the type of summary required. Is it to be a summary that would sketch rapidly the main points expected by a reader trained in an existential metaphysics? Is it to be a telling presentation meant to convince an unbeliever, within a few sentences, that God exists? Is it to be a brief recalling of proofs already familiar to the readers from other sources? Is it to be a merely apologetic reminder to believers that the existence of God is also a subject of philosophical demonstration, a reminder that need not have any interest at the moment in bringing out the cogency of each step of the demonstation? From what viewpoint, in a word, does the summarizing take place?

One basic norm for interpretation can be laid down without hesitation. In the procedure of the *Summa Theologiae* the arguments for the existence of God are not meant to be the ground on which the existence of God is accepted by the reader. It is too late for that. The theological procedure is based upon the word of God. It accepts the fact that God has spoken, and accordingly that God exists. Its only problems in this regard are to know whether the existence of God is self-evident or demonstrable, and if demonstrable to examine the ways in which the demonstration takes place.[56] To abstract even for the moment from its certainty about the existence of God would be to undermine its whole method. It would cease to be theology. Even methodically, then, it is not abstracting from its wholehearted and necessarily presupposed accepting of God's existence. True, in accordance with the set formulae of a scholastic discussion, it proposes the question whether God exists and introduces the negative side of the argument in the standard etiquette of "It seems that God does not exist." The arguments presented for the negative are not all straw men. They are the persistent arguments used by atheists through the centuries.[57] They bring out real problems, and they are faced seriously. Yet for all that, there is no descent to a formally metaphysical procedure in which one's certainty of the existence of God would depend upon the cogency of a philosophical demonstration. The certainty of God's existence is already accepted on supernatural faith, and as long as the procedure remains formally theological his existence is presupposed in the acceptance of divine revelation as the source of theological reasoning.

What, then, is the status of the ways for proving God's existence in the *Summa Theologiae*? They are clearly not meant to convince an otherwise unconvinced reader that God exists. Yet, methodically, they are meant to show how God's existence is proved by reason in abstraction from faith. On the difficulty of this task, St. Thomas has no illusions. In the opening article of the *Summa* he had repeated his assertion that through reason truth about God is attained by but a few, and over a long period of time, and intermixed with many errors.[58] One may be pardoned for suspecting an understatement of the difficulty in these words.[59] St. Thomas is well aware that Aristotle's way of demonstrating the existence of immaterial substances depends for its efficacy upon two false premises.[60] What other thinker outside the light of Biblical revelation could he credit with a metaphysically valid demonstration of God's existence? Yet he can say without the least qualm that the efficacy of the Aristotelian argument from motion becomes clearer if the world has begun in time[61]—an obviously non-Aristotelian premise. He can view the history of philosophy as a gradual progress towards a rational demonstration of the creation of all things by God.[62] He can realize fully that the immobile movent reached by the Aristotelian *Physics* is a sphere soul, and nevertheless conclude his commentary on the work with the statement that *the Philosopher* ends the study in the first principle of all nature, God.[63]

What attitude towards human reasoning do these considerations indicate? All men, as Aristotle noted at the beginning of the *Metaphysics*, naturally desire knowledge. When men believe things on God's word, the Augustinian tradition insisted, they wish to understand what they can do about them. Accordingly the theologian, even though the exigencies of his science do not allow the existence of God to be placed in real doubt, has the task of dealing with human understanding of his topics. One such topic is presupposed by faith and revelation. It is the existence of the God who has made the revelation. The divine revelation itself declares that the invisible things of God are known through the things that have been made.[64] The inquiring mind wishes to know how. The history of philosophy has shown how men have reasoned to a first cause of all things, in various ways.[65] This first cause is, in fact, God. True, the few men who have reasoned to it may be expected to have many errors mixed in with their reasoning, according to the first article of the *Summa Theologiae*. Yet their reasoning has shown them that there is a first cause of all things. This is a characteristic that belongs exclusively to God. To that extent, then, and according to their individual capacity, do these philosophers minister to the desire of the human mind to understand how God is known through reasoning from the things in the visible world.

With this attitude established in St. Thomas, upon what principle will the selection of ways for proving the existence of God be made? Should a strongly summarized form of the existential demonstration indicated by the materials in the *De Ente et Essentia* be given? But no proof of the existence of God developed along those lined existed in western traditions. There was, among others, a proof from motion. It was readily known from Aristotle. It showed that there is a primary movent for the universe. To the Christian, who believed that in God we live and move and have our being,[66] the primary movent could be none other than God. In Aristotle's demonstration, as is to be expected, there were errors, namely the eternity of cosmic motion and the requirement of souls for the heavenly bodies. The efficacy of Aristotle's reasoning was grounded on them. These erroneous tenets could be omitted, however, in the resumption of the proof. But at what price? Something had to be read into the argument to substitute for them and even to make the argument clearer. That, as St. Thomas' lengthier treatments of the Aristotelian argument show,[67] was the viewpoint of existence. But when motion is understood as a process by which new accidents in a thing are brought into existence, it is concerned with actuality that is coming ultimately from subsistent existence as primary movent.

In this setting the requirements of the theological viewpoint could be best met by a skeleton form of the Aristotelian argument from motion. In that skeleton the bone structure of a metaphysically valid demonstration, against the background of St. Thomas' own tenets, remains. The erroneous Aristotelian tenets, upon which it depended for its cogency in its original habitat, are dropped. The skeleton of an argument that St. Thomas in his own existential metaphysics reads as valid, is presented. It is a skeleton that recalls unmistakably a long established and universally recognized way in which the western intellect sought to explain observed cosmic motion through a primary movent. The primary movent, in the Christian setting of the theologian, was God and was recognized by all as such. A way to prove the existence of the primary movent was accordingly a way to prove the existence of God. The *Summa Theologiae* (I, 2, 1–2) had already shown that the existence of God was not self-evident, but that it was demonstrable. The next step was to indicate ways in which it was demonstrated. Five ways, all recognized in the tradition of western philosophy and all acceptable in the metaphysical thinking of St. Thomas, were listed. Of these, the first and more readily convincing was the way that established a primary movent for the immediately evident cosmic changes. It was valid for St. Thomas, it was well-known to his readers. In the skeleton form of the *prima via*, it satisfied both exigencies. What better item could be asked for meeting the requirements of the theological organization of the *Summa* at this particular stage?

How this way of organizing the materials is to be evaluated today from the viewpoint of acceptable theological procedure, is for a professional theologian to judge. From the historical viewpoint, St. Thomas is summarizing an Aristotelian argument in a skeleton form that is acceptable for his own demonstration of God's existence, and that could be expected to win immediate assent from contemporary readers for the rational character of the demonstration. In the situation at the particular time was there any other way of satisfying, within the limits of one short item in a *Summa* article, the two very different exigencies? There was the rigor of philosophic exactitude in a subject that few can penetrate and only with admixture of error, on the one hand, and on the other, the legitimate aspirations of the ordinary theological student to see the human mind reaching out on its own powers to the primary movent of heaven and earth. What better way was there to meet this twofold requirement than the adaptable skeleton structure of the *prima via*?

V

A philosopher's interest in St. Thomas today cannot very well consist in looking for an already organized philosophical synthesis in his writings. There is
none in them to find.[68] The philosopher's task, rather, is the understanding
and explanation of the philosophical tenets used in the theological reasoning,
and their organization and presentation from a strictly philosophical viewpoint.
The philosophical organization will not be the work of St. Thomas, but of the
modern thinker. The *prima via* is far from an exception to this general norm.
For philosophical understanding, it has to be given an organization and presentation very different from that of its original setting. It functions in terms of actuality emerging from potentiality. From a philosophical standpoint, as the
thinking of St. Thomas himself, it has to be read against the metaphysical
background of the all-pervading doctrine that whatever is actual is actual
through existence. In its very starting point new accidental reality is being
brought into existence as things are being moved in the observed world. Upon
the existential character of observed motion and its terminus depends the
metaphysical cogency of the reasoning to something else that is correspondingly
in a state of actuality, and ultimately to actuality that is immediately
recognizable as God. But the only actuality metaphysically recognizable as God
is subsistent existence. Correctly and pertinently, then, is the starting point of
the *prima via* worded "Some things are being moved in this world." Not the
quidditative nature of motion that is expressed in a definition, but the fact that
motion is here and now taking place, as known through immediate judgment,
is the operative factor in the proof's starting point.

The starting point of the *prima via*, accordingly, is the fact of observed motion in its full integrity. It is motion that is actually going on in the sensible
world. The integrity of the fact involves existential actuation. Why, then,
should consideration of the existential actuality be bracketed as the demonstration commences? Existence is known immediately through judgment. It is fundamental for knowledge of sensible things. It is obvious to all. Why was it not
taken into consideration by Aristotle or by any other thinker before St.
Thomas? Why was it not adequately noticed in the text of St. Thomas for centuries afterwards? Why has it been so completely missed by philosophy in
general?

This question brings to the fore the really pertinent problem. If one did not
know through revelation that the proper name of God is being, and did not
work back from the being of God to the being of creatures, could one have ever
realized that the aspect of being is attained through judgment? Gilson seems to
suggest a negative answer[69]—being, as the light in which all the rest is seen,

would itself pass unnoticed did not another source of knowledge, divine revelation, call attention to it. Though a necessary cause, acquaintance with divine revelation obviously need not be a sufficient cause. Thinkers like St Augustine meditated on being as the name of God and interpreted it to mean unchangeableness rather than the actuality known through the composition of judgment. But to what extent is divine revelation a necessary cause? The answer, Gilson adds,[70] is very simple. Just take a verb as a verb. Avoid substituting a noun for it. See this, and no problem arises.—Simple, yes. But no one except St. Thomas did see it. Perhaps the difficulties and admixture of errors in human cognition of God[71] do make the revelation in *Exodus* a practically necessary condition for focusing attention on judgment as the cognition by which being is originally grasped. Accordingly, being is immediately known to all through judgment, and at the same time, in the present state of the human intellect, can go philosophically unnoticed without light from revelation.

If that is the case, one can understand the bearing of Gilson's exhortation to follow St. Thomas in the way from God to creatures.[72] Concentrate on God as known through Christian faith, meditate on him as creator of heaven and earth, follow being as it proceeds from him to creatures. Look at it in them in its temporal flux, contrast it with its eternity in God, and you may thereby be brought to see how it is attained not statically through conceptualization, but dynamically through judgment. Perhaps, then, the correct method for grasping the existential character of the *prima via's* starting point is to "try the theological way—from God to creatures,"[73] to work from "I am who am" to the motion of sensible things.

Perhaps the theological way is indeed necessary, under present habits of human thinking, in order to focus attention upon the existential aspect of observed motion, as immediately known through judgment. In point of fact, there is no record that any man ever attained it through "the philosophical way." But once that focus is attained, one is aware of existential actuality as an aspect immediately known and therefore able to serve as operative factor in the starting point of a genuinely metaphysical demonstration.[74] The probative force rests entirely upon what one sees immediately with one's own intellect in things. Under this direct insight into the starting point, the ancient elements of the *prima via*, like the bones in the valley in *Ezechiel* (37, 1-10), come together again in their basic skeleton form. But now they are given new sinews, filled out with new flesh, covered with new skin, and inspired with entirely new life. The different understanding of the starting point in St. Thomas makes the demonstration a radically different proof from the original Aristotelian argument.

ACTUALITY IN THE "PRIMA VIA" OF ST. THOMAS

The operative feature in the reasoning of St. Thomas' *prima via* (*Summa Theologiae*, I, 2, 3c), one may readily see, is the notion of actuality. The argument consists in analyzing the movement experienced in the sensible world into actuality and potentiality, and explaining it as a process in which something is being brought from potentiality into actuality by a movent already actual in the pertinent respect. Movement tends towards the actuality into which it brings its subject—towards heat, for instance, in wood that is being made warm. It requires a movent that is already hot. The movent, in fact, imparts motion insofar as it is in that state of actuality—in the case of heating, a movent that is already hot. The movent, in fact, imparts motion insofar as it is in that state of actuality—*movet autem aliquid secundum quod est actu*. With this understanding of motion clearly established, the primary movent is shown to be imparting motion without being moved by anything else. In the setting, what else can the conclusion mean except that the primary movent is of itself in a state of actuality from the viewpoint of imparting motion, and is not being brought into that actuality by anything else?

The external framework of the argument is taken obviously enough from Aristotle. With the Stagirite, however, the notions of actuality and potentiality were comparatively simple. Actuality coincided with form, potentiality with matter.[1] Motion, accordingly, terminated in the form that was being acquired. The form was the ultimate actuality towards which the motion tended. But could this be so for St. Thomas? Does not the situation with him become much more complicated? For St. Thomas nothing is actual except through existence.[2] Existence is the actuality of every form, both substantial and accidental.[3] Becoming anything means being moved towards new existence.[4] It is in new existence that every motion terminates.[5]

What do these considerations imply? Can they mean anything else than that the process of bringing something to a new actuality is ultimately a process of bringing it to some new existence? Only by being made to exist can anything, whether substance or accident, be actualized for Aquinas. Existence is the ultimate actuality in which every process from potentiality to actuality must end.[6] There is no way in St. Thomas by which something can be brought into actuality except by being brought into existence.

If this is the overall metaphysical conception of actuality in St. Thomas, is it possible to detach the *prima via* from a setting in which actuality always involves existence? Can the actuality of the primary movent, the actuality that enables it to impart motion without being moved, be anything other than existence itself? Will it not have to be existence that is not being brought into actuality by anything else? Will it not be existence that is there of itself? What else could be considered actual in regard to everything contained in and required by the perfections towards which all the members in the series of things moved are being brought? And is this not enough to show at once its identity with the God who had revealed himself in the verse of *Exodus* (III, 14), quoted in the *Sed contra* of the present article, solely in terms of being: *Ego sum qui sum?*

Some objections may easily arise against this reading of the *prima via*. First, does it not give each accident a corresponding existence of its own, really distinct from the existence of the substance as well as from the nature of the accident? Is not this notion of a distinct accidental existence rejected by leading Thomists of the last four centuries? Secondly, according to the order of presentation followed by St. Thomas, the primary movent is not identified with subsistent existence till several articles later. Does this not mean that St. Thomas *first* establishes the notion of a primary movent in general, and only *later* draws out the conclusion that the primary movent must be its own existence? What justifies an interpreter in reading into the starting point of the *prima via* existential considerations that Aquinas does indeed develop elsewhere, but which he does not even mention in this particular argument? Is not that a subversion of the order given to the demonstration by St. Thomas himself?

Thirdly, if the argument is kept on the purely metaphysical plane of existence, how can it avoid ending as another version of the much controverted ontological argument, quite as the cosmological does in the Kantian setting? Does not every purely metaphysical argument for the existence of God, in fact, ultimately coincide with the ontological argument? Are not the terms "metaphysical" and "ontological" interchangeable even in this respect? Finally, does not an interpretation of the *prima via* as well of the other *viae* in terms of existence mean that they are all merged into one common procedure for proving the existence of God? Is any possibility left for effectively distinguishing the different *viae* one from another?

These objections deserve careful consideration. They are distinct from one another in character. Each calls for separate treatment. Accordingly they will be examined one by one in the following sections of this article.

I

First, does this way of understanding the *prima via* mean that each accident has its own existence, really distinct from the existence of the substance? Undoubtedly it does. A new accident, for instance a degree of heat that did not exist before, is brought into being. There is new existence now over and above the existence of the substance. It is existence that was not there before, existence in which the motion terminates. It is existence that is now really present. It is accordingly really distinct from the substantial existence that was already there and that will remain after the heat, for example, ceases to exist. There is not the least doubt that this reading of the *prima via* means that the existence of an accident is really distinct from the existence of the substannce.

These considerations, however, do not at all mean that a real distinction is in any way being presumed. All that is understood is that the accident exists and that its existence is recognized as really distinct from the existence of the substance. Whether its existence is really distinct from its own nature and remains an open question. Accordingly no real distinction of existence from things either in substance or in accident is presupposed in this understanding of the *prima via*. The question of a real distinction between nature and being can be approached only after the existence of God has been already demonstrated.

Nevertheless, one may rightly insist, will not this view of the *prima via* later have to face a situation in which it will entail the conclusion that the existence of an accident is really distinct from the accident itself as well as from the existence of the substance? If the accident has its own existence, really distinct from that of the substance, will it not come under the further reasoning that everything produced by the first cause, mediately as well as immediately, is really distinct from its own existence? How can this consequence avoid bringing the interpretation into a head on collision with the position of outstanding Thomistic scholars that accidents do not have a really distinct existence of their own, an existence that would be proportionate to their nature and therefore really distinct from substantial existence as well as from their nature?

In St. Thomas himself, however, there are abundant passages that ascribe a superadded and characteristically different existence to the accidents.[7] The existence of any accident is of course naturally dependent upon the existence of the substance in which the accident inheres. The accidental existence is termed *inesse*, and not *esse* without qualification. Yet *inesse* is a kind of *esse*, a way of being. In this framework St. Thomas may be found at times ascribing *esse* to accidents, and at times denying it to them.[8] When understood without qualification, *esse* is naturally refused to accidents. It would make them substances. But that does not at all imply that the *inesse* of the accident is really identical with the *esse* of the substance. Rather, they are two different kinds of existence, unable to coincide in reality with each other. Each is proportionate to the kind of essence it makes exist. If the essence is a substance, the corresponding existence will be accidental.[9] The substance will exist in a new way, by the accidental existence, and in a way that is really distinct from the substantial existence it already possessed. One may also say that the accident itself exists through the accidental existence. But in speaking that way, one is making the accident a subject of predication and thereby representing it as a substance. Nevertheless, one is not deceived for an instant into judging that the accident exists in itself. In saying that the accident exists, one means that the substance is actually being qualified by it. For this the two really distinct existential actualities are required, the *esse* of the substance and the *inesse* of the accident. The *inesse* of the accident is an existence that is really added over and above the existence of the substance.

It may well be that the objections in the more recent Thomistic tradition against the really distinct being of accidents will disappear under more careful clarification. The common objection seems to be that to give an accident an existence of its own is to turn it into a substance. But a substance is an independent nature in respect of receiving existence, while an accident can receive existence only in dependence upon a substance. There is no question of an accident being given an existence that would be naturally independent of another and substantial existence. The accident is not being given *esse* without qualification. It is given only *inesse*. But both these come under the multisignificant notion of existence. In saying that an accident has its own existence, then, one does not at all mean that it exists like a substance. One means only that it is actually modifying a substance. Existence cannot be reduced to a single meaning. Its range is as wide as the multiplicity of essences that specify it.

In saying that motion has existence, then, or in speaking of the existence of motion, one is not saying anything else than that something is being moved. By making motion the subject of predication in the proposition "Motion has existence," one is not at all imagining that motion has existence in itself, like a stone or a tree. To speak about motion and reason about motion one has to think that way. One has to represent motion as a substance. But that does not at all lead one to judge that motion is a substance. All one means is that something is actually being moved. Motion cannot have in reality any existence in separation from the subject in which it is occurring. From a metaphysical standpoint the two propositions "Some things are being moved in this world" and "Motion really exists" are equivalent. They are both expressing the same truth. In English the notion of being, as involved here, is expressed in the verbal form "are being moved." In Latin it is only implied in the passive tense in "aliqua moventur."[10] But no matter how one expresses it, one cannot speak of the existence of motion without thereby meaning that something, in the sense of a substance, is being moved. The statement "Some things are being moved in this world" expresses the existential actuality of motion with all the cogency required for its functioning as the operative feature in a reasoning process. This actuality is not the existence of the substance that was present before the motion started. It is a new existence, accidental in character, and superadded in reality to the already recent substantial existence of the thing that is being moved.

II

A second objection is that according to the order of presentation in the *Summa Theologiae* a primary movent is first demonstrated, and only several articles afterwards is it shown to be identical with its own existence. This is alleged to indicate that the order of procedure is first to establish a primary movent, and then, after further reasoning, to arrive at its identity with subsistent existence. This objection is crucial, and calls for an exceptionally penetrating inquiry into the procedure of St. Thomas in the actual setting of the argument.

What is reached as the immediate conclusion of the *prima via* is described as "aliquod primum movens, quod a nullo movetur, et hoc omnes intelligunt Deum." It is a primary movent in the sense that all understand it to be God. The immediate identification of a primary movent with God may well occasion misgivings, in the light of the argument's Aristotelian background. An Aristotelian primary movent cannot readily be understood as the God revealed in the sacred Scriptures.[11] Accordingly the procedure by which St. Thomas shows that the primary movent is identified with its existence and is unique and infinite in perfection, should be examined carefully. Is this a conclusion drawn by him from the notion of primary movent in general? Or is the primary movent already understood by him as existential actuality in the conclusion of the *prima via*, before any further conclusions are deduced?

The first consequence drawn from the consideration of God as primary movent is that he is not a body:

Primo quidem, quia nullum corpus movet non motum: ut patet inducendo per singula. Ostensum est autem supra quod Deus est primum movens immobile. Unde manifestum est quod Deus non est corpus (*ST*,I,3,1c).

In the second reason given for this conclusion, the argument from actuality and potentiality is now brought to bear upon the primary *being* without explicit mention of the primary movent:

> Secundo, quia necesse est id quod est primum ens, esse in actu, et nullo modo in potentia. Licet enim in uno et eodem quod exit de potentia in actum, prius sit potentia quam actus tempore, simpliciter tamen actus prior est potentia: quia quod est in potentia, non reducitur in actum nisi per ens actu. Ostensum est autem supra quod Deus est primum ens. Impossibile est igitur quod in Deo sit aliquid in potentia (*ibid*).

The reasoning repeats the principle of the *prima via* that what is in potency can be brought to actuality only through a being that is already in actuality. Then, in drawing the consequence that nothing in God is in a state of potentiality, it has a recourse to a conclusion said to be already established, namely that God is the primary being. Where was that conclusion stated? Was it mentioned anywhere in the argument that proceeds from motion by way of actuality and potentiality, the *prima via*? True, what brings something from potentiality to actuality was designated "a being in actuality" (*ens actu*) in the *prima via*, just as it is called *ens actu* here. But does that justify an interpreter in straightway identifying primary movent and primary being with each other? If it does, it would mean that throughout the *prima via* St. Thomas is thinking primarily in terms of being and is definitely regarding his conclusion in terms of being.

But could not the backward reference be to the conclusion of one of the other four *viae*, even though the setting in the present passage is the argument of potentiality and actuality? The most likely perhaps would be the fourth *via*. There God was shown to be *maxime ens*. No one need object to equating *maxine ens* with *primum ens*, even though *primum ens* is not mentioned. The two expressions are obviously equivalent against the Aristotelian background in which the greatest is the cause of all the other instances that share its characteristic.[12] But by the same norm one could likewise equate the expression *primum ens* with the conclusion of the *secunda via*, that God is the first efficient cause—*causam efficientem primam*. Since there is no question, then, of literally equating *primum ens* with anything yet established in the demonstration of God's existence, why not remain within the context of the reasoning through actuality and potentiality? One would then regard the notion *primum ens* as understood in what follows in the *prima via* upon the principle "de potentia autem non potest aliquid reduci in actum, nisi per aliquod *ens actu*." Every movent is a movent insofar as it is an *ens actu*. In this understanding of a movent in the *prima via*, the ensuing stages through the series of movents to the primary movent would require that the primary movent be regarded as the primary *ens actu*. Reasoning later in the setting of actuality and potentiality, St. Thomas could therefore readily refer back to the *primum movens* as the *primum ens*.

Even so, however, what allows the conclusion that in such a first being there can be nothing in potentiality? No reason is explicitly given. One might suggest that if the first being had any potentiality it would require something still prior to itself to actualize this potentiality, and would not be any longer the first movent or the first being. But does this reason hold, just by itself? Today many thinkers, especially against a Whiteheadian background, feel no qualms in acknowledging God as the first being and at the same time allowing change in him and the addition of new real relations.[13] Why, then, might not the primary movent or the primary being be actual of itself, and yet be in potentiality in regard to aspects or virtualities that do not affect its status as primary movent of the series under consideration? Aristotle had an answer carefully worked out. Cosmic motion was eternal and uniform. Any potency whatsoever in a primary movent would introduce possibility of some change, and would therefore fail to account for the eternal uniformity of the cosmic motion.[14] St. Thomas cannot accept the eternity of cosmic motion as a fact. He cannot make his own the Aristotelian reason for the lack of all potentiality in the primary movent. Yet he does make his own, without feeling any strain, the Aristotelian conclusion.[15] How can he do this? No reason at all is given in the present context. But a reason is required, and there must be one understood, if the conclusion of St. Thomas regarding the lack of all potentiality in the primary being is to be accepted as valid. Does the reasoning in the immediately following article (*ST*, I, 3, 2) throw any light upon the ground that allows him to draw this conclusion?

The article (*ST*, I, 3, 2) is meant to show that there is no matter in God. As its first reason it states that matter is in potentiality. But in referring back to the already mentioned assertion that there is no potentiality in God the primary being, it uses the expression "pure actuality" as the equivalent of the notion involved: "Ostensum est autem quod Deus est actus purus, non habens aliquid de potentialitate"(*ST*, I, 3, 2c). That God is pure actuality can hardly be regarded as a new conclusion. It is rather the converse side of the proposition that there is no potentiality present in him. In Aristotle[16] this consideration is not brought out expressly. Yet St. Thomas does not feel the least hesitation in referring to the conclusion explicitly as pure actuality, without any need of explanation. Why does this way of formulating the notion come so spontaneously to St. Thomas' mind?

No answer is to be found in the present article (*ST*, I, 3, 2), nor any further light on the grounds that allow St. Thomas to identify with the Christian God the pure actuality reached through the *prima via*. In the third argument in the body of the present article, God is in contrast to matter described as essentially form: "Est igitur per essentiam suam forma" (*ST*, I, 3, 2c). This stresses the puzzling nature of the whole situation. In Aristotle the separate substances were essentially forms. Yet they were finite and multiple, unlike the Christian God. For St. Thomas himself an angelic substance is essentially a form. But the angelic substance is not pure actuality, since it is in potency to its existence, its accidents, and its operation. A finite separate substance would have for St. Thomas the status of angel. It lacked all potentiality for Aristotle, yet it could not be considered pure actuality in the Thomistic setting. What is causing this crucial difference in the two ways of viewing the primary movent?[17]

In the following article (*ST*, I, 3, 3), nothing occurs that would help elucidate this situation. Then in the next article, the fourth, the problem whether God's essence and being are identical, is presented. The *Sed contra* of the article quotes St. Hilary's well-known dictum that in God being is not an accident but is subsistent truth, and interprets this as meaning that what subsists in God is his existence: "Id ergo quid subsistit in Deo, est suum esse" (*ST*, I, 3, 4). Since *esse* is being used in this setting in express contrast with *essentia*, there need be no hesitation in translating it as "existence." At this point, then, one may urge, is the notion of subsistent existence first introduced into the reasoning, and presented as a conclusion from what has already been established.

Is the situation, however, really that simple? To show that in God essence and existence are the same is a conclusion that well may follow, in the order of theological presentation, from the notion of a primary movent already understood as pure existential actuality. The preceding reasoning had established the primary movent as pure actuality. Could not this be understood as pure existential actuality? The preceding reasoning had established the primary movent as pure actuality. Could not this be understood as pure actuality in the line of existence, and still allow in orderly fashion the further conclusion that it requires identity of essence and existence? In the theological order that is being followed, the present articles all fall under the general heading of the simplicity of God.[18] After God has been shown to be identical with his essence or nature (*ST*, I, 3, 3), a still further simplicity is now being established in the identity of essence and existence. Even though pure actuality is being understood all along as existence only, the order of presentation still calls for the question of its identity with essence in God. The purpose is to treat from all angles the thoroughgoing simplicity of the Godhead.

But does the demonstration of the identity of essence and existence in God, as given in this article, *in fact* presuppose that the primary movent is understood as existential actuality? The first argument in the body of the article follows the strict line of existence and the causing of existence, without reference to the *prima via*. The second argument, however, proceeds in terms of actuality and potentiality. It refers back to the already established conclusion that in God there is nothing potential:

> Secundo, quia esse est acualitas omnis formae vel naturae: non enim bonitas vel humanitas significatur in actu, nisi prout significamus eam *esse*. Oportet igitur quod ipsum esse comparetur ad essentiam quae est aliud ab ipso, sicut actus ad potentiam. Cum igitur in Deo nihil sit potentiale, ut ostensum est supra, sequitur quod non est aliud in eo essentia quam suum esse (*ST*, I, 3, 4c).

The opening sentence of this passage reiterates the fundamental metaphysical doctrine of St. Thomas that existence is the actuality of every form or nature. This is not referred back to any previous proof in the *Summa Theologiae*. It is mentioned as if it is something that has to be everywhere understood. It seems regarded as a factor that always has to be kept in mind. Nothing can be actual unless it is made actual by existence. This holds everywhere. It is accordingly taken for granted whenever actuality is in question. All that is needed is a reminder when actuality is made to bear upon an existential problem. So understood, actuality in its pure state will be incompatible with an essence distinct from existence. The conclusion then follows that God's essence is his existence.

The order in which the conclusions are drawn from the nature of the immobile movent established in the *prima via* is consequently clear enough. First, the immobile movent is found to have no potentiality at all, and accordingly is designated as pure actuality. Secondly, this absence of potentiality requires that the essence of the primary movent be its existence. The latter conclusion was drawn with the presupposition that existence is the actuality of every form or nature.

What does this general picture of the situation in the *Summa Theologiae* indicate? Does it not show pointedly enough that the primary movent in the conclusion of the *prima via* has in fact been understood as actuality that is not being made actual by anything else? This, as has been seen,[19] is what the structure of the *prima via* required. But is any reason given to justify the next conclusion that the primary movent has no potentiality whatsoever? No ground is expressly offered. If the actuality of the primary movent were being understood in the Aristotelian sense of finite form, the conclusion would not follow without the supposition of the world's eternity. If, however, pure actuality is being understood in the framework of a metaphysics in which nothing is actual except through existence, the conclusion follows without difficulty. With the next conclusion, that in God essence and existence are identical, this metaphysical framework is expressly mentioned, and mentioned in a way that implied its presence wherever actuality is concerned. Has it not, then, the aspect of a general doctrine that has to be taken into account wherever actuality is used in a reasoning process? Could anything be considered actual in this context unless it is understood as actual through existence?

If the argument were located in a strictly philosophical context, it could be expected to stress the existential requirement for actuality from the start. As it is, it occurs in a theological proposition that God's existence is rationally demonstrable. The proof from motion, as handed down traditionally,[20] made no mention of existence. The proof is accordingly reproduced in a skeleton form that shows nothing not already contained in the Aristotelian source. In concluding to a movent that has no potentiality whatsoever, the skeleton is vivified in Aristotle by the eternity of cosmic motion and the animate nature of the heavenly bodies. While rejecting these two tenets,[21] St. Thomas is able to retain the conclusion of a primary movent that is pure actuality, and then, treating next in order the divine simplicity, to show that in this pure actuality essence and existence are identical. What is vivifying the skeleton form of the argument in this process of reasoning? Can it be anything else than the ever present understanding that nothing is actual except through existence?

In the theological order of presentation, then, the mention of existence is not required until the explanation of the divine simplicity reaches the question of the identity of essence and existence in God. For the metaphysical understanding of the *prima via*, however, the tenet that existence is the actuality of every form or nature (*ST*, I, 3, 4c) has to be seen in the argument from the beginning. It cannot be eliminated from the requirements for the actuality of the movement going on in the sensible world, without thereby stepping outside the metaphysical universe of St. Thomas. For him a form or nature that is not made actual by existence lacks all actuality, and could not function as the starting point for a proof of God's existence. If in following the theological order, then, you stop at any crucial point in the reasoning and inquire into the metaphysical cogency of the deduction, you will find that actuation through existence is in each case the ground that makes the argument valid. The requirements of a movent other than the thing moved, of pure actuality in the primary movent, of identity of essence with existence, of infinity and of unicity, are all based upon the understanding that actuality is brought about by existence, even though existence is not mentioned till it comes to the fore in a question about the divine simplicity.

This does not at all mean that the whole of Thomism has to be read into any one of its main positions. Far from it. There is a definite order from principles to conclusions, and that order has always to be respected. One is by no means justified in reading into the starting point of the *prima via* doctrines like the real distinction between essence and existence or between essence and operative powers in creatures. These are conclusions that presuppose the existence of God, and accordingly cannot be used in a proof of his existence. But there are other teachings of St. Thomas that pertain to the primal notion of being that is operative in the starting point of any metaphysical argument. One of these is that a thing's nature is what is grasped through the first operation of the intellect, namely through conceptualization, while the thing's being is what is apprehended through the second operation, namely through judgment.[22] Unless a thing has the actuality that is known through judgment, it is nonexistent, it is nothing. In noting at the commencement of the *prima via*, then, that some things are being moved in this world, the text of the *Summa Theologiae* definitely contains a judgment of the existence of this motion, even though existence is not expressly mentioned. St. Thomas is proving one thing at a time, in careful order. But in that order the actualization of natures by existence is not a step that follows as a conclusion from a previous tenet. It is a consideration that is present from the start, and needs but to be alluded to when the theological sequence of problems encounters a question in which existence is expressly mentioned, as in the case of the divine simplicity.

It is hardly correct, therefore, to say that existence is conspicuously absent from the starting point of the *prima via*. The statement that some things are being moved in this world means that motion exists here and now in the sensible universe. The existence of the motion is grasped through one's judgment, just as the nature of the motion is known through conceptualization. Both are apprehended in the knowledge that some things are being moved in the world. The starting point of the *prima via* is the fact of sensible movement as grasped integrally, in regard to both the nature and existence of the motion, with the nature seen as actual through its existence. No matter how limited and precise this starting point may be, it has to include these two factors if it is to ground metaphysical conclusions in the characteristic thought of St. Thomas. So understood it is credited with, and not denied, the meaning that it had in its own historical setting.

III

Thirdly, is there any reason for thinking that this metaphysical view of the *prima via* will make it an ontological argument for the existence of God? Is it true that every purely metaphysical demonstration of God's existence is but another version of the ontological argument? Can this claim be at all substantiated?

Naturally, one has to be careful of words. "Ontological," in the Wolffian framework in which its traditional meaning became fixed, referred to a general notion of being that did not coincide with the nature of any particular being. The recent existentialist conceptions of "ontological" as opposed to "ontic" likewise take "ontological" as referring to being that is not a being. The term "ontological," accordingly, applies readily enough to a nature conceived as abstracting from real existence. The problem, then, whether real existence can be demonstrated with such a nature as a starting point, may be raised. The term "metaphysical," on the other hand, does not have these connotations. Etymologically it means beyond or after the physical. In its historical context it meant by "physical" the sensibly observable world, the universe of things composed of matter and form, or else the treatises dealing with these things. In Aristotelian tradition the preposition "meta" made the term "metaphysical" bear on the separate substances that were beyond or were studied after the world of nature. The history and etymology of the term, consequently, will allow it to bear upon existence that is beyond the natures of things as these are grasped through conceptualization, and that is apprehended only through judgment. The term does not have to be considered synonymous with "ontological."

With this verbal consideration set aside, the ontological arguments themselves may be approached. Historically, they may be ranged under one or the other of two different types. The first is that of reasoning from thought to things. The second is that of reasoning from real natures, found in really existent things, to another existence. It may not always be easy to distinguish sharply between the two ways of reasoning, since the nature that really exists is the nature that is grasped in the concept of a thing. But the two ways may be studied separately in versions that emphasize the one or the other respectively.

The first way of proceeding may be seen clearly enough in the version of the argument given by Descartes. His fundamental norm in this respect is: "When we say that something is contained in the nature or concept of a thing, it is the same as if we said that it is true of the thing, or that it can be affirmed of it.[23] Existence, however, is contained in the notion of God. Therefore the mind is obliged to conclude that God exists: "So from the sole fact that it perceives that necessary and eternal existence is contained in the idea of the all-perfect being exists."[24] From what is perceived in the idea of God, accordingly, one argues to the real existence of God.

Can there be any question of this way of reasoning in the *prima via*? When the actuality of motion and of its term is understood as existence, it is emphatically not regarded as something that could be contained in the concept or idea of motion. Rather, it is something that can be originally grasped only through judgment. It never enters the idea or concept. That "some things are being moved in this world" cannot be known through any concept of motion. It has to be apprehended each time through a different activity of the mind. It can be seen only in the real world, and not in any concept of it. There is accordingly no question of arguing from the content of an idea to the real existence of what is represented by the idea. The reasoning in the *prima via* is from the existence by which motion is made actual here and now in the sensible world, to something that is not being actuated by anything else. There is definitely no passage from the content of thought to real existence.

The second type of ontological reasoning may perhaps be best seen in Duns Scotus. Whether or not one cares to apply the term ''ontological'' to his procedure, at least he himself considered it to be a coloring of the Anselmian argument.[25] From the natures or quiddities of things, known in the real sensible world, he shows the possibility of a first cause. From that possibility, he establishes the existence of this cause on the ground that if the first cause did not exist it would not even be possible, since there would then be no prior cause to make it exist.[26]—This way of arguing is from real nature to existence. With real quidditative perfection as its starting point it argues to real existence.[27] It makes perfections known through conceptualization the basis for reasoning to a nature that contains perfection without limit. In that nature—so it deduces—existence, because a perfection, will be included.

This way of arguing requires a philosophical framework in which all human intellection comes originally through conceptualization. Perfection grasped through conceptualization will when raised to the infinite include accordingly all perfections, not excepting existence. But in a setting in which existence is not grasped originally through conceptualization, this reasoning cannot take place. No matter how far the quidditative perfection is extended, it will never encompass existence. All knowledge of existence comes from a different source, judgment. Only by going back to something known through judgment to exist, can one develop an argument that concludes to the existence of something else. On the basis of quidditative perfection one can never reach existence. Conversely, an argument starting from the existence of something, for instance of motion in the judgment that some things are being moved in this world, is not reasoning from quidditative perfection of things and is definitely not an ontological argument in this second sense of the notion.

A proof that starts from the existence of motion, as grasped through judgment, cannot then be brought under either type of ontological argument. Understood in this existential way, the *prima via* commences with the existence here and now of movement in the sensible world. It centers on the actuality to its ultimate source. It proceeds from the real existence of motion to something that is of itself actual in respect of the perfection required by the starting point. That perfection is existence. The actuality of the primary movent, accordingly, is existence itself. In the reasoning there is no passage to existence either from quiddity or from thought.

IV

Finally, does not this understanding of the *prima via* run the risk of merging all five ways into a common process of reasoning from observed existence to subsistent existence? Does it not do away with all relevant distinction between the different *viae*?

That in all five ways there is the same basic kind of demonstration, namely from real sensible existence to its immediate cause and then to its ultimate cause, need not occasion any difficulty. If the nature of God is existence, one may well expect that the only perfection in creatures to open the way philosophically to God is existence.[28] Basically, then, only the one demonstration will be contained under all five ways, or under whatever number of ways that are selected for its development. But need that prevent the existence of motion from giving rise to a distinctive *via*? The motion involved is accidental motion, the kind of motion that is immediately observable. The examples make that clear enough—the hand moving a stick that moves a stone, wood being warmed to a higher degree of temperature. These are the kinds of motion that are immediately perceived in the sensible world. They accordingly provide the starting point for the "first and more manifest" way, for the most obvious way to develop the basic demonstration. New locations for hand and stick and stone, new degrees of heat in the wood, are observed to come into existence. That the man or the stick or the stone has substantial existence, does not enter into the starting point of the argument.

Only the fact that something is here and now being moved—in other words, the existence of movement in the sensible world—forms, then, the starting point of the *prima via*. Whether or not the stone and the wood are created or uncreated, generated or ungenerated, the starting point of the *prima via* will not be affected. The starting point is restricted to the existence of accidental motion in the sensible world. In this *via*, at least as it is presented in the *Summa Theologiae*, there is no allusion to substances coming into existence. The *via* is concerned only with their accidental motion here and now. The actuality involved in their motion, not the actuality that makes them exist as substances, is what is operative in the *prima via*. From the standpoint of a *via* it is not looking for something that makes substances exist, but only for a movent that is moving them in accidental fashion. The difference corresponds to that of making a car in the factory and making it go on the road. Surely this is enough to distinguish the *prima via* sharply from the second, third, and fourth ways of the *Summa Theologiae*, ways that concentrate on the substantial being of things. From the fifth way it is distinguished clearly enough by the manner in which it remains within the analysis of motion into actuality and potentiality, instead of starting from the way in which the activities of creatures are guided towards a definite goal.

There is no danger, consequently, to the distinctive status of the *prima via* when it interpreted in existential terms. It remains a definite way of presenting the demonstration of God's existence from the starting point of existence known in the sensible world. Any sensible existence will serve as the starting point for the demonstration. But only the existence of accidental motion serves as the starting point for the *prima via*. As long as a real distinction between accidental existence and substantial existence is admitted, the *prima via* will remain distinct from the ways that are concerned with substantial existence of things.

V

The actuality to which the stone or the wood is being brought in the *prima via* is accordingly the existence of an accidental perfection. In the two examples given in the text, it is the existence of an accident in the categories of quality and place respectively. To say that accidents of this kind are being brought into existence is from a metaphysical standpoint the same as saying that things are being moved in the sensible world. Nothing more is presumed in reading the argument from the viewpoint of existence as the actuality of every form or nature. In particular, no real distinction between essence and existence is being read here into the argument. Merely the fact that motion exists, understood in the sense that it is actual through its existence, enters into the starting point. That is a fact that is immediately known through judgment, in which the existence is grasped as actualizing the nature. The existence, so apprehended, is under the general notion of actuality or perfection. In this guise it is seen to be the actuality towards which every motion is ultimately tending.

One may easily, it is true, neglect this existential feature that is dominant in the fact that some things are being moved in the sensible universe. One may concentrate only on what is grasped through conceptualization. In that case the existential side will not become operative in the reasoning. The starting point will be the nature of motion, and the conclusion will remain within the realm of finite form. The primary movent reached will not be a movent from which infinite perfection, unicity, and subsistent existence will follow. One will have the Aristotelian argument from motion, but what internal resemblance will it have with the *prima via* of St. Thomas? If the existential side is made operative, on the other hand, the procedure will be to a movent that is already actual in respect of the perfection towards which the movement is tending. This perfection is ultimately real existence. The actuality of the movent that is not being moved by anything will accordingly be existence, existence that is there in virtue of itelf and not through motion imparted by something else. From this kind of actuality the further conclusions drawn in the *Summa Theologiae*, conclusions namely of pure actuality, identity of essence and existence in the sense that the existence subsists, infinity of all perfections, and unicity, follow with all due rigor. Motion's actuality as grasped originally through judgment enables the *prima via* to arrive at a conclusion readily recognizable as the *Ego sum qui sum* in the Vulgate translation of *Exodus*.

IMMOBILITY AND EXISTENCE FOR AQUINAS

I

What has been called "the awful leap" from finite to the infinite in proving God's existence does not seem even to be felt in the *prima via* of the *Summa Theologiae* (I, 2, 3c), or in the two corresponding *viae* of the *Contra Gentiles* (I, 13), or in the other versions of the argument that have been left by St. Thomas Aquinas.[1] The reasoning flows smoothly from the actuality that is being attained through motion to a movent that is in no way being moved. In view of the difficulty in experiencing any sensation of shock, may not one legitimately ask if a leap has really been made?

Certainly in the reasoning there is no overt preoccupation with a passage from the finite to the infinite. In fact, the terms finite and infinite are nowhere operative in this perspective during the demonstration. The word "infinite" is used to designate a series of movents that would keep receding indefinitely—a possibility that is eliminated in the course of the argument. The word "finite" is also used (*CG*, I, 13, Quarum prima...Si) in reporting Aristotle's reasoning that an infinite number of bodies cannot move in a finite spread of time. But in the sense in which the two terms would imply a start from a finite object and a conclusion to an infinite object, they just do not enter into the proof.

Rather, the procedure is from something that is being moved in the observable world to something that is entirely unmoved. No attention is paid to any consideration that the one must be finite and the other infinite. The movement in the observable world is analyzed into actuality and potentiality. So analyzed, it shows that the observable thing is being moved ultimately by something that is imparting motion without thereby being moved itself. This unmoved movent is at once identified with the God of Christian belief. The procedure is entirely unruffled by any question of a passage from the finite to the infinite. The notions do not seem to affect the progress of its reasoning in any notable way.

Could it be that the Aristotelian framework of the argument is partly responsible for this failure to sense any shock at a leap from the finite objects of the observable world to the infinitely perfect God of sacred theology? In Aristotle, the starting point was undoubtedly finite. It was an object composed of matter limited by form, even though there was no need to call attention to the fact. But with Aristotle the objects reached in the conclusion of the argument were also finite. They were a limited number of separate forms, each confined to its own distinct actuality. There was accordingly no passage from the finite material objects to finite immaterial forms. The procedure was from the finite to the finite, with no occasion to bring the notion of a infinite being into the reasoning. Does this condition of the Aristotelian model, then, allow St. Thomas to close his eyes to a transition that has actually taken place in his own argument? Has it enabled him to speak as though he was unaware that he had made a leap from the finite to the infinite?

Prima facie, the interpretation seems very unlikely. St. Thomas was keenly sensitive to the differences of his own demonstration from that of his Greek predecessor. He knew that he was arguing from different premises.[2] Possibly, he could have realized full well that he had made a leap from the finite to the infinite, have seen no need of adverting to it for the moment, and having left its explanation to a later stage when the question of infinity would be dealt with explicitly. But no such explanation is ever given. No such problem is even faced. There seems no way of finding his own solution when the situation is approached from this angle. Might it not be more advisable, then, to test the possibility of a different aternative? Would it not be more feasible to proceed at first on the assumption that no leap was being made at all in the argument? Could the reason lie in the fact that during the reasoning there is no passage from any finite nature to an infinite nature? Could that be why the two notions of finite and infinite are not operative in the course of the demonstration?

At least, this alternative is worth investigating. Is there any reason why a passage from the mobile to the entirely unmoved has to involve *ipso facto* a transition from the finite to the infinite? Certainly the transition did not occur in the Aristotelian background against which Aquinas is sketching the argument. For Aristotle, the argument led to a plurality of separate forms. Each form was distinct from the others. Each, consequently, was finite in itself. This was in full accord with the Parmenidean setting in which being and finitude coincided. With the Stagirite, separate being was actuality without potentiality. But, as required by the Parmenidean background, it was actuality that was finite in virtue of its very nature as form. Pure actuality, in this understanding of the notion, could be reached without any transition to an infinite object.

With St. Thomas, however, can there be any chance of allowing the presence of finitude in the object reached by the proof's conclusion? Is not this object straightway identified with the infinite and unique God of Christian revelation? Does it not become the basis for concluding to eternity and to other considerations that involve infinity? Can it even for a moment be regarded as finite? From the viewpoint of its openness to nature of the Aristotelian separate movents? Clearly, there is no possibility of interpreting the Thomistic reasoning as a transition from one type of finite object to another type of finite object. The object reached by the demonstration cannot be finite. If a transition from the finite to the infinite is to be avoided, the reason will evidently have to lie in the starting point of the argument. Insofar as it is operative for the reasoning, the starting point will clearly have to transcend the finite.

But how is this possible? At first sight, does not the starting point of the Thomistic demonstration seem definitely located in finite things? Surely the things in the observable world are all finite. The examples used in the argument are clearly finite objects. The stick that is being pushed by the hand, the wood that is being heated by the fire, are undoubtedly finite things. Likewise, the reasoning from motion requires this condition. The mobile thing, from which the argument starts, is a composite of matter and form. It is accordingly able to contain the combination of actuality and potentiality that allows the argument to set out on its way. But it is thereby shown to be a subject limited by a form.

There is not the least doubt, then, that the things from which the argument commences are finite objects. How can they furnish the basis for reasoning that eventually reaches something infinite? The reasoning leads to an unmoved movent. Unlike the unmoved movent of the Aristotelian argument, it at once breaks out into consequences that show it to be infinite. In point of fact it does this in all its locations in St. Thomas. In the *Contra Gentiles*, moreover, the basis from which the further characteristics of God are to be deduced is explicitly noted. It is the thoroughgoing immobility that was reached in the conclusion of the argument from motion.[3] From this immobility the characteristics that involve infinity are reasoned to. If it itself is not something infinite, will there not have to be a "leap" in reasoning from it to the divine perfections that require infinity? Yet how can it be regarded as something infinite in itself, if it is reached by way of the argument from finite mobile things? Must one agree with Suarez[4] that the argument from motion is incapable of reaching an uncreated movent? Or has some new ichor been injected into the argument's starting point by St. Thomas, enabling it to flow out into channels that transcend the finite?

There can, of course, be no question of a buffer region between the finite and the infinite. If a thing is not infinite it has to be finite. It cannot be a *tertium quid*, a denizen of a no man's land located between the two. In nature and individuality, mobile things are undoubtedly finite. No reservation need be made in this assertion. But can the condition of finitude be extended so readily and so uncompromisingly to their existence? On the one hand, their existence is in every case the existence of a stone or a tree or a man or some such other finite object, and is limited in space to the here and in time to the now. On the other hand, it has been possible to say in a Christian context that God is the existence of all things.[5] There seems to be a sense in which the existence of mobile things is not finite but infinite.

The relevance of this consideration should become apparent after a moment's reflection. If, as the texts of St. Thomas imply cogently enough,[6] the actuality towards which all movement tends is existence, will not existence be the supremely operative factor in the argument from motion? Will it not be the actuality that is found to be acquired through motion and that finally is the immobile nature reached in the conclusion of the demonstration? But for Aquinas existence is an actuality that of itself is not finite.[7] Of its own nature it is unlimited. Could this condition, then, not be carried over in some way when existence is limited by a subject into which it is received? Does some aspect of infinity always remain with it? If so, is this the aspect that enables a mobile thing to function as the starting point for the Thomistic *prima via*? Does it allow the reasoning to arrive at an infinite being without involving any leap from the finite? Does it in this way provide an opening or a "clearing" into an order beyond that of finite beings?

At least, these considerations suggest a close, hard look at the starting point of the *prima via*. From their angle does the starting point in fact transcend the condition of finitude, and does it thereby open the way to a nature of infinte perfection, without any need or possibility of a leap from the finite? If existence is what characterizes the starting point in this manner, further problems will arise and will have to be met. Existence, for instance, is not ordinarily a specifying principle. Yet in this case it would have to enter into the specification of the argument from motion. Then, too, if any aspect of infinity is carried over into the existence of mobile things, the problem of keeping their existence really distinct from subsistent existence would seem to become more acute. Finally, after these preliminary difficulties have been considered, the procedure of St. Thomas himself in reasoning from thoroughgoing immobility to aspects that involve infinity call for examination in detail.

II

The first interest, then, requires a good look at the starting point of the *prima via* from the angle of finitude or transcendence of finitude. The starting point is explictly found in observable things, things "in this world" that are in motion. As composites of matter and form, these things themselves are finite.

As in motion, they are in process towards new actuality. The motion ceases when the new actuality has been brought into existence. The actuality towards which motion ultimately strives is accordingly existence.[8] Insofar as it enters into the starting point of the *prima via*, actuality cannot help but involve existence. As the actuality that is ultimately being acquired through motion, the aspect of existence will necessaily condition the starting point.

As being acquired through motion, is the new existence to be considered finite or infinite? The question may seem foolish. But perhaps that is just the trouble. Early in the present century, G. E. Moore noted that many of the most glaring difficulties and disagreements in philosophy arose from the faulty way in which the questions were framed.[9] May this be the case here? To ask whether the fleeting existence of a rainbow or a rose petal is finite, may at first hearing seem to overstep the limits of propriety in posing philosophical questions. Placed that way, the question shuns an affirmative answer. It calls quite obviously for a negative reply. Just as the rose petal has a limited size, a definite shade of color, a particular time and place, so may it be said to have, correspondingly, a finite existence.

Precisely here, however, should suspicions begin to arise. The debates of the last few decades have shown the difficulty in assessing existence as a predicate in a sense that corresponds to predicates like size and color and time and place. In the text of St. Thomas the difficulty in accentuated by the different way in which existence is originally grasped. While the predicates that belong in the categories are first attained through conceptualization, existence on the contrary is not originally known through a concept. Existence is apprehended through judgment, the second operation of the intellect.[10] Only subsequently is existence conceptualized. Even then it is represented under other notions, such as actuality or perfection or "something." The result is that one never acquires an authentic concept of existence, a concept with content characteristic of existence and nothing else. The concept may be elaborated in a way that will pinpoint its bearing and make it focus exclusively upon existence, as in the description "the actuality of all acts, and...the perfection of all perfections."[11] But in itself it does not carry the genuine message of existence, namely the assertion that something does exist. This can be known only through judgment.

Here the difficulties become crucial. Existence as attained through judgment is expressed in speech by the copula "is" or the simple verb "exists."[12] If you try to take what is meant by the "is" and ask whether it is finite or infinite, do you not at once become aware that there is something incongruous about the question? It does not seem to bear properly upon its subject. You are taking a notion that is predicative and making it into the subject of an assertion. Elsewhere the process may be perfectly legitimate. You may take the predicate "white" and turn it quite smoothly into a subject, saying for instance that whiteness is a color or a quality. In this perspective it makes perfect sense to say that whiteness is something finite, a finite quality. But if you apply exactly the same treatment to the notion of existence, you find you are left with an empty concept. You have no content about which you could ask whether it is finite or infinite. True, you can retain content for it by keeping it focused on what was apprehended through judgment, just as in the *prima via* the concept of movement is given existential content by spotlighting movement that is taking place here and now in the observable world. But in regard to the present problem, the focusing on what is attained through judgment merely brings the question back where it started. Is the fact that a golf ball is white something finite or something infinite? The query just does not seem to apply to the content of the "is," to the object distinctively grasped by the judgment. Can the reason be that what the "is" represents is not a "something", and therefore cannot immediately appear as either something finite or something infinite?

These reflections suggest an investigation of the way in which existence comes to be represented as something and known as something. Is the injection of the notion "something" the factor that allows the predicates of finite and infinite to characterize existence? If so, existence will be subject to these predicates in exactly the manner in which it is something. How, then, is existence something? There is no particularly acute problem in the primitive predication of "something" in its regard. Existence is an object of cognition, attained through the cognitive activity of judgment. The object of conceptualization, the other activity of human intellection, is in its most general aspect regarded as a thing, as something. When existence is conceptualized for purposes of study or communication, it accordingly has to be regarded as something, as something that is known and that can be discussed. What could be more natural or normal in view of the workings and exigencies of the human cognitive powers? Through the concept, moreover, attention may be brought to bear on the fact that a thing is existing here and now in the sensible world. The concept, though, just in itself it is entirely without existential content, in this way focuses upon and spotlights what is attained through judgment. It brings that distinctive content directly before the fixed gaze of the inquiring intellect. It allows the intellect to possess in a way manageable for reasoning and discussion the content of the judgment that a thing is existing or that movement is taking place here and now in the observable universe. If the concept ceases to focus upon the fact already known through judgment, it is no longer the means of exhibiting existential content, just as the spotlight no longer makes visible the features of the actress when it is turned away from their actual presence on the stage. But when kept under the focus of the concept, the existence known through judgment leads the mind to knowledge of existence as a nature in God.[13]

In this conclusion of the demonstration of God's existence you finally have existence as a thing.[14] The question may now be legitimately posed. Is existence finite or infinite? The answer, in the context of St. Thomas, is unhesitating. Existence, where it subsists, is infinite.[15] The nature of existence is something that embraces in itself every perfection in unlimited degree.[16] When the question is asked without qualification, the answer is simple and straightforward. Existence is something infinite. An argument that starts with existence and ends with existence should accordingly be moving on a plane that transcends the finite.

However, once existence is participated in other things, does it not thereby become finitized?[17] As found in things in the observable world, is it not a finite actuality, limited by the essence in which it inheres? There is no doubt about the affirmative answer invited by both these questions. Yet the problem does not seem to be met. When existence is established as a real nature, it has the status of something infinite and unique. It cannot be repeated. To be found in other instances, it has to pay the penalty of losing its status as a nature. In all things other than God existence does not enter into the nature it actuates.[18] It always remains other than finite nature. The *only* nature that it discloses is the infinite nature of God.[19] The existence found in observable objects never acquires the status of a finite thing or a finite nature.

When for the purposes of reasoning and discussion, therefore, the existence of finite things is itself represented as something finite, does not the original problem recur? Because it has to be represented in human concepts as something finite? Certainly it cannot function as a finite nature or thing. Outside God existence can never funcion as a nature or thing. While finitized through reception in a limited nature, existence manifests a character of its own that is not an aspect of any finite nature. That character is what enables it to play its distinctive role in the starting point of the demonstration that leads to subsistent being. As operative in the starting point of the argument, then, existence is not appearing in the guise of something limited. It is appearing only as existence, as something whose nature is eventually shown to be infinite. That it is in fact a finitized actuality can be shown only after existence has been established as a real nature that cannot be shared in things as a nature but can be participated through limitation in them by an essence other than itself. Not this limitation, however, but only the character of existence, becomes operative in the argument. The fact that things possess existence, or are being brought through movement into existential actuality, is what counts in the starting point of the demonstration. What *kind* of a thing the actuality is, whether it is finite or infinite, is a question that can be asked only later. It can be asked only after existence has been shown to be a real nature, a nature that can actualize other things through efficient and not through formal causality. But this information comes only after the conclusion of the argument. In the starting point, the existence is not operative as finite or as infinite, but only as existence. It is operative only as a characteristic that opens out into an infinite nature, in the line of efficient causality. Its status as a finitized actuality in observable things is reached only after the "clearing" into subsistent existence has been penetrated. To regard it in the starting point of the argument as something finite would be to make it originally an object of conceptualization, and immediately to short circuit the whole procedure.

There is no question, then, of a leap from something finite to something infinite in the argument. The procedure, rather, is from existence to existence. As originally grasped through judgment, the existence is not given as something finite. It is given merely as existence, an actuality that through reasoning discloses its nature as infinite. Only afterwards is it shown to be a really distinct actuality in the observable thing, and finitized by the things's essence. But in the starting point of the argument it is operative only as existence grasped through judgment, and not as specified in one way or the other in conceptualization.

Lacking any authentic concept of existence, the human intellect is of course unable to reason in this situation from within. It cannot explain the consequences in the way it can account for the properties of a triangle by the essence of the three-sided figure. From what it grasps of the existence of observable things, it can conclude that existence subsists. It knows thereby that existence is a real nature, infinite in every perfection. But *what* existence is, and *what* the perfections are when identified with it, it does not know at all in any characteristic way.[20] Correspondingly, it cannot understand from within how existence is participated. It can know only *that* when existence is participated, existence is no longer a nature or part of a nature, but an actuality other than the nature and finitized by the nature. The questions that the intellect asks about the finitude or infinity of existence have to be posed accordingly in this framework.

Posed in this way, however, the infinity of the divine existence does not appear as something that excludes other existents.[21] The infinite nature of subsistent existence is known only through the existence of observable things. A conclusion that eliminated their existence would be sawing off the branch on which it was posed. As far as Thomistic metaphysics is concerned, the existence of observable things is the only existence that is immediately given. Upon their existence alone rests metaphysical knowledge of subsistent being. From the viewpoint of the metaphysician, then, the starting point cannot be eliminated by the conclusion. Rather, it stands on its own evidence, and is the support upon which the conclusion is maintained.

Nevertheless the temptation is strong to view the problem outside its genuinely Thomistic framework and face it as though the existence of finite things were itself a thing or a nature. From that viewpoint an infinite being would exclude all other beings and accordingly would be an absurd conclusion to reach. Just as whiteness when shared by more golf balls or sugar cubes means more whiteness, so existence when participated by more existents should mean more existence. But is this not regarding existence as a nature that is participated by way of a nature? Can that be done in the Thomistic framework? Is not existence participated purely by means of efficient causality, and in no way through intrinsic formal causality?[22] In bestowing existence the efficient cause makes a thing exist, but without adding anything to the thing in the line of nature. No new nature or additional aspect of a nature is conferred upon the thing through it existential status. Merely a nature other than existence is brought into being. There is no multiplication of a nature, as there is when generic or specific traits are exemplified in new individuals. While more births mean more humanity, how can more effects of an efficient cause really mean more existence? The nature of existence, rather, is entirely concentrated in its primary instance. It cannot be found anywhere else as a nature. How, then, can it be looked upon as increased when other things begin to exist? Is that not regarding it as being shared in the manner of a nature, as for instance whiteness and humanity are shared?

Existence, consequently, is participated by a type of causality, namely efficient causality, that prevents it from being assimilated with the model of perfections that are shared through formal causality. While the process of participation cannot here be understood from within, on account of the lack of any authentic concept of existence, it does make the conclusion sufficiently clear from without that it cannot multiply instances of a nature. More existents do not mean more existence.

But does not the participation of existence mean more things? Undoubtedly it does. If there are more existents, there are necessarily more things in the universe. Yet if the primary existent is all-embracing, if it contains within its own infinity all perfection, how can it leave room for any other things?

The question seems to presume that finite things have some perfection just of themselves. It would be this perfection that might be set off in contrast to the infinite perfection of their primary cause. In the Thomistic framework, however, finite essences have no actuality of their own. Of themselves, their status is that of nothing. They receive all their perfection from an efficient cause. To exercise their own type of causality they do not need actuality, for they specify their existence not as actualities but as potentialities.[23] From the viewpoint of perfection, consequently, the problem is thrown back to the framework of existence, the actuality through which they have their perfections. For the same reason that more existents do not mean more existence, so more things do not mean more perfection added to the already infinite perfection found in their primary cause. They may mean a greater number of perfect things in the universe, but they do not thereby mean that there is more perfection.

The problem, accordingly, is forced back on the character of existence and the way it is known originally through judgment. As things, existents are known through conceptualization. The being that is infinite in every perfection is reached by the metaphysician first as existence, and only later as a thing. The existence is established first, and then is shown to be subsistent and accordingly to be a thing. From a metaphysical viewpoint, therefore, the aspect of thing is secondary in infinite being.[24] The problems of its relation to other things have to be broached on the level of existence. If in the perspective of existence the presence of a unique infinite existence is shown to be compatible with a plurality of finite existents, the question has to be answered. They all may then be considered as a totality of things, without any further query arising how a thing of infinite perfection can allow room for things of finite perfection.[25] Used as a starting point and model, the notion of thing will inevitably involve finitude. It is a notion that generalized the limited natures found in the categories. Only through starting with existence and showing that subsistent existence is itself a thing, is the notion of an infinitely perfect thing established.

The problem of the alleged leap from the finite to the infinite becomes accordingly quite intelligible. To serve as a subject for consideration and discussion, the existence of finite objects had to be represented as itself a finite thing. The illusion is thereby given that the demonstration of God's existence is starting off from something finite. While the thing that is being moved in the observable world is unquestionably a finite object, the existential actuality that is being acquired by the motion is not grasped as a finite thing or nature, but as an actuality that discloses only an infinite nature. As subsistent, existence is finally established as a thing and a nature. It shows itself to be something finite. When actualizing a finite thing, it ceases to be something. Yet it has to be represented as something if it is to be placed in the starting point of the demonstration. Hence arises the temptation to project the argument as a passage from a finite thing to another thing that would be infinite. This, of course, is impossible. Rather, the operative feature throughout has to be located in existence, an actuality that in its nature is infinite only.

III

But if a demonstration of God's existence has to find its operative characteristic in existential actuality, in order to avoid a leap from the finite to the infinite, will not every cogent proof have to be in some way specified by existence? Will not the proof from motion have to be regarded as existential in character and bearing? Yet how can existence specify any intellectual activity or process?

This throws the question into the larger context of the specification of metaphysics as a science. In the Aristotelian tradition, metaphysics is the science of beings as beings. It finds its specifying principle in the characteristic of being. In St. Thomas, being is existence. Metaphysics, accordingly, will have a subject that is characterized by existence. Existence will be its specifying principle. But how is this possible?

Explicitly for St. Thomas, all things come under metaphysics insofar as they coincide in the aspect of being (ratio entis).[26] Common being is accordingly the subject of the science.[27] But how is this "aspect of being" or the notion of "common being" attained by the human intellect? Certainly it cannot be regarded as merely "given"in conceptualization, in the way that aspects such as humanity or quantity or motion are immediately given. Would not a concept so attained be lacking in all content when it attempted to represent being? Would it not extend the notion of "common being" in a way that would bring under it all beings, including God? But for St. Thomas the aspect of being has important content, and God does not come under common being. In the case of being must not the common aspect, then, be attained in a way quite different from the manner in which the specifying principles of other sciences are grasped?

How is the aspect of being, in its basic notion, constituted for Aquinas? It is clearly derived from the actuality of being.[28] This actuality is the being that is originally grasped through judgment,[29] and that has regularly been called existence in the course of the present article. What is apprehended through judgment gives the notion its characteristic content. It gives it content that is able to constitute a subject for a distinctive science, metaphysics. To that extent does existence determine the character and procedure of this discipline. To that extent, accordingly, may it be regarded as specifying the science of metaphysics. True, the notion of specification thereby becomes analogous. As certain essential traits determine the objects of other sciences, so does existence characterize the subject of metaphysics. In this analogous fashion the notion of specification is extended to the existential order. But need there be anything surprising about the introduction of analogy into the constitution of the subject of metaphysics? Rather, is not analogy the condition under which anything enters into the metaphysical realm in the context of Thomistic reasoning?

A genuinely metaphysical aspect, then, is not something that can be indicated or pointed to with the finger, as plants for botany or stars for astronomy. If you try to isolate being in this manner as an object for a science, do you not get something entirely empty of objective content?[30] To reveal characteristic content, the concept of being has to be kept focused on what is known through judgment, that is, on the fact that something exists. It is in this way that the subject of metaphysics is established. Not immediately given in any one activity of the human intellect, it has to be constituted by combining the objects of the intellect's two basic and irreducible operations. Is is something that exists. In the complex notion the "something" is the general object of conceptualization, and is focused upon what the judgment grasps in the knowledge that something exists. May not this situation be correctly designated by saying that the subject of metaphysics has to be established, since it is not immediately given in conceptualization?

This peculiar condition of the subject of metaphysics has two important consequences in regard to the primary instance of being. It means that God does not come under the subject of metaphysics. The subject of metaphysics has to be a combination of two factors. The general object of conceptualization enables it to be common and to provide accordingly the universal character necessary for any scientific subject. The highly particularized existence, as attained through judgment, gives it distinctive content. Both are necessary for the subject of metaphysics. In consequence the primary instance of being, which in itself does not contain the combination of these two factors, does not come under the subject of metaphysics. Rather, it is the principle of the subject of this science. Accordingly common being comes under it, and not vice versa.[31]

The other notable consequence in regard to the primary instance of being is that the demonstration of God's existence is based upon the judgment that something exists here and now in the observable world. Not on anything originally known through conceptualization can a metaphysical reasoning to God be grounded. Existence as grasped through judgment has to be the operative factor. An ontological argument is accordingly impossible. What characterizes a demonstration as metaphysical in the context of St. Thomas, therefore, is its specification by existence grasped through judgment.

What bearing do these general considerations have upon the particular case of the *prima via*? If movement is a process towards existential actuality,[32] it will possess quite obviously the factor that allows it to ground a metaphysical demonstration. That factor, however, will have to be known through judgment. It will have to be the fact that something is here and now being moved in the observable world. Nothing in the essence or nature of movement is able to lead the intellect to an infinite movent. Only the existential feature in the actuality that is being acquired through motion is able to provide the operative characteristic for a demonstration that has to proceed on a level higher than that of finite natures.

If this is the case, may not the existential factor be correctly said to specify the demonstration contained in the *prima via*? Will not the *via* be an argument from existential actuality that is being acquired through movement, to existential actuality that subsists? Will it not thereby allow ample room for other *viae*? Existence can be acquired or shared in different ways. It is bestowed through motion, through creation, through conservation, through concurrence. These, in themselves and in their numerous complications, allow wide scope for distinct ways of proceeding from participated existence to subsistent existence. While the operative force of the demonstration is always in the existential order, the different ways in which existence is bestowed invite different ways of developing the one proof.

Need this assessment of the *prima via*, then, be regarded as an effort to have things both ways at the same time, to keep one's cake and eat it? Does not the subject of metaphysics itself require both the universalizing concept and the existential actuality? In this context is the specification of the *prima via* by both motion and existence anything more than a claim that the argument is metaphysical in character?

IV

How do these considerations apply in the way St. Thomas himself proceeds from the conclusion of an unmoved movent to problems involving its infinity and its existence? The *Contra Gentiles*, in which the argument from motion is developed at its greatest length and in explicit attention to detail, should provide a good means for investigating the sequence of his thought.

In it the arguments are presented as "rationes quibus tam philosophi quam doctores Catholici Deum esse probaverunt."[33] They are offered as ways already established in philosophical and Christian tradition. No original way is promised. In point of fact, they are all regarded here as arising in one way or another from Aristotle, with the exception of the last *via*. For it John Damascene and Averroes are cited (*CG*, I, 13, Ad hoc). What has been reached by these arguments is a primary being, and its conditions remain to be investigated: "Ostenso igitur quod est aliquod primum ens,...oportet eius conditiones investigare" (*CG*, I, 14, init.).

The examination of the conditions of the primary being is to be made chiefly by way of the negative theology. The reason is that the divine substance exceeds any form the human intellect can grasp:

> Nam divina substantia omnem formam quam intellectus noster attingit, sua immensitate excedit: et sic ipsam apprehendere non possumus cognoscendo quid est. Sed aliqualem eius habemus notitiam cognoscendo quid non est (*CG*, I, 14, Est autem).

From the start, accordingly, the object reached by the arguments for God's existence is being regarded as something endowed with *immensitas*. It is something that is beyond measure. The way in which it is beyond measure is specified. It surpasses any form that the intellect can attain, so there is no possibility of apprehending *what* it is. This means, clearly enough that one has no conceptual knowledge of the divine substance. Conceptual knowledge is knowledge of things from the viewpoint of their forms. But because it is immeasureable, the divine substance exceeds all such forms.

From the start, therefore, the object reached by the demonstration is considered to be without measure. Not for a moment is the possibility allowed that it might be a finite form, as in the case of the Aristotelian separate substance. The term "infinite" is not used. Nevertheless the notion expressed by *immensitas* can hardly differ from what is ordinarily meant by infinity. At least it excludes any bounds or limits, in its notion of beyond all measure. The treatment takes place as though one has but to look at the object reached by the demonstration to see that it is beyond measure, just as one has but to look at it to see that it is what all recognize as God.

Negative theology, or procedure by way of removal, must however presuppose something positive to work on. It is true that knowledge of the divine substance is reached more and more as one characteristic after another is removed by the process of human thought: "Tantoque eius notitiae magis approquinquamus, quanto plura per intellectum nostrum ab eo poterimus removere" (*ibid.*) But to offer more knowledge, the process has to consist in removal of limitations that restrict the object's perfection. The human intellect must have attained a positive object that appears under limitations, and that becomes better known as the limitations are gradually removed.

What is that positive underlying and immeasurable object? The article of the *Contra Gentiles* immediately identifies it under the characteristic of immobility, as reached by the *viae* from motion: "Ad procedendum igitur circa Dei cognitionem per viam remotionis, accipiamus principium id quod ex superioribus iam manifestum est, scilicet quod Deus sit omnino immobilis" (*ibid.*, fin). The thoroughgoing immobility reached by the argument from motion is to be the starting point from which limiting traits are to be removed one by one. It itself is placed beyond all limiting measures. It is designated by a word that is negative in form. But what the word signifies in the backward reference to the conclusion of the demonstration from motion is positive enough. It is the "primum motorem separatum omnino immobilem" (*CG*, I, 13, Sed quia). According to the force of the reasoning it is actuality that is not being brought into actuality by anything. Is not this a decidedly positive notion? From its unmeasured and immeasureable richness, consequently, all limiting features are to be gradually removed. The removal of the limiting traits enables the human intellect to understand it in increasing depth.

With immobility as the basis for the reasoning, the first aspect demonstrated of the primary being is its eternity:

Nam omne quod incipit esse vel desinit, per motum vel mutationem hoc patitur.

> Ostensum autem est Deum esse omnino immutabilem. Est igitur aeternus, carens principio et fine (*CG*, I, 15, init.).

From the immobility reached by the argument from motion, the conclusion is drawn that God has no beginning of existence or end of existence. His existence cannot undergo change either by beginning or by ending. To carry this reasoning, the notion of movement has been extended to that of any kind of change (*mutatio*) whatsoever. In the Thomistic argument, accordingly, movement has not been understood as restricted to the process by which matter acquires form. In that Aristotelian perspective the matter was always previously existent, and was being brought to a new form. The extension of the notion to *mutatio* shows clearly enough the location of the reasoning in the traditional Augustinian setting, in which mutability was the characteristic of creatures in contradistinction to God. Against this background, mutability covered change from non-existence to existence, even though there was no subjective potency presupposed.[34] Does not this indicate quite sharply that in the conclusion of the Thomistic argument the notion of the entirely immobile is being understood on a level above that form? Is it not taken in a sense in which the actuality reached by the proof's existence? Though the phrasing is Aristotelian, does not the meaning range beyond the Aristotelian notion of change as the acquisition of form to a setting in which change can denote the attaining of new existence?

St. Thomas is well aware of the basis on which the cogency of the Aristotelian reasoning is laid. The cogency rests on the eternity of time and of cosmic motion. It is from the eternity of cosmic movement that the Aristotelian argument concludes to the eternity of the movent substance. Nevertheless the rejection of the Aristotelian premise does not undermine the conclusion:

> Ostendit etiam Aristoteles ex sempiternitate temporis sempiternitatem motus. Ex quo iterum ostendit sempiternitatem substantiae moventis. ...Negata autem sempiternitate temporis et motus, adhuc manet ratio ad sempiternitatem substantiae. Nam, si motus incoepit, oportet quod ab aliquo movente incoeperit. Qui si incoepit, aliquo agente incoepit.[35]

Even after the denial of the Aristotelian premises regarding the eternity of time and cosmic movement, the argument from motion still holds for St. Thomas. If movement begins, it has to have its beginning through a movent, and ultimately through an agent that had no beginning. An eternal agent, and accordingly an eternal substance, is thereby demonstrated. This conclusion may not seem to rise above the Aristotelian framework, in which a finite form could be an eternal substance. Yet unlike the Aristotelian separate form, the eternal substance reached by the Thomistic reasoning is an agent, an efficient cause. Not feeling himself bound by the premises in the Aristotelian framework, St. Thomas is quite free to substitute other premises and arrive at a different kind of eternal substance. The full force of the difference is not exploited here, as it is elsewhere,[36] but enough appears to show that, just as in the other places, eternity is being conceived in terms of existence: "Est igitur carens principio et fine, totum esse suum simul habens. In quo ratio aeternitatis consistit" (CG, I, 15, Item).

The next stage in the development of conclusions from the immobility of the primary movent is to show that there is no passive potency in God (CG, I, 16). Through demonstration couched in terms of actuality and potentiality, the arguments from motion had reached explicitly an entirely immobile movent. But the conclusion that in the immobile movent there is no potency at all, was not drawn. In the Aristotelian Physics a conclusion of this kind had not been reached. In the Metaphysics, Aristotle did arrive at separate movents about which he was able to draw this conclusion. The eternity of cosmic motion required them to be entirely without potency, even though they did not function as efficient causes. Against his own Christian background, St. Thomas is now drawing explicitly the conclusion that the primary movent has no passive potentiality whatsoever.

The case is introduced in terms of the eternal existence already established in the preceding article. To the extent a substance has admixture of potentiality, it is capable of non-existence. But God, because of his eternity, is not capable of non-existence. Accordingly there is no admixture of potentiality in his substance. Secondly, as primary being and primary cause, God cannot presuppose any actuality prior to himself. But a thing that is in any way potential presupposes some prior actuality. Thirdly, because God is of himself necessary being, he is not subject to any cause and consequently cannot have any aspect of potentiality in his substance. As the primary agent, fourthly, he cannot act in virtue of participating anything else. He has to be active through his own essence. This means that he is active in virtue of his entire self. He has accordingly no admixture of potency, but is pure actuality (CG, I, 16, Item unumquodque).

These arguments, starting with the one from the eternity of God, all understand potentiality in relation to existence and activity. Potentiality, even though introduced in the Aristotelian setting of cosmic movement, is being viewed in the wider setting of potentiality to existence. No difficulty seems felt in this extension of the notion, and no need of calling attention to it seems to be experienced. In a fifth argument, the notion of potentiality is thrown back on the Aristotelian definition of movement, and the same conclusion is immediately drawn from immutability that had already been established for God as a result of the arguments from motion:

> Unumquodque, sicut natum est agere inquantum est actu, ita natum est pati inquantum est in potentia: nam motus est actus potentia existentis. Sed Deus est om-

nino impassibilis ac immutabilis, ut patet ex dictis. Nihil ergo habet de potentia, scilicet passiva (CG, I, 16, Adhuc unumquodque).

In this argument the thoroughgoing immobility of God, as reached in the demonstration from motion and viewed in the wider terms of impassivity and immutability, is regarded as leading to the impossibility of any passively potential aspect in God. The conclusion is meant in the broad sense in which potentiality has been understood throughout the present article. It is regarded as potentiality not only to form but also to existence.

The sixth and final argument also follows closely the steps of the demonstration from motion. But the aspect of existence makes itself felt in the reasoning. What is only in potency does not yet exist, and therefore cannot perform any activity. Accordingly it requires that something prior to itself exist, to bring it from potentiality to actuality:

> ...quia quod est potentia, nondum est; unde nec agere potest. Ergo oportet esse aliquid aliud prius, quo educatur de potentia in actum. ...Ergo oportet devenire ad aliquod quod est tantum actu et nullo modo in potentia (CG, I, 16, Item videmus).

The least that can be said in respect of the potentiality envisaged in all this reasoning is that it ranges considerably beyond the Aristotelian notion. It is spread out in a Christian context in which mutability is the characteristic of creatures, in the sense that they are made from nothing and not from a preexisting potentiality. In this setting potentiality is related to existence and to efficient cause, rather than to form. What is in potency does not exist and cannot act, as is stated in the final argument just quoted. The explicit conclusion that the primary agent is pure actuality is drawn from the consideration that it has to act in virtue of its whole essence. It is shown to be pure actuality because it is in this way an efficient cause. Could the difference from the Aristotelian separate forms be any more striking?

The theme of immobility is then used to show that in God there is no matter, since matter is something potential: "Si igitur Deus est immobilis, ut probatum est, nullo modo potest esse rerum causa per modum materiae" (CG, I, 17, Item materia non fit causa). Likewise, complete lack of potentiality makes a composition impossible, since composition requires at least the potentiality of the parts to form a whole (CG, I, 18). Also, the thoroughgoing immobility of God is used to show that there can be nothing strained or unnatural in him: "Omne in quo est aliquid violentum vel innaturale, natum est ab alio moveri: ...Deus autem est omnino immobilis, ut ostensum est" (CG, I, 19, Item). Further, the impossibility of composition and the complete lack of potentiality in God require that he be his own essence, since individual is related to essence under the aspect of potentiality as to actuality (CG, I, 21).

Then follows the proof that in God essence or quiddity is not other than his existence. The first arguments are from the necessary and independent character of the divine existence, from its simplicity or lack of composition, and from its primacy. But eventually one is brought forward from the aspect of pure actuality in God. Pure actuality, however, is understood in a context in which everything other than existence is regarded as a potentiality for existence. The result is that nothing besides existence could be understood as pure actuality. The restriction of the notion to the existential order appears clearly in the argument:

> *Esse* actum quendam nominat: non enim dicitur esse aliquid ex hoc quod est in potentia, sed ex eo quod est in actu. Omne autem cui convenit actus aliquis diversum ab eo existens, se habet ad ipsum ut potentia ad actum:...Ostensum est autem in Deo nihil esse de potentia, sed ipsum esse purum actum (*CG*, I, 22, Amplius *esse*).

Can there be any question here of deriving the notion of subsistent existence from any non-existential actuality? Can the reasoning be construed as though the argument from motion had reached a conclusion common to both the Aristotelian and Thomistic conceptions of an entirely immobile movent, and that only later the additional conclusion is drawn that the primary movent has to be subsistent existence? Is it not clear from the above text that the immobile movent reached by the Thomistic reasoning was understood from the start as purely existential actuality, since all other actuality is still a potency to its own existence? In the course of the subsequent reasoning no query was framed in terms of proving that the entirely immobile movent was subsistent existence. Rather, the query was framed in terms of lack of any difference between essence or quiddity and existence in God. The conclusion as first expressed is that God has no essence that is not his existence: "Deus igitur non habet essentiam quae non sit suum esse" (*CG*, I, 22, Ostensum). Does not this read as though the divine existence is taken as established, here by the argument from the possible and the necessary, and the query is whether any essence is there in addition to the existence? When the argument from pure actuality as demonstrated through motion is reached, the framework of the reasoning can hardly be regarded as changed. The conclusion accordingly is worded: "Non igitur Dei essentia est aliud quam suum esse" (*CG*, I, 22, Amplius *esse*). The conclusion here takes for granted that the existence has been established, and is showing that in this case the essence cannot be other than it. All continues to proceed as though the argument from motion had arrived at existential actuality, and now this actuality is shown to have no essence other than itself. There is no trace of an attempt to prove that the actuality itself is existential. That is clearly taken for granted.

In the concluding passages of the article the statement of *Exodus*, III, 14, is brought forward. Since the name signifies the nature or essence of a thing, it follows that the divine existence itself is its own essence or nature: Hanc autem sublimem veritatem Moyses a Domino est edoctus...*Ego sum qui sum*. ...Quodlibet autem nomen est institutum ad significandum naturam seu essentiam alicuius rei. Unde relinquitur quod ipsum divinum esse est sua natura vel essentia."[37] The existence is regarded as established. The conclusion drawn is that it is its own essence. If this use of the Scriptural passage is compared with its occurrence in the article in which the *prima via* of the *Summa Theologiae* is located, does not the whole picture make excellent sense? In the *Sed contra* of that article (*ST*, I, 2, 3), God is presented under the designation found in *Exodus*. Accordingly, from St. Thomas' earlier understanding of the Scriptural text in the *Contra Gentiles*, God is presented as existence that is its own essence. In that setting when the immobile movent reached by the *prima via* is at once identified with God, need it be at all surprising that the movent should be regarded as existential actuality? As existential actuality and nothing else,[38] does it not appear without more ado as the *I am who I am* of the *Sed contra* in the article, especially when one considers the understanding that had been given the Scriptural statement in the *Contra Gentiles*?

Finally, in proving that all perfection is found in God, St. Thomas draws the conclusion equally from God's existence and from his pure actuality. The conclusion follows from his existence: "Deus igitur, qui est suum esse, ut supra probatum est, habet esse secundum totam virtutem ipsius esse. Non potest ergo carere aliqua nobilitate[39] quae alicui rei conveniat" (*CG*, I, 28, Omnis). It follows just as readily from pure actuality: "Id igitur quod nullo modo est in potentia sed est actus purus, oportet perfectissimum esse" (*Ibid.*, Amplius unumquodque). In the premises, then, pure actuality, just as does subsistent existence, involves all perfections. It is being understood as existential actuality, not formal actuality. This totality of perfection means that God is infinite: "...eius perfectio omnium generum perfectiones continet, ut supra ostensum est. Est igitur infinitus" (*CG*, I, 43, Omne). The infinity is shown equally from pure actuality (*ibid.*, Item tanto) and from existential actuality (Amplius ipsum). The two seem regarded as coinciding in the fullness of actuality.

The procedure in the *Contra Gentiles*, then, shows clearly enough that what is reached in the conclusion of the arguments from motion is an actuality unlimited by any essence or nature. This, in the framework of St. Thomas' metaphysical reasoning, can be only existential actuality. On the strength of the actuality so reached, the immobile movent is readily shown to be eternal, lacking all passive potentiality, containing the perfections of all things, and accordingly to be infinite.

V

Nowhere in the procedure of St. Thomas in proving God's existence and perfections is there any leap from the finite to the infinite. The operative feature in the starting point is the existential actuality found in sensible things. Of its nature this actuality is infinite. Where it is present in a status other than that of a nature, it is indeed limited by something else, but not at all in virtue of the characteristic it itself discloses. It is on the strength of that characteristic that the demonstration is developed.

In particular, in the reasoning from motion the actuality that is being attained through movement is ultimately existential. Accordingly the actuality that is finally reached in the argument, actuality that is not being actualized by anything, can be only existential actuality. It is existence and nothing else. No authentic concept of it can be formed. It has to be expressed in terms of notions taken from finite natures, such as something, or actuality, or perfection. Here the notion used is that of an entirely unmoved movent, a notion taken from Aristotle's separate finite forms. In itself it does not express existence. But, just as the concepts of something and of actuality and of perfection, it can be kept focused on existential actuality and serve as an apt means of spotlighting the character that enables the object reached by the *prima via* to be identified at once as the *I am who I am* of *Exodus*. No more than any other concept can that of a completely immobile movent have genuine existential content. But like a number of other concepts, it can focus attention on what is concluded from the actuality apprehended through judgment. Just as what is known through the judgment "This table exists" can be taken up again conceptually as "the existence of this table," so the entirely unmoved actuality that ultimately is imparting observed motion can, though existential in character, be indicated by the concept of a completely immobile movent. To be known, however, it has to be seen as cogently required, in the conclusion of a reasoning process, by the movement here and now occurring in the observable world. It may not even for an instant be cut off from the existential starting point, if it is to be validly reached. Pascal[40] noted trenchantly that a metaphysical proof for the existence of God would have force only at the moment the demonstration is being seen. Does not this reflection have striking application in the case of the Thomistic *prima via*? A reservation, of course, is that memory keeps fresh the assent given to conclusions already proved.

AQUINAS ON INFINITE REGRESS.

A note in a recent issue of MIND sees a *petitio principii* in the argument of St. Thomas Aquinas against an infinite series of movents. In that argument the observable movents are described as *moventia secunda*. But the serial order understood in the description "second" does not allow for the possibility of an infinite series of moved movents. The argument therefore presupposes what it undertakes to prove, namely, that there is a first movent in the series.[1]

No one would quarrel with this critique just in itself, absolved as it stands from any concrete background of place and time. But does it at all come to grips with the argument of Aquinas in the argument's own medieval setting? Is it not transferring the demonstration to a quite alien plane of abstract logic, a plane on which the argument was never meant to function? Most philosophers at the present time, as Ryle[2] has noted in one of his apt similes, would liken their activities to the work of the cartographer rather than to that of the detective. But was this the case with the medieval thinkers, and in particular with St. Thomas? Did Aquinas look upon metaphysics as plotting the contours of concepts, or as searching for some one who did something? The descriptions in places like the Proem to the *Commentary on the Metaphysics of Aristotle* show definitely enough that he regarded metaphysics as a search for the ultimate causes of things, causes that at least in part existed separately from the material world. As a Christian he was convinced in advance that the primary movent of things was the God he accepted on faith. But, like the detective already psychologically convinced of the identity of the murderer, he was seeking metaphysical proof that would stand up in a philosophic courtroom. As clues, there lay before him sensible things and their real movement in the external world.

In the Aristotelian example, a stone was being pushed along by a cane, the cane in turn being propelled by a hand. Any other instance of something actually being moved would have served St. Thomas just as well. Aristotle's (*Ph.*, III 1,200b25 ff.) analysis had shown that any movement is of its very nature in potency to something further. Therefore, Aquinas (*In VII Phys.*, lect. 1, Leonine no. 6) interprets, movement is something essentially dependent. It cannot have a "first" or primary instance in its own order. This inherent imperfection gives anything affected by movement, and so any *moved* movent, a secondary status as a movent. Whether a particular series of moved movents is finite or infinite in number, is beside the point. Mathematical order does not enter into the reason for the status of these movents as secondary. Whether they are first or third or fourth or millionth in serial order, or whether in an infinite series they have no serial number at all, they are all *moventia secunda* as St. Thomas understood the expression.

Whether the series of moved movents had a beginning in time or will have an end in time, is indifferent to the argument of Aquinas. Nor would he have anything against indefinitely continued substitution of one moved movent for another.[3] A man could have been driving the car that went into the ditch as well as the woman. On the basis of the closing passages in *De Aeternitate Mundi*, St. Thomas would not see any philosophical objection to an actually infinite number of men and women on hand to take over in turn the wheel. The "endless alternatives of sufficient causes" (Williams, p. 403) do not in any way affect his argument. No matter how auto-mobile or even automotive the horseless carriage may be, it needs a chauffeur to make it go. The chauffeur decides freely to drive it; still according to St. Thomas,[4] his free will needs a mover of infinite efficacy to move it into act. The "microscopic" (Williams, p. 405) act of human free will requires a prior movent just as much as does necessitated movement. In fact, on account of its special indetermination, it requires the movent even more. Considerations like this show how different from the modern outlook is the approach of Aquinas to these problems. Yet his approach has to be respected if his argument is at all to be understood.

The result of the argument is that any movement in each and all of the moved movents, whether they are finite or infinite in number, has to be caused ultimately by a movent that remains unmoved in causing the motion. Because unmoved, it initiates movement absolutely and not in virtue of any prior movent. It may therefore be denominated "first movent." For Aristotle there were many such, for St. Thomas only one. That is a further issue, but it indicates profound difference between the approach of Aristotle and the approach of Aquinas. The point immediately decided by the argument now in question, however, is that any series—whether finite or infinite—of moved movents requires an unmoved movent that is outside their whole order. In the case of a mathematical series, the parallel would be that a mathematical succession, whether finite or infinite, has to be thought by a mathematician who, as the thinker, remains outside the whole order of the mathematical entities in the series.

The *Summa Theologiae* is of course just a *summa*. It restates arguments in summary fashion. In this particular instance the argument summarized is given at greater length in the earlier *Summa contra Gentiles* (I, 13), with references to its Aristotelian sources. In the commentaries of St. Thomas upon those Aristotelian passages his actual meaning has to be sought, and laboriously. There the force of the notions "first" and "secondary" in regard to movents is explained in terms of entitative dependence and independence, not in terms of mathematical order. In that setting the notions do not at all preclude the philosophical possibility of an infinite series of moved movents. Rather, they remain entirely compatible with such a series.

People who recognize the validity of this argument of Aquinas today—and they are legion—face serious challenges from modern philosohy. They have to establish the detective rather than cartographic nature of metaphysics. They have to show that human thought commences not from anything interior to its own workings like a Kantian phenomenon, but from sensible things that have being in themselves in an external world. But one thing the upholders of the argument do not have to presuppose is the impossibility of an infinite series of moved movents. What they have to request is that the argument of Aquinas be not placed in the setting of a nonexistential metaphysics like that of Aristotle, nor on the abstract plane of modern logic. It has to be examined according to the function of metaphysics in the procedure of St. Thomas himself. For Aquinas "the logician considers the way of predicating, and not the thing's existence." The metaphysician, on the other hand, is "a philosopher who seeks the existence of things," and who therefore seeks causes that are entirely outside the formal notion of the thing, namely the motive and the one who did the deed.[5]

SELECTED BIBLIOGRAPHY OF JOSEPH OWENS

The books and articles found herein are especially pertinent to the further study of the theme of this volume of Father Owen's papers on the existence of God.

1. "Up to What Point is God Included in the Metaphysics of Duns Scotus?" *Proceedings of the American Catholic Philosophical Association*, 21 (1964) 165-172.
2. "Theodicy, Natural Theology, and Metaphysics" *The Modern Schoolman*, 28 (1951) 126-137.
3. "A Note on the Approach to Thomistic Metaphysics" *The New Scholasticism*, 28 (1954) 454-476.
4. "The Special Characteristics of the Scotistic Proof that God Exists" *Analecta Gregoriana*, 67 (1954) 311-327.
5. "The Causal Proposition—Principle or Conclusion?" *The Modern Schoolman*, 32 (1955) 159-171; 257-270; 323-339.
6. "The Intelligibility of Being" *Gregorianum*, 36 (1955) 169-193.
7. *St. Thomas and the Future of Metaphysics* Milwaukee; Marquette University Press, (1957), 2nd Printing (1973) 97pp.
8. "Common Nature: A Point of Comparison between Thomistic and Scotistic Metaphysics", *Mediaeval Studies*, 19 (1957) 1-14.
9. "Unity and Essence in St. Thomas Aquinas" *Mediaeval Studies*, 23 (1961) 421-444.
10. "Analogy as a Thomistic Approach to Being" *Mediaeval Studies*, 24 (1962) 302-322.
11. "Existential Act, Divine Being, and the Subject of Metaphysics" *The New Scholasticism*, 37 (1963) 359-363.
12. *An Elementary Christian Metaphysics*, Milwaukee; Bruce Publishing Company (1968) xiv-384 pp.
13. "The *Analytics* and Thomistic Metaphysical Procedure" *Mediaeval Studies*, 26 (1964) 83-108.
14. "Quiddity and the Real Distinction in St. Thomas Aquinas" (Mediaeval Studies, 27 (1965) 1-22..
15. "The Real Distinction of a Relation from its Immediate Basis" *Proceedings of the American Catholic Philosophical Association*, 39 (1965) 134-140.
16. "Aquinas and the Proof from the *Physics*" *Mediaeval Studies*, 28 (1966) 119-150.
17. "The Causal Proposition Revisited" *The Modern Schoolman*, 44 (1967) 143-151.
18. "The Range of Existence" *Proceedings of the Seventh Inter-American Congress of Philosophy*, Quebec, 1 (1967) 44-59.

19. "This Truth Sublime" *Speaking of God*, ed. Denis Dirscherl, Milwaukee (1967) 128-156.
20. *An Interpretation of Existence;* Milwaukee, The Bruce Publishing Company (1968) 153 pp. (paper).
21. "Aquinas—Existential Permanence and Flux" *Mediaeval Studies*, 31 (1969) 71-92.
22. "Metaphysical Separation in Aquinas" *Mediaeval Studies*, 34 (1972) 287-306.
23. "The Content of Existence" *Logic and Ontology*, ed. Milton Munitz, New York; New York University Press (1973) 21-35.
24. "The Primacy of the External in Thomistic Noetics" *Eglise et Théologie*, 5 (1974) 189-205.
25. "Aquinas on Cognition as Existence" *Proceedings of the American Catholic Philosophical Association*, 48 (1974) 74-85.
26. "Aquinas—'Darkness of Ignorance' in the Most Refined Knowledge of God" *Bonaventure and Aquinas*, ed. R.W. Shahan and Francis J. Kovach, Norman: University of Oklahoma Press (1976) 69-86.

NOTES

Notes—Aquinas as Aristotelian Commentator

1 E.g., *In XII Metaph.*, lect. 5, Cathala-Spiazzi nos. 2496-2499; *In VIII Phys.*, lect. 2, Angeli-Pirotta nos. 2041-2044; *In I Eth.*, lect. 9, Spiazzi no. 113; *In I Periherm.*, lect. 14, Spiazzi nos. 195-197; *In III de An.*, lect. 9, Pirotta no. 726; *In I de Cael. et Mund.*, lect. 6, Spiazzi nos. 64-66. Cf.: "Sehr beachtenswert ist die Art und Weise, wie Thomas oft ganz unauffällig an der nikomachischen Ethik Korrekturen vornimmt und auf die Ideen und Ideale des christlichen Ethos hinweist. ... Es liessen sich diese Belege von Korrekturen, die Thomas oft ganz unauffällig an Aristoteles vornimmt, noch bedeutend vermehren." Martin Grabmann, "Die Aristoteleskommentare des heiligen Thomas von Aquin," in *Mittelalterliches Geistesleben* (Munich 1926), pp. 305-306. "In the present case where the reader is the theologian Saint Thomas, the Stagirite's works are read through Christian eyes." M.-D. Chenu, *Towards Understanding Saint Thomas*, tr. A.-M. Landry and D. Hughes (Chicago 1964), p. 209. However, Grabmann (p. 282) can maintain that Aquinas was striving to present an "objective picture" of the Aristotelian doctrine. On the way a medieval commentator may claim to be giving an entirely objective interpretation, and yet not "remain within the bounds of what he had intended in principle," see Chenu, pp. 206-207, n. 9, in reference to Albert the Great.

2 E.g., *In Metaph.* Proem; *In I Eth.*, nos. 2-7; *In Periherm.*, Proem, no. 1; *In de Gen. et Cor.*, Proem, Spiazzi no. 2.

3 *In XII Metaph.*, lect. 5, no. 2496; cf. lect. 10, no. 2598. *In VIII Phys.*, lect. 2, no. 2043. *In I de Cael. et Mund.*, lect. 6, no. 64. On the requirement of souls for the Aristotelian heavenly bodies, see *In II de Cael. et Mund.*, lect. 13, nos. 415-419; cf. *In VIII Phys.*, lect. 21, no. 2479, and *In XII Metaph.*, lect. 4, nos. 2476 and 2536. For the *Ethics*, see infra, n. 43.

4 Victor Preller, *Divine Science and the Science of God* (Princeton 1967), p. 22.

5 Preller, *ibid.* The "articulating" of the positions rejected does not necessarily mean their acceptance by Aquinas in the commentaries. Preller's attitude is: "The closest that Aquinas comes to manifesting a purely philosophical intention is in his commentaries on Aristotle." *Ibid.*

6 J. Isaac, "Saint Thomas interprète des œuvres d'Aristote," *Acta Congressus Scholastici Internationalis Romae 1950* (Rome 1951), p. 356. This would extend to present-day beginners in philosophy.

7 "... procurer à la jeunesse estudiantine un cours complet de philosophie adapté à ses besoins." Isaac, *ibid.* Against these views, see Chenu, p. 214.

8 Isaac, p. 355.

9 E. Cantore, "Critical Study: The Italian Philosophical Encyclopedia," *The Review of Metaphysics*, XXIV (1971), 515.

10 See Isaac, p. 355. Some interesting possibilities for exploration in regard to the "management" of the Aristotelian philosophy in the commentaries are suggested by A. C. Pegis, "St. Thomas and the Nicomachean Ethics," *Mediaeval Studies*, 25 (1963), 1-25.

11 See Angelus Walz, *Saint Thomas d'Aquin*, adaptation française par Paul Novarina (Louvain & Paris 1962), pp. 165-166; 221-222. Chenu, pp. 223-224.

12 For a short survey of the general procedure in the commentary of Aquinas on the *Metaphysics*, see John P. Rowan, *St. Thomas Aquinas, Commentary on the Metaphysics of Aristotle*, 2 v. (Chicago 1961), I, viii-xxiii. The commentary will be referred to according to the numbers in the edition of M.-R. Cathala, revised by R. M. Spiazzi, *S. Thomae Aquinatis, In Duodecem Libros Metaphysicorum Aristotelis Expositio* (Turin & Rome 1964). These numbers are likewise used in Rowan's English translation of the commentary.

13   "... scientia debet esse naturaliter aliarum regulatrix, quae maxime intellectualis est. ... causarum cognitio maxime intellectualis esse videtur... Unde et illa scientia maxime est intellectualis, quae circa principia maxime universalia versatur. ... Unde scientia, quae de istis rebus considerat, maxime videtur esse intellectualis, ..." In Metaph., Proem.

14   Metaph.,Γ 2, 1003b28-1004a20. Actuality and potentiality had been described as attributes following upon being by Albert, Metaph., I, tr. 1, c. 2; ed. Borgnet, VI, 5b. Cf. also Avicenna, Metaph., I, 1D, (Venice 1508) fol.70r2.

15   Metaph., △ 7, 1017b1-9; E 2, 1026b1-2.

16   Cf. Ph., II 2, 193b33-34, and Metaph., E 1, 1026a9-15; K 7, 1064a32-33. The status of the mathematicals had been handed down as that of things dealt with in a science that is sine motu inabstracta, things that cannot be separated (separari non possunt) from matter and motion. Boethius, De Trin., c. II; ed. Stewart and Rand (London & New York 1926), p. 8.11-14.

17   See Aquinas, In Boeth. de Trin., V, 4, Resp.; ed. Bruno Decker (Leiden 1955), pp. 194.14-195.27. At p. 195.15 "God and angels" (cf. p.·165.27) is used in the context in which "God and the intelligences" occurs in the Proem to the commentary on the Metaphysics. In In I Sent., d. 36, q. 2, a. 1, Solut. (ed. Mandonnet, I, 839) the separate movents of the spheres in Averroes seem to be entirely absorbed into the Christian notion of God. Apparently Aquinas experienced little difficulty in seeing the Aristotelian separate substances coalesce in the one Christian God, or on the contrary in regarding them as God and angels together, or in speaking of them as God and the intelligences according to the Neoplatonic tradition as found in the Arabians: "... Platonici ponebant... ordinem superiorum intellectuum separatorum, qui apud nos consueverunt intelligentiae vocari." In II de Cael. et Mund., lect. 4, Spiazzi no. 334.

18   See Avicenna, Metaph., I, 1(Venice 1508), fol. 70r1-v1. St. Thomas seems well enough aware that the Avicennian framework has to be used as an alternate to saying that the primary philosophy treats of the separate substances and then having to add "non tamen solum ea; sed etiam de sensibilibus, inquantum sunt entia, philosophus perscrutatur. Nisi forte dicamus, ut Avicenna dicit, quod huiusmodi communia de quibus haec scientia perscrutatur, dicuntur separata secundum esse,..." In Metaph., lect. 1, no. 1165. At In I Sent., Prol. q. 1, a. 3, Solut. 1 (v. I, p. 12), metaphysics was regarded as divine from the viewpoint of subject in contrast to source of illumination: "Metaphysica autem considerat causas altissimas per rationes ex creaturis assumptas. Unde ista doctrina magis etiam divina dicenda est quam metaphysica: quia est divina quantum ad subjectum et quantum ad modum accipiendi; metaphysica autem quantum ad subjectum tantum." Here the highest causes and the divine are regarded as subject in the wide sense that they are things treated of by metaphysics, even though its source of inspiration is not divine. There is no occasion here for contrasting the subject of the science with the causes and principles of the science from the viewpoint of the science's specification, with reference to Aristotle's philosophical theology.

19   From the viewpoint of inclusion under common being, the angels as creatures have to be regarded as part of the subject of metaphysics, along with spiritual souls. This allows common aspects such as being, unity and plurality, actuality and potentiality, to be found sometimes in matter, sometimes apart from matter. When the separate intelligences are contrasted with common being as its cause or principle, then, they are viewed as coalescing in nature with the Christian God (see supra, n. 17). In the Aristotelian tradition they were called divine, and from this viewpoint would for a Christian have to coincide with the one supreme God. When on the other hand they are regarded as angels and accordingly as creatures, they are all composed of actuality and potentiality, and in this way exhibit unity and multiplicity. For Aquinas, in consequence, both actuality and potentiality are said to follow upon common being, as though by way of a property without which common being cannot be found.

20   "Et qui dicit quod prima Philosophia nititur declarare entia separabilia esse, peccat. Haec enim entia sunt subjecta primae Philosophiae." Averroes, In I Phys., comm. 83G (Venice 1562), fol. 47v1. "Thus, Averroes is the permanent substrate of his commentary on the Metaphysics" — Chenu, p. 215. Cf. supra, n. 18.

21   Aristotle, Metaph., E 1, 1026a19; K 7, 1064b3.

22   "Dicitur enim scientia divina sive theologia, inquantum praedictas substantias considerat." In Metaph., Proem. Cf. "Sic ergo theologia sive scientia divina est duplex. Una, in qua considerantur res divinae non tamquam subjectum scientiae, sed tamquam principia subjecti, et talis est

theologia, quam philosophi prosequuntur, quae alio nomine metaphysica dicitur." *In Boeth. de Trin.*, V, 4, Resp.; ed. Decker, p. 195.6-9. Cf. V, 1, Resp.; p. 166.1-6.

23 "Dicitur autem *prima philosophia*, inquantum primas rerum causas considerat." *In Metaph.*, Proem.

24 The two opposed interpretations of the *Metaphysics*, labeled the "ontological" versus the "theological" interpretation, persist through medieval into modern times. A discussion of the problem may be found in my study *The Doctrine of Being in the Aristotelian* Metaphysics, 2nd ed. (Toronto 1963), pp. 25-26; 35-67; 3rd ed. (Toronto 1978), pp. 25-26; 35-67.

25 Boethius, *De Trin.*, c. II.

26 See Aquinas, *In I Sent.*, Prol., q. 1, a. 1: ed. Mandonnet, I, 6-8, especially "quamvis philosophia determinet de existentibus secundum rationes a creaturis sumptas, oportet tamen esse aliam quae existentia consideret secundum rationes ex inspiratione divini luminis acceptas". *Ibid.*, ad 1m; p. 8.

27 See Bonitz, *Ind. Arist.*, 221a34-61.

28 *In Isog. Porphyr.*, editio secunda, IV, 14; ed. Brandt (CSEL, vol. 48), p. 273.13-15.

29 Cf.: "Quaedam vero sunt, quae quamvis dependeant a materia secundum esse, non tamen secundum intellectum, quia in eorum diffinitionibus non ponitur materia sensibilis, sicut linea et numerus. Et de his est mathematica. Quaedam vero speculabilia sunt, quae non dependent a materia secundum esse, quia sine materia esse possunt, sive numquam sint in materia, sicut deus et angelus, sive in quibusdam sint in materia et in quibusdam non, ..." *In Boeth. de Trin.*, V, 1, Resp.; p. 165.21-27. Here the *esse* is contrasted with the definitions, and means existing in contradistinction to essence. Translation by the English term "existence" is accordingly justified: "Now there are some objects of speculation which depend on matter with respect to their existence, for they can exist only in matter ... There are some objects of speculation, however, which although depending on matter with respect to existence, do not depend on it with respect to their concept, because sensible matter is not included in their definitions." *The Division and Methods of the Sciences*, tr. Armand Maurer, 2nd ed. (Toronto 1958), pp. 7-8.

See also: "Non enim intelligit lineam esse sine materia sensibili, sed considerat lineam et eius passiones sine consideratione materiae sensibilis, ..." V, 3, ad 1m; p. 186.26-28. Cf.: V, 4, Resp.; p. 195.11-12. *Ibid.*, ad 7m; p. 199.14-21.

30 "Sed quia non habet esse a seipso angelus, ideo se habet in potentia ad esse quod accipit a deo, et sic esse a deo acceptum comparatur ad essentiam eius simplicem ut actus ad potentiam. Et hoc est quod dicitur quod sunt compositi ex 'quod est' et 'quo est,' ut ipsum esse intelligatur 'quo est'"—*In Boeth. de Trin.*, V, 4, ad 4m; p. 198.16-20. This is exactly the same doctrine of existence as is found in *De Ente et Essentia*, c. IV (ed. Roland-Gosselin, pp. 34.4-36.3), and in *In I Sent.*, d. 8, q. 5, a. 2, Solut. (ed. Mandonnet, I, 229-230).

31 "Esse enim rei quamvis sit aliud ab eius essentia, non tamen est intelligendum quod sit aliquod superadditum ad modum accidentis, sed quasi constituitur per principia essentiae." *In IV Metaph.*, lect . 2, no. 558. Cf.: "... cum nihil sit essentialius rei quam suum esse." *In I Sent.*, d. 8, expositio Iae partis; I, 209.

32 A discussion of this topic may be found in my article. "The Causal Proposition—Principle or Conclusion?" *The Modern Schoolman*, 32 (1955), 323-327.

33 See *In I Sent.*, Prol., q. 1, a. 2, ad 2m; 1, 10.

34 E.g.: "... quae quidem correspondentia, adaequatio rei et intellectus dicitur; et in hoc formaliter ratio veri perficitur. Hoc est ergo quod addit verum supra ens, scilicet conformitatem, sive adaequationem rei et intellectus." *De Ver.*, I, 1c.

35 "Et ratio sua, quam inducit, est valde derisibilis... Deficit enim haec ratio. *Primo* quidem in hoc, quod cognitio intellectus nostri non est finis substantiarum separatarum, sed magis e converso." *In II Metaph.*, lect 1, no. 286.

36 Unde sunt causa entium secundum quod sunt entia, quae inquiruntur in prima philosophia, ut in primo proposuit. Ex hoc autem apparet manifeste falsitas opinionis illorum, qui posuerunt Aristotelem sensisse, quod Deus non sit causa substantiae caeli, sed solum motus eius." *In VI Metaph.*, lect. 1, no. 1164. Cf. no. 1168, and *In XI Metaph.*, lect. 7, nos. 2264-2265.

While there need not be any doubt that for Aristotle the separate substances are the cause of being for the sublunar world, the Aristotelian text explains this in the order of final causality. Yet Aquinas, showing clear understanding of the way the influence of the separate substances reaches the sublunar world through moving the heavenly bodies, speaks in a way that would strongly suggest the exercise of efficient causality by the separate substances: "Sic enim a substantiis separatis immobilibus ponit Aristoteles procedere et fieri et esse inferiorum, inquantum illae substantiae sunt motivae caelestium corporum, quibus mediantibus causatur generatio et corruptio in istis inferioribus." *In I Metaph.*, lect. 15, no. 237.

37   *In VI Metaph.*, lect. 1, no. 1165, my translation. Text supra, n. 18.

38   "... eadem enim est scientia primi entis et entis communis, ut in principio quarti habitum est." *In VI Metaph.*, lect.1 , 1, no. 1170. Cf. "Eadem enim est scientia quae est de primis entibus, et quae est universalis. Nam prima entia sunt principia aliorum." *In XI Metaph.*, lect. 11, no. 2267. "Et quia ad illam scientiam pertinet consideratio entis communis, ad quam pertinet consideratio entis primi, ideo ad aliam scientiam quam ad naturalem pertinet consideratio entis communis; et eius etiam erit considerare huiusmodi principia communia." *In IV Metaph.*, lect. 5, no. 593.

39   *In XII Metaph.*, lect. 7, no. 2535. The metaphor of "assimilation"seems to have a Neoplatonic background. On the notion of necessity dependent upon the will of the maker, see my article "'Cause of Necessity' in Aquinas' *Tertia Via*," *Mediaeval Studies*, 33(1971), 22-23; 33-39; 44-45.

40   "Et propter hoc secundum fidem catholicam dicitur, quod nihil fit temere sive fortuito in mundo, et quod omnia subduntur divinae providentiae." *In VI Metaph.*, lect. 3, no. 1216. This means clearly enough that on account of the reasons set forth in Aristotle one is able to apply the vocabulary of the Catholic faith to the situation that is being considered.

41   When the three Aristotelian *Ethics* are read strictly against their original Greek pagan background, there can be little if any doubt that they make moral and political philosophy coincide. Political science is the discipline that envisages the supreme good of man and directs to it all other human activities (*E N*, I 2, 1094a27-b7), the good of the individual and the political society is one and the same (2, 1094b7-10), and moral philosophy is a political study (b10-11; *M M I* 1, 1181b28-1182a1). The *Politics* is regarded as continuing the same discipline pursued in the *Nicomachean Ethics* (X 9, 1180b28-1181b24). However, for the view that Aristotle himself broke with "cette confusion platonicienne de la morale et de la politique," see R. A. Gauthier and J. Y. Jolif, *L'Ethique à Nicomaque* (Louvain & Paris 1958-1959), II, 2.

42   See Joseph Mariétan, *Problème de la classification des sciences d'Aristote à St. Thomas* (Paris 1901), pp. 67 (on Boethius); 80-81 (Cassiodorus); 137 (Hugh of St. Victor); 172-173 (Albert the Great). With Albert the vocabulary is exactly the same as that used by Aquinas. In Hugh of St. Victor the term *solitaria* occurs instead of *monastica*, and is used as an alternate for *ethica* and *moralis* in designating the science—see *Disdasc.*, II, 19, (ed. Buttimer) pp. 37.22-38.9; VI, 14, p. 131.15-17. The focus is on the exercise of the virtues, these being regarded as the acts of individuals. Boethius, though still under the influence of Aristotle in giving political science the leading rank among the branches that deal with groups, had given the branch that deals with virtues the first place in introducing the threefold division. See texts and comment in Mariétan, pp. 66-67, nn. 3-4 and 1-2. "Virtues" and the "care of the republic" are accordingly regarded as two different objects for the specification of sciences.

43   *In I Eth.*, lect. 2, no. 31; lect. 9, n. 113; lect. 10, no. 129; lect. 15, no. 180; lect. 16, no. 202; lect. 17, no. 212; *In III Eth.*, lect. 18, no. 590; *In IX Eth.*, lect. 11, no. 1912; *In X Eth.*, lect. 12, no. 2115; lect. 13, no. 2136. The *scientia divina* at no. 31 is quite clearly meant in reference to Aristotle's assertion of the supremacy of metaphysics at *Metaph.*, A 2, 982a16-19 and b4-7, yet the wording remains open to the still higher role of sacred theology in this regard. More surprising, however, is the way Aristotle's secondary happiness, the life of the active virtues, is at no. 2115 located as happiness in this life in contrast to "separate" happiness in the only too obvious sense of happiness after death: "Et per consequens felicitas, quae in hac vita consistit, est humana. Sed vita et felicitas speculativa, quae est propria intellectus, est separata et divina." In the commentary on the *Sentences*, however, the Aristotelian happiness in this life was ranged under contemplation: "Contemplatio autem Dei est duplex. Una per creaturas, quae imperfecta est, ratione jam dicta, in qua contemplatione Philosophus, *X Ethic.*, ... felicitatem contemplativam posuit, quae tamen est felicitas viae; et ad hanc ordinatur tota cognitio philosophica, quae ex rationibus creaturarum procedit." *In I Sent.*, Prol., q. 1,a. 1, Solut.; ed. Mandonnet, I, 7-8. The same is suggested at *In X Eth.*, lect. 11, no. 2110

44 E.g., the reference to the supreme God as the giver of happiness at *In I Eth..*, lect. 14, no. 167. Cf. no. 169, lect. 10, no. 120, and lect. 18, no. 223. See also the example of St. Lawrence at *In III Eth.*, lect. 2, no. 395.

45 *In I Phys.*, lect. 1, no. 3. Cf. nos. 1-6. The framework is dependence or lack of dependence on matter *secundum esse, secundum rationem*. *Ibid.*, no. 3.

46 "Ex hoc ergo quod omne particulare agens presupponit materiam quam non agit, non oportet opinari quod Primum Agens Universale, quod est activum *totius entis*, aliquid praesupponit quasi non creatum ab ipso." *In VIII Phys.*, lect. 2, no. 2000. This is considered to be in accord with the meaning (*intentio*—no. 2001) of Aristotle and with his knowledge of the principle of all being (*totius esse*—no. 2007). The efflux is not movement or change, but emanation from an agent who is acting voluntarily (nos. 2046-2047).

47 E.g., the truth that God made other things on account of himself, yet without need of them for his happiness, *In VIII Phys.*, lect. 2, no. 2051; and the assertion that he can have eternal understanding of non-eternal things, no. 2047. Also the difference of the faith from the position of Anaxagoras, at lect. 3, no. 2067.

48 "Cum autem Logica dicatur rationalis scientia, necesse est quod eius consideratio versetur circa ea quae pertinent ad tres praedictas operationes rationis." *In I Periherm.*, Proem, Spiazzi no. 2. On the problem of logic and the Aristotelian division of the sciences, see Mariétan, pp. 20-25; 179-181.

49 On the bearing of the term "Analytics" for Aquinas, in the sense of bringing a judgment back to the first principles upon which its certainty rests, see *In I Post. Anal.*, Proem, Spiazzi no. 6.

50 *In I de An.*, lect. 2, Pirotta no. 28. Though the commentary on Book I of the *De Anima* is the report of a *lectio* of Aquinas, it is accepted as authentic Thomistic doctrine; see preface in Pirotta edition (Turin 1925), pp. xi-xii.

51 *In II de An.*, lect. 7, no. 319. In the commentary on the *Sentences* a strongly existential explanation of the text had been given: "Alio modo dicitur esse ipse actus essentiae; sicut vivere, quod est esse viventibus, est animae actus; non actus secundus, qui est operatio, sed actus primus." *In I Sent.*, d. 33, q. 1, a. 1, ad 1m; ed. Mandonnet, I, 766. Similarly at *In II de Cael. et Mund.*, lect. 4, no. 334, *vivere* is explained as having two meanings, namely existence (*esse*) and operation. A discussion of the different instances of the use of this Aristotelian passage by Aquinas may be found in A. E. Wingell, "*Vivere Viventibus Est Esse* in Aristotle and St. Thomas," *The Modern Schoolman*, 38 (1961), 85-120.

52 The commentaries in this paragraph have been cited according to the numbers used in the Marietti editions.

53 *ST*, I, 1, 6c,. Cf. "Ita, cum finis totius philosophiae sit infra finem theologiae, et ordinatus ad ipsum, theologia debet omnibus aliis scientiis imperare et uti his quae in eis traduntur." *In I Sent.*, Prol., q. 1, a. 1, Solut.; ed. Mandonnet, I, 8.

54 Cf. expression of this dedication in the *Contra Gentiles*: "Assumpta igitur ex divina pietate fiducia sapientis officium prosequendi, ... propositum nostrae intentionis est veritatem quam fides Catholica profitetur, pro nostro modulo manifestare... et quomodo demonstrativa veritas fidei Christianae religionis concordet". *CG*, I, 2, Assumpta.

55 "Unde illi, qui utuntur philosophicis documentis in sacra doctrina redigendo in obsequium fidei, non miscent aquam vino, sed aquam convertunt in vinum." *In Boeth. de Trin.*, II, 3, ad 5m; ed. Decker, p. 96.18-20. On the topic, see A. C. Pegis, "Sub Ratione Dei: A Reply to Professor Anderson," *The New Scholasticism*, 39 (1965), 141-157.

56 So, for St. Bonaventure, *In I Sent.*, Proem, q. 4, the writer of the *Sentences* was exercising the function not of a scribe or of a compiler or of a commentator, but of an author: "Talis fuit Magister, qui sententias suas ponit et Patrum sententiis confirmat. Unde vere debet dici auctor huius libri". *Ibid.* Resp. This theme in Bonaventure is discussed in John Quinn, *The Historical Constitution of St. Bonaventure's Philosophy* (Toronto 1973).

57 See Pegis, art. cit., pp. 143-146.

58 See Maurice Nédoncelle, *Is there a Christian Philosophy?* tr. Illtyd Trethowan (New York 1960), pp. 85-114.

59 Aquinas states clearly the difference between the two procedures, philosophical and theological: "Vel procedunt ex principiis fidei, ... Ex his autem principiis ita probatur aliquid apud fideles sicut etiam ex principiis naturaliter notis probatur aliquid apud omnes. Unde etiam

theologia scientia est". *ST*, II-II, 1, 5, ad 2m.

The work of James C. Doig, *Aquinas on Metaphysics* (The Hague 1972), appeared after this paper had been completed. Its study of the nature of Aquinas' commentary on the *Metaphysics* bears out the views of the present article, though it does not trace the reasons for the unity of Aquinas' treatment to his theological activities.

Notes—Aquinas on Knowing Existence

1   See, for example, Etienne Gilson, *Philosophie et Incarnation selon saint Augustin* (Montreal: Institut d'Etudes Médiévales, 1947), pp. 10-29; Cornelia De Vogel, "'Ego sum qui sum' et sa signification pour une philosophie chrétienne," *Revue des sciences religieuses*, 35 (1961), 346-354.

2   Gilson, "Propos sur l'être et sa notion," in *San Tommaso e il pensiero moderno*, ed. Pontificia Accademia di S. Tommaso (Rome: Città Nuova Editrice, 1974), pp. 7-17. Jacques Maritain, "Réflexions sur la nature blessée et sur l'intuition de l'être," *Revue thomiste*, 68 (1968), 5-40, reprinted in Maritain's *Approches sans entraves* (Paris: Fayard, 1973), pp. 249-291, with continuous numeration of the footnotes.

3   See Cornelio Fabro, "The Transcendentality of *Ens-Esse* and the Ground of Metaphysics," *International Philosophical Quarterly*, 6 (1966), 389-427; "The Intensive Hermeneutics of Thomistic Philosophy:The Notion of Participation," *The Review of Metaphysics, 27 (1974), 449-491.* J.Donceel, *"Transcendental Thomism,"The Monist*, 58 (1974), 67-85.

4   "Immediate apprehension"—R. Rorty, s.v. "Intuition" in Paul Edwards' *Encyclopedia of Philosophy*, IV, 204a. In Aquinas the word *intuitus* is just as wide. It signifies "the presence of the intelligible object to the intellect in any way whatever"—*In I Sent.*,d.3,q.4,a.5,Solut.; ed. Pierre Mandonnet, I.122. A study of the term in Aquinas may be found in Luigi Bogliolo, "Realismo moderno e realismo tomista," in *San Tommaso e il pensiero moderno* (see supra, n. 2), pp. 47-48.

5   The intuition of existence in judgment with the consequent concept is affirmed also in Maritain's *The Peasant of the Garonne*, trans. Michael Cuddihy and Elizabeth Hughes (New York: Holt, Rinehart and Winston, 1968), p. 138. References to the intuition in Maritain's *Sept leçons sur l'être* (1944) and *Court traité de l'existence et de l'existant (1947)* are given in the study of F. D. Wilhelmsen, *"La théorie du jugement chez Maritain et saint Thomas d'Aquin."* La table ronde, no. 135 (1959), pp. 34-56.

6   Maritain's charge seems to envisage Gilson's *Being and Some Philosophers*, 2nd ed. (Toronto: Pontifical Institute of Mediaeval Studies, 1952), pp. 190-202; cf. Appendix, p. 223. Gilson, though, in the context does not use the term "intuition" for knowledge of existence through judgment.

7   Fabro, "Transcendentality," p. 426. His critique is directed expressly against writers who wish "to make St. Thomas into a Kantian." He suggests that this stand implies stopping "at existence as a fact and a positing of reality," instead of probing it deeply as an actuality. In the later article (supra, n. 3) the transcendental Thomists are charged with "deriving the *actus essendi*, understood in the nominalistic sense of existence, from the act of judgment"—"Intensive Hermeneutics," p. 470, n. 68. Fabro, in contrary direction, regards "existence which is the *fact* of being" as "a 'result' rather than a metaphysical principle" (p. 470).

8   Donceel, art. cit., pp.76-77, in express opposition to "the conception of Neo-Thomism, as brilliantly exposed by such authors as Jacques Maritain and Etienne Gilson" (p. 76).

9   "Cum in re duo sint, quidditas rei, et esse ejus, his duobus correspondet duplex operatio intellectus. Una quae dicitur a philosophis formatio, qua apprehendit quidditates rerum, quae etiam a Philosopho, in III *De anima*, dicitur indivisibilium intelligentia. Alia autem comprehendit esse rei, componendo affirmationem, quia etiam esse rei ex materia et forma compositae, a qua cognitionem accipit, consistit in quadam compositione formae ad materiam, vel accidentis ad subjectum....Sed intellectus noster, cujus cognitio a rebus oritur, quae esse compositum habent, non apprehendit illud esse nisi componendo et dividendo" (ed. Mandonnet, I, 903-904). Cf. *In I Sent., d.19, q.5, a.1, ad 7m; I, 489.* Also *In Boeth. de Trin.*, V, 3c; ed. Decker, p. 182. In the *Summa*

Theologiae, II-II, 83, 1, arg. 3, the aspect of apprehending is clearly stated for both: "…prima est indivisibilium intelligentia, per quam scilicet apprehendimus de unoquoque quid est; secunda vero est compositio et divisio, per quam scilicet apprehenditur aliquid esse vel non esse." What is in the intellect is of course an existent thing (*ens*), regarded from the standpoints of its being and its nature. The first object of conceptualization is accordingly a *being*, and the first object of judgment is that a *thing* exists, thereby excluding the contradictory. See *In I Sent.*, d.8, q.1, a.3, Solut.; I, 200. Likewise the term "comprehend" is used for both the activities, *In I Sent.*, d.38, q.1, a.3, ad 4m; I, 904. But whatever term is used, the role of judgment in regard to existence is neatly stated in the conclusion of an article by Ignatius O'Brien, "Analogy and our Knowledge of God," *Philosophical Studies*, 6 (1956), 104: "Only through judgment have we knowledge of that which is the root of being —namely existence."

10   It is so translated by F. Rahman, "Essence and Existence in Avicenna," *Mediaeval and Renaissance Studies*, 4 (1958), 4, n. 2. On the term's basic notion of "image" and the probable transmission of that notion from the Greek *phantasia* through Stoic and Neoplatonic writers, see M.-D. Chenu, "Un vestige du stoicisme,"*Revue des sciences philosophiques et théologiques*, 27(1938), 64-65. Chenu, p.67, n.3, calls attention to an interesting use of the term by Aquinas himself in the sense of conceptualization as opposed to knowledge through judgment, when saying that God escapes any "formation" by our intellect: "…Deus, formationem intellectus nostri subterfugit"—In III Sent., d.24, a.2, Solut. 1; ed. Maria Fabian Moos, III, 768 (no. 51). What is divine cannot be conceptualized, according to this assertion.

11   See William of Auvergne, *De Trin.*, II (Paris: Peter Auboüin, 1674), Supplementum, p.2b. Nevertheless, the awkward situation caused by the different viewpoint in Aristotle could still make itself felt, e.g.: "Et hoc modo 'an est' probatum est per 'quid est' secundum Averroes"—Albertus Magnus, *Metaphysica*, ed. Bernard Geyer (Aschendorff: Monast. Westfal., 1964), p.303.10-11. Rahman, p.2, notes the presence already in Alfarabi of the tenet that one could know the essence without knowing the existence, contrary to the Aristotelian viewpoint.

12   "…since in everything that exists there is to be considered its quiddity, by reason of which it subsists in a determined nature, and its being, by which it is said of it that it is in actuality" (…cum in omni quod est sit considerare quidditatem suam, per quam subsistit in natura determinata, et esse suum, per quod dicitur de eo quod est in actu)—*In I Sent.*, d.8., q.1, a.1, Solut.; I, 195.

13   The one term *comprehendere* is found for both in the critical edition, *Commentarium Magnum in Aristotelis de Anima Libros*, ed. F. Stuart Crawford (Cambridge, Mass.: Mediaeval Academy of America, 1953), p.455.17—21. On the sources, see p. xi. On the Latin terms as interchangeable for Aquinas, cf. supra, n.9.

14   Elsewhere, *In IX Metaph.*, lect. 11, Cathala no. 1898, the assertion "Socrates is a man" is said by Aquinas to depend for its truth on the composition of human form with individual matter. Here the distinction between common nature and individual is only a conceptual difference.

15   "…not second actuality, which is activity, but first actuality"— *In I Sent.*, d.33, q.1, a.1, ad 1m; I, 766. On the different meaning of the expression *actus essentiae* as found in Albert the Great, see L.-B. Geiger, "La vie, acte essentiel de l'âme—l'*esse*, acte de l'essence d'après Albert-le-Grand," Etudes d'histoire littéraire et doctrinale, 17 (1962), 49–116. Though the expression runs through Albert's writings, it meant (see Geiger, pp. 50-51; 112-113) an actuality participated dynamically yet within the order of formal specification. The dynamism was accordingly understood as belonging to the "essential, not existential" (p.113), order. The participationist motif prompting Albert's use of *actus essentiae* is not enough to explain Aquinas' understanding of the phrase as the existential synthesis grasped through judgment.

16   Cf.: "…esse ipsius sequitur componentia, quae non sunt ipsum esse"—*In I Sent.*, d.8, q.4, a.1, Contra; I, 219. This stand is quite frequent in Aquinas and goes back to Aristotle's (*Metaph.*, Z 17, 104lb28; H2, 1043a2-3) dictum that form as a substance is the cause of being.

17   The combined causality is expressed succinctly in the *Summa Theologiae*, I, 104, 1, ad 1m: "…esse per se consequitur formam creaturae, supposito tamen influxu Dei." Aquinas speaks accordingly of existence in creatures as an effect. Yet he regards it as that by which the creature exists: "ipso formaliter est creatura"—*In I Sent.*, d.8, q.1, a.2, ad 2m; I, 198. This seems sufficient justification for referring to existence as immanent cause" (Gilson, art. cit., p.10) or even "immanent formal cause" (p.13) where the context suggests that existence as a component be described in that way. Cf., "intrinsically activating causality"—Maritain, *Degrees of Knowledge*,

Appendix IV, trans. G.B. Phelan (New York: Charles Scribner's Sons, 1959), p. 437.

18   By the very fact that something is being thought about, it exists in the mind and thereby is actuated through cognitional existence "ad minus enim oportet quod illud de quo aliquid enuntiatur, sit apprehensum; et ita habet aliquod esse ad minus in intellectu apprehendente"—In I Sent.., d.19, 1.5, a.1, ad 5 m; I, 489.   On the three ways in which an individual creature exists for Aquinas, see In I Sent.., d.36, q.1, a.3, ad 2m; I, 836-837; Quodl., VIII, 1, 1, c.

19   It is hard to see how any other interpretation can be given to the rest of the clear words in the text just referred to from In I Periherm., lect. 5, no. 73: "However, the actuality which the verb 'is' principally signifies is the actuality of every form commonly, whether substantial or accidental. Hence, when we wish to signify that any form or act is actually in some subject we signify it through the verb 'is,'..." Trans. Jean T. Oesterle, On Interpretation (Milwaukee: Marquette University Press, 1962), p. 53. The particular synthesis is what the concept "actuality of every form" expresses commonly, though the aspect of synthesizing is not signified "principally" (no. 71). Surely there is no need of "forcing the texts" (Fabro, "Intensive Hermeneutics," p. 470, n. 68) here!

20   In I Sent., d.7, q.1, a.1, 2m; I, 177. Here the term realiter is used to designate the distinction. Cf., d.3, q.4, a.2; I, 115-117, or ST, I, 77, 1.

21   "...essentiam, sive existentiam"...essentia vel esse"—In I Sent., d.8; I, 188 (Lombard. "...non subsistentias, sed existentias"—d.23, q.1, a.2, ad 3m; I, 560.

22   "Sed nomen entis sumitur ab esse rei"—   In I Sent., d.25, q.1, a.4, Solut.; I, 612. Cf."...hoc nomen 'qui est' vel 'ens' imponitur ab ipso actu essendi"—d.8, q.1, a.1, Solut.; I, 195.

23   See supra, n.19. Cf., procedure in CG, II, 53-54.

24   See In I Sent., d.19, q.5, a.2, ad 1m; I, 492. Cf.: "Ex quo patet quod diversa habitudo ad esse impedit univocam praedicationem entis"—De Pot., VII, 7, c. Cf., De Ente text quoted infra, n. 34.

25   "...prima non sunt diversa nisi per seipsa: sed ea quae sunt ex primis, differunt per diversitatem primorum"—In I Sent., d.8, q.1, a.2, ad 3m; I, 198. Cf., SCG, I, 17, In hoc.

26   In I Sent., Prol., q.1, a.2, ad 2m; I, 10. Cf., De pot., VII, 7, c. From the divine existence all created existence flows by way of exemplar as well as efficient causality ("effective et exemplariter manat"—In I Sent., d.8, q.1, a.2, Solut,; I, 198). In God, accordingly, existence has the aspect of an exemplar and efficient cause (a.3, Solut.; I, 200).

27   In this type of analogy the "common nature" has to be present in every one of the analogous existents, not just in the primary instance, and in a different way in each. Neither in notion nor in existence is there equivalence: "neque parificatur in intentione communi, neque in esse"—In I Sent., d.19, q.5, a.2, ad 1m; I, 492.

28   In I Sent., d.8, q.1, a.2; I, 197-198. Nevertheless, the existence by which each thing formally exists is diverse: "...nihilominus tamen in rebus diversis est diversum esse, quo formaliter res est"—d.19, q.5, a.2, Solut.; I, 492. Cf., SCG, I, 26, Item res. The latter is existence as grasped by judgment. On God as the being of all other things, see G.B. Phelan, "The Being of Creatures," Proceedings of the American Catholic Philosophical Association 31 (1957), 118-125.

29   See reasoning attributed to Avicenna, In I Sent., d.8, q.4, a.2, Solut,; I, 222. It may be seen at greater length in De Ente et Essentia, c. IV; ed. Roland-Gosselin, pp. 34.7-36.3.

30   See texts supra, n. 26. On divine vis-à-vis common existence, cf.: In I Sent., d.8, q.4, a.1, ad 1 m; I, 219. De Ente et Essentia, c.V; pp. 37.21-38.20.

31   See supra, n. 4. Gilson's sense of "intuition" is much stricter.

32   See Gilson, Being and Some Philosophers, pp. 190-215. At the beginning of the discussion Gilson states clearly that "every act of intellectual knowledge terminates in an intellection" (p.190), in the one case in a concept, in the other in a judgement. Both are therefore regarded as fundamentally acts of cognition, even though the notion of asserting or positing is emphasized.

33   On existence as "the fact of being", see Fabro, "Intensive Hermeneutics," p. 470, quoted supra, n. 7.

34   In III Sent., d.6, q.2, a.2, Resp.; III, 238 (no. 79). Cf., texts supra, nn. 16 and 17. The existence has of course to be regarded as "resulting" from the individual principles as well as the specific principles of the thing, for the specific nature as such is not different in its individual instances, while the existence is diverse in each—"sed esse diversum est in diversis" (De Ente et Essentia, c.V; p. 37.20-21).

Notes—Judgement and Truth in Aquinas

1   "...selon St. Thomas, le jugement au sens strict est toujours une opération de l'intelligence. Cependant il nous parle souvent d'un 'judicium sensus'; mais ce n'est jamais un jugement véritable, au sens propre. ...Ce n'est pas un jugement au sens propre du terme. Nous avons vu plus haut que le jugement a rapport à l'"esse,'..." P. Hoenen, *La Théorie du Jugement d'après St. Thomas d'Aquin* (Rome, 1946), p. 250. There is an English translation, Peter Hoenen, *Reality and Judgment according to St. Thomas*, tr. Henry F. Tiblier (Chicago, 1952), 210.

2   See Bonitz, *Ind. Arist.*, 409a57-b8; b38-45; 410a31-36. As Latin translation, Aquinas uses both *discernere* and *judicare*, *In III de An.*, lect. 3, Pirotta nos. 603-604.

3   *Ph.* IV 8, 216b19-20. On the text, see W. D. Ross, *ad loc.* The passage was in Averroes, and was commented upon by St. Thomas with the translation *discernere* at *In IV Phys.*, lect. 13, Angeli-Pirotta no. 1047.

4   *In I Sent.*, d.19, q.5, a.2, Solut,; ed. Mandonnet, I, 491. Cf. *ibid.*, a.1, ad 7m (I, 489), where the second operation of the intellect is characterized as bearing upon existence: "secunda respicit esse ipsius." See also *In Boeth. de Trin.*, V, 3c; ed. Decker, 182.9-13.

5   *Supra*, n. 1. Cf.: "Le sens ne peut donc pas atteindre la 'ratio entis' et c'est pourquoi il ne peut attribuer l'"esse,' il ne peut juger au sens strict." Hoenen, p. 251.

6   See *De Ente*, c. III; ed. Roland-Gosselin, pp. 24.1-27.6.

7   *Ibid.*, p. 26.8-10. Cf. *Quodl.*, VIII, 1.

8   The "ratio entis" (*supra*, n.5) would be a distinct object. Since the external senses do not express a species (*Quodl.*, V, 9, ad 2m), they are unable to represent separately the different aspects that do not appear separately in the thing. But even the internal senses that do express species, such as the imagination, cannot abstract aspects that are not sensibly distinct, such as nature and existence. Abstraction belongs to the intellectual level, e.g. "abstrahendo enim formam circuli ab aere, remanet seorsum in intellectu nostro et intellectus circuli et intellectus aeris" (*ST*, I, 40, 3c); "ea vero, quae sunt in sensibilibus, abstrahit intellectus, non quidem intelligens ea esse separata, sed separatim vel seorsum ea intelligens" (*In III de An.*, lect. 11, no. 782).

9   "...in sensu ex hoc quod apprehendit vel iudicat res aliter quam sint"—*ST*, I, 17 2c; "apprehensum per sensum vel imaginationem vel intellectum"—*CG*, II, 47, Item. Cf. below, nn. 13 and 15.

10   Karl Rahner, "Aquinas: The Nature of Truth," *Continuum*, 2 (1964), 65.

11   Rahner, 65. "...for St. Thomas...the transcendental 'a priori' of the spirit (the light of the agent intellect)"—62. Cf. "This light is the *a priori* form under which the spontaneity of the spirit perceives the material sensible"—67.

12   On this point, see my discussions in *An Elementary Christian Metaphysics* (Milwaukee, 1963), 45-56; 249-257; and in *An Interpretation of Existence* (Milwaukee, 1968), 14-43.

13   "...sensus...veram apprehensionem habet de sensibilibus, ut supra dictum est. Quod quidem contingit eo quod apprehendit res ut sunt." *ST*, I, 17, 2c.

14   Hoenen, 250; Hayen, 144-146. The notion may be found elsewhere without the exact expression, e.g. "ex quo iterum consequitur esse omnia per essentiam unum; quod et sensui contradicit" (*In II Sent.*, d.17, q.1, a.1, Solut.; II, 413); "Sic enim se habet intellectus ad iudicandum de huiusmodi, sicut sensus ad iudicandum de sensibilibus communibus vel per accidens." *ST*, I, 17, 3c).

15   E.g., "in esse rei, et in apprehensione virtutis cognoscitivae proportionata ad esse rei" (*In I Sent.*, d.19, q.5, a.2, Solut,; I, 491); "Sed intellectus noster, cujus cognitio a rebus oritur, quae esse compositum habent, non apprehendit illud esse nisi componendo et dividendo" (d.38, q.1, a.3, ad 2m; I, 904). See also *ST*, II-II, 83, 1, arg. 3. The more general notion of apprehension soon came to be restricted to the "first operation" by the addition of the adjective "simplex," e.g., in Henry of Ghent, just as in the more common expression *simplex notitia*.

16   "Mais on observera que toutes les expressions ne doivent pas être prises en rigueur." Hayen, 145.

17   B.J. Muller-Thym, "The Common Sense, Perfection of the Order of Pure Sensibility," *The Thomist* 2 (1940), 321.

18   This seems the only instance given by Hayen, 145, to justify interpretation in a loose sense.

Apprehensio is recognized (*ibid.*) as a term used synonymously here with *formatio,* and therefore distinguished here from *judicium.* It can hardly be regarded as an instance of loose application of terms.

19   *In IV Metaph.,* lect. 14, no. 695. Cf. "Et ideo visus certius et perfectius iudicat de sensibilibus inter alios sensus." *In I Metaph.,* lect. 1, no. 6. The statement "Tactus enim iudicat quod ignis calidus est, non tamen apprehendit propter quid (*ibid.,* no. 30) compares sense judgment with the expertise of experienced persons who do not know the cause of the event.

20   *De Ente,* Proem.; *De Ver.,* I, 1c; *In IV Metaph.,* lect. 6, no. 605.

21   On the expression *imaginatio per intellectum,* see the Latin Averroes, *In XII Metaph.,* comm. 37 (ed. Venice, 1574), fol. 319r2 and vl; *Comm. Magnum in De An.,* ed. F. S. Crawford (Cambridge, Mass., 1953), pp. 6.18-19; 89.23-26; 449.179; and on the Greek equivalents of *formatio,* see Index in Crawford, p. 567, and for instances, pp. 380.38-40, 381.16-17, 449.179-182. Cf. St. Thomas: "Et haec operatio a quibusdam dicitur informatio intellectus sive imaginatio per intellectum." *In I Post. Anal.,* Proem, Spiazzi no. 4.

22   "Secunda vero operatio respicit ipsum esse rei, quod quidem resultat ex congregatione principiorum rei in compositis vel ipsam simplicem naturam rei concomitatur, ut in substantiis simplicibus. Et quia veritas intellectus est ex hoc quod conformatur rei... *In Boeth. de Trin.,* V, 3c; ed. Decker, p.182.9-12. "...significatum eius, quod est esse vel non esse, quod est naturaliter prius enunciatione." *In I Periherm.,* lect. 8, Spiazzi no. 108. "Sed esse compositorum surgit ex componentibus... Verum autem consequitur ens. "*In IX Metaph.,* lect. 11, no. 1903; see also *ibid.,* nos. 1896-1902. Cf. texts above n. 15.

23   On the two different but closely related uses of the term "judgment," see my discussion in *An Interpretation of Existence,* 21-26.

24   "...formae dicuntur invariabiles, quia non possunt esse subiectum variationis; subiiciuntur tamen variationi, inquantum subiectum secundum eas variatur. Unde patet quod secundum quod sunt, sic variantur." *ST,* I, 9, 2, ad 3m. Cf. "Quaedam autem sic recedunt a permanentia essendi, quia esse eorum est subiectum transmutationis, vel in transmutatione consistit"—*ibid.,* 10, 5c, and "dicimus de universalibus, quod sunt incorruptibilia et aeterna, quia non corrumpuntur nisi per accidens, scilicet quantum ad esse quod habent in alio, quod potest non esse"—*In I Sent.,* d.19, q.5, a.3, ad 3m; I, 496-497.

25   "...nomen vel verbum significat simplicem intellectum, oratio vero significat intellectum compositum." *In I Periherm.,* lect. 6, Spiazzi no. 75.

26   In explaining the definition of truth at *CG,* I, 59, Cum enim, St. Thomas expressly attributes the truth to what the intellect expresses: "ad illud in intellectu veritas pertinent quod intellectus dicit, non ad operationem qua illud dicit." In this way he is able to regard the activity as distinguished from its form. But the intellect may also be regarded as known through the cognitional form, and from this viewpoint there is no need to strain a text like that from *ST,* I, 16, 2c, by requiring an abrupt change to a different meaning of *intellectus.* However, there is on the other hand nothing surprising with Aquinas in a change of the type, e.g., "remanet seorsum in intellectu nostro et intellectus circuli et intellectus aeris"—*ST,* I, 40, 3c.

27   *Correspondentia* is used by St. Thomas in this context, though *adaequatio* and *conformitas* are the words that regularly occur: "quae quidem correspondentia, adaequatio rei et intellectus dicitur... scilicet conformitatem, sive adaequationem rei et intellectus"—*De Ver.,* I, 1c.

28   Cf. "For example, the sentence 'I am about to go home,' or 'I am now about to go home,' is true if and only if the person who utters it *is* about to go home at the time he utters it." A. N. Prior, "Fugitive Truth," *Analysis* 29 (1968), 5-8. No matter how fugitive and fleeting, however, truth grounded on temporal being is fixed and stable insofar as it is the firm and unshakable basis of contradiction.

Notes—The Accidental and Essential Character of Being

1   "Dicere quod esse non est essentia rei, sed aliquid constitutum per essentiae principia, est idem affirmare et negare: cum constitutum per essentiae principia nihil aliud sit quam ipsa res ex illis constituta." Siger de Brabant, *Quaestiones in Metaphysicam*, Introductio, q. VII, in the *Reportatio* of Godfrey of Fontaines; ed. C.A. Graiff, *Questions sur la Métaphysique* (Louvain: Institut Supérieur de Philosophie, 1948), p. 16 (14)-(17). On 1272-1274 as the probable date of the *Questiones*, see ibid., Introduction, pp. XXI-XXVII.

2   "...modum tamen ponendi non intelligo." Op. cit., p. 16.25.

3   *De Ver.*, 1,1c: in *Quaestiones Disputatae* (ed. R. Spiazzi, Turin: Marietti, [1949]), I,2b. Cf.: "Unumquodque enim est ens per essentiam suam." *De Ver.*, XXI, 1, arg. 1. "...nulla enim res naturae est quae sit extra essentiam, entis universalis,..." *De Ver.*, XXI, 5, arg. 2, is not challenged in the reply to the *argumentum*.

4   Boethius, *In Cat. Arist.*, Lib. I: *PL*, LXIV, 166BC.

5   *Metaph.*, Δ 7,1017a7-b9; E 2,1026a33-b2.

6   *Metaph.*, K 8,1065b2-3; *Ph.*, II 6.198a7-9.

7   Cf. *Metaph.*, E 4,1027b31-1028a2.

8   "...the accidental is practically a mere name." *Metaph.*, E 2,1026b13-14; Oxford tr.

9   "...the accidental is obviously akin to non-being." Ibid., b21; Oxford tr.

10   Cf. *Metaph.*, E 4,1027b25-34.

11   *In X Metaph.*, lect. 3, no. 1982. In both texts the basic division falls between being as ranged in the categories and being as subject to accidental existence and expressed in the truth of a proposition.

12   See S. Mansion, *Le Jugement d'Existence chez Aristote* (Louvain & Paris, 1946), p. 273.

13   Cf. *De Ente*, c. IV; p. 34.12-14; *In I Sent.*, d.8, q.4, a.2 (ed. Mandonnet, I,222); *In II Sent.*, d.3, q.1, a.1, Solut. (II,87).

14   *In de Hebd.*, c. II; ed. Mandonnet, I,171, except "Currere et esse" for "currere et ens."

15   E.g.: "...sic *ens* esset genus, quod significat ipsum esse." *CG*, 1,25; ed. Leonine, XIII, 76b11-12. "...solus Deus est essentialiter ens, omnia autem alia participant ipsum esse." *CG*, II,53 XIII, 391b-10. "...cum esse Dei sit eius essentia, ut ostensum est, si Deus esset in aliquo genere, oporteret quod genus eius esset *ens:* nam genus significat essentiam rei,..." *ST*, I, 3,5c; ed. Leonine. "...hoc autem nomen ens, significat ipsum esse" *In IV Metaph.*, lect. 2, (ed. Cathala) no. 556.

16   On this topic, see J. Owens, *The Doctrine of Being in the Aristotelian* Metaphysics (Toronto: Pontifical Institute of Mediaeval Studies, 1951), pp. 60-63.

17   On this background, see E. Gilson, *Being and Some Philosophers* (Toronto, Pontifical Institute of Mediaeval Studies, 1949), pp. 52-56.

18   "Gratia igitur et electione omnium quae sunt, et aliud, et melius omnibus his quae sunt ostenditur ipsum esse: non potest igitur accidere esse secundum se, sed necessario omni substantia et accidente melius est,..." William of Auvergne, *De Trin.*, c. VII; (Ed. Orleans & Paris, 1674) II, Suppl., p. 9a.

19   "Et esse de quo queritur per an est, est accidens ei quod ipsa res est, scilicet ei de quo queritur per quid est, omne autem accidens alicui, causatum est; si enim esset ens per se, non esset accidens alii." Algazel, *Metaphysics*, II,3 (ed. J.T. Muckle, Toronto: St. Michael's College, 1933), p. 53.15-17 "...dicemus ergo quod naturae hominis ex hoc quod est homo accidit ut habeat esse: ..." Avicenna, *Metaph.*, V,2A (ed. Venice, 1508), fol. 87vl. "Hoc ergo quod est, ab alio habet esse, et illud quod est, et sic esse hoc modo accidit ei: quia ab alio sibi est:..." Albertus Magnus, *De Causis et Proc. Univ.*, I,8: ed. A. Borgnet, X,377b. On the sense of "following upon" that the Arabian notion bore, see A.-M. Goichon, *La Distinction de L'Essence et de l'Existence d'après Ibn Sina* (Paris: Desclée de Brouwer, 1937), pp. 90-91.

20   Aristotle, *Top.*, I,5 ff.

21   See W. Marx, *The Meaning of Aristotle's 'Ontology'* (The Hague: M. Nijhoff, 1954), p. 43.

22   In Aristotle, *De An.*, II 4,415b13, the context of this expression was that the soul is the formal cause of living things, because according to the Aristotelian doctrine form is the cause of the being of each thing (cf. *Metaph.*, Z 17,1041a28-b 28, which shows how the form is the cause of a

thing's being flesh or a syllable or anything else; similarly H 2,1043a2-3). It is in this formal sense that life is called the being of living things. It is the formal characteristic that distinguishes animate from inanimate things (*De An.*, II 2,413a21-22). "Being" in this context clearly has the meaning of what a thing is. The formal Aristotelian notion of being is brought out definitely enough in the Oxford translation. As "the essence of the whole living body" the soul is its cause: "for in everything the essence is identical with the ground of its being, and here, in the case of living things, their being is to live, and of their being and their living the soul in them is the cause or source. Further, the actuality of whatever is potential is identical with its formulable essence." *De An.*, II 4,415b11-15: Oxford tr.

St. Thomas, however, from the time of his first use of the text in the commentary on the *Sentences,* interprets this being that is the life of the soul as something different from the essence and as the act of the form. As the *actus primus* of the soul it is different from the essence or quiddity just as operation (*actus secundus*) is different from essence. In the *Contra Gentiles,* the notion "life" in the Aristotelian formula is interpreted as meaning the kind of being that proceeds from a special kind of form, namely vital form: "*Vita* enim viventis est ipsum *vivere* in quadam abstractione significatum: sicut *cursus* non est secundum rem aliud quam *currere. Vivere autem viventium est ipsum esse eorum,* ut patet per Philosophum in II de Anima: cum enim ex hoc animal dicatur vivens quod animam habet, secundum quam habet esse, utpote secundum propriam formam, oportet quod vivere nihil sit aliud quam tale esse ex tali forma proveniens." *CG,* I,98; ed. Leonine, XIII, 263a3-12. This interpretation requires that *vivere* be given as its proper sense an existential meaning, instead of its commonly understood sense of operation: "illud ergo esse quod habet res prout est movens seipsam ad operationem aliquam, dicitur proprie vita rei, quia vivere viventis est esse, ut in II *de Anima* dicitur. In nobis autem nulla operatio ad quam nos movemus, est esse nostrum; unde intelligere nostrum non est vita nostra, proprie loquendo, nisi secundum quod *vivere* accipitur pro opere quod est signum vitae;..." *De Ver.,* IV,8c; ed. Spiazzi, *Quaest. Disp.,* I,87b. The difference between the originally accepted meaning of "life" and its proper philosophical sense is explained in the *Summa Theologiae:* "Nam *vitae* nomen sumitur ex quadam exterius apparenti circa rem, quod est movere seipsum: non tamen est impositum hoc nomen ad hoc significandum, sed ad significandum substantiam cui convenit secundum suam naturam movere seipsam, vel agere quocumque modo ad operationem. Et secundum hoc, *vivere* nihil aliud est quam esse in tali natura: et *vita* significat hoc ipsum, sed in abstracto: sicut hoc nomen *cursus* significat ipsum *currere* in abstracto...Quandoque tamen *vita* sumitur minus proprie pro operationibus vitae, a quibus nomen vitae assumitur;..." *ST,* I,18,2c: ed. Leonine. In a subsequent passage, the two senses are merely given as though readily accepted: "...vita dicitur dupliciter. Uno modo, ipsum esse viventis. Et sic beautitudo non est vita: ostensum est enim quod esse unius hominis, qualecumque sit, non est hominis beatitudo: solius enim Dei beatitudo est suum esse.—Alio modo, dicitur vita ipsa operatio viventis, secundum quam principium vitae in actum reducitur;..." *ST,* I-II, 3, 2, ad 1m; ed. Leonine.

"Life," therefore, is given by St. Thomas a technical philosophical sense that is different from its ordinary sense of vital operation. This special philosophical meaning is placed in the being of the soul, which is other than the soul itself. The Aristotelian passage is then explained by saying that the soul is the principle of its own being, just as form in general is the principle of being: "...anima dicitur forma corporis in quantum est causa vitae, sicut forma est principium essendi: vivere enim viventibus est esse, ut dicit Philosophus in II de Anima." *Q. de An.,* a.15, ad 8m; ed. Calcaterra-Centi, *Quaest. Disp.,* II,335a. The clearest explanation of all is found in the *Summa Theologiae:* "...propria forma uniuscuiusque faciens ipsum esse in actu, est principium propriae operationis ipsius. Et ideo vivere dicitur esse viventium ex eo quod viventia per hoc quod habent esse per suam formam, tali modo operantur." *ST,* II-II,179,1, ad 1m; ed. Leonine. Living things operate in such and such a way because they have being through their form. The activities are specified by the form that gives being. This vital specification is considered sufficient to justify the Aristotelian dictum that life is the being of living things.

23   *Quodl.,* III, 1c; ed. Spiazzi, p. 40a. Cf.: "...ita quod quamcumque rationem essendi aliquid habeat, non sit sibi nisi a Deo, sed defectus essendi sit ei a seipso." *In II Sent.,* d.37, p.1, 2.d, Solut.; ed. Mandonnet, II,946. "Ratio autem entis ab actu essendi sumitur, non ab eo cui convenit actus essendi..." *De Ver.,* I,1, ad 3m in contr.; ed. Spiazzi, I,4a.

24 "...de existentia eius in rebus: attribuitur enim Deo quod sit ubique et in omnibus rebus,..." *ST*, I,7, Proem. "Dant enim occasionem falsitatis, eo quod similitudinem eorum gerunt, quorum non habent existentiam." *ST*, I, 17,1 ad 2m; ed. Leonine. "Logicus enim considerat modum praedicandi, et non existentiam rei...Sed philosophus quid existentiam quaerit rerum,..." *In VII Metaph.*, lect. 17, no. 1658; ed. Cathala.

25 "...ei quod fit faciens dat esse." *De Pot*, III, 1, arg. 17m; ed. Mandonnet, II.42a. "Unicuique autem competit habere causam agentem, secundum quod habet esse." *ST*, I,44,1 ad 3m; ed. Leonine.

26 "...sequitur quod aliquid sit sibi ipsi causa essendi. Hoc autem est impossible: quia prius secundum intellectum est causam esse quam effectum; si ergo aliquid sibi ipsi esset causa essendi, intelligeretur esse antequam haberet esse, quod est impossibile:—nisi intelligatur quod aliquid sit sibi causa essendi secundum esse accidentale, quod esse est secundum quid. Hoc enim non est impossibile: invenitur enim aliquod ens accidentale causatum ex principiis sui subiecti, ante quod esse intelligitur esse substantiale subiecti. Nunc autem non loquimur de esse accidentali, sed de substantiali." *CG*, I,22; ed. Leonine, XIII,68b9-21. Cf. *ST*, I,3,4c.

27 *Metaph.*, Z 17,1041a10-b28,

28 *Quaest. in Metaph.*, Introd., p. VII; ed. Graiff, p. 16.21-24.

29 *Supra*, n. 25.

30 "Unde non sic determinatur *esse* per aliud sicut potentia per actum, sed magis sicut actus per potentiam." *De Pot.*, VII,2; ed. Mandonnet, II,254a.

31 See E. Gilson, "Notes sur le Vocabularie de l'Etre," *Mediaeval Studies*, VIII (1946), 152-155.

32 "Certainly in the *De ente et essentia* the essence from which the existence is said to be distinct is the essence expressed in the definition and as this is a positive reality,...it seems clear that St. Thomas did not hold the doctrine that we shall attribute to his maturity when he wrote that work. In his maturity, we shall argue, the essence in the definition would be really identified with the act of being or existence considered as affected by the limit; but the limit itself would be the essence that is really distinct from the act of being." A. Little, *The Platonic Heritage of Thomism* (Dublin Golden Eagle Books, [1951]), p. 193.

33 "Dicemus igitur quod ens et res et necesse talia sunt quae statim imprimuntur in anima prima impressione..." Avicenna, *Metaph.*, I,6A; ed. Venice (1508), fol. 72r2.

34 See supra, nn. 5-11.

35 For Aristotle, *Metaph.*, Γ 2,1003b5-10, privations and negations were called beings on account of their reference to the primary instance of being, *ousia*.

36 "...unaquaeque enim res habet certitudinem qua est id quod est, sicut triangulus habet certitudinem, qua est triangulus, et albedo habet certitudinem qua est albedo: et hoc est quod fortasse appellamus esse proprium. Nec intendimus per illud nisi intentionem esse affirmativi..." Avicenna, *Metaph.*, I,6C; ed. Venice (1508), fol. 72vl.

37 "Set primo modo non potest dici ens nisi quod aliquid in re ponit;...sed sumitur essentia ab ente primo modo dicto; vnde Commentator in eodem loco dicit quod ens primo modo dictum est quod significat essentiam rei." *De Ente.*, c. I; ed. Roland-Gosselin, p. 3: 5-12. W. Norris Clarke, *The New Scholasticism*, XXXII (1958), 266, points out that the first line of this text refers to "*ens*, the composite of essence and existence." The precise difference placed between *ens* in the first sense and *ens* in the second sense, however, is that *ens* in the first sense has an essence, and *ens* in the second sense has not. This is explained by the consideration that *ens* in the first sense "aliquid in re ponit," while *ens* in the second sense "in re nichil ponat." The intelligible nature that is able to be found in reality provides the whole basis for the distinction as sketched here. This intelligible content is positive in the sense of furnishing an object that can be understood or at least known in itself and that can exist in reality. It is "omne illud quod intellectu quocumque modo capi potest" (p. 4.6-7), for instance, a substance. St. Thomas for the moment is primarily interested in dealing with essence as one of the components of *ens*, but at the same time he cannot avoid speaking of it as something that is placed in a category just as *ens* is placed in a category. He accordingly has no hesitation in quoting with approval the statement of Averroes that *ens* in the first sense signifies the essence of the thing (Cf. *In II Sent.*, d.37, q.1, a.2, ad 3m; *Quodl.*, II,3c). To infer, then, that because the first line of the above-quoted text refers to *ens* it "is actually not speaking of essence," seems to leave out of consideration the doctrine of the *De Ente* and the

Commentary on I Sent. (d.22, q.1, a.1, Solut.; ed. Mandonnet, I, 555-557) that essence can be abstracted both with precision and without precision, and the fact that here there is no special reason for remaining strictly within the one type of abstraction. Taken with precision, the essence or nature is not entirely identical with the thing that exists; but taken without precision, it is identical with the same thing, and is what is placed in the category. It can never prescind from its being. One may therefore say indifferently, according to this doctrine of St. Thomas, that an essence or nature is what is placed in a category. The positive character of essence, however, is not sufficient to give an essence the status of a reality when it is considered in abstraction from its being. The Thomistic notion of essence is very different from that of Giles of Rome, who allowed created essence its own intelligibility in priority to the further actuality of existence: "Dicimus enim quod natura creata, licet sit tantae actualitatis quod possit per se intelligi: non sit tamen tantae actualitatis quod possit existere in rerum natura, nisi superaddatur ei actualitas aliqua,   quae communi nomine vocatur esse." *Quodl.,* V,3, (ed. Louvain, 1646), p. 273a.

38   See Roland-Gosselin's edition of *De Ente et Essentia,* p. 11, n. 1. Cf. use of "materia demonstrata" in *In I Sent.,* d.22, q.1 a.1, Solut.; ed. Mandonnet, I, 555-556.

39   E.g.: Est ergo advertendum, abstractionem seu praecisionem intellectus non requirere distinctionem rerum, seu praecisionem alicujus rationis, vel modi, quae ex natura rei antecedat in re ipsa praecisionem intellectus, sed in re simplicissima posse fieri hujusmodi praecisionem variis modis, scilicet, vel per modum formae a subjecto, vel e contrario per modum subjecti a forma, vel per modum formae a forma…Sic igitur abstrahit et praescindit intellectus aliquid ab aliquo tanquam commune a particulari,…" Suarez, *Disp. Metaph.,* II,2,16; ed. Berton (Vivès), XXV. 75b.

40   The geometrical solid, nevertheless, is called a body: "ipse uero tres dimensiones designate sunt corpus quod est in genere quantitatis." *De Ente,* c. II; p. 12, 11-13. It is looked upon as informing an intelligible matter: "Sed accidentia superveniunt substantiae quodam ordine. Nam primo advenit ei quantitas, deinde qualitas, deinde passiones et motus. Unde quantitas potest intelligi in materia subjecta, antequam intelligantur in ea qualitates sensibiles, a quibus dicitur materia sensibilis. Et sic secundum rationem suae substantiae non dependet quantitas a materia sensibili, sed solum a materia intelligibili." *In Boeth, de Trin.,* V,3.Resp.2: ed. Bruno Decker (Leiden: E.J. Brill, 1955) p. 184.12-18

41   "Et quia, ut dictum est, natura speciei est indeterminata respectu indiuidui, sicut natura generis respectu speciei, inde est quod, sicut id quod est genus prout predicatur de specie implicabat in sua significatione, quamuis indistincte, totum quod determinate est in specie, ita eciam et id quod est species, secundum quod predicatur de indiuiduo, oportet quod significet totum illud quod est in individuo essentialiter licet indistincte; et hoc modo essentia Socratis significatur nomine hominis, unde homo de Socrate predicatur." *De Ente,* c.II; p. 20.12-21.1. The problem had been clearly outlined by Plato: "Then while it is one and the same, the whole of it would be many separate individuals at once, and thus it would itself be separate from itself." *Prm.* 131B; tr. Fowler. "…and the third, how in the infinite number of things which come into being this unit, whether we are to assume that it is dispersed and has become many, or that it is entirely separated from itself—which would seem to be the most impossible notion of all—being the same and one, is to be at the same time in one and in many." *Phlb.,* 15B: tr. Fowler.

In the commentary on Boethius' *De Trinitate,* the doctrine of abstraction is expressed as follows: "Et ita sunt duae abstractiones intellectus. Una quae respondet unioni formae et materiae vel accidentis et subiecti, et haec est abstractio formae a materia sensibili. Alia quae respondet unioni totius et partis, et huic respondet abstractio universalis a particulari, quae est abstractio totius, in qua consideratur absolute natura aliqua secundum suam rationem essentialem, ab omnibus partibus, quae non sunt partes speciei, sed sunt partes accidentales." *In Boeth. De Trin.,* V,3, Resp.; ed. Decker, p. 185.20-26. Cf. also *In I Sent.,* d.23, a.1, Solut.; ed. Mandonnet, I,555-556.

42   *De Ente,* c. III; pp. 25.2-26.1. Cf.: "*Tertia* vero est consideratio naturae absoluta, prout abstrahit ab utroque esse; secundum quam considerationem consideratur natura lapidis, vel cuiuscumque alterius, quantum ad ea tantum quae per se competunt tali naturae." *Quodl,* VIII,1; ed. Spiazzi, p. 158b. Although the nature in its absolute consideration is prior to its existing in individuals and in the human mind, in so far as it furnishes the ground for these two states, nevertheless its existing in the divine intellect is prior to it in its absolute consideration: "…et inde est quod hoc quod competit naturae secundum absolutam considerationem, est ratio quare competat naturae alicui secundum esse quod habet in singulari, et non e converso…Similiter etiam intellec-

tus divinus est ratio naturae absolute consideratae, et in singularibus; et ipsa natura absolute considerata et in singularibus est ratio intellectus humani, et quodammodo mensura ipsius." *Ibid.*, p. 159a. Being is its act whether it is considered as abstracted with precision or without precision from its individuals: "Esse enim est actus alicujus ut quod est, sicut calefacere est actus calefacientis; et est alicujus ut quo est, scilicet quo denominatur esse, sicut calefacere est actus caloris." *In I. Sent.*, d.23, q.1, a.1, Solut.; ed. Mandonnet, 1,555. This holds even though simply speaking being is found only in individuals: "...et esse simpliciter non est nisi individuorum; sed determinatio essendi est ex natura vel quidditate generis vel speciei; et ideo quamvis genera et species non subsistent nisi in individuis, tamen eorum proprie subsistere est, et subsistentiae dicuntur...sicut et species, substantiae dicuntur." *Ibid.*, ad 2m; pp. 557-558.

43   For this reason the whole logical order follows upon natures according to the being that they have in the intellect, and not upon those natures according to their absolute consideration: "Non tamen potest dici quod ratio uniuersalis conueniat nature sic accepte, quia de ratione uniuersalis est communitas et unitas, nature autem humane neutrum horum conuenit secundum absolutam suam considerationem...Similiter eciam non potest dici quod ratio generis uel speciei accidat nature humane secundum esse quod habet in indiuiduis, quia non inuenitur in indiuiduis natura humana secundum unitatem ut sit unum quid omnibus conueniens, quod ratio uniuersalis exigit. Relinquitur ergo quod ratio speciei accidat humane nature secundum illud esse quod habet in intellectu." *De Ente*, c. III; pp. 26.11-28.2 The nature according to its absolute consideration, therefore, is proper neither to the metaphysical nor to the logical order, but is common to both. It is difficult to see how in the doctrine of St. Thomas it could be called the "ontological aspect" as opposed to the "logical aspect of the universal"—E. D. Simmons, "In Defense of Total and Formal Abstraction," *The New Scholasticism*, XXIX (1955), 434. On the other hand it is equally difficult to see that the study of the nature in its absolute consideration is a "logical preparation explaining the notion of essence"—W. Baumgaertner. "Metaphysics and the Second Analytics," *The New Scholasticism*, XXIX (1955), 524; or that it can give rise to a "logical" argument "che si può chiamare logicometafisica"—C. Fabro, *La Nozione Metafisica di Partecipazione* (2nd ed., Turin: Soc. Edit. Internaz., 1950, p.218). The argument of St. Thomas to prove the existence of the primary being and the entitative composition of creatures does not start in the logical order and pass over into the metaphysical. It starts with really existent sensible things and sees in them nature's that are common to both the real and the logical orders. There is no question here of a procedure that passes from the logical into the metaphysical order. It merely uses a consideration of nature that is common to both orders.

44   Cf. *De Pot.*, V,9, ad. 16m; *Quodl.*, VIII,1, ad 1 m.

45   In the subsistent being that is reached as a result of this reasoning process, nature and being coincide. To prove that being so exists in itself, is to prove that it is in itself a real nature. It is both *what* exists and the existence. It is both the *what* and the *is*. Hence it is true to say that both subject and predicate coincide in meaning in the statement "Subsistent being exists." Both denote nature as well as existence, when they are reached as a result of the Thomistic argument. But this in no way implies an immediate intuition of the divine existence or nature. "Subsistent being" is not something immediately known by the human intellect, but is attained only through the above reasoning process. Once one knows what it means as a result of the demonstration, however, one thereby knows that it exists in reality. It pertains to the propositions "per se notae, apud sapientes tantum, ut *incorporalia in loco non esse."* (*ST*, 1,2,1c ; ad. Leonine.).

46   The "real" character of the distinction between essence and being is not mentioned by St. Thomas in passages where he is professedly treating the distinction, as for instance in the *De Ente et Essentia*. It is called "real" only several times when it occurs on the occasion of treating other topics. In the commentary on the *Sentences*, on the occasion of explaining the differences between the "now" of eternity, aevum, and time, St. Thomas states: "Actus autem quid mensuratur aevo, scilicet ipsum esse aeviterni, differt ab eo, cujus est actus, re quidem...Esse autem quod mensuratur aeternitate, est idem re cum eo cujus est actus, sed differt tantum ratione; et ideo aeternitas et nunc aeternitatis non differunt re, sed ratione tantum, inquantum scilicet ipsa aeternitas respicit ipsum divinum esse, et nunc aeternitatis quidditatem ipsius rei, quae secundum rem non est aliud quam suum esse, sed ratione tantum." *In I Sent.*, d.19, q.2, a.2, Solut,; ad. Mandonnet, I,471. This text states that the angelic being (*esse aeviterni*) is an act different from its subject in reality (*re quidem*). The difference is in the thing. By contrast, the difference between the two in the case of

God is only a difference of reason (*tantum ratione*). In reality the act is the same as the subject of the act. There is no difference in the thing itself. The difference is set up by human reason in its endeavor to represent the eternal being. The divine being (*divinum esse*), therefore, is not other in reality than its quiddity.—The contrast in this text places its meaning beyond any shadow of doubt. The difference between a finite thing's essence and being is not a difference that is set up by the workings of the human intellect, but is explicitly contrasted with such distinction. It is a difference in the thing itself, independently of any construction of the human intellect in trying to understand that thing. The doctrine here is definite enough, yet it is mentioned in a merely occasional treatment.

Similarly in *De Veritate* St. Thomas writes: "...omne quod est in genere substantiae, est compositum reali compositione;...et oportet quod esse suum sit aliud quam ipsum,..." *De Ver.*, XXVII, 1, ad 8 m; ed. Spiazzi, I,513a. Again the statement is definite, though it is made on the occasion of treating a problem regarding grace. Further, in the commentary on Boethius' *De Hebdomadibus*, the explicit contrast of a real with an intentional distinction is repeated: "...sicut esse et quod est differunt in simplicibus secundum intentiones, ita in compositis differunt realiter;...in simplicibus...necesse est quod ipsum esse, et id quod est, sit unum et idem realiter. Si enim esset aliud realiter id quod est et ipsum esse, jam non esset simplex, sed compositum." *In de Hebd*, c. II; ed. Mandonnet, I,175-176. Real difference is contrasted with a distinction set up by different *intentiones* or concepts of the intellect. The statement is made on the occasion of explaining a text of Boethius.

These texts leave no doubt that for St. Thomas the distinction between essence and being in real finite things may be called a "real distinction." But the occasional nature of these assertions and the lack of mention of it in the passages that professedly treat of being, may well occasion a doubt about how operative the notion "real" is in explaining the distinction. It is a distinction that holds for intentional being (*esse in anima*) just as well as for real being (*esse in re*), and so cannot be narrowed to the characterization of "real distinction."

47   ...et propter hoc a quibusdam dicuntur huiusmodi substantie composite ex quo est et quod est, uel ex quod est et esse ut Boecius dicit." *De Ente*, c. IV; pp. 35. 32-36.3.

48   ...in rebus inferioribus a quibus scientiam capit, in quibus esse non est subsistens, sed inhaerens." *De Pot.*, VII,2, ad 7m; ed. Pession, p. 192a.

49   "Si ergo in angelo est compositio sicut ex essentia et esse, non tamen est compositio sicut ex partibus substantiae, sed sicut ex substantia et eo quod adhaeret substantiae." *Quodl.*, II,3c; ed. Spiazzi, p. 24b.

50   "...diaphanum semper est in ultima dispositione ad lucem..." *CG*, II,19; ed. Leonine, XIII,308b22-23.

51   "...diaphanum est aeri principium lucendi quia facit eum proprium subiectum luminis." *CG*, II,54; ed. Leonine, XIII, 392a23-25.

52   *ST*, I,104,1 ad 1m; ed. Leonine. Cf. *De Pot.*, V.3c.

53   Being is, of course, itself a positive act in the existential order, and is received into a subject that is a positive nature in the essential order. On account of this positive character it is, like goodness, a participated perfection. Unity, on the other hand, is negative in character and so is not considered as participated, but as already present with the very positing of the essence as well as of the being. Transcendental unity is a negation that follows upon *ens*, the essence already constituted as a being: "...unum quod convertitur cum ente, dicitur secundum rationem negationis, quam addit supra ens" (*De Ver.*, XXI,5 ad 7m; ed. Mandonnet, p. 521a). In the same context in which St. Thomas defends against Avicenna the doctrine that everything is essentially one (*unaquaeque res per suam essentiam est una*—ibid., arg. 7; p. 519a), he attributes unity to the essence through itself, and not on account of the accidentally added being: "...unum indifferenter se habet ad hoc quod respiciat essentiam vel esse: unde essentia rei est una per se ipsam, non propter esse suum: et ita non est una per aliquam participationem, sicut accidit de ente et bono"(Ibid., ad 8m; p.521a). The equivocity signalized in the case of unity, therefore, is grounded on unity as a transcendental and unity as the principle of number in the category of quantity. The equivocity of being, on the other hand, stems from the combined essential and accidental character of being in regard to created things. Transcendental unity, on account of its negative aspect, cannot be regarded as a further accident as is the case with being and goodness. The positive character of essence constitutes a ground upon which the unity of a being (*ens*) follows. This does not mean, however, that essence

in its absolute consideration has a unity of its own. The unity follows, negatively, when it is constituted as a being.

54   "Illud autem quod primo intellectus concipit quasi notissimum, et in quod omnes conceptiones resolvit, est ens, ut Avicenna dicit in principio *Metaphysicae* suae. Unde oportet quod omnes aliae conceptiones intellectus accipiantur ex additione ad ens." *De Ver.*, I,1c; ed. Spiazzi, I,2b.

55   *Disp. Metaph.*, XXXI,4,4-6; Vives, XXVI, 236a-237a.

Notes—Diversity and Community of Being

1   *De Ente et Essentia*, ed. Roland-Gosselin (reprint, Paris, 1948), c. V; p. 37.17-21. Cf.: "Ratio enim entis, cum sit diversificata in diversis, non est sufficiens ad specialem rerum cognitionem;..." *In I Sent.*, Prol., q.1, a.2, Solut.; ed. Mandonnet (Paris, 1929), I, 10. "...in diversis rebus est diversum esse, quo formaliter res est;..." *In I Sent.*, d.19, q.5, a.2, Solut.; I, 492. Similarly: "... ratio enim formae in diversis materiis est una, licet secundum esse sit diversa." *De Prin. Individ.*, ed. Mandonnet, *Opuscula Omnia* (Paris, 1927), V, 196.   Strictly speaking, "diverse" is wider than "different": "... prima non sunt diversa nisi per seipsa: sed ea quae sunt ex primis, differunt per diversitatem primorum; sicut homo et asinus differunt istis differentiis diversis, rationale et irrationale, quae non diversificatur aliis differentiis, sed seipsis: ita etiam Deus et esse creatum non differunt aliquibus differentiis utrique superadditis, sed seipsis: unde nec proprie dicuntur differre, sed diversa esse: diversum enim est absolutum, sed differens est relatum, secundum Philosophum, X *Metaph.*, text 13. Omne enim differens, aliquo differt; sed non omne diversum, aliquo diversum est." *In I Sent.*, d.8, q.1, a.2, ad 3m; I, 198. So: "Unde, si fiat vis in verbo, non proprie dicuntur *differre*, sed *diversa esse:* ..." *ST*, I, 3, 8, ad 3m (ed. Leonine). "Sed secundum hoc licet omne differens sit diversum, non tamen omne *diversum* est differens;..." *ST*, I, 90, 1, ad 3m. "Diverse," therefore, may always be used where one would expect "different," e.g.: "Sicut animal quod est diversificatum in diversas species, scilicet in hominem et equum:..." *In X Metaph.*, lect. 10, n° 2112; ed. Cathala-Spiazzi (Turin & Rome), 1950. According to the strict rule, "different" should not be used unless the things share a common genus: "In his autem, quae in nullo conveniunt, non est quarendum quo differant, sed seipsis diversa sunt. Sic enim et oppositae differentiae ab invicem distinguuntur: non enim participant genus quasi partem suae essentiae;..." *CG*, I, 17; ed. Leonine, XIII, 47b4-9. Nevertheless, St. Thomas frequently uses "different" to signify diversity in being, as will be seen in subsequently quoted texts. The distinction between the two terms is a nicety that can hardly be observed regularly in English idiom.

2   "Ainsi, par exemple, la loi du rapport inverse entre l'extension et la compréhension d'un terme vaut parfaitement lorsqu'il s'agit d'un concept univoque; mais que faut-il penser quand il est question d'un concept analogue? Est-il vrai sans nuances que le concept d'être a le minimum de compréhension parce qu'il a le maximum d'extension?"J. Pétrin, "Univocité et analogie dans les lois de la logique," *Angelicum*, XXVI (1949), 248. "Instead of being the emptiest and most abstract of all notions, it is the richest, for everything which is—either material or immaterial—is implicitly included in its content, and nothing real is excluded from its extension."L.J. Eslick, "What is the Starting Point of Metaphysics?", *The Modern Schoolman*, XXXIV (1957), 259.

3   "...particulare dicitur eo quod particulatur in ipso natura communis, cujus partem accipit secundum virtutem qua potest esse in pluribus, quamvis accipiat totam rationem ejus." *In I Sent.*, d.23, q.1, a.2, ad 4m; I,560. On the identity in being of common nature and the subject of which it is predicated, see J. Owens, "Common Nature: A Point of Comparison between Thomistic and Scotistic Metaphysics,"*Mediaeval Studies*, XIX (1957), 6.

4   "...ratio speciei accidat humane nature secundum illud esse quod habet in intellectu. Ipsa enim natura humana in intellectu habet esse abstractum ab omnibus indiuiduantibus;... est de accidentibus que consecuntur eam secundum esse quod habet in intellectu,..." *De Ente*, c. III; pp. 28.1-29.6. As part of a real cognitional operation, however, the species is individuated according to the individuality of the intellectual activity in which the nature has cognitional being: "...tamen secundum quod habet esse in hoc intellectu uel in illo est quedam species intellecto particularis."

De Ente, c. III; p. 28.14-15. Cf. c. III, p. 25.9-10.

In the terminology of abstraction versus separation (see infra, n. 70), being is not "abstract." In the above text from *De Ente* it is called "abstract" quite apparently in the sense of abstract versus concrete as described in the *In de Hebd.*, c. II, (ed, Mandonnet) *Opusc.*, I, 171; cf.: "... ipsum esse significatur ut quiddam abstractum," p. 172; "... ipsum esse significatur ut abstractum," p. 174. "Sic igitur probat auctor quod aeternitas participat esse; ipsum autem esse abstractum est Causa prima, cujus substantia est suum esse." *In Lib. de Causis*, lect. II, (ed. Pera, Turin & Rome, 1955) n°. 55. "Sic igitur si *esse* causatum primum esset esse abstractum, ut Platonici posuerunt, tale esse non posset multiplicari sed esset unum tantum." Lect. IV, n°. 105.

5   "Est etiam quaedam creatura quae non habet esse in se, sed tantum in alio, sicut materia prima, sicut forma quaelibet, sicut universale; non enim est esse alicujus, nisi particularis subsistentis in natura,..." *In I Sent.*, d.8, q.5, a.1, Solut.; I, 227. "...esse simpliciter non est nisi individuorum;..." *In I Sent.*, d.23, q.1, q.1, ad 2m; I, 557. "... in Socrate non inuenitur communitas aliqua, sed quicquid in eo est est indiuiduatum". *De Ente*, c. III; p. 27.1-6. "Universalia enim non habent esse in rerum natura ut universalia sunt, sed solum secundum quod sunt individuata." *Q. de An.*, a.1, ad 2m; ed. Calcaterra-Centi (Turin & Rome, 1953), II, 284b.

6   In St. Thomas, accordingly, there is no immediately facile solution of this problem through distinction of an *esse essentiae* that would coincide in reality with the essence and an *esse existentiae* that is other than it. The whole question is concerned only with being that is other than finite essence.

7   "...esse uniuscuiusque est ei proprium, et distinctum ab esse cuiuslibet alterius rei; sed ratio substantiae potest esse communis: ..." *De Pot.*, VII, 3c; ed. Pession, II, 193b. "Sicut etiam unicuique est proprium esse, ita et propria operatio." *CG*, I, 52; ed. Leonine, XIII, 148b30-31.

8   *De Ente*, c. V; p. 38.8-12. The modeling of the notion *esse commune* on the abstraction of generic natures without precision, may also be seen from the following texts: "...aliquid esse sine additione dicitur dupliciter. Aut de cujus ratione est ut nihil sibi addatur: et sic dicitur de Deo: hoc enim oportet perfectum esse in se ex quo additionem non recipit; nec potest esse commune, quia omne commune salvatur in proprio, ubi sibi fit additio. Aut ita quod non sit de ratione ejus quod fiat sibi additio, neque quod non fiat, et hoc modo ens commune est sine additione. ... et ideo commune est, quia in sui ratione non dicit aliquam additionem, sed potest sibi fieri additio ut determinetur ad proprium; sicut etiam animal commune dicitur esse sine ratione, quia de intellectu ejus non est habere rationem, neque non habere; ..." *In I Sent.*, d.8, q.4, a.1 ad 1m; I, 219. "... ens commune est cui non fit additio, de cuius tamen ratione non est ut ei additio fieri non possit; sed esse divinum est esse cui non fit additio, et de eius ratione est ut ei additio fieri non possit; unde divinum esse non est esse commune. Sicut et animali communi non fit additio, in sua ratione, rationalis differentiae; non tamen est de ratione eius quod ei additio fieri non possit;..." *De Pot.*, VII, 2, ad 6m; II, 192a. "Quia enim id quod commune est per additionem specificatur vel individuatur, aestimaverunt divinum esse, cui nulla fit additio, non esse aliquod esse proprium, sed esse commune omnium; non considerantes quod id quod commune est vel universale sine additione esse non potest, sed sine additione consideratur: non enim *animal* potest esse absque *rationali vel irrationali* differentia, quamvis absque his differentiis cogitetur. ... Unde...concludi potest quod Deus non sit esse commune...." *CG*, I, 26; ed. Leonine, XIII, 82b13-32. "...non est de ratione animalis communis ut habeat rationem; sed nec de ratione eius est ut careat ratione. Primo igitur modo, esse sine additione, est esse divinum: secundo modo, esse sine additione, est esse commune." *ST*, I, 3, 4, ad 1m.

This use of "addition" in St. Thomas has been discussed and traced to its historical origins by Edmund W. Morton, S.J., in an unpublished University of Toronto doctoral thesis (1953), "The Doctrine of *ens commune* in St. Thomas Aquinas," pp. 66-85; 105-121; 184-215; 271-277.

9   *De Ente*, c. V; p. 38.1. On the meaning of "formally" in this context, see infra, n. 23.

10   See *De Ente*, c. II; pp. 12.5-23.7.

11   Aristotle, *Metaph.*, Δ 6, 1016b31-1017a3; cf. 9,1018a13.

12   *De Subst. Sep.*, c. VI, (ed. Perrier, Paris, 1949) no.43. Cf.: "Patet enim quod esse, communequoddam est,... Inde patet quod 'esse' dicit id quod est commune omnibus generibus;..." *In I Sent.*, d.23, q.1, a.1, Solut.; I, 555. "...esse commune ad substantiam et ad accidens,..." *In I Sent.*, d.24, q.1, a.3, Solut.; I, 581. "...omnia existentia continentur sub ipso esso communi,..." *In de Div. Nom.*, c. V, lect. 2, (ed. Pera, Turin & Rome, 1950), n°. 660. "Esse vero quod in sui

natura unaquaeque res habet, est substantiale. Et ideo, cum dicitur, Socrates est, si ille Est primo modo accipiatur, est de praedicato substantiali. Nam ens est superius ad unumquodque entium, sicut animal ad hominem." *In V Metaph.*, lect. 9, n°. 896.

13 H. Renard, "What is St. Thomas' Approach to Metaphysics," *The New Scholasticism*, XXX (1956), 81-83, distinguishes *ens transcendentale* from *ens commune*, on the ground "*that ens commune* is attributable only to being whose essence is not *esse*" (p. 79). Yet St. Thomas' arguments that God is the cause of *ens commune* and is not contained under *ens commune* would apply equally well to *ens transcendentale*; e.g.: "...*ipsum esse* commune est ex primo Ente, quod est Deus, et ex hoc sequitur quod esse commune aliter se habeat ad Deum quam alia existentia, quantum ad tria; primo quidem, quantum ad hoc quod alia existentia dependent ab esse communi, non autem Deus, sed magis esse commune dependet a Deo;... Secundo, quantum ad hoc quod omnia existentia continentur sub ipso esse communi, non autem Deus, sed magis esse commune continetur sub ejus virtute, quia virtus divina plus extenditur quam ipsum esse creatum;... Tertio, quantum ad hoc quod omnia alia existentia participant eo quod est esse, non autem Deus,..." *In de Div. Nom.*, lect. II; (ed. Pera) n°. 660. These arguments are that there is no common *ratio* upon which both God and creatures would be dependent, a *ratio* that would contain them both under itself, and in which both would participate. Rather, God is the nature of being; and all other instances of being are dependent upon Him and are contained under the scope of His power. There is no transcendentally common nature of being, which God and creatures would participate in the order of prior and subsequent. God is not a part of *ens transcendentale*. He is the whole of being. All other being *descends*, and in that sense transcends, from Him. To the extent that its essence allows, it imitates His being. In this way a *community* of analogy (of which God is cause and not part) is established between Creator and creatures. Cf.: "...Creator et creatura reducuntur in unum, non communitate univocationis sed analogiae. Talis autem communitas potest esse duplex. Aut ex eo quod aliqua participant aliquid unum secundum prius et posterius, sicut potentia et actus rationem entis, et similiter substantia et accidens; aut ex eo quod unum esse et rationem ab altero recipit; et talis est analogia creaturae ad Creatorem: creatura enim non habet esse nisi secundum quod a primo ente descendit, nec nominatur ens nisi inquantum ens primum imitatur; ..." *In I Sent.*, Prol., q.1, a.2, ad 2m; I, 10. These considerations help focus interest on the way in which the notion of being is acquired and in which it is known as common. Cf. infra, n. 78. On *ens commune* as essence, see *De Ver.*, X, 11, ad 10m; ed. Spiazzi, I, 218a.

14 *CG*, II, 52; ed. Leonine, XIII, 387a21-24. Cf. *De Pot.*, VII, 2, ad 5m; ed. Pession, II, 192a.

15 "...non precidit designationem materie set implicite continet eam et indistincte, sicut dictum est quod genus continet differentiam;..." *De Ente*, c. II; p. 22.21-23. "... implicite et indistincte continet totum quod in indiuiduo est." *De Ente*, c. III; p. 23.28. Cf. "...non quidem ita quod sit in homine alia res quae sit penitus extra essentiam animalis,... quia id quod determinate et actualiter continetur in ratione hominis, implicite et quasi potentialiter continetur in ratione animalis." *De Ver.*, XXI, 1c; ed. Spiazzi, I, 376a.

16 See *De Ente*, c. II (pp. 13.5-15.3); *In I Sent.*, d.23, a.1, a.1, Solut. (I. 555-556); d. 25, q.1, a.1, ad 2m (I, 602-603). Cf. "... unde in nomine humanitatis, non includitur nec actu nec potentia aliquod individuale principium;...." *In de Div. Nom.*, c.V, lect. 1, (ed. Pera) n. 626.

17 *ST*, I, 3, 5c. "Item, plura individua sub una specie contenta differunt secundum esse, et tamen conveniunt in una essentia." *Comp. Theol.*, c. XIV; ed. Mandonnet, *Opusc.*, II, 8. Cf. supra, nn.6-7.

18 *Q. de An.*, a.1, ad 2m; ed. Calcaterra-Centi, II, 284b. Cf. supra, nn. 4-5.

19 See *De Ente*, c. III; pp. 25.9-29.30.

20 *De Ente*, c. IV; p. 34.12-14. Cf. *In I Sent.*, d.3, q.1, a.1, Solut.; II, 87.

21 "...hoc verbum *est* quandoque in enunciatione praedicatur secundum se; ut cum dicitur, *Socrates est:* per quod nihil aliud intendimus significare, quam quod Socrates sit in rerum natura. Quandoque vero non praedicatur *per se*, quasi principale praedicatum, sed quasi coniunctum principale praedicato ad connectendum ipsum subjecto; sicut cum dicitur, *Socrates est albus*, non est intentio loquentis ut asserat Socratem esse in rerum natura, set ut attribuat ei albedinem mediante hoc verbo, *est*;..." *In II Periherm.*, lect. 2, n. 2 (ed. Leonine).

22 "'Being' is obviously not a real predicate; that is, it is not a concept of something which could be added to the concept of a thing. It is merely the positing of a thing, or of certain determinations, as existing in themselves." Kant, KRV, B 626; tr. N.K. Smith.

23   "...esse est actualitas omnis formae vel naturae:... Oportet igitur quod ipsum esse comparetur ad essentiam quae est aliud ab ipso, sicut actus ad potentiam." *ST*, I, 3, 4c. "...ipsum esse est actualitas omnium rerum, et etiam formarum. ...Cum enim dico *esse* hominis, vel equi, vel cuiuscumque alterius, ipsum esse consideratur ut formale et receptum:..." *ST*, I, 4, 1, ad 3m. "Illud autem quod est maxime formale omnium, est ipsum esse, ..." *ST*, I, 7, 1c. "Esse autem... cum sit formale respectu omnium quae in re sunt,..." *ST*, I, 8, 1c. Cf. *De Pot.*, VII, 2, ad 9m.

24   See *Quodl.*, VIII, 1c. This doctrine of the common nature is radically different from that of Duns Scotus, for whom the common nature exists in individuals as formally distinct from their individual differentiae; see *Op. Ox.*, II, d.3, q.5 & 6, n°. 15; ed. Quaracchi, II, 269-270 (n°. 289).

25   "Sed sciendum est, quod aliquid participatur *dupliciter*. Uno modo quasi de substantia participantis, sicut genus participatur a specie. Hoc autem modo esse non participatur a creatura. Id enim est de substantia rei quod cadit in eius definitione." *Quodl.*, II, 2, 1c; ed. Spiazzi (Turin, 1956), p. 24b. "Unde genus est hoc ipsum quod est species, et non solum aliquid eius." *In X Metaph.*, lect. 10, n°. 2114. Cf.: "Si igitur esse divinum esset formale esse omnium, oporteret omnia simpliciter esse unum." *CG*, I, 26; XIII, 81b3-5.

26   *ST*, I, 4, 2c. Cf.: "Similiter eciam quamuis sit esse tantum non oportet quod deficiant perfectiones relique et nobilitates. Imo habet Deus perfectiones que sunt in omnibus generibus,... set habet eas modo excellentiori ceteris rebus, quia in eo unum sunt sed in aliis diuersitatem habent. Et hoc est quia omnes ille perfectiones conueniunt sibi secundum suum esse simplex;..." *De Ente*, c. V; p. 38.12-20. "...quidquid est entitatis et bonitatis in creaturis, totum est a Creatore: ... Unde oportet quod omnes nobilitates omnium creaturarum inveniantur in Deo nobilissimo modo..."*In I Sent.*, d.2, q.1, Solut.; I, 62." ...cum enim formae rerum sive sint divisim per se stantes, sive uniantur in uno Primo habente esse universalissimum et divinum, manifestum est quod quanto magis appropinquantur ad hoc universalissimum esse formarum, tanto formae sunt universaliores." *In Lib de Causis.* lect. IV, n°. 125 (ed. Pera). "Oportet autem illud quod est causa entis in quantum est ens, esse causam omnium differentiarum entis,..." *De Pot.*, III, 16, ad 4m; ed. Pession, II, 89b. "Igitur si aliquid est cui competit tota virtus essendi, ei nulla nobilitatum deesse potest quae alicui rei conveniat. Sed rei suae quae est suum esse, competit esse secundum totam essendi potestatem:..." *CG*, I, 28; XIII, 86b6-87a1.

27   "... omne esse in se praehabet et in Ipso comprehenduntur et praehabentur *principia omnium entium* et fines; non tamen eodem modo sicut in ipsis rebus, sed Ipse *est super omnia, sicut ante omnia* supereminenter existens. Et quia in Ipso, quodammodo, sunt omnia, quasi in se omnia comprehendente, *simul* de Ipso *omnia praedicantur* et simul ab Ipso omnia removentur, quia *nihil est omnium,* sed super omnia;..." *In de Div. Nom.*, c. V, lect. 2, no. 661; ed. Pera (Turin & Rome, 1950), p. 245b.

28   *Comp. Theol.*, c. LXXI. This theme is frequent enough in St. Thomas; e.g.: *De Pot.*, III, 16; *In Lib. de Causis*, lect. 24, n. 395-399; *CG*, II, 39-45; *ST*, I, 47, 1c; *In XII Metaph.*, lect. 2, n°. 2440.

29   "Si autem hoc modo se habeant res ad unitatem et multitudinem, sicut se habent ad esse: totum autem esse rerum dependet a Deo, ut ostensum est, pluralitatis rerum causam ex Deo esse oportet." *Comp. Theol.*, c. LXXII.

30   "Chaque essence est posée par un acte d'exister qu'elle n'est pas et qui l'inclut comme son autodétermination. ...c'est donc la hiérarchie des actes d'exister qui fonde et règle celle des essences, chacune d'elles n'exprimant que l'intensité propre d'un certain acte d'exister." E. Gilson, *Le Thomisme*, 5th ed. (Paris, 1944), pp.54-55. "Autodétermination" is an exceptionally apt term for this notion, but is difficult to translate into English. "Self-determination," a political and psychological term in English, could perhaps carry its meaning.

31   *Metaph.*, B 3, 998b22-27; Oxford tr. Cf. H 6,1045b1-7. "There is, in any event, nothing univocally and generically common to all beings, and the differences between beings are themselves *beings*. But these specifically and materially different modes of being cannot be actually included in *ens commune* in an explicit way without transforming common being into proper being." L.J. Eslick, "What is the Starting Point of Metaphysics?" *The Modern Schoolman*, XXXIV (1957), 258.

32   *Metaph.*, Z 12, 1037b29-1038a30.

33   *Top.*, IV 2, 122b20-24; *Metaph.*, Z 12, 1037b18-21. The viewpoint in this passage from the *Metaphysics* is still logical, in accordance with the introduction at 1037b8-9.

34   *De Ente*, c. II; p. 16.3-4. Cf.: "...nec differentia forma, set a forma sumpta ut significans totum." Ibid., p. 18.10-11.

35   *In I Metaph.*, lect. 12, 1549. Cf.: "...non hoc modo advenit differentia generi, ut diversa essentia ab eo existens, sicut advenit album homini." Ibid., 1550. "...ultima differentia erit tota substantia rei, et tota definitio. Includit enim in se omnes praecedentes particulas" (1555). "Quod enim in differentia includatur genus, ostensum est, ex hoc quod genus non est sine differentiis. Sed quod ultima includat omnes praecedentes, palam est ex hoc quod nisi hoc dicatur, sequitur quod oporteat 'in terminis.' idest definitionibus, multoties eadem dicere" (1556). "...una erit ultima, ... quae substantiam et speciem definiti comprehendet,..." (1559). "...genus non est praeter differentias,..." (1561). "... differentia nullam formam dicit, quae implicite in natura generis non contineatur,... genus enim non significat partem essentiae rei, sed totum." *In I Sent.*, d.3, q.1, a.6; II, 105. See also *De Subst. Sep.*, c. VI, (ed. Perrier) 41.

36   E.g.: "...differentia non intrat definitionem generis." *CG*, I, 24; XIII, 74b20-21. "Non enim genus ponitur in definitione differentiae, ... Nec etiam differentia ponitur in definitione generis...." *In III Metaph.*, lect. 8, 433. "... omne enim genus habet differentias quae sunt extra essentiam generis; ..." *ST*, I, 3, 5c.

37   *De Ente*, c. II; pp. 17.14-18.2.

38   "... genus praedicatur de differentiis secundum quod sunt in speciebus." *In III Metaph.*, lect. 8, 433. The problem is neatly presented, in terms of the expression and the signification of the differentia, by J. Bobik, "Further remarks upon 'Is Being a Genus,'" *Philosophical Studies* (Maynooth), IX (1959), 73-78. However, in regard to relating genus to differentia, the conclusion "There is no possibility here of relating genus to difference in terms of signification, in addition to expression"(p.76) should not be understood in a way that would exclude the above sense in which genus may be predicated of differentia. "Anything rational is an animal" predicates the genus of the differentia understood as a whole. The differentia here seems taken just as clearly in its proper sense of differentia as it is in the *De Ente* where it is understood as a part and so not able to be identified with the genus in predication: "...cum dicitur animatum, siue illud quod habet animam; non enim determinatur quid sit, utrum sit corpus uel aliquid aliud." *De Ente*, c. II; p.17.9-11.

39   *Top.* VI 6, 144a21-22; 24-25; Oxford tr. Cf. *Cat.*, 5, 3a21-25.

40   *In V Metaph.*, lect. 16, 987. Cf.: "Nam differentia praedicatur in eo quod quale. Et propter hoc, sicut cum dicitur animal rationale significatur tale animal, ita cum dicitur superficies quadrata, significatur talis superficies" (lect. 22, 1121). "... differentiae sunt eius qualitates. Sicut in definitione hominis primo ponitur animal, et bipes sive rationale, quod est quaedam substantialis qualitas hominis" (1122). "... quale invenitur in genere substantiae, secundum quod differentia substantialis dicitur praedicari in *eo quod quale*:..." *In V Phys.*, lect.4, 2. "... qualitatem, inquam, essentialem, secundum quod differentia significat *quale quid."* *In I Periherm.*, lect. 10, 10. "... qualitas quae est differentia substantiae;..." *ST*, I-II, 49,2c.

41   *In Metaph.*, lect. 22, 1123. Cf.: "Genus enim, licet non sit materia, quia non praedicaretur de specie, cum materia sit pars, tamen ratio generis sumitur ab eo quod est materiale in re; sicut ratio differentiae ab eo quod est formale" (lect. 7, 862). "Sicut enim in genere substantiae, differentis, quae praedicatur de genere, et advenit ei ad constitutionem speciei, comparatur ad ipsum ut actus et forma, ita etiam in aliis definitionibus." *In VIII. Metaph.*, lect. 2, 1697. "Nam genus sumitur a materis, et differentia a forma, ..." (lect. 3, 1721). "Et quidem nomen, quo aliquid totum denominatur ab eo quod est materiale in ipso, est nomen generis. Nomen autem, quo denominatur a principio formale, est nomen differentiae. Sicut homo nominatur animal a natura sensibili, rationale vero a natura intellectiva." *In X Metaph.*, lect. 10, 2115. "... differentia advenit generi non *per accidens* sed *per se*, tanquam determinativa ipsius, per modum quo materia determinatur per formam." *In I Periherm.*, lect. 8, 10.

42   *In IV Phys.*, lect. 4, 2. Cf.: "...sive sint partes rationis, sicut sunt genus et differentia, quae sunt partes definitionis: sive sint partes integrales alicuius compositi, sicut ex lapidibus et lignis fit domus."*In I Periherm.*, lect. 12 8.

43   See supra, nn. 15 and 38. Cf. the way in which differentia is predicated of genus at *In VIII Metaph.*, lect. 2, 1697—(supra, 41).

44   "Similite eciam non potest dici quod ratio generis uel speciei accidat nature humane secundum esse quod habet in indiuiduis, quia non inuenitur in indiuiduis natura humana secundum unitatem ut sit unum quid omnibus conueniens, quod ratio uniuersalis *exigit*. Relinquitur ergo

quod ratio speciei accidat humane nature secundum illud esse quod habet in intellectu." *De Ente*, c. III; pp. 27.6-28.2. "Similiter humanitas quae intelligitur, non est nisi in hoc vel in illo homine: sed quod humanitas apprehendatur sine individualibus conditionibus, quod est ipsam abstrahi, ad quod sequitur intentio universalitatis, accidit humanitati secundum quod percipitur ab intellectu, in quo est similitudo naturae speciei, et non individualium principiorum." *ST*, I, 85, 2, ad 2m. Cf. supra, 4.

45   *In X Metaph.*, lect. 10, 2116. Cf.: "Materia enim est pars integralis rei, et ideo de re praedicari non potest." *In VII Metaph.*, lect. 12, 1546. "Si enim in intellectu corporis intelligatur substantia completa ultima forma, habens in se tres dimensiones, sic corpus est genus, ... Si vero in intellectu corporis non accipiatur nisi hoc, quod est habens tres dimensiones cum aptitudine ad formam ultimam, sic corpus est materia" (1547).

46   See supra, n. 38.

47   *De Pot.*, VII, 2, ad 9m; ed. Pession, II, 192b.

48   For the history of the gradual development of the linguistic view of metaphysical problems, see Maxwell John Charlesworth, *Philosophy and Linguistic Analysis* (Louvain, 1959).

49   "Unde in anima invenitur compositio 'esse' et 'quod est,' et non in aliis formis: quia ipsum esse non est formarum corporalium absolute, sicut eorum quae sunt, sed compositi." *In I Sent.*, d.8, q.5, a.2, ad 1m; I,230.

50   The aspect of being arises from the existential act that is other than the thing's essence: "...cum dicitur: *Diversum est esse, et quod est*, distinguitur actus essendi ab eo cui actus ille convenit. Ratio autem entis ab actu essendi sumitur, non ab eo cui convenit actus essendi,..." *De Ver.*, I, 1, ad 3m in contr.; ed. Spiazzi, I, 4a.

51   "...quidditas generis vel speciei non communicatur secundum unum esse omnibus, sed solum secundum unam rationem communem." *In I Sent.*, d.8, q.4, a.2, Solut.; I, 222. Cf. supra, n. 17.

52   *Ens* is used equivocally by St. Thomas for both the act of being and the subject of being. On this topic see J. Owens "The Accidental and Essential Character of Being in the Doctrine of St. Thomas Aquinas" *Mediaeval Studies* XX (1958) 2-10. Cf.: "... essentia dicitur secundum quod per eam et in ea ens habet esse." *De Ente* c. I; p. 1.15-16. "...esse est actus existentis, inquantum ens est." *In I Sent.*, d.19, q.2, a.2, Solut; I, 470. "...cum nomen entis imponatur ab esse,..." *In I Sent.*, d.25, q.1, a.4, arg. 2; I, 611. In texts like these, *ens* is used clearly enough in the sense of that which has being—"what is." It includes both being and essence, and in it, because of that being, the first principle of demonstration is grasped.: "...cum duplex sit operatio intellectus: una, qua cognoscit quod quid est, quae vocatur indivisibilium intelligentia: alia, qua componit et dividit: in utroque est aliquod primum: in prima quidem operatione est aliquod primum, quod cadit in conceptione intellectus, scilicet hoc quod dico ens; nec aliquid hac operatione potest mente concipi, nisi intelligatur ens. Et quia hoc principium, impossibile est esse et non esse simul, dependet ex intellectu entis,... ideo hoc etiam principium est naturaliter primum in secunda operatione intellectus, scilicet componentis et dividentis. Nec aliquis potest secundum hanc operationem intellectus aliquid intelligere, nisi hoc principio intellecto." *In IV Metaph.*, lect. 6, 605.

53   *In I Sent.*, d.23, q.1, a.1, Solut.; I, 555. Cf. *In IX Metaph.*, lect. 11, 1900.

54   *In I Sent.*, d.38, q.1, a.3, Solut.; I, 903. Cf.: "...duplex est operatio intellectus: una quae dicitur intelligentia indivisibilium, qua cognoscit de unoquoque quid est; alia vero, qua componit et dividit, scilicet enuntiationem affirmativam vel negativam formando, et hae quidem duae operationes duobus, quae sunt in rebus, respondet. Prima quidem operatio respicit ipsam naturam rei, secundum quam res intellecta aliquem gradum in entibus obtinet,... Secunda vero operatio respicit ipsum esse rei, quod quidem resultat ex congregatione principiorum rei in compositis, ..." *In Boeth. de Trin.*, V, 3c; ed. Wyser (Fribourg & Louvain, 1948) p. 38.4-12.

55   "Illi autem quidditati non debetur esse nisi per hoc quod suscepta est in hoc vel in illo." *In I Sent.*, d.8, q.4, a.2, Solut.; I, 222. "Sed ista natura sic considerata, quamvis dicat compositum ex materia et forma, non tamen ex hac materia demonstrata determinatis accidentibus substante, in qua individuatur forma; ... *In I Sent.*, d.23, q.1, a.1, Solut.; I, 555. See texts supra, 5. On the designation of matter, cf.: "Et ideo sciendum est quod materia non quolibet modo accepta est indiuiduationis principium, sed solum materia signata; et dico materia signatam que sub determinatis dimensionibus consideratur." *De Ente*, c. II; pp. 10.20-11.3.

56   "...de re judicat, ..." *In I Sent.*, d. 19, q. 5, a. 2, Solut.; I, 491. "... judicium de veritate

sequitur judicium de esse rei et de intellectu." *In I Sent.*, d. 19, q. 5, a. 3, Solut.; I, 495.

57   "Cognoscere autem praedictam conformitatis habitudinem nihil est aliud quam iudicare ita esse in re vel non esse: quod est componere et dividere; et ideo intellectus non cognoscit veritatem, nisi componendo vel dividendo per suum iudicium." *In I Periherm.*, lect. 3, no. 9. It is likewise called *apprehension*, though an apprehension that consists in a composition instead of an incomplex cognition: "*Compositio* quidem quando intellectus comparat unum conceptum alteri, quasi apprehendens *coniunctionem* aut *identitatem* rerum, quarum sunt conceptiones; *diviso* autem, quando sic comparat unum conceptum alteri, ut apprehendat res esse diversas." Ibid., no. 4. "...ratio veritatis in duobus consisit: in esse rei, et in apprehensione virutis cognoscitivae proportionata ad esse rei... . quaelibet res participat suum esse creatum, quo formaliter est, et unusquisque intellectus participat lumen per quod recte de re judicat, ..." *In I Sent.*, d. 19, q. 5, a. 2, Solut.; I, 491. "Sed intellectus noster, cujus cognitio a rebus oritur, quae esse compositum habent, non apprehendit illud esse nisi componendo et dividendo;..." *In I Sent.*, d. 38, q. 1, a. 3, ad 2m; I, 904. Cf. "... Alia autem comprehendit esse rei, componendo affirmationem, ..." Ibid., Solut.; p. 903. "... secundum hanc operationem intellectus aliquid intelligere,..." *In IV Metaph.*, lect. 6, no. 605 (supra, n.52).

L. M. Règis, *Epistemology* (New York, 1959), p. 321, maintains that the judgment is "an act in no way resembling apprehension." Fr. Règis is approaching the problem from the epistemological viewpoint, in which loom large the questions of error, where the intellect judges affirmatively of being that is not there to be grasped, and of demonstrated conclusions and of faith where the intellect correctly judges being that it does not immediately apprehend. In apprehending the being of things through its composing, the intellect plays an active role—"anima vero in quantum de rebus iudicat, non paritur a rebus, sed magis quodammodo agit" (*De Ver.*, I, 10c; ed. Spiazzi, I, 20a), as Fr. Règis (p.317, n. 11) aptly notes, and is able to push its activity further than its immediate apprehension. But the immediate apprehension of being is fundamental to it and is the starting point for its further activities. Though "action, passion, and *existere* are always *acts* whose perfective elements, concept verbs, are always predicates par excellence" (Règis, p. 320), action and passion are predicamental acts that are posterior as accidents to the thing's substance, while existence is an act that is prior to the thing's substance, and is grasped by the intellect in that priority. From the viewpoint of time, the intellect knows the thing simultaneously according to its essence by simple apprehension and according to its existence by judgment. Metaphysically, the judgment is prior, just as the being to which it corresponds is prior in the thing. From the logical viewpoint of a "whole constructed by the intellect" (Règis, p. 319), subject and predicate, even the predicate "being," are prior as the materials for a logical synthesis in the judgment. But these are logical and epistemological considerations and do not at all preclude basic agreement with the assertion "to say that the thing's *existere* is the direct object of judgment is to say that judgment is the act of apprehending this existence" (Règis, p. 322). On the problems involved, see E. Gilson, *Being and Some Philosophers*, 2nd ed. (Toronto, 1952), Appendix, pp. 221-227.

58   "Sed omne esse in se consideratum indivisibile est, ..." *In I Sent.*, d. 19, q. 2, a. 1, arg. 4; I, 466.

59   "Cum igitur esse temporalium mensuretur tempore, videtur quod tempus sit mensura indivisibilis et permanens, et sic non differat ab aeternitate." Ibid.

60   *In I Sent.*, d. 19, q. 5, a. 1, Solut.; I, 486. Cf. "Quorumdam enim esse subjectum est mutationi; et horum duratio tempore mensuratur,..." *In de Div. Nom.*, c, V., lect. 1, no. 627 (ed. Pera).

61   In the *De Principio Individuationis*, this is expressed as follows: "Aliud est in quo salvatur ratio individui apud nos, determinatio scilicet ejus ad certas particulas temporis et loci, quia proprium est esse sibi hic et nunc, et haec detiminatio debetur sibi ratione quantitatis determinatae." *Opusc.*, V. 196 (ed. Mandonnet).

62   "Sicut dicit Philosophus in III *De Anima*, duplex est operatio intellectus: Una quidem quae dicitur indivisibilium intelligentia, per quam scilicet intellectus apprehendit essentiam uniuscuiusque in seipsa; alia est operatio intellectus scilicet componentis et dividentis." *In I Periherm.*, lect. 1, no. 1. "Ubi oportet intelligere quod una duarum operationum intellectus est indivisibilium *intelligentia*: in quantum scilicet intellectus intelligit absolute cuiusque rei *quidditatem* sive *essentiam* per seipsam, puta *quid* et homo vel *quid* album vel *quid* aliud huiusmodi. Alia vero operatio intellectus est, secundum quod huiusmodi simplicia concepta simul

componit et *dividit.*" *In I Periherm.*, lect. 3, no. 3.

63   "...virtus affirmationis et negationis, scilicet significatum eius, quod est esse vel non esse, quod est naturaliter prius enunciatione. ...Cum igitur significare *esse* sit proprium affirmationis, ...*affirmatio est enunciatio alicuius de aliquo,* per quod significatur *esse;*..." *In I Periherm.*, lect. 8, no. 21.

64   See J. Owens, "The Accidental and Essential Character of Being in the Doctrine of St. Thomas Aquinas," *Mediaeval Studies*, XX (1958), 37-39.

65   See supra, n. 23.

66   See supra, n. 30.

67   *In VII Metaph.*, lect. 17, n. 1658. Cf. supra, nn. 44 and 4.

68   On the eternity of the nature in its absolute consideration, as grounded in its being in the divine itellect, see *Quodl.*, VIII, 1, 1; ed. Spiazzi, pp. 158-159.

69   On St. Thomas' own use of "concept" or "conception"in regard to the judgment, see E. Gilson, *Being and Some Philosophers*, 2nd, ed. (Toronto, 1952), Appendix, pp. 222-223.

70   See *In Boeth. de Trin.*, V, 3c; ed. Wyser, pp. 38.13-39.10. Cf.: "Neither the concept of being as a *noun* nor that of being as a *verb* can be the result of an abstraction: for 'being' as a noun implies essentially *habens esse* or *quod est,* and 'being' as a verb implies necessarily the subject of existence whose act it is." L. M. Règis, "Gilson's *Being and Some Philosophers,*" *The Modern Schoolman*, XXVIII (1951), 125.

71   "Omne autem quod recipit aliquid ab aliquo est in potentia respectu illius, et hoc quod receptum in eo est est actus eius." *De Ente*, c. IV; p. 35.19-21. "Sed quia non habet esse a seipso angelus, ideo se habet in potentia ad esse quod accipit a Deo, et sic esse a Deo acceptum comparatur ad essentiam eius simplicem actus ad potentiam." *In Boeth. de Trin.*, V, 4, ad 4m; ed. Wyser, m. 51.4-7.

72   "...sicut esse rei dicitur ens: non quia eius sit aliquid aliud esse; sed quia per hoc esse res esse dicitur, ...eius esse non dicitur ens per aliquod esse aliud ab ipso:..." *De Ver.*, XXI, 5, ad 8m.; ed. Spiazzi, I, 386a. So, for purposes of logic, the subject and its being are represented in separate concepts, and judgment is regarded as a *subsequent* synthesis of them both: "... an act of judgment, whose soul is neither the subject nor quiddity, nor even the verb or the act of existing but the *synthesis* of the two,..." L. M. Règis, *The Modern Schoolman*, XXVII (1951), 125.

73   "Sed individuum dupliciter potest significari vel per nomen secundae intentionis, sicut hoc nomen 'individuum' vel 'singulare,' quod non significat rem singularem, sed intentionem singularitatis; vel per nomen primae intentionis, quod significat rem, cui convenit intentio particularitatis;..." *In I Sent.*, d. 23, q. 1, a. 3, Solut.; I, 563. "...hoc nomen *persona* est commune communitate rationis, non sicut genus vel species, sed sicut *individuum vagum.* Nomina enim generum vel specierum, ut *homo* vel *animal,* sunt inposita ad significantur his nominibus *genus* vel *species.* Sed individuum vagum, ut *aliquis homo,* significat naturam communem cum determinato modo existendi qui competit singularibus, ut scilicet sit per se existens distinctum ab alii. Sed in nomine *singularis designati,* significatur determinatum distinguens: sicut in nomine Socratis haec caro et hoc os." *ST*, I, 30, 4c. So the Aristotelian categories "where"and "when," though denoting a highly particularized circumstance, can be universalized as place and time, and in this way can be defined. Epicurus (*First Letter*, in Diogenes Laertius, X, 72) was aware of the difficulty involved in representing time in a universal concept, and would not allow it to be investigated by reference to any *prolepsis,* as were the other accidents. Kant's stand that space and time are not universal concepts but pure intuitions is well-known.

74   "Multo igitur minus et ipsum esse commune est aliquid praeter omnes res existentes nisi in intellectu solum." *CG*, I, 26; XIII, 82a4-6.

75   *De Ente*, c. IV, p. 34.24-26; p. 35.14-18; c. V, p.37.22.

76   "Inventur enim in omnibus rebus natura entitatis, ...Ergo oportet quod ab aliquo esse habeant, et oportet devenire ad aliquid cujus natura sit ipsum suum esse; alias in infinitum procederetur, et hoc est quod dat esse omnibus, nec potest esse nisi unum, cum natura entitatis sit unius rationis in omnibus secundum analogiam; unitas enim causati requirit unitatem in causa per se;..." *In II Sent.*, d. 1, q. 1, a. 1, Solut.; II, 12-13. Cf. "The metaphysical notion of being, therefore, is analogously common to all beings, in all of whom existence is found properly proportioned to, and as the actuality of, their natures, ...It is a notion which is not reached by abstraction of any quiddity or nature, and which is not knowable, therefore, by any simple apprehension of

essence." L. J. Eslick, *The Modern Schoolman*, XXXIV (1957), 256.

77   "...scilicet ipsum verbum quod est *esse*, et verbum infinitum quod est *non esse*; quorum neutrum per se dictum est significativum veritatis vel falsitatis in re; unde multo minus alia. Vel potest intelligi hoc generaliter dici de omnibus verbis. Quia enim dixerat quod verbum non significat si *est* res vel *non est*, hoc consequenter manifestat, quia nullum verbum est significativum *esse* rei vel *non esse*, idest quod res sit vel non sit. Quamvis enim omne verbum finitum implicet *esse*, quia currere est currentem esse,..." *In I Periherm.*, lect. 5, no. 18. "...verbum EST, quod secundum se dictum, non significat *aliquid* esse, licet significet *esse*. ...illa compositio, quam significat hoc verbum EST, non potest intelligi sine componentibus..." Ibid., no. 21.

78   Unlike a common nature, being is its own primary instance. No common nature can in any way be an instance of itself. Cr.: "Proper universals are not instantiations of themselves, perfect or otherwise." R. E. Allen, "Participation and Predication in Plato's Middle Dialogues," *The Philosophical Review*, LXIX (1969), 147.

79   "Quamvis autem creaturis omnibus communiter det esse, tamen cuilibet creaturae dat proprium modum essendi; et sic... invenitur esse diversimode in diversis, et in unoquoque secundum proprium modum eius." *De Ver.*, X, 11, ad 8m; ed. Spiazzi, I, 218a.

Notes—Aquinas and the Five Ways

1   *ST*, I, 2, 3, c. The impression that the five ways are the only ones recognized by Aquinas, and that all other variations have to be reduced in one way or another to their forms, stems from the Neoscholastic manuals. More than twenty-five years ago this attitude was characterized as "la fidélité opiniâtre des milieux thomistes à la formule des *quinque viae*" by Fernand Van Steenberghen, "Le problème philosophique de l'existence de Dieu," *Revue philosophique de Louvain*, 45 (1947), 5. It was accentuated when a writer who had a new proof of his own to advance felt compelled to designate it as a "sixth way," e.g., Josef Gredt, *Elementa philosophiae aristotelico-thomisticae*, 7th ed. (Freiburg i. Breisgau: Herder, 1973), vol. II, pp. 199-201 (nos. 790-92); and Jacques Maritain, *Approaches to God*, trans. Peter O'Reilly (New York: Harper & Row, 1954), pp.72-83. However, a comprehensive investigation of Aquinas' writings brings to light a number of other "ways" or arguments. These are grouped under eleven headings by Jules A. Baisnée, "St. Thomas Aquinas' Proofs of the Existence of God Presented in their Chronological Order," in *Philosophical Studies in Honor of the Very Reverend Ignatius Smith*, O. P., ed. John K. Ryan (Westminster, Md.: Newman Press, 1952), pp. 63-64, listing frequency of occurrence. Accordingly "other independent proofs which he offers elsewhere" are recognized in Aquinas by Anthony Kenny, *The Five Ways* (London: Routledge & Kegan Paul, 1969), p. 1, and other recent writers. Thirteen "proofs" expressly rejected by Aquinas are listed by Robert Lee Patterson, *The Conception of God in the Philosophy of Aquinas* (London: George Allen & Unwin, 1933), pp. 21-39.

2   See discussion on "The Enigma of the Five Ways," in Edward A. Sillem, *Ways of Thinking about God: Thomas Aquinas and Some Recent Problems* (London: Darton, Longman & Todd, 1961), pp. 55-78. On the notion of one proof though expressed in five different ways, see Michel Guérard des Lauriers, *La preuve de Dieu et les cinq voies* (Rome: Università Lateranense, 1966). For the opposite view, namely that the five cannot be reduced to a single proof, cf. "L'une ne peut être ramenée à une autre, ni les cinq à une preuve unique qui les contiendrait toutes," Louis Charlier, "Les cinq voies de saint Thomas," in *L'existence de Dieu*, ed. le collège dominicain de théologie à La Sarte-Huy (Tournai: Casterman, 1961), p. 189.

3   *SCG*, I, 13. Chronologically, the usually accepted view places the version in the *SCG* about seven years ahead of that in *ST*. The later dating suggested for the *SCG* would not place it that many years after the *ST*. On the present state of the question, see Anton C. Pegis, "The Separated Soul and its Nature in St. Thomas," n. 35, to be published in *St. Thomas Aquinas 1274-1974: Commemorative Studies*, ed. Armand A. Maurer (Toronto: Pontifical Institute of Mediaeval Studies, 1974). This article adds new support for the earlier dating of the *SCG* from development of the Thomistic doctrine on the soul.

4   Aquinas, *In I Sent.*, d. 3, div. lae partis textus; ed. Mandonnet, I, 88. Cf. Pseudo-Dionysius, *On the Divine Names*, VII, 3; *PG*, 3, 872. In Pseudo-Dionysius the statement is brief, namely that we know God "in the removal and the exceeding of all things, and in the cause of all."

5   *In I Sent.*, d. 3, q. 1, a. 3, Solut.; 1, 96. Here *modi* is used for the *viae* described in the *div. lae partis textus* (supra, n. 4). There also, *modus* was used interchangeably for *via*.

6   *In I Sent.*, d. 2, q. 1, a. 1, Solut.; 1, 60-61. Cf. infra, n. 36.

7   See *In II Sent.*, d. 1, q. 1, a. 1, Solut. (2, 12-13); *De Pot.*, III, 5-6; and others listed in Baisnée, pp. 62-63. A discussion of the four *modi* (in the same sense as *viae*) of the Prologue to *On the Gospel of St. John* may be found in Cornelio Fabro, "Sviluppo, significato e valore della 'IV via,'" *Doctor Communis*, 1-2 (1954), 79-82.

8   *On Being and Essence*, IV, 6-7; trans. Armand Maurer, 2d ed. (Toronto: Pontifical Institute of Mediaeval Studies, 1969), pp. 55-57. *In I Sent.*, d. 2, q. 1, a. 1, Contra (I, 59-60; *cf.* second Praeterea, p. 60); *In II Sent.*, d. 1, q. 1, a. 1, Solut. (2, 12-13). In the latter text it is attributed to Avicenna. The argument is used a number of times in the commentary on the *Sentences* to show that God alone is existence while all other things are composed of their nature and of the existence they acquired from him, again with occasional attribution of the argument in some way to Avicenna. The consequences from the arguments for God's existence in later works show clearly enough that Aquinas is placing them in this existential framework, e.g. in *SCG*, I, 22; *ST*, I, 44, 1, c; *Comp. Theol.*, XI. In this framework, to show that existence is a real nature is exactly the same demonstration as the proof for the existence of God. Hence the reasoning in *On Being and Essence* can conclude without further ado "and this is the first cause, or God" (no. 7; p. 57). The reasoning in *ST*, I, 3, 4, c, remains the same as in *On Being and Essence*. See also texts infra, nn. 20-21.

F. Van Steenberghen, "Le problème de l'existence de Dieu dans le 'Scriptum super Sententiis' de saint Thomas," in *Studia Mediaevalia in honorem ... Raymundi Josephi Martin*, ed. B. L. Van Helmond (Bruges: De Tempel, 1948), pp. 331-49, in reaction to the "fétichisme des *quinque viae*" (p. 331, n. 1) and seeking to integrate the ways into the entire syntheses of Aquinas (p. 332), reduces the proofs in the commentary on the *Sentences* to two (p. 349). The first, the way of casuality, is assigned its inspiration in Saints Paul, Ambrose, and Augustine, and is regarded by him as heralding the first three ways of the *Summa of Theology*. The second is called Neoplatonic in character, inspired by Pseudo-Dionysius and Augustine, and heralds the fourth way of the *Summa*. This assessment of Van Steenberghen does not take into account the possibility that what is common to all the Thomistic ways is the new and profoundly original thought of Aquinas, by reason of which the critique of the Anselmian argument "semble être le fruit de son génie personnel" p. 349).

9   *Comp. Theol.*, I, 3, Verardo no. 4, and 11, no. 21. Despite earlier datings based on doctrinal comparisons, the evidence still seems to indicate a later dating, at Paris or Naples, 1269-1273. On this question see James A. Weisheipl, *Friar Thomas d'Aquino: His Life, Thought and Works* (New York: Doubleday & Co., 1974), Chap. 8, no. 60. On the flexibility with which the fivefold arrangement was regarded at Paris in the years immediately before and after the death of Aquinas, see William Dunphy, "The *Quinque Viae* and Some Parisian Professors of Philosophy," published in *St. Thomas Aquinas* 1274-1974 (supra, n. 3).

10   E.g., the "third way" takes over a demonstration from the second: "It is not possible, however, to go on to infinity in necessary things that have a cause of their necessity, just as it is not possible in efficient causes, as has been proven" (trans. Eugene Freeman & Joseph Ownes, *The Wisdom and Ideas of Saint Thomas Aquinas* [New York: Fawcett World Library, 1968], pp. 74-75). The fifth way falls into the framework of the first and third, *ST*, I, 2, 3, ad 2m. Cornelio Fabro, "Sviluppo," p. 80, can find that the second (*ex aeternitate*) way in *On the Gospel of St. John*, Prol., is a fresh synthesis of the first four ways of the *Summa of Theology*. Cf. Van Steenberghen's synthesizing of ways found in the commentary on the *Sentences* (supra, n. 8). The facile synthesizing and interchange of parts would suggest that the five assembly lines come from the same common design. On the problem—which goes back to Cajetan—of reaching a unique conclusion if the five ways are regarded as five different proofs, see Eric Lionel Mascall, *Existence and Analogy* (London: Longmans, Green and Co., 1949), pp. 70-76; Sillem, *Ways of Thinking about God*, pp.29-30; Van Steenberghen, *Hidden God*, trans. Theodore Crowley (St. Louis: Herder, 1966), p. 159.

11   "... the Five Ways ... do not seem to me to express the real nature of St. Thomas' own

thought" (Mascall, *Existence and Analogy*, p. 176). Cf.: "They seem to be the result of a personal reflection by St. Thomas on the historical sources at his disposal; he gathered together what he considered best in tradition" (Van Steenberghen, *Hidden God*, p. 148).

12   *SCG*, I, 13, init,; trans. Anton C. Pegis, in *On the Truth of the Catholic Faith* (New York: Doubleday & Co., 1955), I, 85. For texts giving the historical sources of the "five ways," see René Arnou, *De quinque viis sancti Thomae* (Rome: Gregorian University, 1932).

13   On these questions about the third way, see infra, n. 25.

14   For discussion of these points, see Jean Paulus, "La théorie du premier moteur chez Aristote," *Revue de philosophie*, 33 (1933), 259-94 and 394-424; and my article "The Reality of the Aristotelian Separate Movers," *Review of Metaphysics*, 3 (1950), 319-37.

15   See *SCG*, I, 13, Praedictos. Cf. "From this reasoning, then it is evident that here Aristotle firmly thought and believed that motion must be eternal and also time; otherwise he would not have based his plan of investigating immaterial substances on this conviction" (*Commentary on the Metaphysics of Aristotle*, XII, 5, Cathala no. 2496; trans. John P. Rowan [Chicago: Henry Regnery, 1961], II, 878).

16   "For, if the world and motion have a first beginning, some cause must clearly be posited to account for this origin of the world and of motion. That which comes to be anew must take its origin from some innovating cause; since nothing brings itself from potency to act, or from nonbeing to being. ... if the prime mover is not held to be self-moved, then it must be moved immediately by something absolutely unmoved" (*SCG*, I, 13, 30-32; trans. Pegis). These observations show explicitly how the notion of a "cause" that brings things into being (*esse*) is involved in Aquinas' understanding of the argument from motion, and how easily the argument from efficient causality surfaces in the reasoning.

17   *ST*, I, 3, 4, c. Cf.: "Now no signate form is understood to be in act unless it be supposed to have *being*. ... Wherefore it is clear that *being* as we understand it here is the actuality of all acts, and therefore the perfection of all perfections" (*De Pot.*, VII, 2, ad 9m; Dominican trans.). "However, the actuality which the verb 'is'principally signifies is the actuality of every form commonly, whether substantial or accidental" (*In I Periherm.*, lect. 5, Leonine no. 22; trans. Jean T. Oesterle). See also *Comp. Theol.*, I, 11 (no. 21).

18   Gregory Nazianzenus, *Orat.*, XXXVIII, 7; *PG*, 36, 317B; John Damascene, *De Fid. Orth.*, I, 9; *PG*, 94, 836B.

19   "Et ratio hujus est, quia esse creaturae est ab altero. Unde secundum hoc ducimur in causam a qua est" (*In I Sent.*, d. 3, div. lae partis textus; 1, 88). Cf. Peter Lombard text, d. III, in the same Mandonnet edition of Aquinas' commentary, I, 80-81, for the source also in Ambrose and Augustine.

20   *De Pot.*, III, 5, c; Dominican trans. On the equating, in Aquinas' own thought, of pure actuality with subsistent being, cf.: "Now there is a being that is its own being: and this follows from the fact that there must needs be a being that is pure act and wherein there is no composition" (ibid.)

21   "... et isti fuerunt Platonici. ... Cum ergo omnia quae sunt, participent esse, et sint per participationem entia, necesse est esse aliquid in cacumine omnium rerum, quo sit ipsum esse per suam essentiam, idest quod sua essentia sit suum esse: et hoc est Deus ..."(*In Ev. S.Joannis*, Prol.; ed. Vivès, 19, 670b).

22   See texts cited supra, n. 8. It has been traditionally argued that the procedure in each of the "five ways" is to establish first on existent nature, such as a primary movent or a first efficient cause, and only later (*ST*, I, 3, 4, c) reason that this essence is identical with its existence. The theological procedure, in which God is already accepted on faith as the source of revelation, places the questions in direct reference to the divine essence: "But about the divine essence, the first consideration is whether God exists; the second, how he exists, or rather how he does not exist" (*ST*, I, 2, init.). This direction towards the negative indicates clearly enough that even in the theological procedure the reasoning is in point of fact from the existence, which here is *not* other than the essence. The existence reached is *not* this or that. To interpret the procedure otherwise, not only gives rise to the problem of identifying five different conclusions with each other (see supra, n. 10), but falls into an even more serious difficulty. It means arguing from nature to existence, from the "what" to the "is," a procedure rejected by Aquinas in his critique of the Anselmian argument. In the present case the nature has already been shown to exist. To go on from there in an attempt to

show that it is existence, would mean that existence necessarily appears in what is first known as a nature. But that is the ontological argument. Aquinas' procedure first reaches existence that is not actuating anything else, and then shows that here the existence itself is the nature that subsists.

23 In V Metaph., lect. 2, no. 770; trans. Rowan. On the topic see my articles "Aquinas and the Proof from the Physics," Mediaeval Studies, 28 (1966), 119-50; "Actuality in the 'Prima Via' of St. Thomas,"ibid., 29 (1967), 26-46; and "The Starting Point of the Prima Via,"Franciscan Studies, 5 (1967), 249-84. There is not the least question here of any "nonsensical view that when you have explained a particular motion at a particular time you have to explain also the occurrence of that motion" (Anthony Kenny, The Five Ways, p. 11, n. 1). The motion, like anything other than God, has both its nature and its existence, each requiring its own explanation. The motion itself is known through conceptualization and is explained through concepts. The existence is known through judgment and is explained through agents. Inference on the basis of the nature leads to a finite movent or movents, reasoning from the existence leads to subsistent being.

24 "... sic esset prius seipso, quod est impossibile" (ST, I, 2, 3, c). Existence, as the primary and basic actuality of the thing, has to precede the thing itself from the viewpoint of actuality, even though the thing as a potentiality formally determines the existence. While the "first way" envisages the movement of things already in existence, such as the stone and the cane and the hand, the "second way" focuses on the acquisition of existence by the substances themselves. But both "ways" proceed in line of efficient causality. The overlapping of the two "ways" is noted by Kenny, The Five Ways, pp. 35-36. The first and quite traditional explanation he gives differs from mine inasmuch as he views the first way as starting from the effect, the second from the agent. Yet for Aquinas all the valid ways have to start from the effects, the sensible things: "But having seen sensible things, we arrive at God only by the procedure according to which these things are caused and everything caused comes from some agent cause" (Aquinas, In I Sent., d. 3, q. 1, a. 2, Solut.; 1, 94). (Here the argument from efficient causality is explicitly attributed to Avicenna.)

25 See H. Holstein, "L'origine aristotélicienne de la 'tertia via' de saint Thomas," Revue philosophique de Louvain, 48 (1950), 354-70; and, on the Arabian background, my article "'Cause of Necessity' in Aquinas' Tertia Via," Mediaeval Studies, 33 (1971), 21-45. The literature on the "third way" is extensive, and in recent years has tended to predominate over the attention given the other four ways, apparently because its terminology is more adapted to bring it into line with the cosmological argument. However, even the structure of the "third way" is patently different from that of the cosmological argument. Nor is its basis "the thought that in the fullness of time every possible combination of things will turn up"(Wallace I. Matson, The Existence of God [Ithaca: Cornell University Press, 1965], p. 168). Rather, for Aquinas the basis is that all existent things cannot be contingent, since as contingent they do not account for their own existence. The starting point is the accidental character of their existence, quite as in On Being and Essence. Maimonides is not acknowledged as a source, and there are reasons for questioning any substantial influence of Maimonides' reasoning on Aquinas in this context—see L. Chambat, "La 'tertia via' dans saint Thomas et Aristote," Revue Thomiste, 32 (1927), 334-35. For the contingency argument regarded as "the one basic argument featuring in the Five Ways in as many different guises," see Barry Miller, "The Contingency Argument," The Monist, 54 (1970), 360. The objections to the notion of contingency by D. F. Scheltens, "Contingency and the Proof for the Existence of God," International Philosophical Quarterly, 12 (1972), 577-79, do not come to grips with Aquinas' doctrine that existence is known by a nonconceptual act of the mind, namely by judgment. What is grasped through judgment lies outside all that it knows through conceptualization. This is sufficient to account for contingence as Aquinas views it, and to validate the concept for him, even though a real distinction between a thing and its being is a conclusion drawn after the existence of God has been demonstrated.

26 II 1,993b23-31; IV 4,1008b31-1009a3. Aristotle's clearer formulation of the argument in his lost work On Philosophy based the argument on the grades of goodness. This was not available to Aquinas when writing the Summa of Theology, even though he includes transcendental goodness in the argument. It became known in Latin only after the translation of Simplicius' commentary on De Caelo by William of Moerbeke in 1271. It regarded the proof as taken from the second book of Plato's Republic. For the fragment, see W. D. Ross, The Works of Aristotle, Vol. 12, pp. 87-88. In Aquinas, however, the participation is not of Platonic forms, but of existence and its

transcendental properties. On the existential character of the argument in Aquinas, see Cornelio Fabro, "Il fondamento metafisico della IV via," *Doctor Communis*, 18 (1965), 49-70.

27   *SCG*, I, 13, Ad hoc. In the works of Aquinas this argument enjoys the greatest frequency of all, occurring ten different times—see Baisnée, "Aquinas' Proofs of the Existence of God," p. 63. In the prologue to *On the Gospel of St. John* it is called a "most efficacious way," and is located in "the whole course of nature" (ed. Vivès), 19, 669-70. Unlike the argument from design, this argument does not call on any analogy with mechanisms, but proceeds directly to seek out the cause of the behavior observed in the activities of natural things.

28   Damascene, *De Fid Orth.*, I, 3; *PG*, 94, 795D. Averroës, *In II Phys.*, t. 75 (Venice: apud Juntas, 1562), fol. 75v2.

29   On the history and the philosophical background of the Anselmian argument in the Middle Ages, see Anton C. Pegis, "St. Anselm and the Argument of the 'Proslogion,'" *Mediaeval Studies*, 28 (1966), 228-67; "The Bonaventurean Way to God," ibid., 29 (1967), 206-42; "Towards a New Way to God: Henry of Ghent," ibid., 30 (1968), 226-47; 31 (1969), 93-116; 33 (1971), 158-79; "Four Medieval Ways to God," *The Monist*, 54 (1970), 317-58. The well-known "coloring" of the argument by Duns Scotus, *Ord.*, I, 2, 1, 1-2, nos. 137-39 (ed. Vaticana, 2, 208.16-211.1), makes it accord with Scotus' own proof from God's possibility to his existence. For Aquinas' rejection of the argument, see *ST*, I, 2, 1, ad 2m.

30   *In I Sent.*, d. 3, q. 1, a. 2, ad 1m; 1,94. Cf. *SCG*, I, 11, Ad quartam; *ST*, I, 2, 1, ad 3m.

31   *In I Sent.*, d. 3, q. 1, a. 2, ad 2m; 1,94-95. *SCG*, I, 11, Ad quintam.

32   Given the difference between the nature of God and the nature of human cognitive activity, as known philosophically, it is hard to see how on the philosophical level any immediate experience of God could be possible. "If God does appear in human experience, in so doing he can neither violate his own being nor the characteristic operation of the consciousness of his human host" (Charles E. Meyer, *The Touch of God* [Staten Island, N.Y.: Alba House, 1972], p. 91). Mystical and supernatural manifestations lie beyond the range of philosophy. On the variations of the argument, see Ronald W. Hepburn, s.v. "Religious Experience." in *The Encyclopedia of Philosophy*.

33   Paul Edwards, s.v. "Common Consent Arguments for the Existence of God," in *The Encyclopedia of Philosophy*, 2,154b, notes that there is "no full-length study in any language of the different forms of the Common Consent Argument." Basically it is an argument from authority, rather than a philosophical demonstration.

34   For an appreciation of the moral argument, see John-Henry Wolgrave, "La preuve de l'existence de Dieu par la conscience morale et l'expérience des valeurs," in *L'existence de Dieu* (see supra, n. 2), pp. 109-32. On its forms, see Ronald W. Hepburn, s.v. "Moral Arguments," in *The Encyclopedia of Philosophy*.

35   For the use of this argument by Aristotle, see fragments in Ross, *The Works of Aristotle*, Vol. 12, pp. 85-86.

36   *In I Sent.*, d. 2, q. 1, a. 1, Solut.; 60-61. *De Pot.*, III, 5, c; 6, c. In the latter work the argument is attributed to Plato, but is explained in terms of existence. Likewise in the article of the commentary on the *Sentences*, Contra, pp. 59-60, the argument is developed in terms of entity and existence. Clearly, it is understood by Aquinas not in the original Platonic sense of participation by way of formal causality, but as participation of existence by way of efficient causality.

37   "For every truth that our intellect can grasp is limited, since according to Augustine 'everything that is known is limited by the comprehension of the knower'; and if it is limited, it is determined and particularized. Therefore the first and highest truth, which surpasses all understanding, has to be incomprehensible and unlimited; and this is God" (*On the Gospel of St. John*, Prologue; [Vivès], 19, 670b). See Aug., *De Civ. Dei*, XII, 19. Fabro, "Sviluppo," p. 82, regards this way as a "lieta novità" in Aquinas, carrying expressly the signature of Augustine. But that is no objection to its being read by Aquinas, just as in the case of the other ways, in his own understanding of being and its transcendental properties. The same procedure in regard to the transcendental property of goodness may be seen in *De Pot.*, III, 6, c, where the objective was to show that "all things must be traced to one first principle which is good" (Dominican trans.). A like argument in terms of beauty is given, *In I Sent.*, d. 3, div. lae partis textus, Quarta sumitur; 1, 89.

38   Accordingly for Aquinas there is no problem whatever in seeing that the result of the demonstration is the God of Judeo-Christian belief, the creator of heaven and earth, and whose

first name is being. Hence he can terminate the proof in all its forms unhesitatingly with the words "and this we call God." His procedure does not at all encounter Pascal's inability to see in the metaphysical conclusion the God of Abraham, Isaac, and Jacob, an attitude still widely prevalent, e.g.: "that we can *show* that such a being is God does not seem likely when it is God as conceived by religious believers (rather than metaphysicians) who is to be identified" (James F. Ross, "On Proofs for the Existence of God," *The Monist*, 54 [1970], 217). Others considered the identification as "a species of idolatry" (Charles Hartshorne, "Present Prospects for Metaphysics," *The Monist*, 47 [1963], 190). But given the metaphysical background of Aquinas, there is in this identification no trace of any "exaggeration," not even, as suggested recently, of a "pardonable one"(Thomas P. M. Solon, "Some Logical Issues in Aquinas' Third Way,"*Proceedings of the American Catholic Philosophical Association*, 46 [1972], 82). Against that background subsistent existence, as reached from the actual existence of sensible things, appears at once as identical with the creative and provident God of the Christian creeds.

39   Cf.: "That there was nothing systematic about this alignment of *Five Ways* is clear from a study of the sources" (Van Steenberghen, *Hidden God*, p. 147). Yet it has been claimed that though there is only one proof involved, the five ways are necessary expressions of it: "*Les cinq voies* sont simplement les formes que prend nécessairement *la preuve*" (Guérard des Lauriers, *La preuve de Dieu et les cinq voies*, p. 6). The case, rather, is the opposite. The five different arguments found in preceding thinkers *necessarily* takes on the one existential cast when they are assumed into the metaphysical thinking of Aquinas.

Notes—The Conclusion of the Prima Via

1   *ST*, I, q. 2, a. 3. The reason for the designation "first and more manifest" is sought in the contemporary philosophical situation by A. Boehm: "Nous pensons que c'est le fait que, dans la pensée contemporaine, il était accepté sans difficulté par les philosophes des diverses écoles, qui s'inspiraient, d'une façon ou d'une autre, du néoplatonisme. . ." ("Autour du Mystère des 'Quinque Viae'de Saint Thomas d'Aquin," *Revue des Sciences Religieuses*, XXIV [1950], 229).

2   "Haec enim via probandi primum principium esse, est efficacissima, cui resisti non potest" (*In VIII Phys.*, lect. 3 [Leonine no. 6]).

3   *Compend. Theol.*, cap. 3.

4   Cf. *CG*, I, cap. 13. These are the only sources acknowledged by St. Thomas. For further possible sources, see the Index in R. Arnou's *De Quinque Viis Sancti Thomae* (Rome: Universitas Gregoriana, 1932), p. 103.

5   Cf. J. Paulus, "La Théorie du Premier Moteur chez Aristote," *Revue de Philosophie*, XXXIII (1933), 259-94 and 394-425; A. Nolte, *Het Godsbegrip bij Aristoteles* (Nijmegen-Utrecht: Dekker & van de Vegt, 1940), pp. 126-33 and 172-75.

6   Cf. J. Owens, "The Reality of the Aristotelian Separate Movers,"*Review of Metaphysics*, III (1950), 319-37; *The Doctrine of Being in the Aristotelian* Metaphysics (Toronto: Pontifical Institute of Mediaeval Studies, 1951), pp. 279 ff.

7   *ST*, I, q.2, a.3. Cf.: "Primo autem ponemus rationes quibus Aristoteles procedit ad probandum Deum esse.... Sed quia Deus non est pars alicuius moventis seipsum, ulterius Aristoteles, in sua *Metaphysica*, investigat ex hoc motore qui est pars moventis seipsum, alium motorem separatum omnino, qui est Deus" (*CG*, I, cap. 13).

8   "Sed contra est quod dicitur Exod. III, ex persona Dei: *Ego sum qui sum*" (*ST*, I, q.2, a.3.).

9   "... igitur Metaphysica et naturalis scientia sunt de eodem per accidens; sed de Deo est naturalis magis per accidens, quia summa descriptio, ad quam pervenit de ipso, quasi remotior est a quidditate Dei, quam summa Metaphysici" (*Metaph.*, I, 49; in *Opera Omnia*, ed. Vives [Paris, 1891-95] VII, 37a).

"... sed tam proprietas considerata in scientia naturali quam in ista de effectu, non potest sibi inesse, nisi primum movens sit et nisi primum ens sit; ergo utraque scientia potest probare ipsum esse. Tamen ista immediatius..." (*ibid.*, no. 35, p. 28b).

"Multo etiam perfectius ostenditur primam causam esse ex passionibus causatorum consideratis in Metaphysica quam ex passionibus naturalibus ubi ostenditur primum movens esse. Perfectior enim cognitio et immediatior est de Primo Ente cognoscere ipsum ut *primum ens*, vel ut *necesse esse*, quam cognoscere ipsum ut *primum movens*" *(Opus Oxon.*, Prologus, III, 7, 21; ed. M.F. Garcia [Quaracchi, 1912-14], I, 66 [no. 80c]).

As these statements of Duns Scotus are made in the background of the Arabian controversy regarding the subject of metaphysics, the argument from motion is looked upon as a purely physical argument, pertaining solely to natural philosophy. Cf. Part Two of this article, note 115.

10   "Et ut melius intelligatur quod dicimus, singillatim explanando dicitur, quod primae viae, ex parte motus, sat est quod inferatur, ergo datur primum movens immobile, non curando utrum illud dit anima caeli aut mundi: hoc anim quaeretur in sequenti quaestione.... Omnia enim haec praedicata, scilicet movens immobile... sunt secundum veritatem propria Deo: et ideo, concludendo haec inveniri in rerum natura, concluditur directe, quasi per accidens, quod Deus est, idest, *Deus, non ut Deus, sed ut habens talem conditionem, est;* et consequenter ipsum substratum, scilicet Deus ut Deus, est" *(In ST, I, q.2, a.3, comm. III; ed. Leonine [Rome, 1888], IV, 32b).

11   "Primum medium sumitur ex motu coeli, quo usus est Aristotel., 8 Physic., et illud etiam adhibuit 12 Metaph., text. 26, ubi ex motu coeli aeterno pervenit ad demonstrandum primum motorem immobilem. Hoc autem medium per se ac praecise sumptum multis modis invenitur inefficax ad demonstrandum esse in rerum natura aliquam substantiam immaterialem, nedum ad demonstrandum primam et increatam substantiam..."*(Disputationes Metaphysicae*, XXIX, 1, 7; in· *Opera Omnia*, ed. Vives [Paris, 1856-77], XXVI, 23a).

12   Cf. L.D. Urbano, "La prueba del movimiento y la existencia de Dios," *Ciencia Tomista*, XV (1917), 81; P. Descoqs, *Praelectiones Theologiae Naturalis* (Paris: Beauchesne, 1932-35), I, 293-94; A. Brémond, *Le Dilemme Aristotélicien* (Paris: Beauchesne, 1933), pp. 149 ff.; M.J. Adler, "The Demonstration of God's Existence," *Thomist*, V (1943), 189-91. On the history of this question, cf. M. Chossat, "Dieu (Son Existence)," *Dict. de Théol. Cath. (Paris, 1911)*, IV, 931-34.

13   "*La prima via* appelle donc un prolongement indispensable pour mener jusqu'à Dieu... Bref, la *prima via* est plutôt un acheminement vers la preuve authentique, qui commence là où la *prima via* finit" (F. van Steenberghen, "Le problème philosophique de l'existence de Dieu," *Revue Philosophique de Louvain*, XLV [1947], 164; cf. *ibid.*, 152, 168).

14   *ST*, I, q.2, a.3. Similarly, "Et hoc dicimus Deum" *(CG*, I, cap. 13 [Leonine p. 30, ll. 15-16]). Also, "... et hoc est Deus" *(In I Sent.*, d.3, divisio primae partis—the texts will be found in Part Two of this article, notes 83-84). "... et hoc dicimus Deum"*(Compend. Theol.*, cap. 3). F. van Steenberghen comments: "C'est tout, et quand saint Thomas ajoute aussitôt: 'et hoc omnes intelligunt Deum,' il sait fort bien que cette affirmation est très elliptique et qu'elle demande quelques explications" *(op. cit.*, p. 310).

15   "Certum est enim, et sensu constat, aliqua moveri in hoc mundo. Omne autem quod movetur, ab alio movetur.... Hic autem non est procedere in infinitum: quia sic non esset aliquod primum movens; et per consequens nec aliquod aliud movens, quia moventia secunda non movent nisi per hoc quod sunt mota a primo movente, sicut baculus non movet nisi per hoc quod est motus a manu. Ergo necesse est devenire ad aliquod primum movens, quod a nullo movetur: et hoc omnes intelligunt Deum" *(ST.*, I, q.2, a.3.).

16   "Nihil enim movetur, nisi secundum quod est in potentia ad illud ad quod movetur: movet autem aliquid secundum quod est actu. Movere enim nihil aliud est quam educere aliquid de potentia in actum: de potentia autem non potest aliquid reduci in actum, nisi per aliquod ens in actu: sicut calidum in actu, ut ignes, facit lignum, quod est calidum in potentia, esse actu calidum, et per hoc movet et alterat ipsum. Non autem est possible ut idem sit simul in actu et potentia secundum idem, sed solum secundum diversa: quod enim calidum in actu, non potest simul esse calidum in potentia, sed est simul frigidum in potentia. Impossibile est ergo quod, secundum idem et eodem modo, aliquid sit movens et motum, vel quod moveat seipsum. Omne ergo quod movetur, oportet ab alio moveri. Si ergo id a quo movetur, moveatur, oportet et ipsum ab alio moveri; et illud ab alio" *(ibid).

17   *Ibid.* Text *supra*, n. 15.

18   *Ibid.*; cf. *supra*, n. 16.

19   It has two backward references to *Physics* v, but does not seem to be referred to by any other Aristotelian treatise. On its authenticity and chronology, and the double version of its first three chapters, cf. W.D. Ross' *Aristotle's Physics* (Oxford: Clarendon Press, 1936), pp. 11-19. The argu-

ment demonstrating the primary movent is substantially the same in each of the two versions.

20   *Physics* vii. 1. 241b24.

21   Cf. alternate text, *ibid.*, 242a3; 13.

22   *Ibid.*, 241b40-41 (Ross lineation).

23   *Ibid.*, 241b35-242a49.

24   Simplicius, *In Aristotelis Physicorum Libros Quattuor Posteriores Commentaria* (ed. H. Diels [Berlin: Reimer, 1895]), pp. 1039.13-1040.16, finds this argument and previous Greek treatments of it unsatisfactory. He himself suggests that the basis of the reasoning is that an extended thing as a whole cannot be present to itself as a whole, since it is spread out in parts and so cannot coincide with itself as movent and thing moved (*ibid.*, pp. 1040.30-1041.3). He does not seem any too convinced of his own interpretation, however, and says (*ibid.*, p. 1042.7-9) that a more exact and clearer proof is to follow in Book VIII; cf. pp. 1036.8- 1037.10.

St. Thomas (*In VII Phys.*, lect. 1 [Leonine nos 4-6]) is aware of the Greek and Arabian objections against this proof, but he defends its *propter quid* character against Averroes, who (*In VII Phys.*, 2 [Venice, 1562, fol. 307v2 L]) had classed it as a *quia* argument ("de genere signorum certorum"). The objection that Averroes is answering—namely, that the basic presupposition of the Aristotelian proof does not apply universally since in heavenly bodies or in the Platonic self-moving soul a part could not be imagined to be at rest—is quite legitimately universalized by St. Thomas instead of being restricted to those particular instances.

W.D. Ross, in *Aristotle's Physics* (p. 669), states that the argument is not valid in regard to the dependence of motion on a part of the thing that is being moved. "But Aristotle makes the mistake of supposing that this implies the causal dependence of the movement of AB on the movement of a part of itself ΓB. That this is false is shown by the fact that it is equally true that if AΓ were at rest AB could not be in motion, so that AB's motion, it is were causally dependent on that of ΓB, would be equally dependent on that of AΓ." But that is exactly the force of the argument. The dependence of motion on its parts applies equally to all its parts. It is dependence by way of material causality, as Ferrariensis noted in regard to the interpretation of St. Thomas: "Sunt tamen causa totius in genere causae materialis, et motus partium sunt materia motus totius" (*In Contra Gentiles*, I, 13, comm. IV). Ferrariensis had phrased in the following words what is substantially the same objection: "Quia aliquis posset dicere quod est vera de quiescente ad quietem alterius moventis, non autem de quiescente ad quietem partis. Pars enim est materia totius, non autem quod movet totum" (*ibid.*, comm. III). Cf. also A. Brémond, *Le Dilemme Aristotélicien*, p. 143, n.1, for a similar objection.

25   St. Thomas Aquinas, *In VII Phys.*, lect. 1 (Leonine nos. 2-3).

26   "... sed videtur dicendum quod non sit demonstratio *quia*, sed *propter quid*; continent enim causam quare impossibile est aliquod mobile movere scipsum. Ad cujus evidentiam sciendum est, quod aliquid movere seipsum nihil aliud est, quam esse sibi causa motus. Quod autem est sibi causa alicuius, oportet quod *primo* ei conveniat; quia quod est primum in quolibet genere, est causa eorum quae sunt post. Unde ignis, qui sibi et aliis est causa caloris, est primum calidum. Ostendit autem Aristoteles in sexto, quod in motu non invenitur primum, neque ex parte temporis, neque ex parte mangitudinis, neque etiam ex parte mobilis, propter horum divisibilitatem. Non ergo potest inveniri primum, cuius motus non dependeat ab aliquo priori: motus enim totius dependet a motibus partium, et dividitur in eos, ut in sexto probatum est. Sic ergo ostendit Aristoteles causam quare nullum mobile movet seipsum; quia non potest esse primum mobile, cuius motus non dependeat a partibus: sicut si ostenderem quod nullum divisibile potest esse primum ens, quia esse cuiuslibet divisibilis dependet a partibus" (*ibid* [Leonine no. 6]).

Cf. "Quia vis rationis in hoc consistit, quod, si aliquid seipsum moveat primo et per se, non ratione partium, oportet quod suum moveri non dependeat ab aliquo; moveri autem ipsius divisibilis, sicut et ejus esse, dependet a partibus; et sic non potest seipsum movere primo et per se" (*CG*, I, cap. 13 [Leonine p. 31a, ll. 20-26]).

There has been a long neo-Scholastic controversy commencing in 1888 with A. de Margerie and still continuing (e.g., A. Pechhacker, "Zur Begründung des Kausal prinzips," *Scholastik*, XXV [1950], 518-34) as to whether the "principle of causality" is analytic or synthetic or even (F. Sawicki) a postulate. This controversy has neither an Aristotelian nor a Thomistic background. The causal proposition "Whatever is being moved is being moved by something else," as a universal and necessary truth, is for Aristotle and expressly for St. Thomas, not a "principle" in the modern epistemological sense, but the *conclusion* of a *propter quid* demonstration. The notions of act and potency and participation are the prior conceptions used in proving it.

27 Aristotle *Metaphysics* α.1. 993b24-26.

28 The relation of the particular sciences—including natural philosophy—to the primary philosophy is sketched by Aristotle in *Metaphysics* E. 1. 1025b4-18. The particular sciences take a certain type of being and deal with it, accepting *what* it *is* either as evident or on hypothesis. They do not attempt to assess it in terms of being. The problem of whether or not motion is something essentially imperfect, accordingly, should lie outside the realm of the natural philosopher's inquiry, just as the consideration of contrariety or perfection (*Metaphysics* Γ. 2. 1005a10-13) lies outside the scope of the geometer. The "first" which is denied by Aristotle to motion in *Physics* vi. 5, is, of course, the "first" in a continuum.

29 *Physics* vii. 1. 242a49-243a2.

30 *Ibid.*, 2. 243a3-4.

31 "Si non movetur, habetur propositum, scilicet quod aliquid sit movens immobile; quod est proprietas primi moventis... Erit ergo aliquid primum movens, quod erit prima causa motus: ita scilicet quod ipsum non movetur, sed movet alia" (*In VIII Phys.*, lect. 1 [Leonine no. 1]).

32 *Physics* vii. 1. 250b14-15.

33 *Ibid.*, 251a5-8. For some chronological indications, cf. G. Verbeke, "La Structure logique de la preuve du Premier Moteur chez Aristote," *Revue Philosophique de Louvain*, XLVI (1948), 160.

34 *Physics* viii. 1. 251a8-b10.

35 *Ibid.*, 251b28-252a5.

36 *Ibid.*, 251b10-28.

37 "Et quia omnis motus indiget subjecto, ut hic Aristoteles probat et rei veritas habet, sequitur quod productio universalis entis a Deo non sit motus nec mutatio, sed sit quaedam simplex emanatio. Et sic *fieri* et *facere* aequivoce dicuntur in hac universali rerum productione, et in aliis productionibus. Sicut ergo si intelligamus rerum productionum esse a Deo ab aeterno, sicut Aristoteles posuit, et plures Platonicorum, non est necessarium, immo impossibile, quod huic productioni universali aliquod subjectum non productum praeintelligatur; ita etiam, si ponamus secundum nostrae fidei sententiam, quod non ab aeterno produxeritis res, sed produxerit eas postquam non fuerant, non est necessarium quod ponantur aliquod subjectum huic universali productioni. Patet ergo quod hoc quod Aristoteles hic probat, quod omnis motus indiget subjecto mobili, non est contra sententiam nostrae fidei: quia jam dictum est quod universalis rerum productio, sive ponatur ab aeterno, sive non ab aeterno, non est motus nec mutatio"(*In VIII Phys.*, lect. 1 [Leonine no. 4]).

"Sunt enim huiusmodi rationes efficaces ad probandum quod motus non inceperit per viam naturae, sicut ab aliquibus ponebatur:... inceperunt esse a causa universali totius esse. Ostensum est autem supra, quod productio totius esse a causa prima essendi non est motus, sive ponatur quod haec rerum emanatio sit ab aeterno, sive non. Sic ergo non sequitur quod ante primam mutationem sit aliqua mutatio" (*ibid.* [Leonine no. 18]).

38 "Si ergo ponimus motum non semper fuisse sed est accipere aliquod primum indivisible in motu, ante quod nihil fuit motus; erit etiam accipere aliquod nunc in tempore, ante quod non fuit aliquod tempus" (*ibid.* [Leonine no. 20]).

39 "... quia antiqui naturales non potuerunt pervenire ad causam primam toitus esse, sed considerabant causas particularium mutationum. Quorum primi consideraverunt causas solarum mutationum accidentalium, ponentes omne fieri esse alterari: sequentes vero pervenerunt ad cognitionem mutationum substantialium: postermi vero, ut Plato et Aristoteles, pervenerunt ad cognoscendum principium totius esse.

Sic igitur patet quod non movemur ad ponendum aliquod fieri ex nihilo, quia reputemus ea esse solum entia quae sunt visibilia: sed magis e contrario, quia non consideramus solas productiones particulares a causis particularibus, sed productionem universalem totius esse a prima essendi principio" (*ibid.*, [Leonine no. 5]).

"Sed sicut dictum est, ipsum esse non acquisiverunt per mutationem vel motum, sed per emanationem a primo rerum principio: et sic non sequitur quod ante primam mutationem sit aliqua mutatio" (*ibid.*, [Leonine no. 18]). Cf. *De Substantiis Separatis*, cap. 7; *Opuscula*, ed. Perrier (Paris: Lethielleux, 1949), I, 152-58.

40   St. Thomas is fully aware that Aristotle bases his proof on the *eternity* of motion: "... quia hic in octavo et in *Metaphys.*, ad probandum primum principium, utitur aeternitate motus" (*In VIII Phys.*, lect. 1 [Leonine no. 6]). Cf. "Ex hoc igitur processu manifestum est quod Aristoteles hic firmiter opinatus est et credidit necessarium fore, quod motus sit sempiternus et similiter tempus. Aliter enim non fundasset super hoc intentionem suam de inquisitione substantiarum immaterialium" (*In XII Metaphys.*, lect. 5 [Cathala no. 2496]). St. Thomas maintains, however, that the demonstration is clearer if it can dispense with the eternity of motion: "Si enim mundo et motu existente sempiterno, necesse est ponere unum primum principium; multo magis sempiternitate eorum sublata; quia manifestum est quod omne novum indiget aliquo principio innovante"(*In VIII Phys.*, lect. 1 [Leonine no. 6]). Cf. "Quia si non fuerit mundus aeternus, necesse est quod fuerit productus in esse ab aliquo praeexistente" (*In XII Metaphys.*, lect. 5 [Cathala no. 2499]). Cf. also *CG*, I, lect. 13 (Leonine p. 33b, ll. 10-19).

41   The infinitive *esse* may signify for St. Thomas the essence or quiddity or nature of a thing, or the act of existing, or the truth denoted by the copula. "Sciendum est quod esse dicitur tripliciter. Uno modo dicitur esse ipsa quidditas vel natura rei, sicut dicitur quod definitio est oratio significans quid est esse; definitio enim quidditatem rei significat. Alio modo dicitur esse ipse actus essentiae; sicut vivere, quod est esse viventibus, est animae actus; non actus secundus, qui est operatio, sed actus primus. Tertio modo dicitur esse quod significat veritatem compositionis in propositionibus, secundum quod 'est' dicitur copula: et secundum hoc est in intellectu componente et dividente quantum ad sui complementum; sed fundatur in esse rei, quod est actus essentiae" (*In I Sent.*, d.33, q.1, a.1 ad 1). For Boethius, who is responsible for fixing so much of the Scholastic terminology to technical meanings, *esse* had meant the definition (*In Isagogen Porphyrii*, IV, 14 [*CSEL*, 2d ed., XLVIII, 273, 1. 13]) or the form (*Quomodo Substantiae...* [*PL*, LXIV, 1311]) of the thing. This was entirely in accord with the Aristotelian usage of the Greek infinitive of the verb "to be" to signify form.

42   *Physics* viii. 3. 254a35-b4.

43   *Ibid.*, 256a2-3.

44   *Ibid.*, 254b7-10.

45   *Ibid.*, 254b24-27; 255b32-33.

46   *Ibid.*, 254b27-33.

47   *Ibid.*, 254b33-255b29.

48   *Ibid.*, 255b1-24.

49   *Ibid.*, 255a34-b5.

50   *Metaphysics*, Z 7-8. 1032a12-1034a5; 8. 1050b28-30.

51   "Ergo de prima potentia reducitur in actum cui coniungitur secunda potentia, per aliquod agens, scilicet per docentem. Sed quando sic se habet quod habet habitum scientiae, non oportet quod reducatur in secundum actum per aliquod agens, sed statim per seipsum operatur considerando, nisi sit aliquod prohibens, puta occupatio vel infirmitas aut voluntas" (*In VIII Phys.*, lect. 4 [Leonine no. 3]).

"Haec ergo, scilicet aqua, primo est in potentia levis, et postmodum fit levis in acto; et tunc statim habet operationem suam, nisi aliquod prohibeat" (*ibid.* [Leonine no. 5]).

"... sicut etiam dictum est in qualitate, quod quando est quale in actu, statim tendit in suam actionem; sicut ille qui est sciens, statem considerat, nisi aliquid prohibeat. Et similiter in motu quantitatis; quia ex quo facta est additio quanti ad quantum, statim sequitur extensio in corpore augmentabili, nisi aliquid prohibeat"(*ibid.*, [Leonine no. 7]).

52   *Physics* viii. 5. 256a2-b3.

53   *Ibid.*, 256b3-27. W.D. Ross (*Aristotle's Physics*, p. 669) takes the immobile movent at 256b24 as referring to God. But comparison with 257b26-258b4 shows that Aristotle is thinking of the immobile movent as part of the self-movent; that is, as a soul. The Stagirite notes that Anaxagoras therefore correctly said that the Mind must be impassible and unmixed, since Anaxagoras makes the Mind the source of motion; that is, efficient cause. But Aristotle does not say that his own immobile movent here is unmixed or separate from the animated body.

54   *Ibid.*, 256b27-257a27. That something which is "at rest"(*eremoun*) could cause motion is not taken into consideration by Aristotle. "At rest" means the privation of motion in something mobile. It does not refer to immobile being. *Eremia* is found only in mobile things. Cf. *Physics* iii. 2. 202a4-5; iv. 12. 221b9-14; v. 2. 226b15-16 and 6. 229b24-26; vi 3. 234a31-34 and 8. 239a12-

14. St. Thomas is well aware of this distinction (cf. *In VIII Phys.*, lect. 3 [Leonine no. 2]); nevertheless in the present text (*Ibid.*, lect. 5. 9 [Leonine no. 13]) he takes this argument as concludng in its first member to something "immobile." He likewise gives this same interpretation at *CG*, I cap. 13 (Leonine p. 32b, ll. 19-24).

55   *Physics* viii. 5. 257a27-b32.

56   *Ibid.*, 258b4-9.

57   *In VIII Phys.*, lect. 5 (Leonine nos. 9-11).

58   "Ubi considerandum est quid Aristoteles prius in sexto probavit quod in motu non est aliquid primum,... quia tunc loquibatur de motu in communi, et de mobili secundum quod est quoddam continuum, nondum applicando ad determinatas naturas. Et secundum hoc sequeretur quod non esset aliquid primo motum, et per consequens nec aliquid primo movens, si movens sit continuum: et ita etiam non esset aliquid primo movens seipsum. Sed nunc iam Aristoteles loquitur de motu, applicando ad determinatas naturas: et ideo ponit aliquid esse primo movens seipsum" (*ibid.*, [Leonine no. 6]).

59   *Physics.*, viii. 6. 258b16-24; 259b1-20.

60   *Ibid.*, 258b26-259a20.

61   *Ibid.*, 259a20-b31.

62   *Ibid.*, 260a1-19.

63   *Ibid.*, 10. 266a10-267b26.

64   Cf. summary of the reasoning *ibid.*, 6. 259a29-b1.

65   "Est autem sciendum quod hae rationes, quibus Aristoteles probare nititur primum motum esse perpetuum, non ex necessitate concludunt: potest enim contingere absque omni mutatione primi motoris, quod non semper moveat, sicut supra ostensum est in principio huius octavi" (*In VIII Phys.*, lect. 6 [Leonine no. 8]).

66   For example: "Et huius diversitatis ratio est, quia motores superiorum orbium non constituuntur in suo esse ex sua unione ad corpora, et eorum connexio est invariabilis; et ideo quamvis corpora orbium moveantur, ipsi non moventur per accidens" (*ibid.* [Leonine no. 6]). The pluarlity of such immobile movents as established by the Aristotelian argument is not questioned: "Est etiam attendendum quod, quia nullum movens motum potest causare motum continuum sempiternum, ideo in XI *Metaph.* probare intendit multitudinem motorum immobilium secondum multitudinem caelestium motuum, quasi illa consideratio sequatur ad istum" (*ibid.*, lect. 10 [Leonine no. 8]).

67   Cf. Aristotle *Physics.*, viii. 6. 258b16-259a8. St. Thomas: "Potest autem aliquis sic procedere. Omne quod potest quandoque esse et quandoque non esse, est perpetuum: sed primum movens, cum sit immobile, ut ostensum est, non potest quandoque esse et quandoque non esse; quia quod quandoque est et quandoque non est, generatur et corrumpitur; quod autem generatur et corrumpitur, movetur: ergo primum movens est perpetuum. Aristoteles autem de hac ratione non curat: quia potest aliquis dicere si vult, quod in quibusdam contingit quod quandoque sint et quandoque non sint, absque hoc quod generentur et corrumpantur per se loquendo, et per consequens absque hoc per se moveantur" (*In VIII Phys.*, lect. 6 [Leonine no. 5]).

68   Cf. *supra*, nn. 39-40. St. Thomas himself builds upon everything, except the subsistent act of *esse*, as being in potency to *esse*. Speaking independently of Aristotle, he says: "Substantia autem simplex quae est ipsum esse subsistens, non potest esse nisi una, sicut nec albedo, si esset subsistens, posset esse nisi una. Omnis ergo substantia quae est post primam substantiam simplicem, participat esse. Omne autem participans componitur ex participante et participato, et participans est in potentia ad participatum. In omni ergo substantia quantumcumque simplici, post primam substantiam simplicem, est potentia essendi" (*In VIII Phys.*, lect. 10 [Leonine no. 13]).

"Omne enim quod non est suum esse, participat esse a causa prima, quae est suum esse.... Unde sicut motus perpertuus demonstrat infinitam virtutem motoris, non autem ipsius mobilis; ita et perpetua eius duratio demonstrat infinitam virtutem causae a qua habet esse" (*ibid.* [Leonine no. 14]). On the two senses of *generatio* and *corruptio*, cf. *De Veritate*, V, a.2 ad 6.

69   In this part of the commentary, God is mentioned explicitly only when St. Thomas is treating the comments of Alexander and Averroes (*In VIII Phys.*, lect 10 [Leonine no. 14]).

70   "Et sic terminat Philosophus considerationem communem de rebus naturalibus in primo principio totius naturae, *qui est super omnia Deus benedictus in saecula. Amen*" (*ibid.*, [Leonine

no. 9]. Cf. Javellus, *In Metaph.* XII, 3 (Venice, 1568, fol. 322v2).
71   Cf. W.D. Ross, *Aristotle's Metaphysics*, I, xxvii-xxviii and II, 384.
72   *Metaphysics* A. 6-7. 1071b3-1072b14. St. Thomas notes: "... necesse est enim, si primum movens movet sicut primum intellectum et desideratum, quod primum mobile desideret et intelligat ipsum. Et hoc quidem verum est secundum opinionem Aristotelis, inquantum caelum ponitur animatum anima intelligente et desiderante" (*In XII Metaphys.*, lect. 8 [Cathala no. 2536]).
73   *Metaphysics* A. 9. 1074b15-35.
74   *Ibid.* 8. 1073a14-1074a17.
75   *In XII Metaphys.*, lect. 5 (Cathala no. 2496). Text *supra*, n. 40.
76   "Sed quamvis rationes probantes sempiternitatem motus et temporis non sint demonstrativae et ex necessitate concludentes, tamen ea quae hic probantur de sempiternitate et immaterialitate primae substantiae, ex necessitate sequuntur. Quia si non fuerit mundus aeternus, necesse est quod fuerit productus in esse ab aliquo praeexistente. Et si hoc non sit aeternum, oportet iterum quod sit productum ab aliquo. Et cum hoc non possit procedere in infinitum, ut supra in secundo probatum est, necesse est ponere aliquam substantiam sempiternam, in cujus substantia non sit potentia, et per consequens immaterialem"(*ibid.* [Cathala no. 2494]).
77   "Si autem primum movens est sempiternum et non motum, oportet quod non sit ens in potentia; quia quod est ens in potentia natum est moveri; sed quod sit substantia per se existens, et quod substantia ejus sit actus" (*ibid.*, lect. 6 [Cathala no. 2518]).
78   "... assimilatio autem ad id quod est volens, et intelligens, cujusmodi ostendit esse Deum, attenditur secundum voluntatem et intelligentiam, sicut artificiata assimilantur artifici, inquantum in eis voluntas artificis adimpletur: sequitur quod tota necessitas primi motus subjaceat voluntati Dei" (*ibid.*, lect. 7 [Cathala no, 2535]).
79   "Sed nec etiam potest dici quod in corpore caelesti sit virtus infinita, etsi infinito tempore esse habeat; quia in eo non est virtus activa sui esse, sed solum susceptiva" (*ibid.*, lect. 8 [Cathala no. 2550]).
80   Quanto autem aliquod principium perfectius intelligitur, tanto magis intelligitur in eo effectus ejus; nam principiata continentur in virtute principii. Cum igitur a primo principio, quod est Deus, dependeat caelum et tota natura, ut dictum est, patet, quod Deus cognoscendo seipsum, omnia cognoscit"(*ibid.*, lect. 11 [Cathala no. 2615]).
81   "Et hoc est quod concludit, quod est unus princeps totius universi, scilicet primum movens, et primum intelligibile, et primum bonum, quod supra dixit Deum, qui est benedictus in saeculorum. Amen" (*ibid.*, lect. 12 [Cathala no. 2663]).
82   "Dicit enim quod ex creaturis tribus modis devenimus in Deum: Scilicet per causalitatem, per remotionem, per eminentiam. Et ratio hujus est, quia esse creaturae est ab altero. Unde secundum hoc ducimur in causam a qua est" (*In I Sent.*, d.3, divisio lae partis textus).
83   "Prima ergo ratio sumitur per viam causalitatis, et formatur sic. Omne quod habet esse ex nihilo, oportet quod sit ab aliquo a quo esse suum fluxerit. Sed omnes creaturae habent esse ex nihilo: quod manifestatur ex earum imperfectione et potentialitate. Ergo oportet quod sint ab aliquo uno primo, et hoc est Deus" (*ibid.*).
84   "Secunda ratio sumitur per viam remotionis, et est talis. Ultra omne imperfectum oportet esse aliquod perfectum, cui nulla imperfectio admisceatur. Sed corpus est quid imperfectum, quia est terminatum et finitum suis dimensionibus et mobile. Ergo oportet ultra corpora esse aliquid quod non est corpus.
      "Item, omne incorporeum mutabile de sui natura est imperfectum. Ergo ultra omnes species mutabiles, sicut sunt animae et angeli, oportet esse aliquod ens incorporeum et immobile et omnino perfectum, et hoc est Deus" (*ibid.*).
   Cf. "Omne autem quod recipit aliquid ab aliquo est in potentia respectu illius, et hoc quod receptum in eo est est actus eius. Ergo oportet quod ipsa quiditas uel forma que est intelligencia sit in potencia respectu esse quod a Deo recipit, et illud esse receptum est per modum actus" (*De Ente*, cap. 4; ed. Roland-Gosselin [Kain, Belgique: Le Saulchoir, 1962], p. 35, ll. 19-23).
85   Cf. n.37 in the first part of this article (The Modern Schoolman, XXX [Nov., 1952], 43-44); *De Pot.*, III, a.2.
86   "Primo autem ponemus rationes quibus Aristoteles procedit ad probandum Deum esse. Qui hoc probare intendit ex parte motus duabus viis" (*CG*, I, cap. 13; p. 30a6-9). For a schema of

the use made by St. Thomas of the Aristotelian proofs, cf. J. Paulus, "Le caractère métaphysique des preuves thomistes de l'existence de Dieu," *Archives d'Histoire Doctrinale et Littéraire du Moyen Age*, IX (1934), 146.

On the background in Averroes for dividing the Aristotelian arguments into these two *viae*, cf. the critique of Paulus' article by D. Salman, *Bulletin Thomiste*, IV (1935), 607-8.

87   "Omne quod movetur , ab alio movetur. Patet autem sensu aliquid moveri, utputa solem. Ergo alio movente movetur. —Aut ergo illud movens movetur, aut non. Si non movetur, ergo habemus propositum, quod necesse est ponere aliquod movens immobile. Et hoc dicimus Deum. —Si autem movetur, ergo ab alio movente movetur. Aut ergo est procedere in infinitum; aut est devenire ad aliquod movens immobile. Sed non est procedere in infinitum. Ergo necesse est ponere aliquod primum movens immobile.

"In hac autem probatione sunt duae propositiones probandae: scilicet, quod *omne motum movetur ab alio*; et quod *in moventibus et motis non sit procedere in infinitum*" (*CG*, I, cap. 13; p. 30a10-b8).

88   *Ibid.*, pp. 31b9-31a57. Cf. Aristotle *Physics* viii. 5. 257b6-13.

89   *CG*, I, cap. 13; pp. 30b17-31a2.

90   *Ibid.*, pp. 31b19-32a7.

91   "Praedictos autem processus duo videntur infirmare. Quorum *primum* est, quod procedunt ex suppositione aeternitatis motus: quod apud Catholicos supponitur esse falsum.

"Et ad hoc dicendum quod via efficacissima ad probandum Deum esse est ex suppositione aeternitatis mundi, qua posita, minus videtur esse manifestum quod Deus sit. Nam si mundus et motus de novo incoepit, planum est quod oportet poni aliquam causam quae de novo producat mundum et motum: quia omne quod de novo fit, ab aliquo innovatore oportet sumere originem; cum nihil educat se de potentia in actum, vel de non esse in esse.

"*Secundum* est, quod supponitur in predictis demonstrationibus primum motum, scilicet corpus caeleste, esse motum ex se. Ex quo sequitur ipsum esse animatum. Quod a multis non conceditur.

"Et ad hoc dicendum est quod, si primum movens non ponitur motum ex se, oportet quod moveatur a penitus immobili" (*ibid.*, p. 33b6-27).

92   *Ibid.*, pp. 32a12-33b5. Regarding "immobile" at p. 32b19-24, cf. n. 54 above.

93   "... cum nihil educat se de potentia in actum, vel de non esse in esse"(*ibid.*, p. 33b18-19). The pure act reached by this argument (cf. résumé at end of *CG*, I, cap. 16) is interpreted in the existential sense: "Ostensum est autem in Deo nihil esse de potentia, sed ipsum esse purum actum. Non igitur Dei essentia est aliud quam suum esse" (*CG*, I, cap. 22; p. 68b37-39).

94   Cf.: "Cum igitur esse sit communis effectus omnium agentium, nam omne agens facit esse actu; oportet quod hunc effectum producunt inquantum ordinantur sub primo agente, et agunt in virtute ipsius" (*CG*, III, cap. 66; ed. Leonine, XIV, 188a18-22).

95   "Posteriores vero philosophi, ut Plato, Aristoteles et eorum sequaces, pervenerunt ad considerationem ipsius esse universalis; et ideo ipsi soli posuerunt aliquam universalem causam rerum, a qua omnia alia in esse prodirent, ut patet per Augustinum. Cui quidem sententiae etiam catholica fides consentit. Et hoc triplici ratione demonstrari potest: quarum prima est haec.... Cum ergo esse inveniatur omnibus rebus commune, quae secundum illud quod sunt, ad invicem distinctae sunt, oportet quod de necessitate eis non ex se ipsis, sed ab aliqua una causa esse attribuatur. Et ista videtur ratio Platonis...." (*De Pot.*, III, a.5). Cf.: "Sed causa primi gradus est simpliciter universalis; ejus enim effectus proprius est esse" (*In VI Metaphys.*, lect. 3 [Cathala no. 1209]).

96   "Est autem ponere unum ens, quod est perfectissimum et veracissimum ens: quod ex hoc probatur, quia est aliquid movens omnino immobile et perfectissimum, ut a philosophis est probatum. Opertet ergo quod omnia alia minus perfecta ab ipso esse recipiat. Et haec est probatio Philosophi" (*De Pot.*, III, a.5).

97   "Est autem ponere aliquod ens quod est ipsum suum esse: quod ex hoc probatur, quia oportet esse aliquod primum ens quod sit actus purus, in quo nulla sit compositio. Unde oportet quod ab uno illo ente omnia alia sint, quaecumque non sunt suum esse, sed habent esse per modum participationis. Haec est ratio Avicennae" (*ibid.*).

98   "Videmus enim omnia quae moventur, ab aliis moveri.... Hoc autem in infinitum procedere impossibile est. Cum enim omne quod movetur ab aliquo, sit quasi instrumentum quoddam primi moventis, si primum movens non sit, quaecumque movent, instrumenta erunt.... Oportet

igitur primum movens esse, quod sit omnibus supremum, et hoc dicimus Deum" (*Compend. Theol.*, cap. 3).

99   "Omne enim quod possibile est esse et non esse, est mutabile: sed Deus est omnino immutabilis, ut ostensum est, ergo Deum non est possibile esse et non esse" (*ibid.*, cap. 6).

100   "Deus autem nullo modo est motui subjectus, ut ostensum est, non igitur est in Deo aliqua successio, sed ejus esse est totum simul.... Deo autem nihil deperit, nec accrescit, quia immobilis est, igitur esse ejus est totum simul. Ex his duobus apparet quod proprie est aeternus"(*ibid.*, cap. 8).

101   "Item, ostensum est quod Deus est actus purus absque alicujus potentialitatis permixtione, oportet igitur quod ejus essentia sit ultimus actus: nam omnis actus qui est circa ultimum, est in potentia ad ultimum actum: ultimus autem actus est ipsum esse. Cum enim omnis motus sit exitus de potentia in actum, oportet illud esse ultimum actum, in quod tendit omnis motus..." (*ibid.*, cap. 11). Cf. texts in n. 139 below

102   "In quocumque enim aliud est essentia, et aliud esse ejus, oportet quod aliud sit quo sit, et aliud quo aliquid sit, nam per esse suum de quolibet dicitur quod est, per essentiam vero suam de quolibet dicitur quid sit. Unde et definitio significans essentiam, demonstrat quid est res..." (*ibid.*).

103   "Deus enim est suum esse, ut infra patebit. Sed quia nos non scimus de Deo quid est, non est nobis per se nota: sed indiget demonstrari... per effectus" (*ST*, I q.2, a.1).

104   "Secundo, quia esse est actualitas omnis formae vel naturae: non enim bonitas vel humanitas significatur in actu, nisi prout significamus eam *esse*. Oportet igitur quod ipsum esse comparetur ad essentiam quae est aliud ab ipso, sicut actus ad potentiam. Cum igitur in Deo nihil sit potentiale, ut ostensum est supra, sequitur quod non sit aliud in eo essentia quam suum esse" (*ibid.*, q.3, a.4).

Cf. "Quaelibet autem forma signata non intelligitur in actu nisi per hoc quod esse ponitur. Nam humanitas vel igneitas potest considerari ut in potentia materiae existens, vel ut in virtute agentis, aut etiam ut in intellectu; sed hoc quod habet esse, efficitur actu existens. Unde patet quod hoc quod dico esse actualitas omnium actuum, et propter hoc est perfectio omnium perfectionum" (*De Pot.*, VII, a.2 ad 9).

"Quia vero actualitas, quam principaliter significat hoc verbum EST, est communiter actualitas omnis formae, vel actus substantialis vel accidentalis..." (*In I Periherm.*, lect. 5 [Leonine no. 22]). Cf. also *CG*, II, cap. 54.

105   Cf. the text in n. 101 above and those in n. 139 below.

106   "Dicendum quod *esse* dupliciter dicitur: uno modo, significat actum essendi; alio modo significat compositionem propositionis, quam anima adinvenit coniungens praedicatum subjecto. Primo igitur modo accipiendo *esse*, non possumus scire esse Dei, sicut nec eius essentiam: sed solum secundo modo. Scimus enim quod haec propositio quam formamus de Deo, cum dicimus *Deus est*, vera est. Et hoc scimus ex eius effectibus, ut supra dictum est" (*ST*, I, q.2, a.4 ad 2). Cf. *CG*, I cap. 12; *De Pot.*, VII, a.2 ad 1.

107   Cf. "Quicquid enim non est de intellectu essentie uel quiditatis hoc est adueniens extra et faciens compositionem cum essentia sine hiis que sunt partes essentie intelligi potest. Omnis autem essentia uel quiditas potest intelligi sine hoc quod aliquid intelligatur de esse suo; possum enim intelligere quid est homo uel fenix et tamen ignorare an esse habeat in rerum natura" *De Ente*, cap. 4; ed. Roland-Gosselin, p. 34, 11. 7-14.

"In quocumque enim est essentia, et aliud esse ejus, oportet quod aliud sit quo sit, et aliud quo aliquid sit, nam per esse suum de quolibet dicitur quod est, per essentiam vero suam de quolibet dicitur quid sit. Unde et definitio significans essentiam, demonstrat quid est res..." (*Compend. Theol.*, cap. 11).

108   Cf. E. Gilson, *Being and Some Philosophers* (Toronto: Pont. Inst. of Mediaeval Studies, 1949), pp. 190 ff. L.-M. Régis, approaching the question from the *logical* analysis given by St. Thomas, writes: "If we admit that 'to exist' can and must be known in and by a concept of apprehension, we also admit that there is a second knowledge of 'to exist' which comes after the first, controls, and completes it. This affirmation, an act of judgement..." (The Modern Schoolman, XXVIII [Jan., 1951], 125).

Recent studies have shown that *as a matter of fact* St. Thomas never arrives at the distinction between essence and *esse* through reasoning from the limitation of act by potency."Ce n'est, en effet, que postérieurement à la découverte de la composition essence-*esse* dans le créé, que Saint Thomas applique à cette composition le couple puissance-acte" (J.D. Robert, "Le Principe 'Actus non limitatur nisi per potentiam subjectivam realiter distinctam,'"*Revue Philosophique de Louvain,* XLVII [1949], 68). *"Thus act and potency take on the aspect of limitation only as a kind of post factum* consequence, so to speak, not as a first principle" (W. Norris Clarke, "The Limitation of Act by Potency," *The New Scholasticism,* XXVI [1952], 192).

109   "Sed dicendum est quod cum duplex sit intellectus operatio, ut supra habitum est, ille qui dicit nomen vel verbum secundum se, constituit intellectum quantum ad primam operationem, quae est simplex conceptio alicuis, et secundum hoc, quiescit audiens, qui in suspenso erat antequam nomen vel verbum proferretur et eius prolatio terminaretur; non autem constituit intellectum quantum ad secundam operationem, quae est intellectus componentis et dividentis, ipsum verbum vel nomen per se dictum: nec quantum ad hoc facit quiescere audientem.

"... Probat autem consequenter per illa verba, quae maxime videntur significare veritatem vel falsitatem, scilicet ipsum verbum quod est *esse,* et verbum infinitum quod est *non esse;* quorum neutrum per se dictum est significativum veritatis vel falsitatis in re..." (*In I Periherm.,* lects. 3 and 5 [Leonine nos. 17-18]).

110   Cf. *De Ente,* cap. 1; ed. Roland-Gosselin, p. 2, l. 8 and p. 3, l. 10.

111   "Secunda vero ordinatur ad tertiam: quia videlicet oportet quod ex aliquo vero cognito, cui intellectus assentiat, procedatur ad certitudinem accipiendam de aliquibus ignotis" (*In I Periherm.,* proem. [Leonine no. 1]).

112   Cf. Cajetan: "Cum autem de Deo scimus *an est,* dicimur scire esse quod significat veritatem propositionis, et nescire esse Dei: non quod terminus ultimus cognitionis nostrae sit esse propositionis, ut objectio intellexit (quoniam terminus est esse Dei, non absolute, sed ut respondet veritati propositionis); sed quia per hanc cognitionem non cognoscitur esse Dei propria questione qua est secundum se cognoscibile, quia non scitur per *quid*" (*In ST,* I, q.2, a.4, comm. v). Ferrariensis, *In CG,* I, cap. 12, comm. III: "... sed cognoscimus esse quod significat compositionem intellectus, idest, cognoscimus esse Deo convenire ut actualitatem essendi..." A.-D. Sertillanges, on the other hand, seems to minimize this bearing of the truth of the proposition on the actual *esse* of God: "Nous savons qu'il est; mais dans cette proposition: Dieu est, le verbe être ne signifie point l'être réel, l'être considéré à la facon d'un attribut; il n'est que le lien logique d'une proposition vraie... Cette affirmation: Dieu est, est une affirmation vraie, non comme *qualifiant* Dieu au titre de l'être; mais comme *exigeant* Dieu en se fondant sur l'être" (*S. Thomas d'Aquin, Somme Théologique, Dieu,* [Paris: Desclée, 1926] pp. 383-84. Cf. also *Le Christianisme et les Philosophes* (Paris, Aubier), p. 269.

113   Cf. *CG,* I, cap. 14; *ST,* I, q.3, init. Also: "Inde est quod prima rerum principia non definimus nisi per negationes posteriorum; sicut dicimus quod punctum est, cujus pars non est; et Deum cognoscimus per negationes, inquantum dicimus Deum incorporeum esse, immobilem, infinitum" (*In X Metaphys.,* lect. 4 [Cathala, no. 1209]).

The case in general against as existential interpretation of the *prima via,* to quote a recent work, is that in the text "the literal development, the words and the statements, are not about composition of essence and existence nor do they speak of creation" (William Bryar, *St. Thomas and the Existence of God* [Chicago: Henry Regnery Co., 1951], p. vii). But neither does any other of the *viae* speak of these, though they are involved in the probative force of the other four. The force of the *prima via,* as has been seen, lies in its treatment of act and potency. The act towards which sensible motion (as understood by St. Thomas) ultimately tends is existential, as is sufficiently clear from the preceding and following context and from comparison with other versions of the argument; so the pure act reached by the *prima via* can be only the subsistent act of existing. Far from being "simply an extraordinarily loose literary rendering of St. Thomas' theme of the composite essence-existence and of the dependence of the composite on a creator God" (Bryar, p. vi), the *via* is a close and cogent expression of how actually existent motion has to originate from pure subsistent act, which (in the procedure of St. Thomas) can be only existential. The *via* is not explaining the creation of things, but the *motion* of things.

A particular objection is that "the argument for the second premise appears to operate by way of a presupposition of a multiplicity of agents, such a multiplicity being in fact incompatible with the creation or conservation *ex nihilo*" (Bryar, p. vii). But how is it incompatible with imparting *motion* that terminates in existential act? The reasoning is concerned not with creation or conservation, but with *motion* (at least, as the *via* appears in the *Summa Theologiae*). In St. Thomas' doctrine, the *proper* effect of the *primary* agent, *esse*, is imparted through motion *mediately:* "Igitur esse est quod agentia secunda agunt in virtute agentis primi" (*CG*, III, cap.66; cf. also the text from this chapter quoted, n. 139 below). In saying that the *prima via* is metaphysical and therefore deals with *being*, one should keep in mind that the *being* so meant is the *esse* of motion and its terminus. Likewise Mortimer Adler's conclusion that "hence no corporeal substance can *efficiently* cause the being of anything" ("The Demonstration of God's Existence," *The Thomist*, V [1943], 217), holds in creation and conservation, but not entirely in mediate causality through motion.

Bryar, using the tools of symbolic logic, finds that the text of the *prima via* allows three interpretations or explications, which "yield three demonstrations with a certain common likeness" (*St. Thomas and the Existence of God*, p. 150). None of the three coincides exactly with either of the traditional alternatives (*ibid.*, p. vii).

114   "Et scito quod ista quaestio est subtilissima, et propria antiquis metaphysicis: a modernulis autem valde aliena, quia tenent non solum in omni re, essentiam identificari existentiae illius"(*In ST*, I, q.3, a.4, comm. I [ed. Leonine, IV, 42b]).

115   Cf. Avicenna, *Metaphys.*, I, 1 (Venice, 1508, fol. 70a-b) and Averroes, *In I Phys.*, 83 (Venice, 1562, fol. 47va) and *In II Phys.*, 26, (fol. 59ra). In Aristotle the principle that no science establishes its own subject (*Posterior Analytics*, i, 10. 76b11-13) seems restricted to the particular sciences and does not apply to the primary philosophy. Cf. *Metaphysics*, E. 1. 1025b7-8 and St. Thomas, *In VI Metaphys.*, lect. 1 (Cathala no. 1151).

116   Cf. Cajetan, *In ST*, I, q.2, a.3, comm. I (ed. Leonine, IV, 32a).

117   *CG*, I, cap. 13 (ed. Leonine, p. 3348-52).

118   *In ST*, I, q.2, a.3, comm. III (ed. Leonine, IV, 32b). The text is given in note 10. Cajetan's interpretation, however, does not by any means represent a unanimous Thomistic tradition at the time. C. Javellus writes: "Quantum ad rationes B. Tho. Aduerte quod licet expositor teneat has rationes non efficaciter concludere expresse Deum esse, quoniam prima et secunda non deducunt nisi ad primum corpus, id est, caelum, et animam intellectiuam, et similiter aliae non concludunt, sed tantum concludunt quaedam praedicata quae pro veritate sunt propria Deo non curando quomodo vel qualiter sint tamen sequendo doctrinam Capr. I di. 3 q. 1 melius est quod sustineas has esse sufficientes..." (*In I ST*, 2, 3 [Lyons, 1588] p. 8b33-40). Javellus (*In Phys.* VIII, 3, [Venice, 1555, fol. 194vb-195ra] and *In Metaphys.*, XII, q.3 [Venice, 1568, fol. 320vb-322vb) maintains that St. Thomas does not conclude to the first principle from physical motion only, but goes on to metaphysical motion, which is necessary for the demonstration.

119   Cf. nn. 40 and 91, 45 and 112 above.

120   *Disp. Metaphys.*, XXIX, 1, 17 (ed. Vives, XXVI, 25-27). Cf. *ibid.*, XVIII, 7, 36 (XXV, 642a) and 52 (648a).

121   "Dato etiam quod quilibet intelligat hoc nomine *Deus* significari hoc quod dicitur, scilicet illud quo maius cogitari non potest; non tamen propter hoc sequitur quod intelligat id quod significatur per nomen, esse in rerum natura; sed in apprehensione intellectus tantum. Nec potest argui quod sit in re, nisi daretur quod sit in re aliquid quo maius cogitari non potest: quod non est datum a ponentibus Deum non esse" (*ST*, I, q.2, a.1 ad 2).

122   The Anselmian argument criticized by St. Thomas is not exactly the same as the Cartesian. "That than which nothing greater can be thought" is a notion that is indefinite rather than positively infinite. Descartes (*Meditations*, ed. Ch. Adam and P. Tannery [Paris, 1897-1910], III, 48-49 and IX, 36), on the other hand, means his idea of God to be not merely a negation of the finite, but a true idea of the infinite objectively and representatively.

123   "... videtur non nimis improprie dici posse *sui causa*. Ubi tamen est notandum, non intelligi conservationem quae fiat per positivum ullum causae efficientis influxum, sed tantum quod Dei essentia sit talis, ut non possit non semper existere" (*Primae Responsiones*, 143; ed. Adam-Tannery, VII, 16-19 and IX, 87).

124   *Disp. Metaphys.*, XXIX, 1, 2-6 (ed. Vives, XXVI, 22-23).

125   *Ibid.*, 7 (p. 23a).

126   *Ibid.*, 8-17 (pp. 23-26).

127   *Ibid.*, 7 (p. 23a).

128   *Ibid.*, XVIII, 7, 4 (ed. Vives, XXV, 632). Cf. *ibid.*, 19 ff. (635 ff).

129   "Quia ergo vanum est Aristotelem adducere hic ad conclusionem hanc generaliter proban-

dum, quod nihil movet se, cum in simplicibus motis nihil valeat, sicut in potentiis animae, cum etiam in quibuscumque quantis..." (*Metaphys.*, IX, 14, 16 (ed. Vives, VII, 595a]).

"... et sensui concordat quod grave a se movetur, et secundum Aristotelem in 8. Physicorum: *Fatuum est quaerere rationem, ubi habetur sensus;* et concordat rationi... et movet actione aequivoca, et ipsum est capax termini illius actionis; ergo sic movebit se" (*ibid.*, 10 [589b-90a]).

Cf. also *Opus Oxon.*, I, 3, 9, 3, 27-30 (Quaracchi, I, 453-56 [no. 501]); II, 2, 10 (II, 196-208 [nos. 199-208]); II, 25, 1 (II, 687-95 [nos. 3-15]).

130   "... praecise sumendo utrumque actum scilicet virtualem et formalem, virtualis perfectior est; quando tamen est limitatus, non est ita perfectus, ut omnem potentiam subjecti excludat respectu formalis, quia ille formalis aliqua perfectio est, inquantum distinguitur a virtuali, et ita secundum illum proprium grandum ejus non perficeretur subjectum, quod haberet solum virtualem" (*Metaphys.*, IX, 14, 22 [ed. Vives, VII, 599b]).

131   *Ibid.*, 10-13 (589-92). As to Aristotle, see the texts in notes 46 to 49 above.

132   "... ex ratione actus virtualis et formalis, numquam est repugnantia quod insint eidem, quia tunc ubique esset repugnantia"(Scotus, *Metaphys.*, IX, 14, 22 [ed. Vives, VII, 599-600]).

133   Aristotle *Metaphysics* Z. 7-9, 1033a24 ff. nn. 47-51 above.

134   "... et sic agens quodcumque aequivocum est in actu respectu effectus, non formaliter habens actum similem, quia tunc non esset agens aequivocum, sed virtualiter habens, quia scilicet formaliter habet eminentiorem. Secundum quid igitur est in potentia, et secundum quid in actu? Respondeo, est in potentia secundum terminum motus, in actu secundum principium activum aequivoce respectu termini" (*Metaphys.*, IX, 14, 18 [ed. Vives, VII, 596b]).

Neglect of the Scotistic and Aristotelian background (e.g., A. Breuer, *Der Gottesbeweis bei Thomas und Suarez* [Freiburg: St. Paulusdruckerei, 1929] pp. 11-12) makes the treatment in Suarez seem very superficial.

135   Cf. Scotus: "Si dicatur quarto, quod generans movet, quomodo effectus in actu erit sine causa in actu? Dices, dedit virtutem. Verum est, generavit, et quando generavit, fuit; nunc non est, quomodo nunc movet? (*Metaphys.*, IX, 14, 10 [ed. Vives, VII, 589b]). Suarez: "... nulla causa agens particularis habet a se virtutem agendi, sed ab alio supposito, neque etiam potest per se agere sine concursu superioris causae, ut infra constabit ex his quae de Deo et prima causa dicemus" (*Disp. Metaphys.*, XVIII, 7, 52 [ed. Vives, XXV, 648a]).

For a discussion of the "actus virtualis," cf. the fifth part (chap. 20) of L. Fuetscher's *Akt und Potenz* (Innsbruck: F. Rauch, 1933); and for a treatment following it into a modern background, P. Descoqs, *Praelectiones Theologiae Naturalis* (Paris: Beauchesne, 1932-35), I, 306-10.

These reflections may help to understand Aristotle's preoccupation (e.g., *Metaphysics* Λ.5. 101a15-16 and *De Generatione Animalium* i.2. 716a16-17) with the role played by the sun and the heavens in generation.

136   Still further removed from the *prima via* is the cosmological argument criticized by Kant (*Kritik der reinein Vernunft*, A603-12). This argument has its starting point not in things in themselves, but only in phenomena, which of course have much less actuality than that which emerges even from the Aristotelain analysis of sensible things. The cosmological argument is therefore from its very start an argument radically different from the *prima via* of St. Thomas. Similarly, any interpretation which starts from a "réification statique"(E. Le Roy, *Revue de Métaphysique et de Morale*, XV [1907], 132) of the acts involved in sensible motion does not at all approach the thought of St. Thomas.

137   "Ex hoc autem apparet manifeste falsitas opinionis illorum. qui posuerunt Aristotelem sensisse, quod Deus non sit causa substantiae caeli, sed solum motus ejus" (*In VI Metaphys.*, lect. 1 [Cathala no. 1164]).

"Ex quo patet quod quamvis Aristoteles poneret mundum aeternum, non tamen credidit quod Deus non sit causa essendi ipsi mundo, sed causa motus eius tantum, ut quidam dixerunt" (*In VIII Phys.*, lect. 3 [ed. Leonine, no. 6]).

"Non ergo existimandum est quod Plato et Aristoteles propter hoc quod posuerunt substantias materiales, sea etiam coelestia corpora semper fuisse, eis substraxerint causam essendi" (*De Substantiis Separatis*, cap. 7; ed. J. Perrier, no. 53 [*Opuscula*, I 157]).

A glance at these texts should be sufficient to discourage any attempt at applying a "development" theory to the present problem—namely, that as St. Thomas studied the Aristotelian texts more closely and more directly, he gradually came to realize that the Stagirite's prime movent was not the Christian God.

138   F. van Steenberghen, *Revue Philosophique de Louvain*, XLV (1947), 310.

139   "Dicimus enim non entia esse intelligibilia vel opinabilia, aut etiam concupiscibilia, sed non dicimus ea esse mota. Quia, cum moveri significet esse actu, sequeretur quod non entia actu essent actu; quod patet esse falsum" (*In IX Metaphys.*, lect. 3 [Cathala no. 1806]).

"... verbi gratia, si dicatur, quod omne quod est in potentia, reducitur ad actum per ens actu, et ex hoc concluderetur quod Deus esset ens actu, cum per ipsum omnia in esse educantur" (*De Pot.*, VII, a.7).

"In omni autem actione esse in actu est principaliter intentum et ultimum in generatione: nam, eo habito, quiescit agentis actio, et motus patientis. Est igitur esse proprius effectus primi agentis, scilicet Dei: et omnia quae dant esse, hoc habent inquantum agunt in virtute Dei"(*CG*, III, cap. 66 [ed. Leonine, 188b5-11]). Cf. *CG*, II, cap. 6.

A doctrinal exposition of the existential nature of the conclusion is to be found in the "Third Observation" to the *prima via* in Gerard Smith, S.J., *Natural Theology* (New York: Macmillan, 1951), pp. 108-14.

Notes—The Starting Point of the Prima Via

1   "The Conclusion of the *Prima via*," *The Modern Schoolman*, XXX (1952-53), 33-53; 109-121; 203-215. See above pp. 142-168 ed.

2   "Sed contra est quod dicitur *Exodi* III, ex persona Dei: *Ego sum qui sum.*" St. Thomas, *ST*, I, 2, 3. On the solidarity of this interpretation of the Scriptural text with Christian philosophical tradition, see C. J. De Vogel, "'Ego sum qui sum' et sa signification pour une philosophie chrétienne,"*Revue des Sciences Religieuses*, XXXV (1961), 346-354. It is St. Thomas' own understanding of the text rather than its meaning in the original Hebrew, that is pertinent here. This way of viewing the conclusion of the *prima via* gives the answer to the question of Walter Kaufmann, *Critique of Religion and Philosophy* (New York, 1958), p.108, who, after noting that in Aristotle the argument infers the existence of over forty unmoved movents, asks: "Is not Thomas arbitrary in supposing that there is but one?" It is hardly a case in which "logical argument has been forsaken" (ibid.) and the threat imposed that one must either understand this to be God or be burnt. One should follow out rather the implications of Kaufmann's correct observations that we become involved in St. Thomas' own metaphysics in this adaptation of Aristotle's argument (ibid.), that "the premises must be interpreted as containing a great deal of Aquinas' metaphysics in a nutshell" (p.111), and that the *prima via* "is in fact a world view in miniature" (p.109), not able to be assessed independently of St. Thomas' metaphysics as a whole. The understanding of the *Summa* form as a summary of reasoning developed elsewhere is familiar enough; e.g."Ea enim quae in Summa Theologica summatim Angelicus exponit multa praesupponunt quae alibi fusius tradit." A. Bogliolo, "De Numero Viarum S. Thomae ad Probandum Existentiam Dei," *Doctor Communis*, III (1950), 192.

3   "...aliquod primum movens, quod a nullo movetur: et hoc omnes intelligunt Deum." *ST*, I, 2, 3c. In book *lambda* (6, 1071b 18-20) of the *Metaphysics*, Aristotle, while not using the expression "pure actuality," concludes to a nature that is actuality alone: "...even if it acts, this will not be enough, if its essence is potency; for there will not be *eternal* movement, since that which is potentially may possibly not be. There must, then, be such a principle, whose very essence is actuality" (Oxford tr.). Having established this kind of substance on the basis of the *eternity* of cosmic motion, Aristotle can go on to the question (ibid., 8, 1073a 14-15) whether it is one or more than one, and, if more than one how many.

4   Against the Platonic background, the possibility of a self-movent as primary movent had to be excluded. The wording of the conclusion in the *Summa Theologiae* does exclude it. The *Contra Gentiles* (I, 13, Sed quia Deus) expresses the Aristotelian conclusion as follows: "Oportet igitur esse *primum motorem separatum omnino immobilem, qui Deus est.*"

To regard creatures as potential in respect of existence and operation is not to presuppose a real distinction between the creature's essence and existence, but merely to take account of the fact that sensible things begin to exist and cease to exist, start activities and end them.

5   Cajetan, *In ST*, I, 2, 3, comm. III (ed. Leonine, IV, 32b), and F. Van Steenberghen, *Dieu Caché* (Louvain & Paris, 1961), pp. 187; 216-220, require a further reasoning process to show that the primary movent is God. Duns Scotus (*Ord.*, I, 2, 1-2, no. 58; ed. Vaticana, II, 164. 5-165. 3) has to make use of a "coloring" (ibid., nos. 137-139; II, 208. 16-211. 1) of the Anselmian argument to establish the existence of the primary efficient cause. For Kaufmann, on the other hand, a critical examination shows that the primary movent is not the God of the Bible: "What Thomas describes is clearly not the God of Job, nor the God of Abraham, Issac, and Jacob." Op. cit., p.135; cf. pp. 115-116.

6   See *ST*, I, 2, 1, ad 2m. Fundamental in this respect is the radical distinction between the sources of knowledge of quiddity and knowledge of existence for St. Thomas: "Cum in re duo sint, quidditas rei, et esse ejus, his duobus respondet duplex operatio intellectus. Una...qua apprehendit quidditates rerum...Alia autem comprehendit esse rei,..." *In I Sent.*, d. 38, q. 1, a. 3, Solut.; ed. Mandonnet, I, 903. Cf.: "Sed intellectus noster...non apprehendit illud esse nisi componendo et dividendo" (ibid., ad 2m; I, 904). Likewise: "Prima quidem operatio respicit ipsam naturam rei...Secunda vero operatio respicit ipsum esse rei,...*In Boeth. de Trin.*, V, 3c; ed. Decker, p. 182. 6-10. The twofold origin of intellectual knowledge prevents quidditative cognition, even when represented in expansion to the infinite, from passing over to the existential realm on the strength of its own content.

7   Art. cit., *The Modern Schoolman*, XXX (1953), 212-214. See above pp. 166-168 Ed. Cf. "...les *cinq voies* sont probantes. Lorsqu'elles enchaînent: 'Il y a du fini, du contingent; celui-ci dépend dans son être d'une cause qui le transcende; donc cette cause existe et elle est l'être même, c'est-à-dire Dieu,' elles ont validement prouvé l'existence de Dieu." J. Defever, *La Preuve Réelle de Dieu* (Paris, 1953), p. 8.

8   T.C. O'Brien, in *The New Scholasticism*, XXXVIII (1964), 271. Cf. "...la notion clef *d'esse*, ou acte d'être, n'est invoqué dans aucune d'entre elles. E. Gilson, "La preuve du 'De ente et essentia,'" *Doctor Communis*, III (1950), 258. Gilson contrasts the respective starting points: "Au lieu de la contingence métaphysique de l'existence par rapport à l'essence finie, saint Thomas part d'une évidence physique et sensible" (ibid.). On the other side: "Uno è infatti in tutte le Vie il punto di partenza, cioè la creatura considerata metafisicamente,...Insomma le cinque Vie ci appaiono come altretanti aspetti o forme di un unico argomento." I. Bonetti, "Indole metafisica delle prove dell'esistenza di Dio," *Doctor Communis*, III (1950), 115.

9   "...sicut calidum in actu, ut ignis, facit lignum, quod est calidum in potentia, esse actu calidum...sicut baculus non movet nisi per hoc quod est motus a manu." *ST*, I, 2, 3c. The example of the cane is taken from Aristotle, *Ph.*, VIII 5, 256a 6-32. That of fire and heating is used at *Ph.*, VIII 1, 251a 29-32. "Wood", however, fits in rather as an example of something being burnt; cf. *Mete.*, IV 9, 387a 18, and *Ph.*, VIII 1, 251a 15-16 and 251b 32-33.

10   *Ord.*, I, 2, 1-2, nos. 56-58; II, 161. 10- 164. 14. The preoccupation of Scotus is to have premises that are necessary, not contingent — "sic procedendo ex necessariis" (no. 56, p. 162. 5), "et sunt ex necessariis" (no. 58, p.164. 15).

11   *Ph.*, III 1, 201a 10-11. Cf. VIII 1, 251a 9-10. The Aristotelian definition is explicitly mentioned by St. Thomas in his earliest use of the argument from motion in proving the unchangeableness of God, *In I Sent.*, d. 8, q. 3, a. 1, Contra & Solut.; I, 211. It is included in the argument as presented in *CG*, I, 13, *Tertio*. See also texts infra., n. 16.

12   "Nihil enim movetur, nisi secundum quod est in potentia ad illud ad quod movetur; movet autem aliquid secundum quod est actu. Movere enim nihil aliud est quam educere aliquid de potentia in actum." *ST*, I, 2, 3c. The notion that a thing "imparts motion insofar as it is in actuality" is stated as though it could be taken for granted in the Aristotelian setting of the argument, in which any nature exercises its activity as long as nothing is hindering. See *Ph.*, VIII 4, 255b 3-256a 3. So, in *De Pot.*, II, 1C, St. Thomas regards the notion as a consequence of the communicative nature of actuality: "Dicendum, quod natura cuiuslibet actus est, quod seipsum communicet quantum possibile est. Unde unumquodque agens agit secundum quod in actu est." On the explanation through "virtual act," see R. Effler, *John Duns Scotus and the Principle "Omne quod Movetur ab Alio Movetur"* (St. Bonaventure, N. Y., 1962), pp.81-89.

13   "In praecedentibus enim libris *Aristoteles* locutus fuerat de motu in communi, *non applicando ad res;* nunc autem inquirens an motus semper fuerit, *applicat* communem considera-

tionem motus ad esse quod habet in rebus." *In VIII Phys.*, lect. 1, Angeli-Pirotta no. 1975.

14 "Est igitur communis suppositio in Scientia Naturali, quod motus habeat esse in rebus." Ibid., no. 1976.

15 "Sed sicut dictum est, ipsum esse non acquisiverunt per mutationem vel motum...et sic non sequitur quod ante primam mutationem sit aliqua mutatio." Ibid., lect. 2, no. 2046. Because motion can begin to exist ("incipiat de novo esse motus," ibid.) in a way other than through a preceding motion, it need not be eternal for St. Thomas. The existential viewpoint in the approach to the consideration of motion enables St. Thomas to reason about the eternity of the world in a way so different from that of the Aristotelian *Physics.*

16 Aristotle, *Ph.*, III 2, 201b 31-32; VIII 5, 257b 8-9; *De An.*, II 5, 417a 16. Cf.: "Sed hic loquitur de motu *secundum quod est actus imperfecti* id est existentis *in potentia.*" St. Thomas, *In VIII Phys.*, lect. 1, no. 1779. "...est actus imperfectus, quia est actus ejus inquantum adhuc est in potentia." Ibid., lect. 10, no. 2218. See also references infra, n. 17.

17 *Ph.*, III 1, 201a 16-18; b7-13. Cf.: "Ipse igitur actus imperfectus caloris in calefactibili existens *est motus*; non quidem secundum id quod iam actu tantum est, sed secundum quod iam in actu existens habet ordinem in ulteriorem actum: quia si tolleretur ordo ad ulteriorem actum, ipse actus quantumcumque imperfectus, esset terminus motus et non motus, sicut accidit cum aliquid semiplene calefit." St. Thomas, *In III Phys.*, lect. 2, no. 560. See also nos. 559 and 561.

18 "Quaelibet autem forma signata non intelligitur in actu nisi per hoc quod esse ponitur." *De Pot.*, VII, 2, ad 9m. "Quia vero actualitas, quam principaliter significat hoc verbum EST, est communiter actualitas, omnis formae, vel actus substantialis vel accidentalis,..." *In I Periherm.*, lect. 5, Leonine no. 22.

19 "...esse est actualitas omnis formae vel naturae: non enim bonitas vel humanitas significatur in actu, nisi prout significamus eam esse." *ST*, I, 3, 4c. "Nihil enim habet actualitatem, nisi inquantum est. Unde ipsum esse est actualitas omnium rerum et etiam ipsarum formarum." *ST*, I, 4, 1, ad 3m.

20 "Hoc autem est esse, ad quod generatio et omnis motus terminatur: omnis enim forma et actus est in potentia antequam esse acquirat." *CG*, II, 52. Item cum omne. Cf.: "Generatio per se loquendo est vis in esse, et corruptio via in non esse: non enim generationis terminus est forma, et corruptionis privatio, nisi quia forma facit esse et privatio non esse: dato enim quod aliqua forma non faceret esse, non diceretur generari quod talem formam acciperet." *CG*, I, 26, Item generatio. See also *In IV Metaph.*, lect. 2, no. 551.

21 See Aristotle, *Metaphysics Z* 17, 1041b 7-28; H 3, 1043b 13-14; 6, 1045a 29-33.

22 The Platonic source material is collected in René Arnou, *De Quinque Viis Sancti Thomae* (Rome, 1932), pp. 11-20. On Scotus, see supra, n. 10, and on Cajetan and Suarez my discussion in art. cit., *The Modern Schoolman*, XXX (1953), 203-211. See above pp. 153-166 Ed. Kant's (*KRV*, B 632-640) reduction of the argument, under the title of "cosmological proof," to the ontological argument, is well-known. The same process may be seen in C. D. Broad, *Religion, Philosophy and Psychical Research* (London, 1953), pp. 176-189, with the express reduction of the cosmological argument "historically, to a physical argument of Aristotle's about motion" (p. 183).

23 "Calor enim facit calidum esse, et aedificator facit domum esse. Conveniunt ergo in hoc quod causant esse, sed differunt in hoc quod ignis causat ignem, et aedificator causat domum....Et propter hoc dicitur...quod primus effectus est esse, et non est ante ipsum creatum aliquid." *De Pot.*, VIII, 2, c. Cf. texts on primacy of being, infra, n. 49.

24 Cf. "...cum volumus significare quamcumque formam vel actum actualiter inesse alicui subiecto, significamus illud per hoc verbum EST." *In I Periherm.*, lect. 5, no. 22.

25 "...ultimus autem actus est ipsum esse. Cum enim omnis motus sit exitus de potentia in actum, oportet illud esse ultimum actum, in quod tendit omnis motus." *Comp. Theol.*, I, 11.

26 T. C. O'Brien, *Metaphysics and the Existence of God* (Washington, D.C., 1960), p.253, claims "St. Thomas himself states that that God is subsistent *esse* is proved (*probatur*) by reason of His being the unmoved mover," in the sense that "the formalities involved must be distinct in order that there be proof." The text referred to is: "Unde si esset unus calor per se existens, oporteret ipsum esse causam omnium calidorum, quae per modum participationis calorem habent. Est autem ponere aliquod ens quod est ipsum suum esse; quod ex hoc probatur, quia oportet esse aliquod primum ens quod sit actus purus, in quo nulla sit compositio" (*De Pot.*, III, 5). There is no mention of the unmoved mover, the reason is given as that of Avicenna, and the example of the

"calor per se existens" would model it on the *quarta via* rather than on the *prima via*. The reasoning seems to proceed directly to a pure actuality that is subsistent existence, without any composition. Fr O'Brien likewise claims that "the same thing is said" in *Comp. Theol.*, cc. 3, 6, and 11. Yet there is no mention of subsistent being in cc. 3 and 6; and in c. 6 the reasoning seems modeled rather on the *tertia via*. In c. 11, the reasoning is from being as the ultimate actuality to which motion tends (text supra, n. 25) and from being as ultimate actuality the conclusion is "oportet igitur, quod essentia divina, quae est actus purus et ultimus, sit ipsum esse." There is no reasoning in these texts from a primary movent to subsistent being.

The claim (O'Brien, p. 252) that the text of St. Thomas "Et propter hoc moveri non attribuitur non existentibus...Quia, cum moveri significet esse actu, sequeretur quod non entia actu essent actu" (*In IX Metaph.*, lect. 3, Cathala no. 1806) is "simply irrelevant" to the existential interpretation of the starting point of the *prima via*, would mean that St. Thomas is remaining strictly within Aristotle's understanding of the expressions used. What the text states is that "being moved" is not attributed to nonexistents, since it means to be in actuality. The text from the *Contra Gentiles*, apparently brought under the same charge of irrelevance (O'Brien, p. 252, n. 122), occurs in a setting that requires "esse in actu" to be interpreted according to St. Thomas' own doctrine of being: "In omni autem actione esse in actu est principaliter intentum, et ultimum in generatione: nam, eo habito, quiescit agentis actio et motus patientis" (*CG*, III, 66, Adhuc). The motion ceases when what is *initially* intended, namely the being of the effect, has been attained.

One may with Aristotle, Scotus (see Effler, op. cit., pp. 90-91), or Suarez unhesitatingly acknowledge the existence of things and still proceed unaware of the distinctive problems to which existence, when taken as originally grasped through judgment, gives rise. Scotus (*Ord.*), I, 2, 1-2, no. 56; ed. Vaticana, II, 161. 9-162. 5) can note the contingency of produced existence, and yet deliberately set aside the actual existence as operative in his proof that God exists.

27   William P. Alston, "The Ontological Argument Revisited," *The Philosophical Review*, LXIX (1960), 454.

28   "...est sicut esse proprium rei." Avicenna, *Metaph.*, I, 6c; fol. 72vl (Venice, 1508). So, in Giles of Rome, *Quodl.*, V, 3 (Louvain, 1646), p. 273a, a created nature has actuality of its own, sufficient to make it intelligible, but to which further actuality is added to make it exist: "Dicimus enim quod natura creata, licet sit tantae actualitatis quod possit per se intelligi: non sit tamen tantae actualitatis, quod possit existere in rerum natura, nisi superaddatur ei actualitas aliqua, quae communi nomine vocatur esse."

29   See texts supra, n. 6, and *ST*, II-II, 83, 1, arg. 3 (infra, n. 30). For convenience today the distinction between the two acts of cognition may be expressed as the distinction between conceptualization and judgment. In St. Thomas' own terminology, however, the word "concept," as a general term for the *verbum* expressed in any act of human intellection, is applied likewise to what is expressed in a judgment. For a discussion of this question, see E. Gilson, *Being and Some Philosophers*, Appendix, 2nd ed. (Toronto, 1952). pp. 217-223.

30   "Sed intellectus noster, cujus cognitio a rebus oritur, quae esse compositum habent, non apprehendit illud esse nisi componendo et dividendo." *In I Sent.*, d. 38, q. 1, a. 3, ad 2m; ed. Mandonnet, I, 904. "Secunda vero est compositio et divisio, per quam scilicet apprehenditur aliquid esse vel non esse." *ST*, II-II, 83, 1, arg. 3. "Intellectus enim habet judicare, et hoc dicitur sapere et apprehendere, et dicitur intelligere." *In III De An.*, lect. 4, Pirotta no. 629. "...secundum hanc operationem intellectus aliquid intelligere." *In IV Metaph.*, lect. 6, Cathala no. 605.

31   "Esse autem nostrum habet aliquid sui extra se: deest enim aliquid quod jam de ipso praeteriit, et quod futurum est." *In I Sent.*, d. 8, q. 1, a. 1, Solut.; ed. Mandonnet, I, 195. On this topic, see my discussion in "Diversity and Community of Being in St. Thomas Aquinas," *Mediaeval Studies*, XXII (1960), 289-297. See above pp. 97-131 Ed.

32   See texts supra, nn. 6 and 30.

33   Supra, n. 27.

34   Texts supra, nn. 18, 19, 24-26. In the sixth edition of *Le Thomisme* (Paris, 1965), p.97, n. 85, Gilson writes: "Je n'admets plus ce que j'écrivais alors (p. 119): 'les preuves thomistes de l'existence de Dieu se développent immédiatement sur le plan existentiel'; ce n'est pas exact si l'on entend par là, comme je l'entendais alors, que ces preuves supposent admis l'*esse* thomiste." The scope of this revision, as the words themselves testify, is limited to an existential level that would

start the demonstration with the real distinction between a thing and its being. Gilson's footnote goes on to explain clearly that only after the proof for the existence of God is one able to acquire knowledge of the real distinction between essence and being in creatures. In the fifth edition of *Le Thomisme* (Paris, 1944), p. 119, after the completion of the proof, Gilson mentioned that "les preuves thomistes de l'existence de Dieu rejoignent un autre ordre de considérations," in which the distinction between essence and existence in caused beings is shown. It was quite possible, and was in fact the experience of more than one reader, to go through Gilson's treatment of the *quinque viae* in the fifth edition without finding anything to imply that an understanding of the "plan existentiel" (p. 119) or "ordre existentiel" (p. 60) commenced with a real distinction between essence and existence. Rather, the statements there seemed based clearly on existence as immediately known through judgment (cf. pp. 61-62), without any attempt to show that existence was really distinct from essence. On the distinctions made in St. Thomas' procedure in this question, see my article "Quiddity and Real Distinction in St. Thomas Aquinas," *Mediaeval Studies*, XXVII (1965), 1-22.

35   "Whatever else is true, in the two *summae* St. Thomas wrote theology, and the philosophy that in these works if *formally* theology and *only materially* philosophy." A.C. Pegis, "*Sub Ratione Dei*: A Reply to Professor Anderson," *The New Scholasticism*, XXXIX (1965), 153. The whole article (pp. 141-157) is a cogent demonstration of this tenet and a discussion of its crucial bearing upon the modern interpretations of St. Thomas.

36   "In an early work, the little treatise *On Being and Essence*, St. Thomas asked the meaning of essence and existence as metaphysical notions." A. C. Pegis, *St. Thomas and Philosophy* (Milwaukee, 1964), p. 3.

37   *De Ente et Essentia*, Prooemium; ed. Roland-Gosselin, pp. 1-2.

38   Supra, n. 36.

39   "They...wrote many purely philosophical discussions." A. C. Pegis, *The Middle Ages and Philosophy* (Chicago, 1963), p. 23. This sentence was meant as part of a summary of Gilson's reflections.

40   *De Ente*, c. I; p. 3. 13-14. There seems no other way of translating *ens* conveniently here than by "being." In this sense "being" denotes all that exists, in the way "all existence" would signify all existents. The inconvenience is the use of "being" to translate *esse* later in the work. J. Bobik, *Aquinas on Being and Essence* (Notre Dame, 1965), uses "being" to translate *ens* and "existence" to translate *esse*. This use of two different verbs tends to obscure the common notion that runs through both expressions, for existence is the only kind of being in St. Thomas.

41   "...causatum dico sicut a causa efficiente." *De Ente*, c. IV; p. 35. 7-8.

42   "...oportet quod sit aliqua res que sit causa essendi omnibus rebus ex eo quod ipsa est esse tantum;...et hec est causa prima que Deus est." *De Ente*, c. IV; p. 35. 13-19.

43   "Dialectic," as St. Thomas understood the term against the Aristotelian background, meant reasoning from probable premises, and resulted not in scientific knowledge but in belief or opinion. See *In Post. Analyt.*, Prooemium, Leonine no. 6. In the present sense, however, "dialectic" studies the formal sequence in which one notion follows upon another, a sequence that is necessary and not just probable. From this viewpoint it may be compared with St. Thomas' view of mathematical sequence in regard to abstraction from existence: "Unicuique autem competit habere causam agentem, secundum quod habet esse. Licet igitur ea quae sunt mathematica habeant causam agentem, non tamen secundum habitudinem quam habent ad causam agentem, cadunt sub consideratione mathmatici." *ST*, I, 44, 1, ad. 3m.

Though existence lies outside the order dealt with by logic, this does not at all mean that reasoning based on existence can escape the control of logical rules. To reject logical criticism of an argument on the score that the argument itself is not about logical relations would of course be "mere impertinence," as noted by Peter Geach, "Nominalism," *Sophia* (Melbourne), III (1964), 10. Geach refers to an unidentified discussion of the *tertia via* of Aquinas. The issue, however, is the same as in the *prima via*, or in the *De Ente et Essentia*. It is whether aspects dealt with by logic or by mathematics or by a phenomenology or by a dialectic of concepts can lead to a cause external to the thing immediately known. A negative answer does not at all imply that the structure of an argument from the thing's existence can elude the norms of logic. Conversely, correct logical structure of a proof, say for the historical existence of Socrates, does not make it an argument in the realm of logic.

44   The extensive controversies in recent years on the ontological argument and existence as a predicate make this situation very noticable. The various positions brought to the fore in the contemporary discussions may be seen in the collection *The Ontological Argument*, ed. A. Plantinga (New York, 1965).

45   See reference to the reduction of the "cosmological" argument to the ontological in Kant and C. D. Broad, supra, n. 22. The impasse arises from the impossibility of having a further concept determine the general concept of existence to express the fact that something does exist. "There is no concept whose addition to that of existence can make it signify actual existence, because no concept can signify it." E. Gilson, *Being and Some Philosophers*, 2nd ed. (Toronto, 1952), p. 198.

46   See *De Ente*, c. IV; p. 34. 7-14. The starting point is the nature of sensible things, of which existence is not a part.

47   *ST*, I, 47, 1, ad 3m. As the distinction here is between demonstration and probable reasoning, it does not bring out any reason why demonstration from effects should be excluded. The common aspect that enables the effects to serve as middle term, in this case being, constitutes them all under the one means of demonstration.

48   "...quia sic aliqua res esset causa sui ipsius." *De Ente*, c. IV; p. 35. 8. To impart existence means to make something exist. So, in regard to the divine causality: "...ipse est principium dans esse, et per consequens creans omnia alia quae ad esse sunt superaddita." *In I Sent.*, d. 37, q. 3, a. 2, Solut.; ed. Mandonnet, I, 874. "...Deus simul dans esse producit id quod esse recipit." *De Pot.*, III, 1, ad 17m. "...ex hoc ipso quod quidditati esse attribuitur, non solum esse, sed ipsa quidditas creari dicitur." Ibid., 5, ad 2m.

49   "Primus autem effectus est ipsum esse, quod omnibus aliis effectibus praesupponitur..." *De Pot.*, III, 4c. "Primus autem effectus Dei in rebus est ipsum esse, quod omnes alii effectus praesupponunt, et supra quod fundantur." *Comp. Theol.*, c. LXVIII. "Id autem quod est commune omnibus intelligentiis distinctis est esse creatum primum, de quo quidem praemittit talem propositionem: Prima rerum creatarum est esse et non est ante ipsam creatum aliud." *In Lib. De Causis*, IV; ed. Saffrey, p. 27. 8-11. Cf. "Omnis enim nobilitas cuiuscumque rei est sibi secundum suum esse." *CG*, I, 28, Omnis enim. It is true that the *notio entis* precedes the "two-fold content of the notion of *ens*, essence and *actus essendi*," as Fabro, "The Transcendentality of *Ens-Esse* and the Ground of Metaphysics," *International Philosophical Quarterly*, VI (1966), 426, notes. But this is because the intellect has to conceive each of the components as an already constituted "something."

50   "Ad quod dicendum, quod accidens dicitur hic quod non est de intellectu alicujus, sicut rationale dicitur animali accidere; et ita cuilibet quidditati creatae accidit esse, quia non est de intellectu ipsius quidditatis." *In I Sent.*, d. 8, expos. Iae partis textus; I, 209. "Et quod Hilarius dicit, dico quod accidens dicitur large omne quod non est pars essentiae; et sic est esse in rebus creatis..." *Quodl.*, XII, 5c. Cf.: "...esse est accidens, non quasi per accidens se habens, sed quasi actualitas cujuslibet substantiae." *Quodl.*, II, 3, ad 2m.
Accidentality and priority, it is important to keep in mind, are here first intention notions. They are notions obtained by precisive abstraction (cf. *De Ente*, c. II; pp. 12. 5-23. 4), and are concerned directly with what is found in the real world. They are here not second intention notions, like individual, species, differentia, genus. Accidentality is found in the real world, for instance in quantity or action or relation in respect of substance. Likewise, priority is found in the real world, for instance in substance with regard to predicamental accidents. The accidentality and priority, therefore, characterize existence as found in the real sensible world. They are not just the relations between concepts formed in the human mind. Yet the direct knowledge that the accidentality and priority of existence is real, does not immediately show a real distinction between existence and thing. Sensible things are known to acquire existence and lose existence, and to be definable without inclusion of existence, even though no real distinction between their essence and existence is evident. Likewise their existence, known in this initial way as really accidental, cannot be regarded as following upon an already posited nature. It is known as prior in reality to the nature even though it is not known as really distinct from it. The situation, accordingly, does not justify the assertion "il n'y a pas de preuve plus directe ni plus profonde de l'existence de Dieu que la distinction réelle entre l'essence des choses et leur existence,..." St. -M. Gillet, *Thomas d'Aquin* (Paris, 1949), p. 67.

51   See text supra, n. 15.

52   Aristotle, *Ph.*, VII 1, 241b 24. See St. Thomas, *In VII Phys.*, lect. 1, Angeli-Pirotta nos. 1776-1778.

53   Cf.: "Et quia omne quod est per aliud reducitur ad illud quod est per se sicut ad causam primam,..." *De Ente*, c. IV; p. 35. 11-13. The model is the standard Aristotelian example of fire as the primary instance of heat, and accordingly the cause of heat for all other things; see Aristotle, *Metaph.*, a. 1, 993b 24-26. So St. Thomas: "...omnia ignita per participationem reducuntur ad ignem, qui est per essentiam talis." *In Joan.*, Prol.; ed. Vivès, XIX, 670b.

54   Gilson, *Le Thomisme*, 6th ed., p. 93, n. 80, draws attention to the absence of the word "cause" in the *prima via*. Yet in explaining the force of the original Aristotelian argument, St. Thomas makes the notion "cause" carry the burden of the reasoning: "...aliquid movere seipsum nihil aliud est quam esse sibi causa motus. Quod autem est sibi causa alicuius, oportet quod *primo* ei conveniat; quia quod est primum in quolibet genere est causa eorum quae sunt post. Unde ignis, qui sibi et aliis est causa caloris, est primum calidum." *In VII Phys.*, lect. 1, no. 1777. The *primum movens* is accordingly the primary cause of motion: "Erit *ergo* aliquid primum movens, quod erit prima causa motus,..." Ibid., lect. 2, no. 1782. In general: "omne quod movetur habet causam sui motus." *In VIII Phys.*, lect. 12, no. 2266. Cf. *causa, causat, causetur* in *CG*, I, 13, Quod autem necesse, ff.

The general status of the proposition "whatever is being moved is being moved by something else," in thirteenth century thought, may be found sketched briefly in Effler, op. cit., p. 19.

55   If today the term "demonstration" be restricted technically to an argument in which every premise is expressed, it will no longer apply directly to the *prima via*. But in the sense in which "proofs can be regarded as shorthand notations for demonstrations," in the word of Irving M. Copi, *Symbolic Logic* (New York, 1954), p. 215, there seems no reason for refusing to call the *prima via* a true demonstration. In the scholastic terminology of the *Summa Theologiae* (I, 2, 2-3) and of the *Contra Gentiles* (I, 13), the argument for the primary movent is described indifferently as "proving" and as "demonstrating."

56   *ST*, I, 2, 1-3. Cf. *In I Sent.*, d. 3, q. 1, aa. 1-3; I, 90-97; *CG*, I, 9-13.

57   *ST*, I, 2, 3, args. 1-2. In modern language, these two arguments have been summed up as "God is scientifically unnecessary and ethically impossible." E. Borne, *Atheism*, tr. S. J. Tester (New York, 1961), p. 25.

58   "Quia veritas de Deo per rationem investigata, a paucis, et per longum tempus, et cum admixtione multorum errorum homini perveniret..." *ST*, I, 1, 1c.

59   "Mais il est tout aussi avéré que personne, en dehors de la révélation, n'a réussi à se faire une conception pure et ferme de Dieu." J. Defever, *La Preuve Réelle de Dieu* (Paris & Brussels, 1953), p. 7.

60   "Et *praeterea*, perpetuitate temporis et motus quasi principio utitur ad probandum primum principium esse..." *In VIII Phys.*, lect. 2, no. 2043. Cf. ibid., lect. 1, no. 1990; *In XII Metaph.*, lect. 5, no. 2496; *CG*, I, 13, Praedictos. A comparison of the Aristotelian argument with the formulations of the proof from motion given by St. Thomas may be found in my article "Aquinas and the Proof from the 'Physics,'" *Mediaeval Studies*, XXVIII (1966), 119-150.

61   "Si enim mundo et motu existente sempiterno, necesse est ponere unum primum principium, multo magis sempiternitate eorum sublata." *In VIII Phys.*, lect. 1, no. 1991. "Quia si non fuerit mundus aeternus, necesse est quod fuerit productus in esse ab aliquo praeexistente." *In XII Metaph.*, lect. 5, no. 2499. "...ex suppositione aeternitatis mundi, qua posita, minus videtur manifestum quod Deus sit. Nam si mundus et motus de novo incoepit, planum est quod oportet poni aliquam causam quae de novo producat mundum et motum:...cum nihil educat se de potentia in actum, vel de non esse in esse." *CG*, I, 13, Et ad hoc.

62   See *De Pot.*, III, 5c.

63   "Et sic *terminat Philosophus* considerationem communem de rebus naturalibus in Primo Principio totius naturae, *qui est super omnia Deus...*" *In VIII Phys.*, lect. 23, no. 2550.

64   *Rom.*, I, 20. Cf. St. Thomas, *In I Sent.*, d. 3, q. 1, a. 3, arg. 1; I, 95. *In Boeth. de Trin.*, V, 4c; ed. Decker, p. 194. 17-27. *CG*, I, 12. *ST*, I, 2, 2, Sed contra.

65   See *ST*, I, 44, 1c. Cf. *De Pot.*, III, 5c; *De Subst. Sep.*, I-II; *In Joan.*, Prol.; ed. Vivès, XIX, 669b-670b.

66   *Acts*, XVII, 28. "Et hoc modo intelligendum est verbum Apostoli dicentis, *in ipso vivimus*,

movemur et sumus: quia etiam nostrum vivere, et nostrum esse, et nostrum moveri causantur a Deo." *ST*, I, 18, 4, ad lm. "...esse et vivere et moveri, non attribuuntur rebus in Deo existentibus secundum esse quod in ipso habent, sed secundum esse quod in seipsis habent a Deo,..." *In I Sent.*, d. 36, q. 1, a. 3, ad 4m; I, 837.

For a recent discussion of "proof" and "way," see M. Guérard des Lauriers, *La Preuve de Dieu et les Cinq Voies* (Rome, 1966), especially the outline of the proof's stages on p. 37.

67   *In VIII Phys.*, lect. 1-2, nos. 1990-2046; *In XII Metaph.*, lect. 5, nos. 2496-2499; *CG*, I, 13, Et ad hoc—cf. "Nam, si motus incoepit, oportet quod ab aliquo movente incoeperit" (ibid., I, 15, Ostendit). Cf. *In I Sent.*, d. 8, q. 3, aa. 1-3; I, 210-215.

68   "The modern student can see the principles that enabled St. Thomas to transform Aristotle, but he cannot find the philosophy that St. Thomas would have built had he chosen to be a philosopher." A. Pegis, *St. Thomas and Philosophy* (Milwaukee, 1964), p. 85. So, in regard to the *quinque viae:* "Les désaccords trop réels sur le sens des preuves tiennent d'abord à ce qu'on les a traitées comme des démonstrations philosophiques....il veut simplement mettre à la disposition des théologiens, soit une, soit quatre, soit cinq des manières principales dont les philosophes ont procédé pour démontrer cette vérité." E. Gilson, *Le Thomisme*, 6th ed., p. 90. "...c'est dans les perspectives du théologien qu'il a vu les cinq voies." Louis Charlier, "Les cinq voies de saint Thomas," in *L'Existence de Dieu*, ed. collège dominicain à La Sarte-Huy (Tournai, 1961), 182.

69   "Mais enfin comment faire voir ce principe? Il n'y a peut-être pas de réponse, car la lumière est cela même en quoi l'oeil voit le reste." E. Gilson, "La preuve du 'De ente et essentia,'" *Doctor Communis*, III (1950), 260.

70   "St. Thomas a donc accepté de Moyse la vérité sublime que Moyse avait accepté de Dieu, mais il a fallu son génie métaphysique pour la comprendre au sens où lui-même l'a comprise. Et pourtant, comme c'était simple! Il n'y avait qu'à prendre un verbe pour un verbe au lieu de lui substituer un nom. Car le *maxime proprium nomen Dei* est un verbe." Ibid. There is something peculiar, however, about the verb "to be." Its present participle, "being," can be used for both the actuality itself and the subject that has the actuality, just as in Latin (or French or Italian) the infinitive is used for both. This situation does not occur with other verbs.

71   *ST*, I, 1, 1c. Cf.: "Unde necesse est ad naturalem rationem recurrere, cui omnes assentire coguntur. Quae tamen in rebus divinis deficiens est." *CG*, I, 2, Contra.

72   "This impasse is an invitation to us to give up the philosophical way—from creatures to God—and try the theological way—from God to creatures." E. Gilson, *Elements of Christian Philosophy* (New York, 1960), p.131.

73   Ibid. It should be obvious that this way of concentrating upon being does not at all mean turning philosophy into theology or starting metaphysical demonstration from anything not immediately known to human cognition. No theological premise whatsoever is introduced into the reasoning.

74   "C'est qu'en effet une affirmation médiate d'existence ou d'être, comme l'est la preuve de l'existence de Dieu, ne peut être médiatisée que par l'*etre* des choses du monde de notre expérience immédiate, en tant précisément que cet être est exigence de l'affirmation d'un autre être." D. de Petter, "La charactère métaphysique de la preuve de l'existence de Dieu," *L'Existence de Dieu*, ed. collège dominicain (Tournai, 1961), p. 168. This is quite a different approach from that of a philosophical rationalism seeking a sufficient reason for the world, e.g.: "...some real Being of such a kind as to constitute the reason for the existence of the universe," Wallace I. Matson, *The Existence of God* (Ithaca, N. Y., 1965), p. 56. Not so much a reason for its existence, but rather the efficient cause that made it exist, is being sought. Hence arises the requirement of an observed existent as the starting point. Matson, however, suggests that "it is particularly appropriate that God's existence should be demonstrable by the intellect unaided by the senses." Ibid. However, even though the evidence of existence is regarded as sensible, should it be called physical in either the strict Aristotelian sense of "physical," or in the sense associated with modern science? It is certainly beyond the scope of Aristotelian matter and form. It is likewise independent of physical interpretations of the cosmos at any particular period: "Interpreted in this literal way, the first way becomes independent of any scientific hypothesis as to the structure of the universe. The starting point is the existence of change." E. Gilson, *Elements of Christian Philosophy*, p. 67.

Notes—Actuality in the Prima Via

1   The equation of form with actuality and of matter with potentiality may be seen clearly enough in Aristotle, *Metaph.* H 2,1042b9-1043a28, and the other passages listed by Bonitz, *Ind. Arist.*, 251a16-20 and 785b55-61. On the skeleton form that underlies the argument from motion both in Aristotle and in the different versions of it in St. Thomas Aquinas, see my article "Aquinas and the Proof from the 'Physics'," *Mediaeval Studies*, 28 (1966), 122-148.

2   "Nihil enim habet actualitatem, nisi inquantum est:..." *ST*, I, 4, 1, ad 3m. "...vita et scientia, et alia huiusmodi, sic appetuntur ut sunt in actu: unde in omnibus appetitur quoddam esse." *ST*, I, 5, 2, ad 4m. "Quaelibet autem forma signata non intelligitur in actu nisi per hoc quod esse ponitur." *De Pot.*, VII, 2, ad 9m.

3   "...unde ipsum esse est actualitem omnium rerum, et etiam ipsarum formarum." *ST*, I, 4, 1, ad 3m. "...esse est actualitas substantiae vel essentiae." *ST*, I, 54, 1c. "Quia vero actualitas, quam principaliter significat hoc verbum' EST, est communiter actualitas omnis formae, vel actus substantialis vel accidentalis,..." *In I Periherm.*, lect. 5, Leonine no. 22. "Unde patet quod hoc quod dico *esse* est actualitas omnium actuum,..." *De Pot.*, 7, 2, ad 9m.

On the immediate background of actus essentiae in Albert the Great, see L. G. Geiger, "La vie, acte essential de l'âme—l'*esse*, acte de l'essence d'après Albert-le-Grand,"*Etudes d'histoire littéraire et doctrinale*, 17 (1962), 49-116. Geiger notes that this formula does not give rise to any new problem in Albert: "On la trouve d'un bout à l'autre de son œuvre. Les formules, en se répétant presque identiques, montrent qu'Albert exprime là une thèse dont le fond ne semble jamais avoir fait problème pour lui:..."*Ibid.*, p. 50. The notion seems to stem from the illustration of light as used to explain being—see Geiger, p. 50, n. 11, and p. 13, n. 195. A glance at the source indicated by Geiger in Anselm shows how the expression could easily arise: "Quemadmodum enim sese habent ad invicem lux et lucere et lucens, sic sunt ad se invicem essentia et esse et ens, hoc est existens sive subsistens." *Monologion*, c. VI; ed. F. S. Schmidt (Seckau, 1938), p. 20.15-16. So, with Albert: "...sicut lucere refertur ad actum, ita et esse." *In III Sent.*, d. 2, a. 5; ed. Borgnet, 28, 27a. As long as no attention was paid to the way in which being is originally grasped through judgment, the conception of being that was expressed by the infinitive *esse* could be equated with the actuality expressed by other infinitives and then transferred from the level of operation to the level of primary actuality, without encountering any new problems.

4   "Licet alicui existenti accidat motus, tamen motus est praeter esse rei. Nullum autem corporeum est causa alicuius rei nisi inquantum movetur...Nullum igitur corpus est causa esse alicuius rei inquantum est esse, sed est causa eius quod est moveri ad esse, quod est fieri rei." *CG*, 3, 65, Adhuc licet. Cf. Comp. Theol., I, 11.

5   "Hoc autem est esse, ad quod generatio et omnis motus terminatur: omnis enim forma et actus est in potentia antequam esse acquirat." *CG*, II, 52, Item cum omne.

6   "Ultimas autem actus est ipsum esse. Cum enim omnis motus sit exitus de potentia in actum, oportet illud esse ultimum actum in quod tendit omnis motus." *Comp. Theol.*, I, 11, Verardo no. 21.

7   E.g. "Quia enim omnia accidentia sunt formae quaedam substantiae superadditae, et a principiis substantiae causatae; oportet quod eorum esse sit superadditum supra esse substantiae, et ab ipso dependens; et tanto uniuscuiusque eorum esse est prius vel posterius, quanto forma accidentalis, secundum propriam rationem, fuerit propinquior substantiae vel magis perfecta." *CG*, IV, 14, Leonine no. 7c. The relevant texts throughout the works of St. Thomas have been collected and discussed in an unpublished doctoral dissertation by Barry F. Brown, "The Being of Accidents according to St. Thomas Aquinas," University of Toronto, 1966.   From a comprehensive study of the texts, Dr. Brown concludes: "The accidental being is therefore really distinct from substantial being. Any attempt to identify the two is to forget that for St. Thomas, change is the reduction of potency not only to formal act, but also to that entitative act that is given by the formal act, be it accidental or substantial. And to forget this is to make St. Thomas implicitly deny the reality of accidental change itself. An accident *depends* in being upon substance; it is *not* one in being with it." *Ibid.*, pp. 218-219 (quoted with permission of the author). For the modern commentators who oppose this interpretation, see *ibid.*, pp. 281-283, nn. 31-39.

8   Compare, for instance these two texts from the *Summa Theologiae*: "Ad cuius evidentiam,

considerandum est quod in quolibet novem generum accidentis est duo considerare. Quorum unum est esse quod competit unicuique ipsorum secundum quod est accidens. Et hoc communiter in omnibus est inesse subiecto, accidentis enim esse est inesse" (I, 28, 2c) and "Accidens vero non habet esse, sed eo aliquid est, et hac ratione ens dictur" (I, 90, 2c). The reason lies in the way an accident, when considered by itself and made the subject of predication, has to be represented as a substance while lacking the being of a substance: "Pro tanto autem videntur accidentia in abstracto significata esse est alteri inesse, et non est possibile aliquid eorum separari a substantia; et ideo quando significantur in abstracto quasi sint secundum se entia et a substantia videtur quod sint non entia." In VII Metph., lect. 1, Cathala no. 1253. Cf. In V Metaph., lect. 9, no. 894.

9   E.g. "...sicut se habet substantia ad esse sibi debitum, ita et qualitas ad esse sui generis conveniens." In III Sent., d. 1, q. 1, a. 1, Resp.; ed, Moos, III, 8 (no. 12). Cf. CG, IV, 14, 7c (text supra, n. 7).

10   For St. Thomas every finite verb implicitly contains the notion of being: "Quamvis enim omne verbum finitum implicet esse, quia currere est currentem esse,..." In I Perihem., lect. 5, no. 18. "Quia vero quaedam praedicantur, in quibus manifeste non apponitur hoc verbum Est, ne credatur quod illae praedicationes non pertineant ad praedicationem entis, ut cum dicitur, homo ambulat, ideo consequenter hoc removet, dicens quod in omnibus huiusmodi praedicationibus significatur aliquid esse. Verbum enim quodlibet resolvitur in hoc verbum Est, et participium. Nihil enim differt dicere, homo convalescens est, et homo convalescit, et sic de aliis." In V Metaph., lect. 9, no. 893.

11   The plurality of the Aristotelian separate substances, as opposed to the unicity of the Christian God, should be enough to raise suspicions. Even today, however, a warning against confusing the philosophy of St. Thomas with that of Aristotle seems necessary, and is strongly worded by Gilson: "Nous avons dit et répété sur tous les tous pendant des siècles, que la philosophie de saint Thomas d'Aquin était celle d'Aristote. Ceux qui l'ont dit ont fini par le faire croire, et le pis est qu'eux-mémes l'ont crû. Beaucoup le croient encore aujourd'hui, à tel point qu'ils tiennent presque pour une hérésie la proposition pourtant évidente que la philosophie de saint Thomas d'Aquin n'est pas celle d'Aristote. Le langage est le même, la technique de la démonstration est semblable, mais le contenu de la doctrine est différent." E. Gilson, "Trois leçons sur le Thomisme et sa situation présente," Seminarium, IV (1965), 692-693.

12   "...a thing has a quality in a higher degree than other things if in virtue of it the similar quality belongs to the other things as well (e.g. fire is the hottest of things; for it is the cause of the heat of all other things)..." Metaph. α 1,993b24-26; Oxford tr. This passage of Aristotle, referred to explicitly by St. Thomas in the quarta via (ST, I, 2, 3,c; cf. CG, I, 13), can equally well be phrased by him in terms of the first in a genus as cause of the rest: "...illud quod est primum in quolibet genere, est causa omnium eorum quae sunt post, ut dicitur in II Metaphys." ST, III, 56, 1c. The general procedure may be seen clearly enugh in the Contra Gentiles: 'Ostensum est supra aliquid esse quod per se necesse est esse, quod Deus est. Hoc igitur esse quod necesse est, si est alicui quidditati quae non est quod ipsum est,...' (I, 22). Necessary existence has been reached as the first cause (CG, I, 15, Amplius), and then this existence is shown to belong to no quiddity that is not itself. The reasoning is from existence to identity with essence, and not from an essence to identity with existence.

13   E.g. "God is primordially one, namely, he is the primordial unity of relevance of the many potential forms: in the process he acquires a consequent multiplicity, which the primordial character absorbs into its own unity." Alfred N. Whitehead, Process and Reality, reprint (New York, 1941), 529. This is meant in express contrast to the Aristotelian 'unmoved mover' and the traditional Christian transcendent creator; see ibid., 519. For the position that real relations to the world are possible in God, see W. E. Stokes, "Is God Really Related to this World?", Proceedings of the American Catholic Philosophical Association, 39 (1965), 145-151. Fr. Stokes' conclusion is: "Between a philosophy of creative act which excludes the possibility of the real relation of God to the world and a modal philosophy which demands reciprocal relations between God and the world, it is possible to posit a 'third position': a philosophy of creative act with real but asymmetrical relations between God and the world." Ibid., 151.

14   Metaph. Λ 6,1071b17-20. Cf. Ph. VIII 6,258b10-259b28; 10,267b2-5.

15   Cf.: "Et ad hoc dicendum quod via efficacissima ad probandum Deum esse est ex suppositione aeternitatis mundi, qua posita, minus eidetur esse manifestum quod Deus sit. Nam si mun-

dus et motus de novo incoepit, planum est quod oportet poni aliquam causam quae de novo producat mundum et motum: quia omne quod de novo fit, ab aliquo innovatore oportet sumere originem; cum nihil educat se de potentia in actum, vel de non esse in esse." *CG*, I, 13. "Si enim mundo et motu existente sempiterno, necesse est ponere unum primum principium; multo magis sempiternitate eorum sublata; quia manifestum est quod omne novum indiget aliquo principio innovante." *In VIII Phys.*, lect. 1, Leonine no. 6. "Ex hoc igitur processu manifestum est quod *Aristoteles* hic firmiter opinatus est et credidit necessarium fore, quod motus sit sempiternus et similiter tempus. Aliter enim non fundasset super hoc intentionem suam de inquisitione substantiarum immaterialium. ...tamen ea quae hic probantur de sempiternitate et immaterialitate primae substantiae, ex necessitate sequuntur. ...necesse est ponere aliquam substantiam sempiternam, in cuius substantia non sit potentia, et per consequens immaterialem." *In XII Metaph.*, lect. 5, nos. 2496-2499.

16   References, supra, n. 14.

17   St. Thomas refers to God as a "form" in the same way that he speaks of the divine "nature" or "essence"—namely, as something identical with the divine existence: "Et ideo cum omnium quae dicuntur de Deo natura vel forma sit ipsum esse, quia suum esse est sua natura, propter quod dicitur a quibusdam philosophis, quod est ens non in essentia,..." *In I Sent.*, d. 35, a. 1, a. 4, Solut.; ed. Mandonnet, I, 819-820. Yet he can also speak as though the existence and the quiddity were two distinct "forms": "...forma a qua imponitur, scilicet esse, non multiplicatur in eis. ...Sed quidditas sive forma, a qua sumitur nomen rei in divinis, consideratur dupliciter." *Ibid.*, d. 25, q. 1, a. 4, Solut.; I, 612. The reason, of course, is that human intelligence has to represent existence and nature under two different concepts, each of which has its own formal aspect. With existence, this formal aspect is that of perfection or actuality, or more vaguely, of "something." Even though existence has to be expressed in this way, however, it is kept clearly apart by St. Thomas from any quidditative element, whether genus or differentia: "Quod additur alicui ad designationem alicuius designatione essentiali, non constitui eius rationem, sed solum esse in actu: *rationale* enim additum *animali* acquirit animali esse in actu, non autem constituit rationem animalis inquantum est animal; ...hoc autem, scilicet esse in actu, est ipsa divina essentia, ut supra ostensum est." *CG*, I, 24, Item quod.

18   "Primo ergo inquiratur de simplicitate ipsius, per quam removetur ab eo compositio." *ST*, I, 3, init. The procedure, accordingly, is to take what has already been established, and "remove" composition, in the sense of showing that none of the composition found in creatures is present in God. The procedure can hardly be conceived as allowing the insertion of existence into the nature of a primary movent that had been known only in terms of a quidditative concept. Yet that is what the requirement of a "prolonging" for the *prima via* would seem to demand.

19   See supra, opening paragraph of the article. Gilson, while allowing that this interpretation is philosophically unobjectionable, urges an historical difficulty: "Assurément on peut interpréter la première voie comme la preuve d'une première cause efficiente du mouvement. C'est ce que presque tout le monde fait. La première voie devient simplement alors un cas particulier de la seconde, celui où l'effet dont on cherche la cause efficiente est le plus manifeste de tous. Il n'y a à cela aucun inconvénient philosophique, mais il y en a un historique, car il ne semble pas que telle sit été l'intention de saint Thomas lui-même. En effet, si la *prima via* est un cas particulier de la *secunda via*, il n'y a pas cinq voies, mais quatre..." E. Gilson, "Prolégomènes à la *Prima via*, *Archives d'histoire doctrinale et littéraire du moyen âge*, 30 (1963), 56. Cf.:"On peut prouver l'existence d'un Premier Moteur et refuser d'admettre qu'il soit un Premier Efficient; s'il n'a pas créé le monde, par exemple, et si la metière est, come lui, une cause première incréé, le cosmos peut lui devoir l'ordre sans lui devoir l'être." Gilson: "Trois leçons sur le problème de l'existence de Dieu," *Divinitas*, 1 (1961), 43.

20   See texts in R. Arnou, *De Quinque Viis Sancti Thomae ad Demonstrandam De Existentiam* (Rome, 1932). However, as St. Thomas first approachs the traditional ways of proving God's existence, he shows no hesitation in interpreting them from the common viewpoint of the reception of existence in creatures: "Harum autem diversitas sumitur secundum vias deveniendi ex creaturis in Deum, quas Dionysius ponit,... Dicit enim quod ex creaturis tribus modis devenimus in Deum: scilicet per causalitatem, per remotionem, per eminentiam. Et ratio hujus est, quia esse creaturae est ab altero. Unde secundum hoc ducimur in causam a qua est." *In I Sent.*, d. 3, div. Iae partis textus; ed. Mandonnet, I, 88. For St. Thomas it seems perfectly legitimate to retain the skeletal

structure of an Aristotelian argument and read into it his own existential meaning; e.g.: "Unde sicut est idem mobile secundum substantiam in toto motu, variatur tamen secundum esse, sicut dicitur quod Socrates in foro est alter a seipso in domo; ita nunc est etiam idem secundum rationem quam accepit prioris et posterioris. Sicut autem motus est actus ipsius mobilis inquantum mobile est; ita esse est actus existentis, inquantum ens est." *In I Sent.*, d. 19, q. 2, a. 2, Solut.; I, 470. In Aristotle the meaning was that a thing remains the same in substance while changing in accidents: "This is an identical *substratum*... but it has different *attributes*—as the sophists assume that Coriscus' being in the Lyceum is a different thing from Coriscus' being in the market-place." *Ph.* IV 11,219b18-221; Oxford tr. "In the Lyceum" and "in the market" were the examples of the category of place used in the *Categories* (4,2a1-2), and the Boethian usage allowed "esse aliquid" to signify an accident (see St. Thomas, *In Boeth. De Hebd.*, lect. II, Calcaterra nos. 26-28). Yet into what originally meant accidental change of place, St. Thomas can unhesitatingly read the meaning of change in existential actuality. The skeleton remains the same, but it now supports different flesh.

21   See *CG*, I, 13, Praedictos autem.

22   "Cum in re duo sint, quidditas rei, et esse ejus, his duobus respondet duplex operatio intellectus. ...Alia autem comprehendit esse rei, componendo affirmationem, quia etiam esse rei ex materia et forma compositae, a qua cognitionem accipit, consistit in quadam compositione formae ad materiam, vel accidentis ad subjectum." *In Sent.*, d. 38, q. 1, a.3, Solut.; ed. Mandonnet, I, 903. There is still a tendency to take rather lightly this basic doctrine of St. Thomas; e.g.: "One interpretation, quite widespread among Neo-Thomists, tries to resolve the question with a good deal of elegance: just as in simple apprehension essence is grasped, so too in the judgment *esse* is grasped. ...But let it be said for the peace of all of us: these and other similar texts do not treat at all of our precise question: they deal with the characteristic function of the two operations of the mind which divide the two-fold content of the notion of *ens*, essence and *actus essendi*. Therefore, the *notio entis* precedes them both, just as, in fact, *ens* precedes *res* and *verum* in the grounding of the transcendental." C. Fabro, "The Transcendentality of *Ens-Esse* and the Ground of Metaphysics," *International Philosophical Quarterly*, 6 (1966), 425-426. It is perfectly true that the human intellect has to conceive both existence and essence in terms of a composite *ens*. In that sense the *notio entis*, as the notion of a composite, is prior to both. But this does not at all mean that in the thing itself existence is denied priority to thing and to everything else in the thing. Through one's immediate judgments existence is grasped in sensible things into the priority it exercises over all it actuates. It does not follow as a transcendental upon the composite *ens*.

23   "Cum quid dicimus in alicujus rei natura, sive conceptu, contineri, idem est ac si diceremus id de ea re verum esse, sive de ipsa posse affirmari." *2ae Resp.*, Def. IX; A-T, VII, 162.8-10.

24   "...ita ex eo solo quod percipiat existentiam necessariam et aeternam in entis summe perfecti idea contineri, plane concludere debet ens summe perfectum existere." *Principia*, I, 14; A-T, VIII, 10.15-18.

25   *Ord.* I, d. 2, pars 1, q. 1-2, no. 137; ed. Vaticana, II, 208.16. Cf.: "Hoc probatur primo de esse quiditativo...Et tunc arguitur ultro quod sit, loquendo de esse existentiae:..." *Ibid.*, no. 138; pp. 209.8-210.3.

26   "...quo prius aliud esse includit contradictionem, sic in quantum primum existit." *Ibid.*, no. 59; p. 165.9-10. Cf. no. 138; p. 210.5-8.

27   On perfection as the ground for concluding to actual existence, see Scotus, *ibid.*, nos. 53 (pp. 158.3-159.6) and 131-135 (pp.206.6-208.7). A discussion on this point may be found in my article "The Special Characteristic of the Scotistic Proof that God Exists," *Analecta Gregoriana*, 67 (1954), 321-322.

28   *Esse*, according to the repeated assertions of St. Thomas, is the characteristic effect (*effectus proprius*) of God in creatures. It should therefore be the one effect that in virtue of itself points in the direction of God.

Notes—Immobility and Existence

1   For other versions, see *In I. Sent.*, d.3, div. lae partis textus (ed. Mandonnet, I,88-89); d.8, q.3, a.1, Contra (I,211); *In VII Phys.*, lect. 1-3, Angeli-Pirotta nos. 1759-1799, with *In VIII Phys.*, lect. 1-23, nos. 1966-2550; *In XII Metaph.*, lect. 5-7, Cathala-Spiazzi nos. 2488-2535; *Comp. Theol.*, I, 3, Verardo no. 4; I, 11, no. 21.

2   See infra, n. 35.

3   *CG*, I, 14, Ad procedendum. On the way immobility is understood, see infra, n.34.

4   *Disp. Metaph.*, XXIX, 1, 7-16; ed. Vivès, 26, 23-26.

5   Dionysius the Pseudo-Areopagite and St. Bernard are cited for this assertion by Aquinas, *In I Sent.*, d.8, q.1, a.2; ed. Mandonnet, 1, 197-198. For St. Thomas' own explanation, see also *CG*, I, 26. A discussion of it may be found in the paper of the late Msgr. G.B. Phelan, "The Being of Creatures," *Proceedings of the American Catholic Philosophical Association*," 31 (1957), 118-125; reprinted in *G.B. Phelan: Selected Papers*, (Toronto, 1967), 83-94.

6   A study of the texts may be found in my article, "Actuality in the *Prima Via* of St. Thomas," *Mediaeval Studies*, 29 (1967), 26-46. See above pp. 192-207 Ed.

7   E.g.: "Ipsum esse absolute consideratum infinitum est: nam ab infinitis et infinitis modis participari possibile est." *CG*, I, 43, Amplius ipsum.

8   E.g., *Comp. Theol.*, I, 11, no. 21. See supra, n. 6.

9   See *Principia Ethica* (Cambridge, 1903), pp. vii-viii.

10   The texts may be found assembled and discussed in my article "Diversity and Community of Being in St. Thomas Aquinas," *Mediaeval Studies*, 22 (1960), 284-295.   See above pp. 97-131 Ed.

11   *De Pot.*, VII, 2, ad 9m; Cf. *ST*, I, 3, 4c (Secundo); *In I Periherm.*, lect. 5, Leonine no. 22.

12   See *In I Periherm.*, lect. 3, nos 9-13; lect. 5, nos. 8-22.

13   The proof may be found developed in terms of existence (*esse*) in *De Ente et Essentia*, c. IV; ed. Roland-Gosselin, pp. 34.7-35.19. The overall point at issue in the passage to show that the angelic forms (*intelligencie*) are not entirely incomposite. Yet in the course of the reasoning it proves "quod sit aliqua res que sit causa essendi omnibus rebus ex eo quod ipsa est esse tantum" (*ibid.*, p. 35.13-14). The demonstration occurs frequently in the commentary of St. Thomas on the first book of the *Sentences*, e.g., *In I Sent.*, d.2, q.1, a.1, Contra, Praeterea ejus (ed. Mandonnet, I, 60); d.8, q.4, a.2, Solut. (I,222). That creatures have their existence from another is the common reason given for all three ways mentioned by Dionysius for reaching God: "Dicit enim quod ex creaturis tribus modis devenimus in Deum: scilicet per causalitatem, per remotionem, per eminentiam. Et ratio hujus est, quia esse creaturae est ab altero." *Ibid.*, d.3, div. lae partis textus (I, 88).

14   St. Thomas has no hesitation in referring to God as a *res*. See text quoted from *De Ente*, supra n. 13. Cf.: "…res illa quae Deus est, est quoddam esse subsistens," *In I Sent.*, d.2, q.1, a.3, Solut,; I, 67.

15   "Sed esse non receptum in aliquo, non est finitum…" *In I Sent.*, d.8, q.5, a.1, Contra; I, 226. "…illud quod non habet esse receptum in aliquo, sed subsistens, non habet esse limitatum, sed infinitum, sicut Deus." *In III Sent.*, d.13, q.1, a.2, Solut. 2; ed. Moos, III, 402 (no. 46). "…habet esse non limitatum." *Ibid.*, d.14, a.4, ad 3m; III, 465 (no. 180). "…cuius esse est infinitum." *CG*, II, 21, Amplius cum. See also supra, n. 7, Cf. *Comp. Theol.*, I, 18, no. 35.

16   *In I Sent.*, d.2, q.1, a.2, Solut.; I, 62-63. *De Ente et Essentia*, c. V; pp. 38.12-39.3. *CG*, I, 28. *ST*, I, 4, 2. *Comp. Theol.*, I, 21, nos. 42-43. Cf. *In De Div. Nom.*, c. V, lect. 1, Pera nos. 629-631; lect 2, nos. 661-662.

17   See *De Ente et Essentia*, c. V; p. 39.6-24.

18   "Vnde oportet quod in qualibet alia re preter eam aliud sit esse suum et aliud quiditas uel natura seu forma sua." *De Ente*, c. IV; p. 34.30-32. A discussion of the texts on this topic may be found in my article "Quiddity and Real Distinction in St. Thomas Aquinas," *Mediaeval Studies*, 27 (1965), 14-19.

19   "Sane esse omnium dixerim Deum…sed causale, non materiale." St. Bernard, *In Cant.*, Iv; PL, 183, 798B. Similarly "Deus est esse omnium non essentiale, sed causale." St. Thomas, *In I Sent.*, d.8, q.1, a.2, Solut.; I, 198. Cf. supra, n. 5. On the Platonic background, see: "…eo modo loquendi utitur quod Platonici utebantur qui esse separatum dicebant esse existentium, inquan-

tum compositiva per participationem abstractorum participantur. Et quod causaliter sit intelligendum, apparet per hoc quod subdit quod *non solum existentia* sunt ex Deo, *sed* etiam *ipsum esse existentium est* ex Deo..." *In De Div. Nom.*, c. V, lect 1, no. 630.

20   On this topic see A. C. Pegis, "Penitus Manet Ignotum," *Mediaeval Studies*, 27 (1965), 212-226.

21   Outside the Thomistic framework, however, the difficulty can become insuperable. Cf.: "The hard question for the Thomist is then whether or not I, with my peculiar fragment of existence, do not in fact stand over against God with his Existence. The Thomists sometimes speak as though they meant to hold that all Existence is god, in him or from him. But it is not clear then how I can exist." Paul Weiss, *Modes of Being* (Carbondale, Illinois, 1958), 191 (no. 3.08). "The classical doctrine, of course, regarded deity as exclusively actual (*actus purus*). ...All that God has power to be, that, it was held, He is. ...God, on the contrary, is supposed to know and will what He elicits in the world, and indeed to love His creatures. That so many could think they believed this, and at the same time could hold that, no matter what world there is, God remains in exactly the same state, is to my mind one of the great oddities in human development." Charles Hartshorne, *The Logic of Perfection* (Lasalle, Ill., 1962), 35-36.

22   "...non sic est in rebus quasi aliquid rei, sed sicut rei causa quae nullo modo suo effectui deest." *CG*, I, 26, Quartum. Cf. texts supra, n. 19. The latter texts seems to stress efficient causality in this regard. Nevertheless the commentary on the *Sentences* means to include also exemplar causality, that is, extrinsic formal causality: "et ideo esse divinum dicitur esse omnium rerum, a quo omne esse creatum effective et exemplariter manat." *In I Sent.*, d.8, q.1, a.2, Solut.; I, 198. Exemplar causality is the type mentioned expressly in the *Contra Gentiles* article: "Ex hoc vero quod dixit quod divinitas est *esse omnium*, ostendit quod a Deo in omnibus quaedam divini esse similitudo reperitur." *CG*, I, 26, Huic. Cf.: "Unde ipse est exemplaris forma rerum." *In I Sent.*, d.2, q.1, a.2, Solut.; I, 63.

23   "Unde non sic determinatur *esse* per aliud sicut potentia per actum, sed magis sicut actus per potentiam." *De Pot.*, VII, 2, ad 9m.

24   In the context of St. Thomas, accordingly, it can hardly be correct to prefer "the reality of God" to "the existence of God," at least if the etymology of "reality" as coming from *res* 'thing' is respected. Peirce, on account of his own understanding of existence, advocated that preference: "I will also take the liberty of substituting 'reality' for 'existence.'. This is perhaps overscrupulosity; but I myself always use *exist* in its strict philosophical sense of 'react with the other like things in the environment.' Of course, in that sense, it would be fetichism to say that God 'exists.'" Charles S. Peirce, *Collected Papers of Charles Sanders Peirce*, ed. C. Hartshorne and P. Weiss (Cambridge, Mass., 1935), VI, 340 (6.495). Cf. *ibid.*, 311-341. (nos. 452-496). The influence of this diction continues, e.g.: "The question is whether the existence of God—or better, the reality of God—is..." E. Fontinell, "postscript," in *Speaking of God*, ed. Denis Dirscherl (Milwaukee, 1967), 158. On the etymology of *res* for Aquinas, see *In I Sent.*, d.25, q.1, a.4, Solut.; I, 611-612.

25   In this perspective one may concede that "God and creatures have nothing in common as regards their essence"—J. Bobik, "Some disputable Points Apropos of St. Thomas and Metaphysics," *The New Scholasticism*, 37 (1963), 418. Although St. Thomas himself regards existence as essence in God, he does not consider the tradition predicating essence of God to be basically different from the Avicennan assertion that God has no essence: "Hae autem opiniones, quamvis in superficie diversae videntur, tamen non sunt contrariae, si quis dictorum rationes ex causis assumit dicendi. Quia primi consideraverunt ipsas res creatus...et ideo dixerunt, quod Deus est esse sine essentia,..." *In I Sent.*, d.2, q.1, Solut.; I, 69. Cf. *De Ente*, c. V; p. 37.14-16. Having nothing in common from the viewpoint of essence, God and creatures are not comparable strictly as things. They are comparable from the standpoint of existence—God is the primary instance, creatures are secondary instances. Creatures, because of their essences, diversify the existence they receive. To try to find a ground for diversification directly in subsistent existence, which is infinite in its inclusiveness, seems to render insoluble the problem how any room is left for other existents. The diversification has to be explained entirely from the side of finite essences.

26   See *In I Sent.*, Prol. q.1, a.2; I, 9-10.

27   *In Boeth. de Trin.*, V, 4, Resp.; ed. B. Decker, 194-195. *In Metaph.*, Proem.

28   E.g.: "esse est actus existentis, inquantum ens est." *In I Sent.*, d. 19, q.2, a.2, Solut.; I, 470. cf. "Sed nomen entis sumitur ab esse rei." *In I Sent.*, d.25, q.1, a.4, Solut.; I, 612.

29 Cf.: "...secunda respicit esse ipsius." *In I Sent.*, d.19, q.5, a.1, ad 7m; I, 489. "Alia autem comprehendit esse rei,..." *In I Sent.*, d.38, q.1, a.3, Solut.; I, 903. "Secunda vero operatio respicit ipsum esse rei,..." *In Boeth. De Trin.*, V, 3, Resp.; ed. Decker, 182.9-10.

30 E.g,: "The reason that Existence must be empty, diaphanous, blank, and in sum, *nil*, resides in its definitory contrast with Essence. ...There is no *nature* left for Existence,..." Donald C. Williams, "Dispensing with Existence," *The Journal of Philosophy*, 59 (1962), 753.

31 "...omnia existentia continentur sub ipso esse communi, non autem Deus, sed magis esse commune continetur sub eius virtute,..." *In De Div. Nom.*, c. V, lect 2, no. 660.

32 See *supra*, n. 6.

33 *CG, I, 13, Ostenso.* Cf. *In I Sent.*, d.3, div lae partis textus (I, 88-89), where the three ways are presented as those of Dionysius. Theological methods, proceeding on the strength of God's revelation, presupposes his existence. Its interest, from St. Thomas' viewpoint, is to examine the proofs, just as it examines any other materials offered it.

34 See the standard texts of St. Augustine assembled in Lombard's *Sentences*, Dist. VIII, cap. 1-7, in *Libri IV Sententiarum* (Quaracchi, 1916), I, 57-64. Cf.: "Si creata, utique et mutabilia sunt." John Damascene, *De Fide Orth.*, I, 3, 126; PG, 94, 795. Nevertheless the Aristotelian conception of motion may be seen influencing the traditional Christian demonstration of God's existence before the thirteenth century. In a text pointed out by Beryl Smalley from Herbert of Boseham, *Liber Melorum*, III, 8 (PL, 190, 1357), the coupling of actuality with movement seems to me to indicate Aristotelian conditioning, even though the notion of mobility is meant to be in accord with *Wisdom*, VII, 24. The text is: "Quare et juxta philosophorum demonstrationem certissimam necesse est ut ab aliquo immobili omnis hic sensibilis mundi procedat motus. ...prima et summa causa est sicut omnis actus et omnis motus, juxta quod scriptum alibi quod manens immobilis dat cuncta moveri."

35 *CG*, I, 15, Ostendit, Cf. I, 13, Praedictos. See also In *XII Metaph.*, lect. 5, no. 2499; lect. 8, no. 2536.

36 *In I Sent.*, d.8, q.2, a.1-2; I, 201-206. *Ibid.*,d. 19, q.2, a.1-2 I, 465-472. *In XI Sent.*, d.2, q.1, a.1 II, 61-65. *In De Div. Nom.*, c. X, lect. 3, nos. 860-875. *In Lib. de Causis*, Prop. 2 (ed. Saffrey, 1954, 11-16). *ST*, I, 10, 1-3.

37 *CG*, I, 22, Hanc autem. Cf. *ST*, 1, 2, 3, Sed contra.

38 Cf.: "...a primo ente quod est esse tantum, et hec est causa prima que Deus est." *De Ente*, c. IV; p. 35.17-19. "...quod Deus est esse tantum." *Ibid.*, c. V, p. 37.21-22.

39 In this sense "nobilitas" seems meant to reflect the aristocratic Greek notion of *arête* and corresponding adjective (see Aristotle, Cat., 8, 10b5-9) *Spoudaios*, as may be seen in St. Thomas, *In I Sent.*, d.2, q.1; a.2, Praeterea (I, 62), where the concept of the perfect is based on the teaching of *Metaph.*, Δ 16, 1021b21-24, with the comments of Averroes, *ad loc.*, comm. 21 (Venice, 1574), fol. 130vl-131rl.

40 "The metaphysical proofs of God are so remote from the reasoning of men, and so involved, that they have but little force; and if this should be helpful to some persons, it would be so only during the moment they are seeing the demonstration." *Pensées, 543 (ed. Chevalier).*

Notes—Aquinas on Infinite Regress

1 C.F.J. Williams, "*Hic autem non est procedere in infinitum...*"MIND, lxix (1960), 403.

2 Gilbert Ryle, "The Theory of Meaning", in *British Philosophy in the Mid-Century*, ed. C.A. Mace (London, 1957), p. 264.

3 "Hence it is not impossible that man be engendered by man in infinitum." *Summa Theologiae*, I, 46, 2, ad 7m. The *Contra Gentiles*, I, 13 (ed. Leonine), v. XIII, p. 33b10, concedes that the argument is "most efficacious" when the perpetual series of moved movents, as understood by Aristotle, is admitted. Cf. *In VIII Phys.*, lect. 2, Leonine no. 4.

4 *Contra Gentiles*, III, 89; *Summa Theologiae*, I, 83, 1, ad 3m; I-II, 10, 4c.

5 "Logicus enim considerat modum praedicandi, et non existentiam rei. ... Sed philosophus qui existentiam quaerit rerum, finem vel agentem, cum sint extrinseca, non comprehendit sub quod quid erat esse." *In VII Metaph.*, lect. 17, Cathala-Spiazzi no. 1658.

INDEX

William of Auvergne, 65,67,68
Williams, C. F. J., 229

Index of Latin & Greek Words and Phrases

ab altero, 154
abstracta atque separabilis, 6
actus entis, 67
actus essendi, 22,159
aliquis homo, 88
an est, 57,59
an sit, 159
a quolibet esse, 89
auctor, 4
apprehensione tali, 39

causum efficientem primam, 197
cognoscat, 40
collatio, 40
communia sensibilia, 40
competit, 57
complexorum vel enuntiabilium, 44
credulitas intellectus, 120

Deus et intellectuales substantiae, 5
Deus et intelligentiae, 5
diaphanum, 92
discernit, 40
diversum in diversis, 97
duplex operatio, 43

einai, 7,108
ens, 22,53,54,55,56,57,60,61,62,63,64,
    66,67,70,71,72, 77,78,79,80,81,95,117,
    118,128,129,179,180
ens actu, 197,198
ens commune, 160
ens homo, 8
ens per se, 79,81

enunciatio, 47
enuntiatio, 120
esse, 7,8,55,56,61,62,63,64,65,66,67,68,69,
    70,71,72,73,74, 76,78,91,96,100,101,129,
    148,151,153,154,156,157,159,
    167,168,195
ens commune, 100
esse commune, 100,130
esse divinum, 130
esse essentiae, 96,176
esse existentia, 96
essens, 78
esse rationis, 81
esse rei, 71
esse tantum, 130
esse universale, 100
essentia, 78
esse ex nihilo, 153
esse in rerum natura, 162
essere (Italian), 69
etant (French), 22
existentia, 29,72
ex parte motus, 160

fides, 120
formatio, 38,39,43,46
formatio quidditatum, 39

generans, 164
genus praedicabile, 114
genus subiectum, 114

homo, 8
homos, 54

imaginatio intellectus, 117,118
immensitas, 220,221
inabstracta, 6,61,62,64,67,69,72,78,79,80,82
in alio existens, 125
in concreto, 61,62,67,69,79,80,82
in esse, 195
intellectualis, maxime, 4
intellectus, 100
ipsum esse, 157
ipsum suum esse, 157

krisis, 34
kritike, 34
krinein, 34

logos (Greek), 7

maxime ens, 197
modi, 134
mores, 13
movere, 41
mutatio, 154,222

natura entitatis, 72
natura essendi, 72
non-esse, 156
notio entis, 22,32
nuntiabile, 120

opos estin (Greek), 20
ousia (Greek), 78,84,152

pati, 78
patiens, 78
per accidens, 56,58,65,66,79,143
per se, 56,79,92,93,94
praeter, 57,64,68,73,86,91,136
preter esse, 97
primum ens, 197
propter quid, 145,183

quale quid, 110,114
quasi per accidens, 143
quid, 24
quidditas, 24
quid est, 57,59
quid sit, 159

quo, 61
quod est, 61,68,91

ratio, 41,72
ratio entis, 31,41,72,116,218
ratio essendi, 72
reduci in actum, 183,185
removens prohibens, 164
res, 22,39
res divinae, 6

secundum esse, 5,7,8,10,98,99
secundum esse et rationem, 15
secundum rationem, 5
sensus communis, 40
separata a materia secundum esse et
    rationem, 6
species mutabilis, 153
substantia, 78

tertium quid, 210
to on, 108
totum, 86,87

variatio, 122
verum, 22
via, 153,155,156,166,205,219
viae, 134,154,161,193
vox, 54

Zoion, 54